FACTORY

Mick Middles is the author of nineteen books, most of which have concentrated on Manchester's music artists from punk to the present. He was the Manchester correspondent for *Sounds* magazine and his work has appeared in publications as diverse as the *Guardian*, *Daily Telegraph*, the *Express*, *Manchester Evening News*, *The Face*, *Kerrang*, *Classic Rock*, *Record Collector* and *Rock'n'Reel*. He lives in Warrington.

FACTORY
The Story of a Record Label

Mick Middles

Published by Virgin Books 2009

2 4 6 8 10 9 7 5 3

First published in Great Britain in 1996 by
Virgin Books
Random House, 20 Vauxhall Bridge Road,
London SW1V 2SA

www.virginbooks.com
www.rbooks.co.uk

Addresses for companies within The Random House Group Limited can be found at:
www.randomhouse.co.uk/offices.htm

The Random House Group Limited Reg. No. 954009

A CIP catalogue record for this book is available from the British Library

ISBN 9780753518250

The Random House Group Limited supports The Forest Stewardship Council [FSC], the leading international forest certification organisation. All our titles that are printed on Greenpeace-approved FSC certified paper carry the FSC logo. Our paper procurement policy can be found at www.rbooks.co.uk/environment

Mixed Sources
Product group from well-managed forests and other controlled sources
www.fsc.org   Cert no. TT-COC-2139
© 1996 Forest Stewardship Council

Typeset by TW Typesetting, Plymouth, Devon
Printed and bound in Great Britain by CPI Bookmarque Ltd, Croydon CR0 4TD

For Lindsay

CONTENTS

Acknowledgements

Thanks are especially due to Anthony H. Wilson, without whom . . .

Thanks also to the following: Rob Gretton, Steve Morris, Peter Hook, Bernard Sumner, Gillian Gilbert, Vini Reilly, Bridget Chapman, Yvette Livesey, Rebecca Boulton, Deborah Curtis, Jon Savage, Johnny Rogan, Paul Morley, Jon The Postman, Mark E. Smith, Steve Burke, Martin Ryan, Brinner, Buzzcocks, Mike Pickering, Kevin Cummins, Simon Topping, Derek Ryder, Dave Haslam, Colin Sinclair, Kay Carroll, Alan Erasmus, Peter Saville, Bruce Mitchell, Derek Brandwood, Roger Eagle, Tony Michaelides, Tina Simmons, John and Ro Barratt, Eric Jackson, Len Brown, Andy Spinoza, Gonnie Rietveld, Craig Cash and Caroline Hook. Special thanks also to Kathryn Turner.

I must draw attention to the following books and publications: *England's Dreaming* by Jon Savage (Faber and Faber), *Buzzcocks – The Complete History* by Tony McGartland (IMP), *The Hacienda Must Be Built*, edited by Jon Savage (IMP), *Unknown Pleasures and Wayward Distractions* by Brian Edge (Omnibus Press), *And God Created Manchester* by Sarah Champion (Wordsmith), *Manchester Evening News*, *Sounds*, *NME*, *Melody Maker*, *The Face*, *Vox*, *Select*, *Mail On Sunday*, *The Wire*, *City Life*, *City Fun*, *Out There*, *Shy Talk*, *Ghast Up*, *Girl Trouble*, *Sniffin' Glue* and the *Financial Times*.

And finally, a huge thank you to Mal Peachey, Hannah MacDonald and Wendy Brown at Virgin.

Illustrations

Tony Michaelides – independent record plugger (and Piccadilly Radio DJ) who pulled Factory into the heart of the record industry machinery (*Karen Middles*)

Dave Haslam and Nathan McGough (*Kevin Cummins*)

Barney in action (*Stephen Wright*)

The Other Two, destined for a rural idyll on the Cheshire/Derbyshire border (*Richard Lohr*)

Chapter One

Introduction

THE GIST OF IT

'Do New Order still exist, Rob?'

It was a simple thing to ask, and one might reasonably expect the manager of New Order – the bear-like, professionally distant Rob Gretton – to be able to provide some kind of answer. Nevertheless, it obviously caused Rob problems, for he swilled the question around his head, gazing intently at the ceiling of the cafe bar, exhaling like a cynical car mechanic inspecting a fifteen-year-old Austin Maestro, shrugging twice and sipping from his raspberry-flavoured mineral water. Finally, encouragingly, he pushed his glasses slowly up to the bridge of his nose, and placed his open palms on the table in front of him.

'Well,' he exclaimed in his familiar dull, soft tone, his forehead creased with concentration, 'it depends on what you mean by "exist".'

I stared at him, in complete silence for a full 30 seconds. I had known Rob Gretton – famed idiosyncratic band manager, ex-director of Factory Records, latterly managing director of Factory's world-famous Haçienda nightclub and owner of a whole string of tiny mid-nineties record labels – since the mid-seventies, when we both attempted to gain lowly footholds in the rapidly evolving Manchester punk scene; Gretton as local DJ and yours truly as music press correspondent. On numerous occasions, some of them recounted in the pages of this book, we sank disgracefully into an alcoholic mist together – rather sweetly at times, like two teenagers sharing a bottle of Woodpecker on a street-corner bench, firing half-baked maxims this way and that.

And yet it would probably be easier to prise teeth, I mused, rather than words, from Rob's mouth on this day, 22 October 1995. He had changed. Always a cool customer, he was now painfully though politely detached, and seemed to have stretched a little – as perhaps we all have – towards caricature.

'I don't speak to them much,' he continued (genuinely I believe), attempting to explain why my questions had been bouncing off him like wooden arrows off a stationary Chieftain tank. 'I get busy, I get tired, I'm getting fat [hence the mineral water]. New Order is, like, not an everyday issue any more. I have meetings with breweries to attend to . . . things like that. I don't suppose my life is all that exciting any more. Maybe the band will get together and record again one day . . . maybe they just won't bother. Maybe it just isn't as much fun as it used to be? Who knows? They are all off doing their own things; I don't think they communicate with each other much really. They are all very different people these days.' He paused thoughtfully and then added, 'Perhaps they never had that much in common.'

To look, for the first time, at Gretton's whitened and wispy face and his large frame clasped rather scruffily in faded black denim, it would be difficult to imagine that this is a man whose arrogant aloofness has thoroughly and famously disarmed all manner of smart-assed music business executives, especially in America. Indeed, at a rough guess, you may well pin him down to be, say, a man who runs a stall at record fairs, or a tobacconist perhaps. If you honed in on his rather optimistic Manchester City match appraisals, you would probably be rather surprised to be informed that, as the gossip columns once proclaimed, this is a man who once befriended and partnered Quincy Jones on the American legend's Malibu pool table.

'So, you're doing a book on us lot, are you?' he drawled gruffly. 'About time, I suppose. What's the angle?'

THE SLANT OF IT

It is, in the main, the tale of two bands, two cities and one record label. The two bands are Joy Division and the band they would evolve into, New Order. Despite being musically quite the antithesis of each other, they remain famously linked and etched into legend by the tragic suicide of Joy Division's lead singer, Ian Curtis.

The two cities, Manchester and Salford, can similarly be viewed as one – geographically if not culturally – for they clasp each other tightly on a map, like a fat auntie (Manchester) clutching her tiny Salfordian niece.

The record label, Factory, at least for the major part of the tale, clutches nobody. It is profoundly, aesthetically aloof: arrogantly self-centred rather than parochial; an 'independent' believing itself to be at the centre of the universe; a mess of indecision and squabbling; an accountant's worst nightmare; a resting home for aesthetic waifs and strays; a breeding ground for unlikely genius; a graveyard for the trendily uninspired; an unofficial scouting agency for the major labels; a label that has always been and, even though now finally under the umbrella of London Records, remains profoundly loved and loathed, perfect and absurd, pretentious and streetwise, friendly and aloof, open and elitist. It is not the greatest label in the world, nor the most artistically sussed, and it is certainly not the most commercially aware. Its overall roster has been rather fat and cumbersome; it has been hip and unhip, trendy and hackneyed. It has always, however, retained a wholly idiosyncratic identity.

It has always been Factory. Had things been different, had the original directors of Factory Records employed a severe business-like strategy rather than submitting to the pulse of their hearts, and had Factory Records become a music industry success story, then the company would have somehow lost stature rather than gained it.

Factory's reputation was initially forged in the late seventies, principally by the position achieved by its leading band, Joy Division, who defied the odds to create a small body of works of such rare, haunting beauty. The sad echo of Joy Division created a base from which the emergent New Order, still blessed with an unlikely measure of raw talent, would evolve into one of the great musical units of the eighties and, perhaps, the nineties. The Joy Division/New Order story has been told many times before, but never, the author hopes, has it been placed so securely in the context of the surrounding area, the surrounding bands and musicians, the surrounding, at times rather suffocating, culture and, of course, the surrounding twin cities.

The core of the story, naturally, belongs to Factory founder Tony Wilson; a charismatic television presenter and journalist from the north-west of England whose enthusiasm and drive has fired the label through the best of times and, most definitely, most famously, the worst of times. As if to parallel the label, Wilson is an intelligent though often untethered cannon; entertainingly complex, often contradictory, but always, at least in the experience of this writer, helpful, thought-provoking and great fun. Not everyone would agree.

Factory's strength lies in its absurdities; in its often rather self-destructive love of extremes; in its socialistic belief that worthwhile art is to be found in the most unlikely places and can be produced by the most unlikely people. Could any other label have seen, so early, the true worth of the wild, hedonistic Happy Mondays? Could any other label possibly spend seventeen years nurturing the weird, beautiful, wholly aloof 'stable' band, Durutti Column – hardly a band at all and mostly just the end result of the musicianly dexterity and aesthetic musings of one man, Vini Reilly, with absolutely no possibility of large commercial returns? Could any other label commit itself to placing the comparative 'low art' of rock music in such stylish, hugely expensive and wholly innovative packaging and extend this belief to create three beautiful Manchester buildings – the Haçienda, Dry Bar and their infamous Charles Street headquarters, all ventures which would heavily contribute to the label's deafening public collapse at the start of the nineties?

What follows then is not the ultimate story of New Order, Joy Division, Factory, Tony Wilson, the Haçienda or Manchester culture, nor does it trudge wearily from release to release, from day to day, from band to band. It is just a book about those things. Shedding a different light from a new angle, and perhaps, if nothing else, dispelling some of the flavour of the label and period, from 1976 up and into the nineties, during which Manchester enjoyed unprecedented musical success. This book doesn't, however, claim that Manchester is any better, musically or culturally speaking, than any other city. But it is, like Factory, different.

ROB GRETTON, 1995

If the first glimpse of the Haçienda's interior is famously mind-blowing – it still is, I believe, even in these days where hi-tech low-brow nightclubs sit on street corners in every parochial town in Britain – then one's first view of the exterior is, and always has been, profoundly anti-climactic. Especially during daylight hours, when its heartbeat, the relentless dance-floor thump, doesn't seep through the walls and drift down Whitworth Street. It seems like nothing: a featureless corner arc of a building, barely competing, in aesthetic terms, with the City Arms opposite, let alone the vast structure of G-Mex or Gothic trickery of the Midland Hotel, or the rising beauty of the new international concert hall, all to be found looming majestically to the rear. As this book was being written, the entire area, it seemed, was swarming with hard-hatted and besuited architects and dust-emplastered workmen. Cranes, to the rear, kept a watchful eye while swaying left and right. The canal strip that zips past the back of the club is landscaped and pristine these days, peppered by cafe bars which, in summer, allow their tables to spill out on to the waterside, hoping to attain a little Mediterranean ambience. This is the very heart of Manchester regeneration. A furious, bustling mess of activity. A joyous optimism abounds, though cynics, understandably, wonder just how the ratio between the rejuvenated workplaces and the actual work which is supposed to miraculously spring to life within them can possibly remain in balance. Nevertheless, the decay that had been encroaching for 30 or 40 years at least, seems to have been stalled.

'Well, even the Haçienda is going to be altered . . . the façade is being refitted. In a couple of weeks time it will be covered in scaffolding. We have to rise to stay in tune with the surrounding area,' stated Rob Gretton, rather wearily, as if his entire life had been encumbered by marauding workmen. He was sitting in the Alaska cafe bar, gazing ruefully across Whitworth Street towards the regeneration. 'This area is going to be really amazing . . . quite upmarket. It's ironic, really, considering it was really the pits when we first moved into the Haçienda, and before that, when Joy Division would rehearse around here. It was really dour then but we kind of liked the area . . . it had a certain atmosphere.'

I had met Rob, half an hour earlier, in the offices of his latter-day record company, Rob's Records, situated directly above the Haçienda. Inside, it's pretty much the archetypal record company office: whirring faxes, a video blasting away, racks of boxed CDs, a floor strewn with demo tapes and videos and a coffee table boasting, among others, the last six months of well-thumbed *Music Week*s. Rob looked quite grand, sat among such a trendy mess, orchestrating his now curious little empire. Rob's Records, after being initially flushed by the success of the dance act, Sub Sub, had 'levelled' a little. Nevertheless, a tireless entrepreneurial spirit had remained, hand in hand with a devotion to 'local' music. Three pristine new labels had just been launched from the nerve centre of Rob's. Manchester Records, devoted to the noisy indie band industry; Blue Records, an intriguing swing and soul black music label; and Pleasure, for matters of a sonic, ambient and techno nature. Despite the need to push these new angles as hard as is humanly possible, Rob, clinging to his state of enigma as if his life depended on it, resolutely refused to talk to the circulating pop journalists. Even Manchester's *City Life* magazine began a Rob's Records feature that very day with the words, 'New Order manager Rob Gretton doesn't like being interviewed, so all the talking is done by right-hand man, Pete Robinson . . .' I showed this article to Rob and he ummed and arrred appreciatively for a full five minutes before lapsing, once again, into his familiar ocean of guarded silence.

'It's difficult, these days,' he told me, 'to make any real impact in music. There is so much going on. I often think back to the early Factory days and think how lucky we were. If we had happened along in the nineties, even with Joy Division, we probably would have never got it off the ground. There was only a tiny few bands so all you had to do to get known was climb on to a stage a couple of times and you'd be an important part of the scene.'

Why is it, I asked him, that he remained so dedicated to deflecting and ducking press attention?

'I'm just shy,' he replied, smiling, and I didn't believe him for a second. 'I don't like attention . . . I don't like people looking at me. I just like to get on with life, quietly, in my own way.'

And it has served him well, his own way. Still manager of New Order – if, indeed, there still be such a thing – where the back catalogue will be worth managing for an eternity; still 60 per cent shareholder in the Haçienda. 'I'm down there every night until the early hours. You *have* to keep an eye on things.'

FACTORY TOO, 1996

Anthony H. Wilson bounded into the office of Factory Too with cheery aplomb; a million ideas, as ever, forming and fading in his head, a million things to do, crammed into his diary. It is a small, cubic office, effectively maintained by manager Bridget Chapman, then the likeable, amiable, approachable, unpretentious face of Factory Too, latterly to depart for the duller but perhaps rather more comforting surrounds of Polydor. I waited twenty minutes but it was a pleasant twenty minutes, surveying the current base of Factory – a new place for the acorns to gather. It is a suitably modernistic office, though resolutely modest, at least by the flamboyant standards of the old Factory. But it still seems upbeat and, with its enormous live-in-me sofa and orchids flowing from thick glass vases, still manages to appear modestly elegant. The coffee table, naturally, was adorned with exact replicas of the magazines on the table over at Rob's, pinning down the nature of the business. Boxes of CDs, however, seemed thin on the ground, hinting that a typical and, by now, rather sweet Factory meanness is still in operation, despite the looming patriarchal shadow of London Records. To illustrate this, Bridget, despite offering to furnish me with the latest single by Factory Too band Hopper, suddenly realised that there wasn't one to be found anywhere in the office. Bad timing, perhaps. I couldn't tell, although I couldn't and still can't resist nodding back to that moment in the Factory Club in 1979 when nobody could present me with a copy of a new single by Factory band the Distractions, despite the fact that in 24 hours I would be writing a *Sounds* 'singles' page.

'Tony's ever so upset about the music press failing to warm to Hopper,' Bridget stated, while emptying Wilson's waste-paper basket. 'Oh don't worry, don't worry . . . he will be here in a minute. I'll ring him . . . shunt him along a bit . . . don't worry . . . he's always a bit late.'

A typically Factoryish string of wild-haircutted callers poked purposefully into the room during my wait, asking for cheques, delivering demo tapes, slapping down artwork. If I had stayed long enough, even Vini Reilly would have appeared in the door frame, hanging around, having a smoke . . . this, it seemed, his second home.

Wilson, when he finally arrived, was at his most engaging, politely breaking off our conversations to answer the phones while Bridget hovered in the next room, deflecting hassles and prising a little space into his day.

'The main thing about me . . . about me and Factory,' he stated, curling into the sofa, booted, black suited, sunglassed and armed with strong coffee, '. . . erm . . . the main thing is that I have always been so lucky, so incredibly lucky, to have been able to work with a number of people who are cleverer than me. Truthfully. I believe that I have just one talent. I am a very good television presenter. In that role I am in full control. I know what I am doing . . . that is me. But I can't write songs or manage bands or create great artwork or do so many things, so I arm myself with the best. I do believe, incidentally, that this is, artistically, the finest city in the world . . . musically the most fascinating . . . it's just such a fucking great place.'

Aaah, yes. I had waited ten minutes for the first Tony Wilson swear word. He was always very good at swearing, Tony, and I'm afraid his verbal lapses pepper this text a little. But he does swear well, as if to establish a link between his middle-class lifestyle and his Salfordian roots. A little patronising, perhaps, for the often breadline, bedsit artists who have enriched his Factory lifestyle, but he intends the link fondly.

'There is such a power in this city,' he enthused, with almost alarming passion, 'and there always has been, but in terms of music, the whole thing hasn't stopped since '76, since Buzzcocks. It is amazing how it just rolls on. I was meeting some business people not long ago at Manchester Airport. I think we were attempting to get them to put money into the city. And they said that they had heard of the Madchester rave scene of the late eighties/early nineties and had also heard that it had died. I agreed that Madchester had died, but explained to them that Manchester had arguably the top adult pop band in the world (Simply Red), the most exciting rock band (Oasis), and the top teen pop band (Take That). Not bad, is it?'

MANCHESTER – THE LOOK OF IT

From one of the Pennine foothills, which tentatively form a semi-circle to the east, Manchester doesn't look much of a city at all. The cityscape, if one dares call it such, is a mere piffling gathering of dull rectangular buildings, neither daunting nor enigmatic. It does not arrest the attention like, say, the gruesome bowl of Sheffield, or drain your joy like the darkly brooding towers of Leeds as you sweep down the M62. More pertinently, it does not twang the heartstrings like neighbouring Liverpool, with its Liver buildings, its rejuvenated docklands, its brash whiff of salt and the omnipresent and ghostly notion that, once, the young John Lennon tramped among the streets.

Thankfully, this underwhelming cityscape – and it underwhelms still, whichever way your train may trundle towards it – tells an extraordinary lie. For the architectural power of Manchester cannot be glimpsed from afar. Indeed, you sometimes have to strain to see it from nearby, as your train snakes through brick-strewn wastegrounds before halting in the dull modernity of Piccadilly Station or the rather more romantic ambience of Victoria. You simply have to disembark, hunch your shoulders to the breeze and the rain, and spend at least half a day with your head angled upwards.

And it *is* powerful architecture, too, and orchidaceously beautiful, though Mancunians, as they drift about their daily business, don't notice it all that much. Sightseeing is for tourists – the people who can often be seen open-mouthed in disbelief as their attention is gripped, vice-like, by a striking piece of nineteenth-century architecture. Indeed, the *Encyclopaedia Britannica* does not lie when it describes Manchester city centre as '. . . an outdoor museum of styles from Greek Classical to tall steel-framed structures.' Forget the latter, for tall steel-framed structures can be found in multitudinous huddles – in Perth or Birmingham. But Manchester's nineteenth-century legacy – now that really is worth celebrating.

It was, in those days, undisputedly Britain's second city. Its extraordinary ostentatious city centre is the result of an outrageous spree of commercial 'keep up with the Joneses'. Firms would entice architects from across the globe. Hence, you would find offices like Gothic castles, warehouses like Venetian palaces. The offices of the prestigious Manchester Ship Canal Company were, for no reason other than sheer flashy braggadocio, given a Grecian colonnade, and the celebrated town hall, designed by Alfred Waterhouse, has often been described as 'the ultimate in Victorian Gothic fantasy'.

Such industrial-age boasting, of course, rather belied the fact that, like Glasgow, Leeds and London, the jewels of the city centre were surrounded by a dark collar of poverty. The legacy of which lingered through the ages – not in the architectural brilliance but in the air in Ancoats, Salford, Hulme and, where the Haçienda and Factory are both situated, in Knott Mill.

It lingers still.

But it remains a city of invention and innovation. Rekindle an ageing Mancunian's dormant pride and he or she will eventually stop talking about the great teams of United or City and move on to the invention of the computer, the atom bomb, about Mr Rolls meeting Mr Royce in the Midland Hotel, about Engals, The Hallé Orchestra, the Battle of Peterloo. Elderly men, deep into their third pint of Boddingtons, will talk wistfully about Crossley Engines. Those in middle age might recall the great days when Manchester was regarded as the nightclub capital of Europe, in the fifties and sixties, of the r'n'b boom – Merseybeat – which the city shared with Liverpool. Those in the younger half of life will talk with equal pride about Buzzcocks, Joy Division, the Smiths, Stone Roses, Happy Mondays, Madchester, Oasis. Maybe they will begin a familiar and, I fully understand, thoroughly irritating boast. 'This is the hippest city in the world,' they might state, and their observation would be constantly backed up by the city's love/hate omnipresence in the glossy youth culture magazines. 'You should see it on Saturday night, it's wild, maaan.'

And so, perhaps, it always was. Consider this snippet, borrowed from a book entitled *Manchester and the Textile Districts in 1894*, by Angus Bethune Reach. The book was a construction of a series of articles which originally surfaced in the *Morning Chronicle*.

In returning, last Sunday night, by the Oldham Road, from one of my tours, I was somewhat surprised to hear loud sounds of music and jollity which floated out of public house windows. The street was swarming with drunken men and women and with young mill girls shouting, hallooing and romping with each other. Now I am not one of those who look upon the slightest degree of social indulgence as a downright evil, but I confess, that last Sunday night in the Oldham Road astonished and grieved me. In no city have I ever witnessed a scene of more open, brutal and general intemperance. The public houses and gin shops were roaring full. Rows and fights and scuffles were every moment taking place within doors and in the streets. The whole street rung with shouting, screaming and swearing, mingled with the jarring music of half a dozen bands.

Chapter Two

Early Warnings

LIKE STARTLED GAZELLES, they scampered into Peter Street. Three of them. Nervous eyes flashing like cats. Spidery legs clasped in spandex, their identical shock-red locks lifting up and off their foreheads, and flowing down before flaring across their shoulders. They were a startling sight. A primary-coloured rebellion. They were unaccustomed, however, to being seen about town so early. Evening would normally begin for them at 10 p.m., when they would taxi to the other side of the city, to the basement club which snuggled beneath the city's defunct Corn Exchange, behind the disappointing cathedral. The club, their spiritual home, was called Pips and, once inside, they would sway, with caricature campness towards the infamous Roxy Room, a self-explanatory haven in which they would pose and pout and kiss and prance about and generally wallow in glorious parodic glam.

Not since David Bowie had played Stretford's soulless Hardrock, back in '73, had they attended a rock gig. And to attend a gig at the Free Trade Hall was rather like surging straight into enemy territory. For the Free Trade Hall, when not famously occupied by the Hallé Orchestra, was Manchester's archetypal dour rock venue. Like Sheffield's City Hall, or Leicester's De Montford, the Free Trade was all too often filled with those sexually repressed types who would trundle, heads bowed, hands buried into combat jackets, legs garbed in frayed Wrangler flares flowing over biro-scribbled pumps. The progressive rock fans, loyal and bowed, would worship their heroes from their respectful seats high in the gods, politely clapping guitar solos, resolutely refusing to 'nod off' during the obligatory drum break. But this night was, somehow, different. Not at all like the America/Poco bash, or Sabbath's triumphant return. On this night, a vastly disparate audience came to the Free Trade Hall. Not only would the Bowie freaks mix uneasily in the bar with straggly-hair rockists, they would be forced, also, to mingle with straight-faced disco trendies, twentysomething couples gazing adoringly into each other's eyes and menacing pockets of clean-jeaned car mechanics, fitters and turners. It was, at least in the eyes of the Bowie freaks, an all too dangerous cocktail, a strange and volatile mix. All assembled to sample the delights of Lou Reed.

Reed had, unwittingly, drawn an audience from every wayward angle of Manchester street culture. His *Transformer* album, flushed by the power of Bowie, had penetrated deeply, gaining him a barrage of unlikely fans, most of whom would never have heard of the subversive genius of the Velvet Underground. *Berlin*, his famously introspective follow-up, had penetrated less deeply although the recent live album, *Rock'n'Roll Animal*, with its – to Velvet purists – unforgivable hard rock base, had stretched his appeal into the vast progressive field. The portents were . . . well, interesting.

Things began meekly enough; Steve Hunter's guitar slashing through 'Sweet Jane', Reed, black-clad and bleached-haired, humorously sashaying his way across the stage, to and fro, taunting the wild gathering at the front, their arms stretched out and upward in a state of crazed worship. There was, however, an unusual menace in the undertone. All the Free Trade Hall employees noticed it, for their proud venue, with all its architectural power and historical resonance, more often than not had a calming effect on rock audiences. On this occasion, however, a tension flowed around the hall. Reed's broad appeal had cut across no small number of, frankly, rather stupid rock barriers. It felt exciting – it didn't feel safe. Reed was able to camp it up to full effect. The songs, though performed with none of the ad lib adventures that had typified his performances of old, were punched across in dour-faced rockist manner. Reed seemed to enjoy the band's reactionary grunge, especially the power it seemed to hold over the audience. Only during the absurdly camp finale, 'Goodnight Ladies', was the show allowed to break into pure theatre. Caned and top-hatted, at last he seemed to fit the narrow description of him – 'the king of glam' – that had graced the unlikely preview in that evening's *Manchester Evening News*.

Ten minutes after Reed had left the stage, the obligatory chants for an encore, fuelled by a rising tension, darkened into a dull roar. Suddenly, the clapping hands had changed to clenched fists. Screams rang out as a fight rippled through the stalls before crashing horribly into the stage front . . . and then another . . . and then another. Somebody clambered on to the stage, grasped a microphone, and found himself surrounded by a furious road crew who, in turn, were beaten back in a flurry of fists and a partial stage invasion. '*Get off my equipment, cunt!*' screamed the tour manager, three times, before retreating into the dressing room. Local television journalist Tony Wilson stood, quaking in the stalls, loathing the violence and yet somehow sensing that a barrier had been crossed, that a change had begun. In the stalls, also, somewhere, stood Ian Curtis, fresh into town from Macclesfield, and like Wilson, thrilled and repulsed in equal measure.

As the fighting – not as serious as it initially appeared – settled down to a muffled growl, both left the hall, not quite knowing what had taken place. Behind them, three pencil-thin Bowie fans were seen, at the stage front, scrambling from the subsiding fracas, tripping over the splintered wood and tumbling into the aisle. That night, in the Roxy Room of Pips Disco, they would pout and spin and sing heartily into a dead microphone, a microphone that, they informed the assembled oddities, had been used earlier in the evening by Lou Reed.

That Lou Reed gig, though one of the most notorious Manchester gigs of the mid-seventies, wasn't the only sign that things had started to change. At the very same hall, twelve months later, a startled Dr Feelgood – the biggest and by far the most vigorous exponents of Essex r'n'b – performed before a swaying, rolling, numbingly volatile crowd, more akin, the band remarked, to a 'derby match' football crowd than the kind of rock audiences who would normally sway to the jerky movements of guitarist Wilko Johnson.

'The crowd were phenomenal,' gasped the late, great singer, Lee Brilleaux, before adding, 'Is it always like that in Manchester?'

It wasn't always like that, of course. Far from it. But the twist into an early kind of punk had begun. The crowds had begun to mix, although rather more messily and certainly more violently at some of the smaller venues, the ex-cinemas and the bingo halls, which sat absurdly amid the partly demolished inner-city areas. The Electric Circus, dangerously positioned in a darkened street in Collyhurst, and three miles away, within earshot of the Belle Vue Speedway Stadium, a staid, white wreck of a building, the Stoneground, developed a reputation for downbeat drug dealing, smalltime criminality and a wholly courageous booking policy.

Local music, in any influential sense, hadn't really existed in Manchester, not since the mighty blast of Merseybeat – as much a Mancunian concept as Liverpudlian – which folded so disappointingly in the mid-sixties, leaving vast circuits, heavily beaded with all manner of venues, wholly redundant. A smattering of largely derivative, smalltime bands – Stackwaddy, the Purple Gang, Son Of A Bitch – had pottered away, ineffectively isolated from the city's few success stories. 10cc, of course, who alone bridged the gap so innovatively between Merseybeat and the mid-seventies, and the unfathomable and distant success of Oldham's Barclay James Harvest. Mere pockets of success. Nothing solid. For so long, there had been no real reason to actually physically start playing in a band as the gap between local halls and dizzy success just wasn't expected to happen. Rock stars, it had long since been concluded, were hallowed beings who hailed from somewhere else – America or the south of England – and owned fish farms in Hertfordshire.

But to gain a true perspective, one has to begin in 1973, in the unlovely mining town of Leigh, with a young, elfin-faced schoolboy named Pete McNeish, a compact and complex mixture of shyness and precocity who had already started to write wry, teasing, innuendo-stacked love songs, spiced with campness as would befit the glam pop of the era. In May 1973, McNeish formed the smartly named Jets Of Air, whose debut live performance at the local All Saints church hall included a tasteful and measured mixture of his own songs, plus numbers by Lou Reed, David Bowie, Roxy Music and, rather dangerously perhaps, the Velvet Underground.

Two years later, McNeish, while studying for an HND electronics course at the Bolton Institute of Technology, formed a music society with the intention, mainly, of finding like-minded students who would wish to sit around listening to the massively innovative electronic disco of the German band Kraftwerk. Through this tiny, insular though rather significant college society, McNeish met Howard Trafford, a fellow student who required some kind of electronic soundtrack for a soon-to-be-aborted art video. Later the same year, Trafford placed a scribbled note on the college noticeboard requesting 'MUSICIANS REQUIRED ... ESPECIALLY EUPHONIUM PLAYERS ... TO PERFORM A VERSION OF SISTER RAY'. Intrigued, McNeish instantly replied. The pair, using numerous, transient musicians, would attempt to cover and perfect – if such a thing is possible – a set comprising mainly of songs from Iggy Pop And The Stooges' unholy repertoire.

In February of 1976, after excitedly soaking in a Neil Spencer-penned *NME* review of the ramshackle new band, the Sex Pistols, who had supported Eddie and the Hot Rods at the Marquee, McNeish and Trafford immediately departed for London. They stayed with Trafford's old pal from Leeds Grammar School, Richard Boon, then studying art at Reading University. The intention was to track down the Sex Pistols.

The pair couldn't possibly have known it, but in excitedly purchasing a copy of the London what's on guide, *Time Out*, on Friday 20 February 1976, they had already taken their first step into the annals of punk legend. It was Trafford, apparently, who stopped dead on the pavement when his feverish leafing through the pages – they were hunting mentions of the Sex Pistols – came to rest on a review of the television programme *Rock Follies*, the tale of the Julie Covington-led all-girl rock band. Everyone, surely, who has enjoyed a mere passing interest in punk rock must surely know that the article's headline read, 'FEELING A BUZZ, COCKS?'

'Buzzcocks!' stated Trafford, instantly metamorphosing, one likes to think, into the Beefheartian persona Howard Devoto. McNeish, likewise, would melt into the more familiar Pete Shelley.

That afternoon, their rather quaint search for the Sex Pistols was rewarded after their phone call to the *NME* office had provided them with the office number of Pistols manager Malcolm McLaren. It was McLaren himself, somewhat charmed by this northern quest to discover his band, who informed them of two impending gigs, at High Wycombe College of Further Education that very night and the next day at Welwyn Garden City. Shelley, Devoto and Boon dutifully attended both gigs, and to these three and to so many others who would catch the band live during the following six months it was as if they had managed to touch some kind of magic, some strange power that lay certainly not in the musicianship, and not merely in the attitude either. There was something beyond that, something less obvious.

Pete Shelley: 'It was a specialness . . . I mean, initially we were struck by just how "normal" the band were. They seemed like nice blokes even, apart from when John was being abusive, and yet, well, they just seemed like the centre of everything. They held the power. It was so obvious . . . I could never explain it. We got to know them a little and almost immediately started planning to bring them to Manchester. The idea was to put them on at the Lesser Free Trade Hall and our band, Buzzcocks, would provide the support . . . that is, if we could find a rhythm section in time.'

They couldn't, as it turned out. Despite a disastrous two-song gig at Bolton Institute and a furious attempt to find suitable musicians via an advert in the listings magazine, *New Manchester Review* (Devoto, unpaid and over-enthusiastic, had been compiling 'pub rock' listings for the mag), they failed to fall into a steady line-up before the first of two appearances by the Pistols at the Lesser Free Trade Hall, taking place on Friday 4 June 1976.

Devoto had hired the hall for £32. Not bad for such a featureless shell, though tagged on to the main hall it lacked any trace of shabby grandeur. McLaren, however, was ecstatic.

Standing like a manic bus conductor in the dead centre of Peter Street, clad head to toe in black leather, using his natural aggressive enthusiasm he coaxed, grabbed, bundled and conned every passing youngster into the building, up the stairs, and past Pete Shelley who had adopted the role of doorman. This was not to be the gig that would alter the course of Manchester musical history. (Indeed, many people would be immediately alienated by the heavy metal thrash of support act, Solstice, crashing their way through 'Nantucket Sleighride'.) The main event would come in the same venue on Tuesday 20 July, when the Sex Pistols would be furiously supported by local glam-punk brats Slaughter And The Dogs and, making their shambolic debut, Buzzcocks.

TUESDAY 20 JULY 1976

A glass smashed into the neck of the man who would soon be called Ed Banger. Dazed, though not generally the kind of chap one would wish to unduly aggravate, Eddie Garrity turned round to see the sneering face of Johnny Rotten, soon to be engulfed in a raucous bundle of his London followers, a tumbling, spitting ball of a gang, falling through the doors of the bar as well as falling into a 'Cockney' football chant. The Slaughter And The Dogs fraternity, not unaccustomed to such battles, fell heavily into the fray before the entire human mess splintered into disparate fractions; bickering, punching, spitting around the hall and along the adjoining catacomb of hallways.

Pete Hook: 'I'd dragged my mates Terry Mason and Barney and Barney's wife down to both gigs ... it was more wild than nasty, fists were flying all over the place at one point though I always get those two gigs mixed up. I was so impressed, though. I saw McLaren, dressed all in leather ... I thought he looked incredible.'

And so would most attendees, though it would remain obvious that whatever strange music had hovered around the Sex Pistols would certainly sprinkle among the tiny crowd – although, naturally, a couple of hundred thousand would claim attendance – who included three future members of Joy Division, Mick Hucknall, Steven Morrissey, and practically every subsequent Mancunian luminary, all drawn to the strange howl and mocking leer of Johnny Rotten and his inept, sub-metal backing. The whole inelegant mess was captured imperfectly on the swiftly distributed bootleg, *The Good Time Music of the Sex Pistols*, the record being the pirate product of some quick Mancunian thinking. It was a small victory, but this much-prized vinyl would represent Manchester ripping off London for a change. Not much to boast about, but it was a start.

Chapter Three

Of Sweet Salford and Sad Suburbia: Anthony H. Wilson

T HE M602 CUTS MERCILESSLY into the heart of Salford. For a mile it forms a rigid parallel with Eccles New Road, once a darkly evocative drag, lavishly 'pub peppered' and at all hours warmly flanked by busy pavements. In later years, the road would seem joyless, barely peopled at all and profoundly devoid of former grandeur or purpose. Today, the two great roads merge to form a huge clockwise crawl which half-heartedly seems to signify the centre of something. From this point, the traffic slithers testily down and into the 'back end' of Manchester. More often than not, progress is slowed even further by outbreaks of illogically placed traffic cones, guiding drivers this way and that, proving the catalyst for a never-ending state of mass road rage. The old Salford, or at least a memorable little corner of it, seems merely a ghostly echo here now, on this drag. This is Regent Road. Infamous today for its twin states of gridlock and madness. Infamous for other things, too, things associated all too easily with nineties street culture.

Back in the fifties, at 448 Regent Road – right there, on the site of the roundabout – stood the tobacconist shop belonging to the Wilson family. It was a lively little shop blessed with, naturally, an aromatic allure and a good deal of amiable chat. It was also, of course, something of a male preserve, a place to linger – in such times, a veritable male oasis in a string of female-dominated retail outlets like the Co-op or the chemist.

Anthony H. Wilson, born in Salford's Hope Hospital in 1950, lived through his intriguing early years in this tobacconist's and, although moving to Marple, near Stockport, at the age of five, would still spend most Saturdays up and into his teens lurking mischievously in the shop's oak-panelled corners, soaking in the delicious smells of fresh tobacco and generally observing the nuances of severe, working-class Salfordian life.

Marple proved something of an antithesis to all that for this precocious Catholic boy. Marple was, and to this day remains, quite the epitome of Cheshire leafiness balanced, as it is, between Manchester's darkened sprawl and the hills of nearby Derbyshire. It is a commuter heaven, boasting a small, lively centre, two railway stations and a series of infamous canal locks – and little else. Although attending primary school in Marple, Anthony's links with Salford were kept alive by his weekly visits to the shop, and he never felt truly at home as he sauntered wearily through Marple's ever-pleasant, although in his young eyes, profoundly dull suburbia. As far as Wilson was concerned, and as far as he is still concerned, his character is shot through with 'city boy' vision – street suss, perhaps. He recognised this back then, before he could recognise the lure of detached or semi-detached superiority. The 'magic', for Wilson, lay back in Salford, in the darkened, Gothic, distinctive, mesmerising Salford that crumbled steadily away as fifties clearance schemes took a firm hold and Anthony H. Wilson ambled wryly through childhood.

The 'city boy' aspect of Wilson's character could only be accentuated when, upon passing his eleven-plus with flying colours, he attained a scholarship at De La Salle, the Catholic grammar school situated – to Wilson's delight – in the heart of Salford. Hence, from the age of eleven, Wilson would join the commuter set.

The selection system which operated in regard to Manchester and Salford's famous 'direct grant' Catholic grammar schools was both bewildering and curiously logical. Fifty per cent of a school's intake would soak in children from the immediate locality while the other half would be filled by the brightest kids from the satellite towns of Warrington, Wigan, Macclesfield, Stockport, and their respective neighbourhoods. The commuter trains, buses, and trolley buses of Cheshire and Lancashire would be swelled by this often unwelcome intake of riotous schoolchildren, and rarely would they travel to the schools nearest their homes. Such common sense just wouldn't seem fitting, somehow. It can, therefore, be ascertained that a certain degree of streetwise worldliness would be nurtured by daily forays across Manchester city centre, and out, by a second bus or train, into Hulme, Moss Side, Whalley Range or, in Wilson's case, Salford.

Musically, Anthony would, from the age of ten, nurture a love affair with the guitar, an instrument that he never quite managed to fully tame. His first instrument was swiftly purchased, at the alarming cost of £4.15s, from Mameloks on Manchester's Oxford Road, before attending a series of fraught lessons above the store. (Later, from the demolished sixties bombsite of Mameloks and surrounding shops, would spring the BBC's New Broadcasting House.) By the time Wilson had reached thirteen, his musical horizons had widened and he had begun to strum a Watkins Rapier, red and shiny.

Naturally, considering this fondness for the guitar and his ear for the better music of the era, his initial hero was the American solo guitarist, Duane Eddy. For the same reason, he also enjoyed the Shadows, principally because of Hank Marvin, although he was, in true rock tradition, not at all enamoured with the beaming, bleached juvenility of Cliff Richard. People may smirk when today Wilson recalls his Shadows affections but, in effect, in the early days the band were poised at the cutting edge of the British r'n'b boom. (Although, their slide into blandness would begin, somewhat ironically, at Manchester's Free Trade Hall when, then named the Drifters, they backed Richard shortly after recording 'Livin' Doll'.) Much to Wilson's delight, the Shadows line-up included, as well as Marvin, Jet Harris on bass (the English James Dean, complete with mean, moody leer and an omnipresent black leather jacket) and Tony Meehan. Harris and Meehan would soon leave the Shadows and Wilson's affection would travel with them. He feverishly purchased Jet Harris and Tony Meehan records, Besamo Mucho (with Meehan on drums) and Applejack, and placed them lovingly next to his Beatles and Shadows EPs.

So began Wilson's secondary love affair; not just with the guitar or guitar music, but with record sleeves. He simply adored the picture sleeves of the day, running his fingers across their enticing glossiness, feeling them, smelling them and, when in a record shop, all too often buying them. He liked record shops too, and of course the multitudinous adventures and pleasures that could be gained inside them. He frequented Denis Violet's – the old Manchester City and United centre forward – record shop in Manchester, the infamous record section of Lewis's department store (he bought a Duane Eddy single from there) and a couple of record shops in Salford, one near his father's shop and the other on Chapel Street.

Tony Wilson was always, by his own admission, 'a lousy guitarist'. His comical attempts to recreate his favourite sounds – the Animals' 'Don't Let Me Be Misunderstood' proved to be his favourite '64 song – failed to prevent him from trying, endlessly trying, back in Marple in the back room. It was partially his passion for guitar which turned his attention towards the American folk boom of the early to mid-sixties. He would pluck through inept finger pickin' routines to the sound of Joan Baez and the young Bob Dylan. Wilson's precocious mind would be stirred by a somewhat unexpected influx of lyrical intelligence. Suddenly, the traditional r'n'b mess of sexual innuendo and juvenile angst hardly seemed fulfilling. Barely into his teens, Wilson found himself leafing mesmerically through the pages of Kerouac and Ginsberg, Burroughs and Faulkner. Standard student reading fodder although, unusually, Wilson was more attracted to the descriptions and visions of America than any soul-searching profundities on behalf of the writers. This Americanisation would colour his cultural life for a full ten years. Not for Wilson the dour insular rumble of progressive Brit-rock, or even the brash popisms of the glam boom. In fact, almost to the point of obsession, he fully immersed himself in America and Americana, with the exception of Rod Stewart's *Every Picture Tells A Story*, and, indeed, the Faces. Though loath to admit it, he even purchased Ronnie Wood's dire solo effort, *I've Got My Own Album To Do* on cassette (although, years later, he would sellotape the recording holes and symbolically use it to tape the first A Certain Ratio album). His only early seventies regret was his incredible and seemingly lone failure to pick up on David Bowie.

'I really did miss out on that,' he would later say, shrugging, his black spot seeming all the more remarkable considering his addiction to the Velvet Underground, Lou Reed and Iggy Pop, all strongly linked with the Bowie phenomenon.

These American leanings carried him through Cambridge University, where he would eventually graduate with an English degree – after a spell editing the university newspaper – and a sudden, unpremeditated hunger to become immersed in the strange world of television media.

'I have absolutely no idea where the notion to become involved in television came from,' he confesses, 'though it was pretty simple. Things just seemed to fall in place for me.' Wilson, charged with volcanic ambition to carve his way into television, trained as a television journalist at ITN, took time out to work as a scriptwriter for the then unparalleled *News at Ten*, became 'Item editor' on *First Report* (now *News at One*), and then moved home to precociously usher his way into a presenter's chair on the north-west news/magazine programme, *Granada Reports*, in 1973.

In Wilson's eyes, especially considering his aversion to British rock which, by 1975, had evolved into a clear-cut loathing of the 'pub rock' boom, Hatfield And The North and all those deadening London outfits, rock music had hit an all-time low. On *Granada Reports* he would continue to drop in unscheduled plugs for Bruce Springsteen or Iggy Pop although, in general, his enthusiasm seemed to noticeably wane. (Much to the relief, as it happened, of the older *Granada Reports* viewers, rather more magnetically attracted to the genial slippers'n'glasses bonhomie of his fellow presenter, Bob Greaves, than to Wilson's trendy and pacy rhetoric. Grannies seemed to like him though. 'They all want to make him a big dinner,' stated one producer at the time.)

Granada Reports was, to some, alarmingly adventurous in those days. Wilson was initially sent out to perform semi-comic reports from the more idiosyncratic corners of the north-west or, as often seemed the case, to act out a kind of 'adult John Noakes' role with a series of mildly risky sojourns into 'adventure activities'. Many people still harbour fond memories of Wilson clumsily stumbling off a Goyt Valley hillside, barely attached to a hang-glider and crashing, to terrific comic effect, into a sheet of bracken.

'I think, overall, I had a good relationship with the people of the north-west. It has changed a good deal since,' he states, before adding, 'I mean, I would get approached in shops and things but it was always a bit more intense for Bob [Greaves] . . . he was more of a favourite uncle whereas I was brought in as the slightly wayward son.' It never escaped Wilson's attention that he had, in effect, picked up the baton from a whole string of legendary TV presenters who, likewise, cut their teeth on the same programme, albeit in a rather less flamboyant earlier version. Brian Trueman, Ray Gosling and, lest we forget, Bill Grundy, to name just a few. Nevertheless, throughout Britain – up until this day, the Granada press office forcibly impress upon me – *Granada Reports* (later renamed *Granada Tonight*) has been regarded as the most innovative if not hard-hitting news magazine programme in the country. Wilson's attempts to drag youth culture into the format would, naturally, be chiefly thwarted, the mysterious hierarchy at Granada allowing Wilson his little youthful 'eccentricities' but not, quite rightly, letting them flavour the output. Occasionally though, things would slip through. Greaves, as ever the steadying force, would be heard to announce, 'I know Tony Wilson has strong thoughts about music. Maybe we will hear them one day, but for now he is off to a Derbyshire hillside where . . .' More infamously, perhaps, were the occasional pop interviews which often seemed gloriously out of place.

'Why are you so miserable?' he asked Leonard Cohen, rather obviously.

'I'm not miserable, I am just pissed off,' came the unexpected reply, as the unusual wide shot captured the sight of Greaves creasing with laughter.

Years later, Greaves would be similarly amused when Wilson attempted to interview the bolshy figure of John Lydon, then promoting the early, and much loved in Manchester, version of PiL.

'He talks very slowly, doesn't he,' exclaimed Greaves of Lydon, after the somewhat painful exchange.

'Well, maybe that's because Johnny isn't restricted by time schedules like you and me,' explained Wilson.

The musical content improved, if only slightly, during Wilson's brief stint presenting the local arts review show, *What's On*, which proved to be quite unexpectedly anarchic, manic, wacky and, to the eyes of the Manchester and Liverpool-based students, rather cool. (One remembers a spectacular appearance by the often unfathomably surreal Manchester comedic outfit, Alberto Y Lost Trios Paranoias, whose unsteady, anarchic performance proved genuinely disturbing, at least for those viewers who hadn't been pre-warned.)

What's On was to prove portentious for Wilson, whose wry style of presentation seemed to have finally slotted neatly into its niche. This didn't escape the attention of Granada boss David Plowright who, in an attempt to create an alternative to *Top of the Pops* – the BBC's monopolisation of the pop chart had long been a thorn in Granada's side – organised a pilot show for Wilson in the autumn of 1975. Taking its name from a Nick Lowe single – Lowe, a credible drop-out from the ashes of the dreaded Brinsey Swhartz *was* a bit pub rocky, come to think of it – the programme would be entitled *So it Goes*. After the pilot, however, Plowright duly abandoned all hope of an attack on *Top of the Pops*. The programme, although adored by Plowright, who duly noticed the ripples of excitement it produced through the more Bohemian elements in the Granada building, had proven too esoteric, too anarchic, and rather too humorous to be capable of instigating any chance of future prime-time exposure.

'We had to put a good deal of comedy into it,' admits Wilson, 'like having a Clive James slot, simply to disguise the fact that there was absolutely no decent fucking music to be found ... not in England, at the end of 1975. I was so desperate to do something of musical or cultural importance, so incredibly desperate to make something that I would actually want to watch, and yet, ironically, I didn't feel that anything that the young were listening to was of particular interest.'

Prime time was out of the question. This didn't worry Wilson too much, for in the mid-seventies, British rock music was still gripped by feverish and mindless snobbery and Wilson, allergic to any traces of encroaching blandness, was partly relieved by the decision to grant *So it Goes* a late-night Sunday evening slot. It may be crap, he told himself (incorrectly), but it will surely be hip (incorrect on both counts).

As Christmas 1975 unfolded messily, Wilson was wondering just how he was going to keep the dreaded pub rock 'explosion' at bay – although Dr Feelgood, it must be noted, were redefining English r'n'b in a noble manner and the Sensational Alex Harvey Band had finally proven that progressive rock, if not literally 'progressive' at all, could hold a deep sense of humour, and a sense of anarchy, too. Not that this cut much ice with Wilson, who kept his eyes firmly glued on America. And America, he decided, would just have to feature heavily in his new programme, if, indeed, it was going to achieve any degree of credibility. After all, for the first time in his life he was poised to break through on a network scale. No longer, perhaps, could he drive 30 miles to the south in order to escape his localised, though undoubtedly intense, television fame. An eerie prospect? A nice thought or a weird notion? He couldn't decide. As it turned out, it would be all of these things. For Christmas, Wilson received a gift from, in his words, 'An old Deadhead junky friend from Cambridge . . . great guy.' Quite how much thought went into this gift is unclear, but it was significant and, for Wilson that year, quite mind-blowing. True enough, it was an American LP. What's more, it was an album that came directly from the most esoteric corner of the punk scene that had begun to rage so flamboyantly in New York. The album was Patti Smith's *Horses*. For so many people who would be involved with or affected by the English punk scene, a change of mind and attitude began, strangely, the moment their respective needles touched down on to that Patti Smith vinyl. Wilson, by no means an expert on the New York scene, played the album repeatedly all Christmas. For him, even though he wasn't aware of it, the new wave had begun.

In February, Wilson ripped open a scruffy brown package which had arrived in a muddle of *Granada Reports* mail, to discover a battered New York Dolls album sleeve. With the sleeve came the message: 'Dear Mr Wilson, I have heard about your show. It's wonderful news. Please, could we have some music like this?' It was signed Steven Morrissey, Stretford. Wilson was both intrigued and bemused. He had never heard of the New York Dolls but, impressed by the precocious enthusiasm of the Stretford upstart, promised himself that he would, indeed, find out more. The suffocating and repressive schedule that was swamping him at the time – and has continued to swamp him ever since – prevented him, alas, from replying to young Mr Morrissey. He remembered the package, however, and would have remembered it even if the sender hadn't eventually progressed to the status of world superstar.

Two months later, as Wilson was wading manically through the often rather fraught filming of *So it Goes*, a third incident advanced his punk education. Again, it came in the form of a package. This time it was a tape containing three songs, if indeed 'songs' can be regarded an adequate description. It was little more than a murky demo tape, through the mud of which a singer screamed and a guitarist slashed through chords with heady though rather artless aplomb. The sender was called Howard Trafford. The band was the Sex Pistols. 'The Pistols are gonna play the Lesser Free Trade Hall on June 4th ... you MUST see them,' the words screamed from the page.

Actually, Wilson had found himself thrown into another, somewhat less well-documented punk experience, one month before the Lesser Free Trade Hall gig, in unlikely Portwood, an unlovely warehouse area on a darkened edge of Stockport. An area cherished in sepia-tone photographs depicting flat-capped workers and chubby wives immersed in Victorian drudgery, but cherished nowhere else. The event in question took place in a club called the Garage, directly opposite the future site of Toys 'R' Us. It was a gig, a strange gig, all the stranger perhaps, due to the tab of acid Wilson had dropped that very afternoon. The gig featured a glam-cum-punk band, Slaughter And The Dogs. A brash, vivacious if somewhat inelegant quartet, profoundly dripping the local street culture of their home area – the Manchester overspill estate of Wythenshawe. Wilson had been alerted to the local rise of the 'Dogs' by a pushy young chap, also a Wythensharian, named Martin Hannett, who had previously visited the presenter at Granada. Hannett had produced an album by the Belt and Braces Trucking Company, and had attempted to get a plug on *So it Goes*. Wilson, naturally, had been rather more interested in this young crowd, Slaughter And The Dogs.

It was a distinctly weird gig, taking place in a dank, blackened Stockport cellar. Upon entering, Wilson had found himself encircled by numerous, apparently unconnected psychopaths and styleless, parochial examples of the 'fag' end of glam rock, latterday Bowie clones and Iggy freaks. Wilson, settling at the rear, found himself 'strangely charmed' as he soaked in the massive surge of youthful energy which flowed so passionately, if ineptly, from the stage. It was little more than local band rock – but local band rock with such attitude. Pop history would, in time, erase the push and verve of Slaughter And The Dogs (and so few people ever managed to catch them at their best), but they will surface again later in this book, and as far as Wilson was concerned, predated those infamous Sex Pistols' appearances by four weeks. Staggering from the club, head still afloat from the acid and fuelled further by alcohol, Wilson decided that he had just experienced his second truly historic rock happening – his memories of *that* Lou Reed gig still causing him to fall, at the merest hint, into a state of repetitive anecdotal bliss.

So it Goes was up and running by mid-1976 and, as six shows had been recorded *before* Wilson's attention had been grasped so heartily by the Dogs and later the Pistols, it was, arguably, though certainly in Wilson's perspective, the *worst* possible time in rock history to kick-start a young, precocious, anarchic rock show. Had the programme emerged six months later, then it would have been effortlessly precious. As it turned out, and as Wilson regarded 90 per cent of the music featured on the show as 'total shit . . . I hated it all . . .', the result proved little more than a messy cultural hotch-potch which strongly veered towards the comedic. Wilson's sardonic tones couldn't quite disguise the fact that, due to his long-standing American bias, 'Album of the Week' spots were devoted, rather absurdly, to the likes of Willy Nelson. Though, the then chaotically satirical Dr Hook proved great fun, if hardly ground breaking. However, with six shows in the can and the Lesser Free Trade Hall embedded in Wilson's consciousness . . . with punkism's swilling about inside him, making a mockery, in part, of his Cambridge background and certainly tainting his busy daily routine with a certain amount of guilt. ('Fuck off, Wilson,' screamed Slaughter And The Dogs singer Wayne Barrett, in a timely fit of inverted snobbery, before adding, 'A punk is supposed to be a pauper, so fuck off, you posh git, you mean nothing to us.')

Such things worried Wilson. The fact that, despite his Salfordian roots – and he would cling to Salford, rather than

Marple, throughout his career – he might just aspire to and succeed in climbing up, out and above the unholy punk maelstrom, he temporarily and naïvely saw this as a positive drawback, and such guilt would never fully leave him. Culturally, therefore, he aspired hopefully downwards, an aspiration that, perhaps, would eventually be fulfilled with the success of Happy Mondays. But 1976, unlike 1990, was awash with inverted snobbery. Punks, that tiny tribe, were carving some kind of pride from dole-queue, tower-block existence. Wilson's alienation from this would swell considerably during the next six months.

However, with punk's howl ringing in his ears, and irritated by the knowledge that he had attended the wrong Lesser Free Trade Hall gig, he set forth on 17 June 1976, with a *So it Goes* researcher in tow, for Walthamstow Assembly Hall, where the Sex Pistols had been ushered in to support Ian Drury and the Kilburns and the Stranglers – whose short set was truncated because, in light of the faulty equipment, they believed they might be electrocuted. It was another strange gig – the pub rock, albeit the credible pub rock of Ian Drury, through to the macho bandwagonning of the Stranglers, to the Pistols, the real thing. Upon entering and paying the 95p admission price, Wilson encountered the strange sight of a cavernous hall, sparsely filled with no more than 35 people, all standing in a singular, semi-circular line in front of the stage. As he approached the stage, this semi-circle proved to be the trajectory of Johnny Rotten's spit. Rotten, in fine, legendary form, had decided to treat the entire event with the kind of contempt it probably deserved. The Sex Pistols, however, had yet to fall so perfectly into image. This fact, Wilson noted, was proven by the antics of guitarist Steve Jones who, dressed in a white jumpsuit and whirling his right arm around in windmill fashion, had yet to escape his Pete Townshend fixation. The Pistols, decided Wilson that night, were undoubtedly the coolest rock band of all time – no one could possibly seem more threatening – but there was a little way to go. Though deciding to book the band for *So it Goes*, he remained slightly less emphatic than Howard Trafford or the young journalist named Parsons, who had commandeered his attention, back in May, at a Roundhouse Patti Smith gig, furiously impressing on Wilson the importance of this new London band.

In the autumn, with *So it Goes* stuttering through a series of clumsy Sunday evening slots, attracting along the way a whole mass of critical slatings – only Chris Dunkley in the *Financial Times*, ironically enough, believed the show to be remotely worthy – the music press, en masse, regarded Wilson as, as one so elegantly stated, 'a northern prat'. Wilson was asked to compère a gig at the Wythenshawe Forum. On the bill would be Slaughter And The Dogs, a local band called Wild Ram – (soon to twist into Ed Banger And The Nosebleeds), and Gyro. The entire affair was patched together by the Manchester agency Music Force, a Wythensharian huddle of musicianly folk which included Martin Hannett, the saxophonist Tosh Ryan and Alberto Y Lost Trios Paranoias drummer, Bruce Mitchell. Wilson accepted the invitation despite being noticeably upset by a review of *So it Goes* which had appeared in listings magazine, *New Manchester Review*. 'So it Goes is Granada's answer to the 5 O'Clock Shop,' it sneered. Below a byline pseudonym, Wilson could sense the writer's real name . . . Martin Hannett. Feeling suitably betrayed, Wilson duly stormed up to a startled Hannett before the show. '*Did you write that review?*' he screamed, before adding, in a manner most unbecoming for a high-profile local television presenter, '*Well . . . fuck you!*'

Hannett was dumbfounded. Nevertheless, his revenge, he swiftly decided, would be instant. Wilson did indeed compère that gig, while spending much of the evening fending off people who kept pushing towards him, intent on informing him that Hannett was waiting for him in the car park with his fists in the air. (One eye-witness report described the maniacal figure of Hannett stomping around the car park, pounding his fists into the side of the headlining band's Ford transit, repeatedly screaming the word 'Cunt!', although this does seem, even for Hannett whose eccentricities so entertainingly spice this entire story, rather an 'over-reaction'.)

'Typical Martin,' Wilson jokes. 'He just wanted a fight . . . I must admit I chickened out of that one . . . I slipped quietly away. I wasn't much into scrapping with crazed Wythensharians.'

THE WYTHENSHAWE CONNECTION

Wythenshawe's curious importance in the history of Manchester music cannot be understated. Initially the largest overspill estate in Europe, its inelegant sprawl bridges a fat gap between Manchester's increasingly decaying Victorian suburbs and the select Cheshire countryside. It has always had to live with the hardest of reputations – local phone-in disc jockeys on Manchester's Piccadilly Radio would even cherish a rather derogatory joke about the new language – 'monosyllabic Wythensharian' as it was known – whenever the obligatory late-night drunken caller would find him or herself blurting obscenities over the air. But this, the cruellest of jokes, belied the fact that to this day Wythenshawe remains quite cleverly at the cutting edge of Mancunian youth culture.

Wythenshawe's musical pedigree is surprisingly impressive. It is probably most succinctly captured within the tale of the area's most successful though still surprisingly faceless pop star, Mike And The Mechanics singer Paul Young, whose tumultuous career stretches the length of Wythenshawe musical folklore and neatly crosses the initial stirrings of Factory at one point. Born in 1947, in the Benchill district, Young exercised his vocal chords before his mother, Blanche, actually gave birth. His startling scream from the womb became manifest in a story in the *Manchester Evening News*.

A natural singer from boyhood, he surprised nobody by prominently featuring in various school and church choirs and, indeed, by fronting his first band, Johnny Dark And The Midnights, at the age of fourteen.

'We were the first real band in Wythenshawe,' he states. 'We had three rhythm guitars all plugged into one microphone and we would play skiffle and chart hits. I thought, This is it, we are the first Wythenshawe pop stars. I can have a big house, buy another one for my parents and drive about in limos . . . God, we were naïve.'

Young's career swerved, rose and dipped through numerous musical guises. He took up vocal duties with Wythenshawe's most promising stab at sixties fame, the Toggery Five, one of the truly great under-achieving Manchester bands of all time. The Toggery Five, as their name implied, were, sartorially speaking, the hippest, most street-sussed beat group in Britain. Indeed, no other band so effectively mirrored the latent pride of their particular area – the first real Manchester personification of working-class attitude – and the ripples caused by their unparalleled 'kudos' would seep influentially into the myriad social circles of that huge overspill estate, if nowhere else. Unfortunately, their tale of woe – largely just missing out on hit songs that were briskly picked up by the Hollies – typified the Merseybeat era, a time when numerous managers and agents grew noticeably and arrogantly fat and a multitude of musicians were left to scramble for the slim pickings as the scene faded. When the Toggery Five's guitarist, Frank Renshaw, left the group for the comparative safety of Wayne Fontana's Mindbenders, Young's career twisted into weirdness, in pace with the times, as the late sixties approached. After a stint singing in front of a Luton-based combo who would soon become Jethro Tull, Young found himself back in Wythenshawe, hanging loosely around an unholy huddle of local musicians, including saxophonist Tosh Ryan, legendary bluesman Victor Brox, and Hughie Flint, later to form McGuinness Flint with Gerry Rafferty. This by now garishly garbed gang evolved rather messily into an avant-garde psychedelic band called the Electric Circus. The band wouldn't, however, manage to take their Zappa-esque bleatings out of the Wythenshawe garages. A spell in Germany, playing with such heavyweights as Ritchie Blackmore and Buddy Miles, preceded an horrific two years, reunited with Frank Renshaw as the Trini Lopez cabaret outfit with the dull name Young and Renshaw. After a spell as failed bland popsters – with Cook and Greenaway – Young and Renshaw evolved, more locally, into – a new one for Wythenshawe, this – a Buddhist-Tibetan unit called the Mandalla Band. This was the point when Young met the brash, young music arranger, Martin Hannett. Hannett joined the band – Renshaw left, rather swiftly – and began to poke about with the possibilities, eventually moulding the sound into something rather less left-field. Indeed, a soft, American-style, melodic rock band. It was quickly decided that the name, the Mandalla Band, had been eclipsed by this new sound and many hours were spent in name-searching horror. This problem ended when Hannett's partner, Susannah O'Hara, walked in with a copy of the novel, *The Ballad Of Sad Cafe*. Sad Cafe, of course, were absurdly misplaced in the scheme of things. As the Manchester punk scene would rage all around them, they soon found themselves locally representing Manchester's punk antithesis, the so-called 'Didsbury set'. These were a locally influential network of media-based ageing trendies who, with their fondness for real ale, vegetarian restaurants and broadsheet newspapers – their wisdom became manifest in the magazine *New Manchester Review* – would, if nothing else, set up the blueprint for the more successful what's on magazine of later years, *City Life*.

The Wythenshawe influence on the record label that Wilson would form, Factory Records, would be massive. From the beginning (the Durutti Column) up to date, the very heart of Factory – its streetwise and stylish cool – would be provided, in part, by Salford, and in the main, by Wythenshawe. Throughout the period covered by this book, Wythenshawe lies omnipresent – a brooding, ragged undertone.

Wilson was unaware that he had already met the musician – indeed, the central musicianly force – around whom Factory Records would be constructed. In order to notice this, he would have had to cast his mind back to his traumatic involvement in the Slaughter And The Dogs/Wild Ram gig and, in particular, the boyish, comparatively mild-mannered guitarist of Wild Ram, perhaps the only musician on the growing Manchester punk scene who could actually 'play' to a high standard – Vini Reilly.

Reilly was, and still is of course, a profound oddity. His idiosyncratic feel and ear for music was inherited from his father, an in-house piano player. The family lived, without the lure of television sets, in strikingly rough areas of Withington and later Wythenshawe. His father would trundle away on the keyboard, expertly imitating the music of Fats Waller (black classical music, as Vini would later call it). He was good, too, although being unable to read a note of music and having no inclination to either, he was rather adrift in an era when learning music meant studiously poring over songbooks. Vini would stand on tiptoes, soaking in his father's tinkering, straining to see his hands caressing the keys. When returning home from school at lunchtimes, Vini would seize the opportunity to perform alone, and on one glorious occasion discovered the power of 'major thirds' while playing 'Trains And Boats And Planes'. One month later, rather absurdly, he had perfected Beethoven's 'Moonlight Sonata', playing it by ear in C sharp minor. This was curious. For Reilly had no idea why he should choose to play it that way, rather than the more obvious A minor. He knew nothing at all about key signatures. 'Something,' he eerily states, 'guided my hands.'

His parents, stunned by their son's obvious natural talent, sent him for piano lessons with a professor of music at Manchester's Royal Northern College, and he went willingly. Reilly, however, had spotted a red, plastic Beatles guitar languishing temptingly in the local Co-op. Though his parents seemed willing to purchase this for him, his older brother, Frank, regarded the guitar as 'stupid' and financed the purchase of a three-quarter size wooden guitar which at least looked like a semi-serious instrument. At precisely the same time, one of Reilly's classmates was having lessons with an eccentric German woman based in Didsbury, named Mee Mee Flecture. Vini tagged along one day, more out of curiosity than intent. After being invited to play, and picking precociously through two pieces, Mee Mee grabbed Reilly by the scruff of the neck, offering to teach him – as she knew his parents could ill afford lessons – for free. She was a hard task master, ordering him not only to attend the lessons twice a week but loading him with homework which would encroach rather dangerously on his schoolwork. Not that Vini minded. Twice a week he would wander from his rough council estate in Withington to the comparatively plush and leafy Didsbury, more often than not failing to avoid the derision and indeed violent assaults from predatory 'Crombie' kids, who so expertly controlled both areas. The sight of a small, slightly girlish boy carrying a guitar was too good an opportunity to miss. Vini doggedly stuck at it.

'I don't know what made me persevere. It is the only thing I have ever stuck at . . . and the fact that I would get the shit kicked out of me on a regular basis only strengthened my reserve,' states Vini.

Vini picked up a number of unusual influences along the way. His brother, for instance, owned a record by a Brazilian troupe called Los Indiano Traviollas, which contained the most poignant guitars he had ever heard. Spending most of his fourth school year in bedroom isolation – in true rock genius manner – he decided that, rather than take 'O' level music or indeed any 'O' levels other than English Language and Literature, he would, for better or worse, forge a career out of composing and playing his own stuff.

To his parents' concern, his schooling had taken a turn for the worse. Aged fifteen, Vini Reilly had, for all intents and purposes, 'gone off the rails' emotionally and intellectually speaking. Physically, he wasn't in such bad shape. He practised judo and staggered his friends by having trials for Manchester City and yet refusing to take things any further, preferring to spend the time with his guitar. (Later he was to learn that Manchester guitarists Johnny Marr of the Smiths and Jez from A Certain Ratio had also turned down further trials at roughly the same time.)

Vini Reilly's first musical unit would comprise of just himself and a bizarre local flute-playing musician called Gamma (a kind of punk rock Ian Anderson). Gamma proved to be a huge influence on Reilly, as well as an eccentric soulmate. Together they began writing the weirdest of songs, many songs; all in 15/8, utilising the most unlikely method of phrasing. Throughout '74/'75 they would try this rather awkward collection of songs out with the accompaniment of numerous bewildered drummers and bass players, none of whom could seem to bend their musicianly prowess around such wayward ditties. Eventually, reverting to a duo, they would perform a series of bizarre dates at working men's clubs, British Legion clubs, Irish clubs and downbeat pubs.

'Those gigs taught me so much,' says Reilly, 'because we played to people who were more accustomed to seeing people singing Frank Sinatra songs very badly. In a sense, that defined my musical stance, and possibly the stance of Factory later on because I always believed that people would accept a far more diverse music form than they would normally come in contact with. The fact was that these people could tell that we could actually play our instruments. That fact managed to gain us respect . . . and we always went down really well.'

Using a Reliant three-wheeler, the couple would jump on to and often gatecrash the somewhat sad 'Talent Competition' circuit, performing songs such as 'Jumpin' Jack Flash' and 'Summertime', with Reilly on guitar and the flute-playing Gamma leaping, with unprecedented vigour, around the venues. Gamma/Reilly, as they became known, won every competition they entered. Using the solid notion that they wouldn't turn anything down, no matter what state of decrepitude the venue was in, or how notoriously aggressive the clientele might be, Gamma/Reilly performed at an extraordinary range of venues, from Trafford British Legion to a local mental hospital to the comparatively plush surrounds of the Oaks, a disco-cum-cabaret pub in Chorlton Cum Hardy.

Reilly, blessed with angelic looks and hair which flowed down his back, would often find himself mistaken for a girl, or at least a boy on the make, and would fend off numerous less than gentlemanly advances. Advances which, more often than not, would be of an aggressively sexual nature.

'I was accosted every day in every pub all the time. Smelly men would rub up to me,' he later muses, totally without feeling.

* * *

The gang that would evolve into the entourage that surrounded Wild Ram and later Ed Banger And The Nosebleeds, and would later splinter into numerous Factory-orientated projects, began as a small, vicious circle in Wythenshawe. Vini had started to hang about with brothers Vinni and Mike Faal, a notorious though amiable couple, and Donald Johnson, later to grasp considerable esteem as A Certain Ratio's exceptional drummer. From this nucleus, a sizeable gang was formed, comprising mainly of the black Wythensharians, all of whom, sensing Reilly's unease with the white gangs of the area, instantly took to him, forging friendships that would last until this day. Mike and Vinni Faal would, to Reilly's delight, write songs together, and almost to relieve the everyday boredom, a band of sorts was formed. With Donald on drums and Vini supplying a funky bass, this ramshackle combo would perform succinct sets in Moss Side 'drop in' centres and a trickle of somewhat severe 'black' clubs – Vini Reilly, to his delight, being accepted as a kind of 'honorary Wythensharian black'. The band – Donald, Vini, Vinni and Mike – briefly adopted the glam monicker, Lady. Their existence was, to say the least, precarious. Often their sets would end in a mess of furious in-band squabbling. For Vini, however, the short-lived Lady would provide him with a unique 'out of body' experience. This occurred during a particularly dangerous gig at Wythenshawe's Red Rose pub, on a ubiquitous Sunday afternoon. The pub, 'rough as owt', was filled with bickering families, most of whom were sitting, staring in disbelief at the guitarist who was winding his way through a series of Santana riffs. That, in itself, might seem pretty incongruous, if not surreal, but Vini Reilly soon found himself floating up to and drifting along the ceiling. Instantly he panicked. Not because of his predicament, for he rather enjoyed the isolated serenity, but because he didn't trust his body to continue for much longer without playing a bum note. With this in mind, the soul of Vini Reilly hurriedly scampered back down into its correct, earthly position. A state which, he will earnestly inform you nowadays, has not altered since.

The band imploded messily, as most bands do, although before the dust had settled Vini received a note from Vinni Faal, asking him to phone soon. 'It's about work!' stated the note. With considerable trepidation, Reilly telephoned, to discover that Faal had started to manage three young lads who had recently left school and desperately needed a guitar player to complete the line-up. Although initially tentative, Reilly was struck by the absolute 'uncontrollability' of the trio – Eddie Garrity, Toby Toman and Pete Crookes.

'They were punk, naturally punk, before I had heard of punk,' exclaimed Vini. 'They really were the wildest lads I had ever come across. Completely, utterly, mental . . . and this madness seemed attractive to me. I found them exciting. It was a genuine expression. We became known as Wild Ram. It seemed a fitting name, as did Ed Banger And The Nosebleeds which came later.'

Vini, however, was poised between two extremes at the time. Part of him wished to explore this new, exciting rock: he had heard all about Slaughter And The Dogs, of course, and found the chance to join their Wythensharian rivals, Wild Ram, a genuinely exciting prospect. Nevertheless, being just about the only musician on the as yet embryonic punk circuit who could actually play, he also nurtured musicianly notions of a higher degree. He wanted to play jazz, believing it, naturally, to be a more fitting expression of his talent. He had heard about a group of jazzers who performed, weekly, in jam-session manner, at Manchester's jazz pub, Band on the Wall. Named Both Hands Free, they seemed, to Vini, to offer a gloriously open door for a fresh input. In truth, they were a pretty insular bunch of cynical session musicians who had no intention of letting a precocious young oik step in and steal their admittedly rather dim and fantastically localised limelight.

'Sure, kid, you can jam with us,' they told him. 'Come back next week.' So after five weeks of rejection, Reilly turned up with his Wythenshawe entourage in tow. This entourage included Slaughter And The Dogs sidekick, Rob Gretton, Vinni and Mike Faal, and numerous and dubious hangers-on. Mostly, this fearsome crew merely wished to see Vini play. Upon discovering, however, that the young guitarist had been snubbed yet again, and noticing also that Vini's small frame seemed incapable of holding in his simmering anger, Rob Gretton, Vinni and Mike Faal proceeded – in true Wythensharian style, for Vini's friends from the hardest edges of the hardest areas were profoundly Wythensharian – to stamp their way through the club, threatening all and sundry while promising to break the sax player's legs.

Thankfully, despite the evening's charged atmosphere, a full-scale riot was mercifully averted. This was, perhaps, just as well. For as Vini wandered disappointedly towards the exit, guitar clasped sullenly beneath his arm, the club manager sidled menacingly up to him and, placing a threatening, gangsterish arm around his shoulders, informed Vini – be it in a spirit of bluff or a genuine threat – that he had strong connections in the Manchester underworld and that if Vini or his friends were to come back into the club and attempt any kind of intimidation, they would simply 'disappear' and nobody – least of all the police – would ever find them again. This somewhat corny warning still manages to chill Vini Reilly. There was, he noted, something in the club manager's tone that hinted that his words carried a certain amount of weight. That was the night that Vini Reilly decided that the sedate, introspective, intellectually adventurous world of a jazz musician might not be for him. He decided to dedicate himself to a less dangerous medium. Punk rock.

Feeling that the name Wild Ram might seem 'a bit pub rocky', the lads swiftly altered it to the rather unpleasant though apt Ed Banger And The Nosebleeds. By this time, late 1976, they were well and truly immersed in punk's invigorating swirl. Toby, Pete and Eddie had attended the Lesser Free Trade Hall while Vini's rebellious muse had been stirred by the Pistols' memorable appearance on *So it Goes*.

Vini's rash introduction to Slaughter And The Dogs, the band who would instigate a fearsome local rivalry with Ed Banger And The Nosebleeds, would remain as a terrifying image; a vision implanted at the back of his mind. To pay for guitar strings, he worked, fairly casually, as a gardener in the Parks Department, and as a petrol pump attendant. The former job provided him not only with ready cash but with a neat circle of rather uncompromising acquaintances, with whom he would too easily spend it. A favourite jaunt would be a trip to a depressing 'pint 'n' a shag' disco, the Riverside, in Didsbury's Palatine Road.

The disco had few pretensions – hessian wallpaper, crudely assembled cocktails, flat bitter and, more often than not, a raging, uncontrollable clientele. Vini would attend each Friday, slotting alongside a trickle of tough, unpretentious 'fighting lads' from the Parks Department. Most fights, however, would evolve into little more than a flurry of fists and multiple bloody noses, inevitably followed by the ritualistic and massively inebriated 'bonding' session with the enemy. On one night, however, things became rather more out of hand. The fight, which began in the dead centre of the room, surged recklessly towards Vini and his friends who naturally seemed only too happy to be swept into the centre of the chair-crashing scrum. Vini ducked and bowed, however, as the fight darkened considerably and bottles were smashed against the wall and thrust towards his face and chairs crashed painfully into his back. Within seconds it had become clear that the fight was swiftly descending into serious riot, and then in dramatic slow motion, Vini noticed one guy turn towards him. In his hand, which hovered with savage intent, glistened the blade of a knife. That was the moment, as it always is, when the fight truly darkened. The guy, his face twisted with unfathomable hatred, lunged forcedly at Vini who somehow managed to scuttle free and scamper into the comparative safety of the central scrum.

Two weeks later, as Vini was finishing his shift on the pumps, a white van belonging to local PA owner and bass player, John Gibson, called round to pick him up on the way to a gig. For the first time, Wild Ram would be sharing van, PA and gig with Slaughter And The Dogs. As Vini excitedly clambered into the rear of the van, he came face to face with a member of the Dogs circle – the very person who had pulled the knife on him. For a while they merely stared silently at each other, before their tension was brushed aside in the prevailing camaraderie.

'We never mentioned it . . . ever,' Reilly states, 'and he turned out to be a thoroughly decent chap. I still see him to this day. Always very polite, very nice indeed. It's amazing to think he was once capable of standing in front of me, in that disco, apparently willing to kill me.'

Ed Banger And The Nosebleeds were not intellectually innovative popsters like Buzzcocks, or brash glam kids like Slaughter And The Dogs, or pushy bandwagoners like the Drones. They were not like any of these bands. They were genuinely, completely, utterly, uncontrollably crazed – Ed in particular, who, with absolutely no sense of self-preservation would think little of jumping on to a table mid-performance, grabbing a guy's beer and pouring it over his girlfriend. Often such actions would result in near tragedy.

'Ed would get beaten up all the time,' says Vini. 'I mean really, really beaten up . . . kicked repeatedly in the head . . .

everything . . . and then he would just get up and walk away. He was simply amazing. I have no idea how we managed to stay alive. They were fantastically exciting, wild, crazy, disorganised mad times.'

The Nosebleeds, perhaps fittingly, would spend most of their days flitting around in the wake of Manchester's leading punk band, Buzzcocks. Reilly noted that Buzzcocks, despite their seemingly innocuous personalities, would cause near-violent hysteria within the straight progressive rock clubs and halls in which they played. Mostly, the Nosebleeds would play the same venue the following week, and, as short-haired punks, would be forced to endure the full wrath of the crowds. All of which, naturally, they encouraged to the full, Ed being quite possibly the most confrontational singer in the country. Inside their ramshackle touring van (an old ambulance) were positioned four handy, ever-ready mike stands, one for each member to grab and hastily beat off the assembled gatherings. 'There were always crowds waiting for us after the gig . . . just wanting to smash us to bits. Sometimes it got quite messy,' says Reilly.

Vinni Faal, self-appointed manager of Ed Banger And The Nosebleeds, approached Tosh Ryan with a view to getting a single out on the Dogs' house label, Rabid Records. Ryan, flushed by the positive reviews of the Slaughter And The Dogs single, was more than happy to provide the necessary funds. Not that, however, these would add up to more than half a day in a local eight track. Two songs were recorded; the bolshy 'Ain't Been To No Music School' – a sarcastic slap in the face of Sad Cafe, who had behaved in an obnoxiously pop-star manner towards them while sharing a bill at a Chorlton venue, the Oaks – and the self-explanatory punk-rock rant, 'Fascist Pigs'. On the strength of this single, which received a ripple of critical applause in the music press, and probably because their name sounded intriguing, Ed Banger And The Nosebleeds found themselves invited to perform, with Sham 69 in support, at London's all-important Roxy venue. It was, to say the least, an 'interesting' London debut. To the band's delight, Sid Vicious and assorted friends, again intrigued by both the name and their fearsome word-of-mouth reputation, managed to attend. However, the Wythenshawe crew were in no mood for gentle camaraderie. Two close associates of the band – allegedly Vinni Faal and Rob Gretton – wandered around the cellar club, smacking people totally at random in the face, before offering the explanation, 'We're from Manchester ... YOU take notice!' This somewhat overtly enthusiastic form of promotion managed to stir up an intense degree of hatred within the club which was hardly softened by Vini's insistence that the band should play nothing other than the two aforementioned numbers, over and over again. Needless to say, all hell broke loose and to the band's delight, their final chord proved to be the rallying cry for a mini-riot.

'It felt like punk. We thought, the Dogs, Buzzcocks and the Drones will never top this,' says Reilly. Unfortunately, despite gaining the admiration of the Roxy's infamous owners and being instantly invited back, the performance would fail to break into punk's biased history books and Ed Banger And The Nosebleeds would attain infamy only as a vehicle that would, at one time or another, carry an unlikely band of musicians who would find success in later years. Reilly, who jumped ship sensibly when the fires of punk had swiftly burnt away, would gain cult respect as the central force of Durutti Column, the initial and constant 'point of balance' of Factory Records. Drummer Toby (Phillip Tolman) would progress to percussion duties in the legendary Ludus and, more famously, Primal Scream. Following Eddie Garrity's departure – by 1993, having changed his name to Eddie Baskerville, he would become the scourge of the Glasgow comedy/music circuit – the vocal spot would be briefly adopted by the same shy and gangly young man who had once sent Wilson the New York Dolls album sleeve – namely Steven Morrissey – and even more absurdly, Vini's guitar position would be occupied by Wythenshawe musician, Billy Duffy, latterly of the Cult.

Chapter Four

From Safety to Where?

L IKE WILSON, PETER HOOK was born in Salford – Salford Royal rather than Hope Hospital – and spent his first three years blissfully ignorant of the uncomfortable turbulence of his family, in a two-up, two-down, within hopping distance of Eccles New Road. His parents split up when Peter was four and, along with his half-brother Chris and full brother Paul, he lived with his grandmother until his mother remarried two years later. During this two-year spell, things settled into normality, enlivened only by his one, glorious, unforgettable Christmas when his mother was courting and he duly received a whole sackful of toys. 'More toys,' he still states, 'than you could fill a wall with.'

This fairly dull Salfordian normality wouldn't last long, however. Upon securing a prestigious position at the Jamaican Glass Company, Peter's stepfather duly whisked the family to the Caribbean before the bright, precocious child reached his seventh birthday. For three and a half years, Peter Hook found himself living in, it must surely have seemed, a whole different universe. They settled in Kingston in a large wooden veranda'd house, enveloped in towering trees and complete with servants.

'It was a simply brilliant place to grow up,' he states, dismissing any notions of juvenile homesickness. 'Just like one big adventure playground.'

Peter Hook's world, enticingly landscaped in lush green rather than the dispiriting grey of Salford, suddenly seemed full of possibilities, and his precocity was duly rewarded at the local 'private' school – part of the Jamaican Glass deal – when, driven by close contact with the teachers, he would catch up with the strikingly advanced class. (Hence, at the age of six, he found himself struggling through his $13 \times$ table.) Not a hint, not a drop, not a trace of racism would cloud either his school life or his playful activities at home, on Phoenix Avenue. This was never an issue, possibly because his stepfather was the only white person in the neighbourhood who would deliberately surge out in the evenings, intent on enjoying the conviviality of the local shabeens, the predominantly black shanty bars. As such, the Hooks were warmly accepted into the community. Significantly, perhaps, the drinking sojourns paid extra dividends, for theirs was the only house on Phoenix Avenue not to be ransacked during their three-and-a-half year stay. They were wealthy by comparison, even to their fellow workers, for they owned the only television in the neighbourhood. Although a merciful escape, the TV also meant that the house would be under constant siege from television-hungry neighbours. This would prove mildly irritating and even occasionally distressing, as in the time when Hook and his brothers, strangely uninvited to a birthday party next door, had to watch the fun from the distance of their veranda, only to find the entire throng switching, post-party, to the Hooks' front room for a television session. Hook's most vivid memory would, quite naturally, be the moment that President Kennedy was shot. He was sitting there, sweating away in his island idyll, surrounded by a warm pocket of neighbourly friendship, dreading the fact that once news of the shooting crackled from the local radio sets, the entire area would surely want to cram into his front room to watch the endless re-runs of the events in Dallas.

When his stepfather's contract eventually ran out, Hook's mother pursuaded him not to renew it, and her pangs for Salford would also prevent the family from relocation to Birmingham on their return to Britain. Even at the age of nine, Hook could feel the cold splash of culture shock and, duly unsettled, he sank tentatively back into life at his gran's two-up, two-down, just off Regent Road. His only relief was at Regent Road Primary School, where his advanced state of education provided him with a lofty cushion on which he sailed effortlessly through his eleven-plus. Only two pupils passed from Regent Road that year, by which time the family had moved to another two-up, two-down in neighbouring Ordsall, on the edge of Salford's rapidly fading dockland. Hook would remain in the house until the age of nineteen when, due to his mother's refusal to be rehoused as the area crumbled to a brick-strewn bombsite, it became (somewhat conspicuously) the only house left standing as the area succumbed to the inappropriately named Slum Clearance Scheme. Indeed, throughout his teens, the entire social structure of Salford would be famously wrestled away, to be crammed into an ultimately vacuous and – as time would tell – ill-conceived tower-blocked 'Utopia'. Salford simply drained away.

Peter Hook met Bernard Dicken (latterly Sumner and for a short while, as a punky affectation, Albrecht, although from this moment on the pair would be known to all around as Hooky and Barney) at Salford Grammar School. Although not in the same stream – Hooky was in 'Lancaster', Barney in 'Gloucester' – the pair would find themselves equals on the unholy schoolyard hierarchy. They were not, for instance, the school bullies but, rather intelligently, they became 'mates' of the school bullies. They 'attached' themselves to the top of the ladder, never to 'do the beating', which was often cruel and extreme, but never to be beaten. Their close association to the 'top dogs' provided a lasting security. Hooky's lofty position had been achieved, simply, by the fact that the 'other' successful Regent Road boy, Dave Ward, happened to adopt the role of 'cock of the school'. Levelly, Barney had entered the grammar school as the ex-primary school mate of 'Baz Benson', who became the 'second cock'. This dual social position proved neatly fortuitous and served to not only provide the enviable security which the two boys gloatingly relished, but tended also to throw them together as 'coat carriers', perhaps. Through this role they developed a sense of 'comic arrogance'. They were untouchable, and as if not wishing to waste their privilege, they duly ran riot – a state of affairs which would eventually result in striking under-achievement at 'O' level stage. Hooky, despite his brooding sharpness, passed just one 'O' level (English), although to this day he believes he was cheated out of technical drawing (the exam teacher, 'a right dopey bastard', forgot to provide them with part two of the exam until ten minutes before the end). Barney passed English and, most naturally for him, art.

Salford's weakening strings of community affected Barney perhaps even more profoundly, for the hollowness of social dismantling would remain with him, and even in later years help to colour the music of Joy Division.

Barney: 'I have thought about this more and more over the years. I can't speak for the others, especially Ian, but I do perhaps think that some of the darkness of Joy Division's music can be traced back to those younger days. When I was very young I was living in Lower Broughton, Salford. We were right near the River Irwell which was disgusting, and there was a chemical factory at the end of the street with oil drums lying around all over the place. So it was pretty grim. But there was always a strong sense of community. The young kids would stay up, like I did, playing in the street until really late at night. There would be a little old lady in each doorway, gossiping, looking over the kids. When it all came down, we were shifted across the river to a tower block. In my young state I thought the new home was brilliant, but the loss would hit me later on. All my childhood memories were wiped away when they cleared out the old Salford.'

Their outside-of-school activities – limited because of the prevailing menace of night-time Ordsall – began at the age of thirteen, when they would both attend North Salford Boys' Club, latching on to the late embers of the skinhead cult. Strangely, considering the prevalence of soul music in the area at the time, especially in the local youth clubs and discos, neither of them latched on to soul at all, although born from their skinhead affiliations they enjoyed a brief flirtation with Trojan reggae. The balance between the pair was rather cruelly shattered, strangely by the British government, as they both approached their fifteenth birthdays (Barney's on 4 January and Hooky's on 13 February). Both had set their hearts on attaining Lambrettas, the essential post-skinhead fashion accessory. Unfortunately, the age limit was swiftly raised to sixteen – fifteen still, for anything below 50cc – as the new year dawned. Barney, having lied – stating his birthday had been on the 4th December – was allowed to purchase and ride one, while for Hooky, the prospect of an agonising scooterless year began to weigh heavy. Naturally, the pair fell into the prevailing 'suedehead' chic: Crombie overcoats, Barathea blazers, two-tone 'tonic' trousers, Stead and Simpson brogues ('Royals'), Prince Of Wales check trousers, electric blue parallels and, to express allegiance to the notoriety of their area, 'Salford' stone-coloured 24-inch parallels.

Eventually, both 'ensembles' were duly completed by scooters, Barney proudly sitting aloft a Lambretta GP 200, notable for its distinctive side-panel stripes, and Hooky the similar though stripeless SX 200. Both boys enjoyed the scooters and would spend evenings 'fiddling' in oily backyards, Barney adding, at one point, a Phillips fuel injector which provided, albeit unexpectedly, a Batmobile flash of flames from his exhaust.

Until able to blag their way into pubs and clubs, the pair wouldn't spend too many hours on Salford's gruesome night-time streets where 'grammar school' lads were prime targets. After a spell in neighbouring Broughton, apparently less risky, they finally managed to join the revellers who flooded the streets of Manchester city centre by night, surging excitedly into the Roxy Room at Pips, lounging in darkened corners, apeing the Bowie freaks, allowing the sounds of Roxy Music, Iggy Pop, Lou Reed, Sparks and Queen to soak into their beer-hazed consciousness. For a while, and much to Barney's disgust and no doubt the delight of his friends, he suffered from a bout of parental strictness, and had to be back in his house before 11.30 p.m.

'He would always cop off and then have to make excuses and leave. He would always be gutted,' states Hooky, still smirking.

Still resisting the distant lure of soul, the lads began, as lads would, listening to heavy rock. The usual stuff: Deep Purple, Led Zeppelin ... They saw Led Zeppelin in concert at Stretford's unatmospheric Hard Rock venue, an experience which, rather ironically, caused Hooky to be physically sick after his balance had been unhinged by near exposure to the bass speakers. In 1976, Hooky had started working at Manchester Town Hall and had nurtured a feverish addiction to music papers. Each Wednesday he would stare from his office window, watching the midday deliveries which would bring the NME, Sounds, Melody Maker and Record Mirror to the Albert Square newsagents. At lunchtime he would devour all four, already living the music scene in his head.

After owning a series of decrepid Mark 10 Jaguars – his lifelong passion – he finally discovered one capable of travelling long distances and duly took four mates to Cornwall. During this raucous sojourn, he was glancing through the *NME* when his attention was arrested by an advertisement for the Sex Pistols at the Lesser Free Trade Hall. He had heard about the Sex Pistols. He had heard, also, about the tension and fighting that all too often, accompanied their gigs. He simply had to go and find out for himself.

The day after the Pistols' second Lesser Free Trade Hall gig, Pete Hook bought himself a bass guitar for £35. (Barney already had a guitar, and had clumsily started to wrap his fingers around the first basic chords.) In a spirited effort to catch up, Hooky bought and immediately sank into – and indeed, still swears by – *The Parma Hughes Book of Rock'n'Roll*.

'It was dead good,' he states, 'because it had little stickers that you put on your guitar neck, so it was dead easy to learn. We were still fired up by the fact that the Pistols had been so crap although, years later, I played that Pistols bootleg and the funny thing is they weren't that bad at all. The sound was crap, but the playing . . . that was a damn good rhythm section. Still, who am I to ruin an old myth?'

The Hook's house finally succumbed to compulsory purchase on the week that Hooky had secured a job at the Manchester Ship Canal Company, and the family moved to Little Hulton. This was something of a relief to Hooky, who had often returned to the Ordsall house at lunchtimes just to check if it had been burgled. On Friday nights, he would stay at Barney's house, principally because of its close proximity to Manchester city centre. Together the pair would strum away – ineptly, of course – with Barney attempting to teach basic bar chords to Hooky.

Hooky: 'We were both shit. I never thought we'd even manage the basics.' Nevertheless, they persisted, with Barney using a tiny practice amp and Hooky wired up through the gramophone belonging to Barney's gran, using the input wires on the arm. Despite such comic makeshift equipment, they would soon surprise themselves by picking up the basics with relative ease. Duly encouraged, they began to put in the hours.

Barney: 'I think it was fair to say that the music, though we were crap, was immediately an escape. It always is . . . just reading the music papers, getting into it . . . it's an escape from real life. And real life was hitting me quite hard at that point. I had started to work at Salford Town Hall, sticking down envelopes, sending out rates. It was immensely depressing. It felt like all the fun had just drained away, and Salford was just horrible at that point. The music just seemed like light relief.'

The practising would continue during the following weeks, heavily fuelled by their feverish scanning of music papers and early fanzines, their enthusiasm, naturally, fired by the unfolding spice of punk, and the infinite and previously unheard-of possibilities which seemed to lie beyond the basic formation of a band. Seeking a vocalist would prove almost impossible. An old school friend, Martin Gresty, rather nervously attempted the task – in fact, he was offered the dubious role – but after securing a job at a local nuts and bolts factory, never bothered to contact the pair again.

IAN CURTIS – THE ENIGMA

Ian Curtis, though born in Old Trafford, was brought up in Hurdsall, an ungainly sprawl on the fringe of Macclesfield, twenty miles to the south of Manchester. Macclesfield was, and indeed still is, a strange, rather self-contained town, drifting alone amid the greenery of the lush Cheshire plain on one side and the darkly looming Peak District to the rear. Macclesfield has great wealth – it is an ex-silk manufacturing town – and the villages which stretch prettily to the west (known as the 'Hollywood' of Manchester) are encircled with Cheshire leafiness and contain stockbrokers, top footballers, ageing rock stars and green-clad countrymen. By contrast, the inner town comprises a myriad of tightly-knit streets and ex-mill-worker two-up, two-downs. The character of Macclesfield has been forged from these two extremes: the wealthy, by day, flocked through the town's exclusive furniture stores, while by startling contrast, a rather wild and parochial revelry raged in the streets at night, providing Macclesfield with twin and not necessarily deserved reputations of Cheshire snootiness and milltown roughness.

Despite this, Curtis's childhood was enjoyably dull, flavoured only by various and fleeting obsessions. A love of speedway, football and music enlivened his daytimes. Although hardly immersed in a violently changing inner-city paradox like Sumner, a curious parallel did occur when the Curtis family moved to the superficial Utopia of an unlovely and latterly hugely detested flat-block near the town centre. Ian fared better at school than Hooky and Barney, gaining seven 'O' levels despite nurturing a growing obsession with music. Again, like his Salfordian counterparts, his Crombie-clad days failed to lead him into the heart of soul music – an odd omission, considering the weekly Macclesfield exodus to the infamous and nearby all-nighter, the Torch, in Stoke-on-Trent, just one stop along the London line. Instead he soaked in the darker edges of glam – the Velvet Underground, MC5, Iggy Pop.

Ian Curtis married Deborah Woodruff in August 1975 at Henbury, Macclesfield, and their somewhat turbulent and edgy relationship is honestly recounted in Deborah Curtis's book, *Touching From A Distance*, in which the central struggle of a young man, split between a wife and a daughter and a burning, penniless obsession to make an impact on the rock stage seems, in retrospect, hopelessly doomed from the word go. Deborah, although not quite sharing Ian's almost total immersion in the bubbling punk scene, willingly followed his obsession, travelling with him to the infamous Mont de Marson punk festival in Bordeaux and many times to the semi-derelict venue on the cold north edge of inner-city Manchester, the Electric Circus.

'Ian was wired up the first time I can remember,' recalls Hook. 'He seemed really edgy but I guess that was understandable because it was when the Pistols were at the Electric Circus. There had been a load of football fans who had turned up, chucking bricks and spears at us on the way in ... all those Pistols gigs were tense. But it was at the Electric Circus, during the earlier punk gigs, that we got to know Ian. He said he had a sort of band, but it was just him and a guitarist messing about, and we were a guitarist and a bassist, so it just didn't seem to fit. We went through various drummers and singers ... we got some right fucking space cadets. We just seemed to attract complete lunatics. It was becoming really desperate but one day Ian just came over and told us that his guitarist had left. It just kind of fell together like that. Suddenly we were rehearsing down at the Black Swan pub in Salford ... and the Great Western.'

Chapter Five

Fear and Loathing . . . in Collyhurst

THE ELECTRIC CIRCUS

The electric circus, the venue so often cited as being the true catalystic heart of the Manchester punk scene, was a dump. Before the warmth and energy of punk, it was an icy, soulless, cynical rock venue, crumbling steadily to match the bombsite appearance of the surrounding terrain. Opposite, across the blackness of Collyhurst Street – and no other street in Manchester ever looked so profoundly black – stood a line of pre-war low-rise flats, all proud and jagged like broken teeth. During the Circus's latter days, the days of new-wave notoriety, the flats would prove to be a useful venue for the local Dickensian oiks, some no more than six years old, who would hurl bricks, stones and breezeblocks down from top-storey windows, on to the ubiquitous line of punks who formed a queue below. But that was in 1977 and the Electric Circus had already reached its all-time low just twelve months previously. In those days it was a downbeat resting home for the plethora of third division rock bands who hastened the sad end of the 'progressive era'. The bands had stark asexual names: the Enid, Tractor, Ray Philips Woman, Stackwaddy, Spider . . . all bound by self-imposed concepts, desirous as they were of endless insular soloing. The crowds were often Spartan, always sub-dued, and would gather their Newcastle Brown bottles from the bar, glowing red in the corner, and clasp these prizes to their chests as they moved stageward, never bursting into any form of bodily rhythm or, God forbid, sexual dance. These were occasions for the head – cerebral inward soul searching or just an excuse to get quietly, as they would say in such times, 'rat-arsed'. In darkly lit corners they would purchase blocks of Moroccan Gold or Red Lebanese or blotting paper acid. Indeed, it was a dope hole – a decaying dope hole at that. How odd then, that so many of these people would later, after a good deal of browbeating, become the true force of the Manchester punk scene.

But this really *was* the all-important venue. The Lesser Free Trade Hall was merely a one-off; a two-off. Some people still claim that the Ranch Bar, a dug-out disco adjoining Foo Foo's Palace, on Dale Street, was the purest heart of the Manchester scene, with its cheery bonhomie and continuous Teddy boy problem. The Ranch was a tight, small circle, where you could relax, purchase *Shy Talk* fanzine from Steve Shy (Burke), the editor, who lurked sullenly behind the bar, and fall into conversation with all manner of freaked-out accountants-cum-Iggy Pop lookalikes, spill the beans with a Buzzcock or snigger with a Dog.

But this was, mainly, relaxation. The true spirit, the true core, the most openly accessible arm of the Manchester punk revolution, cited by Mr J. Lydon to this writer as being the most important music force of the seventies, could be found only in that crumbly ex-bingo hall, two miles to the north of the city centre. (In later days, as film directors would strive to capture the essence of punk in some kind of cinematic glory, often with blandly surreal results, the archetypal punk venue of their dreams would, indeed, closely resemble the Electric Circus.

These directors, however, never had to walk back to the city centre at 1 a.m., past bedraggled armies of drunkards and sundry perverts. They never had to sit on psychopath-filled all-night buses, attempting to slide your studded dog collar beneath your mohair jumper and physically straining to play down your beloved and often day-glo punkisms in the face of glassy-eyed, stupid, stubborn, vicious late-night Mancunian downbeat revellers.)

In 1976, as the second of two strikingly hot summers faded rapidly into a blustery August, the Electric Circus became the frontline of the local music revolution. The 'long-hairs' who had settled so fittingly into the Circus's celebrated seediness, were alerted to battle, not at all willing to allow the punk explosion in through those paint-peeled doors. It became an issue; a matter of principle. The old progressive notions hadn't quite died. Musicianship, especially of the self-indulgent ilk, was still the God of that hall. However, in a somewhat comedic reflection of the pages of the music press, punkisms began to infiltrate slowly. Occasionally, people would be seen wearing – gasp – drainpipe Wranglers. This may not seem such a shocking notion in 1996, but twenty years previously it was positively irresponsible to wander about minus the below-knee flare. People could be, and often were, especially in and around the Electric Circus, openly attacked for displaying such daring. How odd that the great liberating rock venue of Manchester's musical history would begin its days in such a reactionary mood. The irony was, of course, that it was precisely this reactionary status that would provide the venue with the necessary frisson during the early punk gigs. The Sex Pistols' notorious 'Anarchy Tour' would, thanks to the spate of massively reported cancellations, reach the Circus twice. On both occasions, attendance at the gig would be enwrapped in evocative tension, if not downright and genuine personal danger.

Collyhurst Street seemed even blacker than usual on those occasions, a blackness accentuated by sheer white, blinding street lights casting an eerie glow which wrapped so coldly around the venue. And then, of course, the sounds . . . the noises. Smashing glass would always seem to lurk in the soundtrack as you wandered along Collyhurst Street. The imagination would flare: it was Warriors . . . it was romantic black and white West Side Story . . . it was . . . it felt as if it was slap-bang in the heart of the most dangerous area in the most dangerous city in the world. For a punk or aspiring punk or punkette, such images would stack together to form a glorious vision. It was heightened awareness and razor-sharp tension. As one approached, racked in nerves, a sub-human bouncer would beckon you inside, as if ushering you into the most dubious strip joint in Soho. Once inside, aggressive stares would soak in your appearance, taking note of your spiky haircut, your tight jeans, your mohair sweater. Grizzle-chinned, slant-eyed drunks would be slouched over the bar, leering at you menacingly as you approached, slapping down their plastic pint pots as you stuttered your order. You felt, especially on those two Pistols dates, as if you were simply glowing with 'specialness'. There was a magic, of sorts. A magic that could only be enhanced more and more by each manic stare, by each threatening jibe. It was almost as if they, the punk haters, were actually feeding this magic.

When the Pistols finally made it to the stage, a flu-ridden Rotten would cast inhuman and confrontational stares across the hall. Stares that were returned by showers of lager, spit, beer glasses and bottles. Only the stageside huddle would accept and revel in the music. The truth is that, had the Pistols played to adoring hordes, had their every wayward chord been accepted by the majority of the Circus audience as an exquisite primal punky scream, then these two gigs would have – especially in the shadow of the Lesser Free Trade Hall – become less than legendary. As it was, to be there was enough. The Sex Pistols and their courageous band of followers survived the ordeal. That, in itself, also felt rather special.

The Damned suffered a similar fate in January 1977. Their appearance, although advertised hurriedly in that Monday night's *Manchester Evening News*, was a 'fill in'. They had swiftly replaced the Circus's favourites, the Enid, that very afternoon. This little switch did not go down too well with the locals. The band, following a spirited and courageous set, exited the stage to a rousing and undeserved chorus of 'SHIT! SHIT! SHIT!' Rat Scabies, as volatile as ever, his hand streaming blood after an unfortunate clash with a cymbal, lashed out at several goading long-hairs on the way to the dressing room, which was, terrifyingly, directly through the crowd at the rear of the hall. Three minutes later, this same crowd could be seen whirling, swaying and crashing ecstatically around the dancefloor to the sound of Black Sabbath's 'Paranoid', which blasted from the speakers. This, one presumed, was their idea of bona fide rock music – music which, to the untrained ear and even to fairly trained ears, seemed pretty indistinguishable from the lovely and well-played racket produced by the Damned. It was an absurd evening but an evening, none the less, that proved to be the pivotal moment of the Electric Circus, if not the whole Manchester scene. From that night onward, punk seeped rapidly into the club. Suddenly, the bass players of the visiting bands were not sullen gormless types with waist-length hair and loon pants. Soon enough, the haircuts which bobbed about in the audiences began to shrink and shrink until a dominant norm of aggressive spikiness was achieved. As the new-wave singles flooded the market – each week saw a new, though by today's standards, small batch of releases – so they were reflected in the Electric Circus disco. Illicit substances changed also, although not as violently as people might think. Dope would still do the rounds but it was soon to be universally partnered not by acid but by amphetamines.

THE MANCHESTER PUNK SCENE

It was small, tiny, miniscule, insular, cliquish and yet spiced by competitive energy. In 1996, as a thousand British bands battle to climb Brit-pop's rather boring hierarchy, and as dance music continues to rage, and as record releases simply gush into every available corner of the market, it is difficult to imagine just how tiny the 1976–7 punk scene was. Just to be able to play in a band, however ineptly, and clamber on to some rickety stage, would be enough to gain importance on the local scene, secure copious mentions from local writer Paul Morley in the *NME*, play a pop-star role while numerous inebriated fanzine editors attempted backstage interviews, and generally hang around the more desirable city nightspots, urging involvement, hoping to be seen, desperate to be recognised.

Buzzcocks, naturally, lay at the very heart of all this. At parties, whether in Salford terraces, city-centre cellar clubs, or in Gorton pub rooms, they would be somewhat embarrassed to find punk sycophancy positively swirling around them. Since their Lesser Free Trade Hall debut, they had found themselves thrown – too early, really – into the heart of the national punk scene. Infamous gigs with the Sex Pistols – most famously, the Screen on the Green bash in Islington on Sunday 29 September 1976, which also proved to be the first public appearance of the Clash – had caused the band to seep fully into the pages not only of the national music press but firmly into the print of *Sniffin' Glue*, the most central and influential fanzine of them all. Ironically enough, it was the London appearances which truly helped to cement the core of punk Manchester. (And, lest we forget, the elitist contingent who surrounded the Clash quite deliberately ignored Buzzcocks and their small following at Screen on the Green, a quite pathetic attitude which again served to strengthen the resolve of the Buzzcocks' inner circle.) Perhaps Buzzcocks' most influential local gig took place in the unlikely confines of the Holdsworth Hall on Manchester's Deansgate, which also proved to be the debut of London teen punks, Eater. Buzzcocks singer Howard Devoto appeared with bleached hair, nail varnish and Vivienne Westwood trousers. Numerous newcomers to punk, high on tabloid punk frenzy, seemed confused by Buzzcocks' lack of speed-freak punk credentials. The band held a curiously effeminate air and displayed an unsettling penchant for the avant-garde wander-ings of Captain Beefheart, quite the antithesis, in fact, of macho punk strutters like, say, the Clash. And they sang love songs. This was a strange band, indeed. The Manchester crowd, delighted to discover that their local heroes just happened to be the most idiosyncratic punk band of them all, basked in the reflected glory like a typing pool basking in the Torremolinos sun. There was a streak of genuine envy from London – and admiration from the extremely sussed Johnny Rotten – which aimed towards Buzzcocks. None of the second division copyists from the capital, from the aforementioned Eater to the Billy Idol-fronted Chelsea, or indeed the Clash, could claim such an individualistic stance. Buzzcocks owed little to the Ramones. This proved important. In fact, it proved vitally important to Ian Curtis, who, in an intriguing parallel to Steven Morrissey of Stretford – a low-key backstage agitator – drifted wisely into orbit around Buzzcocks.

It had been on Thursday 9 December 1976 that Ian Curtis, garbed in a khaki jacket with the word 'HATE' scribbled across the rear, drifted through the darkness of Collyhurst Street into the Electric Circus, and forced himself – quite a feat, this – into conversation with Pete Shelley. Curtis was awestruck. Shelley, he was startled to discover, seemed overtly normal, in a camp sort of way. Shelley dressed like a garage attendant, admittedly in Harlem, and though charming, didn't seem to be dripping in the kind of charisma that the young Curtis naturally associated with pop stardom. 'I was disappointed, in a way,' he told this writer, twelve months later. 'When I first met Shelley ... yes, I was slightly disappointed because he was really the first pop star I had ever met ... and he wasn't a star at all. I know that was the point of punk but I was still very much a punter. I still thought a rock gig was Led Zeppelin at Earls Court. It seemed most unsettling to me that, during the punk upsurge, one could just go into a bar and find yourself in conversation with the people who were supposed to be our heroes. It sounds daft now, and I hope, I honestly do hope, that I will always be approachable, if I make it, that is. And Pete Shelley really did speak to me, at length. It blew my mind, it really did.'

It wasn't a bad gig to attend, for it was the night that the *Sniffin' Glue* gang, up from London for the first time and keen to grasp the lowdown on the Manchester scene before the music weeklies could take a firm hold, also attended, and painted a somewhat disappointingly thin, barren, illiterate picture of Manchester's gossipy elite within the pages of their fanzine. Buzzcocks, in their purest form, in their purest 'live' form, lasted until the night of Thursday 9 December 1976, when they supported the Sex Pistols on the Anarchy Tour. This would prove to be the last gig that Devoto would play with the band. Nineteen days later, still with Devoto in command, they would drift nervously – so, so nervously – into Indigo Studios in Gartside Street, Manchester, in which they would record the all-time classic punk EP, 'Spiral Scratch'. More importantly, at least to this particular story, the producer of the tracks would be the artistically unhinged, distinctly hippyish Martin Zero (Hannett). Buzzcocks, although musically inept, and illiterates in the softly lit world of the recording studio, managed *not* to make complete fools of themselves, though many times during the session they sank into collective embarrassment. Nevertheless, they slashed and smashed their way through the recordings, their rawness, much to their surprise, actively encouraged by this strange man who sat so enthusiastically behind the mixing desk. Hannett, they noted, didn't seem in the least bit phased by the band's frequent 'bum' notes. Indeed, he seemed to relish their presence. 'It's the spirit I want,' he would say. 'Your spirit, that's what we need here.' Not for the last time in his career, Hannett would find himself in exactly the right studio with exactly the right band at exactly the right time.

Though, in effect, little more than demos, something staggering did occur in that studio. The recordings – 'Breakdown', 'Time's Up', 'Boredom', 'Friends Of Mine' – would slap naïvely on to vinyl and would become essential punk listening, and from a northern perspective, a most welcome parallel to the Pistols. This may, in part, be because of the sharp, incisive, distinctive, Beefheartian lyricism of the clearly unhinged Devoto. It could also be because of the brash, young, slashing guitar'n'thumping drums of the band, whose musical naïveté actually empowered the recordings, but it could also have had something to do with the awesome 'ear' of Hannett – I refuse to call him Zero – who managed to filter the zest and the blind energy of the musicians on to that tape without allowing the whole thing to fall into the kind of muddiness which would, and still does, taint a million half-formulated demo tapes. 'Spiral Scratch' clasped the heartbeat of the era in the manner of a latterday and significantly more sophisticated dance track. Hannett isolated each instrument – including Devoto's voice – and pieced it together in its most simplistic form. It was sharp, direct, effective. What, to Devoto, Shelley, Diggle and Maher had seemed like a perfectly natural process, was a production of sheer inspiration . . . or luck. The initial odds were on the latter. Hannett's later work, especially with Joy Division, would prove it to be the former. This crazed, manic, wayward, troubled, oft-inebriated man, who still allowed his hair to fall untrendily down his face and had seemed so at home among the ageing Didsbury set, had reached directly into the heart of the punk phenomenon. Once on vinyl, the record would be packaged swiftly in the front room of Buzzcocks' manager Richard Boon's house in Salford. The paper cover sported a Boon-taken Polaroid of the band. The entire artefact, which kick-started Boon's New Hormones record label, becoming the perfect example of punk's stumbling DIY culture. It was sensibly priced at one pound.

Ian Curtis, among many others, listened in a state of awe to this silly little thing. This crappily packaged dirge would sit proudly next to his Led Zeppelin albums and, more trendily, his reggae singles snatched from his frequent forays into the record shops of multi-cultural Hulme. Buzzcocks were special to Curtis but so, I suggest, was Martin Hannett, perhaps the greatest cataclysmic record producer of all time. Joy Division was born, in a sense, back in 1977, when Curtis, Sumner, Hook and Morris first slapped that recording on to their Dansettes. That is where it began.

Martin Hannett, as previously mentioned, ran Music Force, with Susannah O'Hara, from an office situated in a Bohemian terrace block on Oxford Road, in the heart of Manchester's studentland. The office reflected Hannett to perfection – cigarette dimps were piled into pyramidal stacks above the ashtrays, beer cans were strewn across the floor, and Hannett would sit centrally, talking with manic intensity into the phone while engulfed in cigarette smoke and other more exotic fumes.

Downstairs could be found the offices of *New Manchester Review*, a sober 'what's on' magazine dedicated to serving the trendy, post-grad media areas of Didsbury and Chorlton and very little else. *New Manchester Review* was suffering the same battles as the Electric Circus. Reactionary by nature, it fought hard to fend off the encroaching 'punkisms' within the music section, initially confining bands like Buzzcocks and Slaughter And The Dogs to the 'pub rock' section (although Devoto had actually spent time compiling the celebrated 'pub rock' section and for a short while New Hormones operated out of the same office). But the magazine, a forerunner to *City Life*, wasn't stupid. Despite a defiant attempt to strike a blow for 'old rock' by voting Sad Cafe the *New Manchester Review* Band of the Year, in 1977 they allowed young writers – Paul Morley, Dick Witts, Steve Forster, Bob Dickinson, Ian Wood – to slowly take command of the editorial. And of the founders, *New Manchester Review* would produce a future editor of the *Observer*, a *Daily Telegraph* sub-editor and a smattering of national journalistic success. For many of the young Manchester bands, it was the first place where they could excitedly discover their names in print, initially in the listings, then among the reviews and then, so proudly, in the features section.

Despite the often-cited notion that Manchester was a musical 'hot bed' during the punk era, there just weren't that many bands. With Devoto lying low for a while, the local scene was a tight elitist circle. The Fall came; stark and severe, intellectual and inept, the musical equivalent of a well-thumbed sci-fi novel. Mark E. Smith sang about mental hospitals and working-class paranoia. They came from Prestwich, a curious mix of crumbling, Jewish, wealthy abodes and dank sub-student flat-blocks. The area, the damp atmosphere, the cultural mix, the omnipresent religious undertone, the dope-smoky bedsit interiors and stark featureless local pub rooms and the struggles of a young band attempting to grasp a fair slice of national attention and a good deal of local, as well as sometimes in-band bitching, soon combined to flavour the unparalleled songwriting of Mark E. Smith. Most punks, initially, believed the Fall to be uncompromising streetwise communists. That was the most popular theory. Most punks, of course, were wrong.

The Worst, who, proudly, were incapable of playing a single note cleanly, were nevertheless entertaining purveyors of minimalistic punk cacophony. Managed by Ranch Bar barman and fanzine editor Steve Shy, they proved to be a precursor to hardcore. Unable to play anything remotely resembling a tune, they relied on solid thrash and complemented this with a mean, black leather spiky look which, five years later, would be ingloriously celebrated by the likes of GBH and Discharge. The Worst's main claim to fame was the overstated fact that the drummer owned a Chad Valley drum kit. Their ineptitude, however, failed to prevent them attaining a full-page feature – courtesy of Jon Savage – in *Sounds* and an influential band of admirers which included Siouxsie Sioux, the Slits, and Salfordian poet John Cooper Clarke. The Worst were fun and nurtured the habit of being in the right place at the right time, their Preston-based singer, Ian, gracing the cover of the aforementioned Sex Pistols' Lesser Free Trade Hall album cover as well as being featured, bizarrely, in a *Sunday People* exposé of new-wave excess and tagged 'King of the Punks'. There are those – who look back, I sense, through warped-lensed spectacles – who cite the Worst as being the full manifestation of Manchester punk. This is only true if one saw aesthetic value in the sheer hopelessness of their position. Unlike Buzzcocks or the Fall or Sad Cafe even, the Worst actually enjoyed languishing in a total lack of ambition. They were, to an extent, the 'real thing'.

This could be seen as missing the point, for down in London, Siouxsie And The Banshees would evolve from a similarly ramshackle base, but had both sexual charisma and an immense sense of aspiration. Aspiration, in the hardcore world of the Worst, was simply a sell-out. Their greatest night, perhaps, took place in the disco adjoining the towering Chorlton pub, the Oaks, an unlikely interim venue which would host classic, tightly packed gigs by Buzzcocks, Siouxsie And The Banshees and the Heartbreakers. The Worst decided, mid-set, to abandon their music performance and attack their young sixteen-year-old bass player, Dave. Pinning him to the floor and producing a pair of scissors – it was obviously pre-meditated – they proceeded to snip away at the hapless punk's hair until the essential uneven spikiness was finally achieved.

'THE WORST WERE FAAAANTASTIC,' gasped Paul Morley, coiled into the back seat of our car, on the way home afterwards. 'No one else can hold a candle to them,' he continued, 'except, of course, the Slits. They are the only London band left with any true credibility . . . I have an interview with them and it's nothing more than a series of bleeps. The Slits and the Worst . . . they are the only truly valid punks left.'

Nineteen years later, sitting in an unlikely pub in the Snowdonia climbing village of Capel Curig, Morley's closest journalistic agitator from the punk era, the London-based Jon Savage, would make a similar though retrospective remark.

'I always remember, when I first came to Manchester, that the Worst were rather good. In fact, I found them to be incredibly inspirational,' he remarked.

MORLEY AND THE PRESS GANG

'COME TO THE ELECTRIC CIRCUS, TONIGHT, TO SEE MANCHESTER'S NUMBER ONE PUNK BAND.'

These were the words which screamed from a hand-scribbled poster, slapped to the window of a second-hand bookshop in

Stockport. The shop, dusty and unwelcoming actually, would soon gain an abnormal degree of infamy. For it was in there that Paul Morley – sharp, precocious, enwrapped in teen arrogance and positively exploding with ambition – would famously allow his entrepreneurial vision to become humbly manifest within a second-hand record section.

Six months previously, he could often be seen, loon-panted and long-haired, carting a bass guitar through Stockport's barren precinct, more for effect than actual intent to play. Morley's initial writings surfaced in his own, glossy fanzine, *Out There*, produced at great cost – £75. (Morley wished to stake a claim for 'glossiness', a touch of glamour in a xeroxed world, so he borrowed the money from his father.) *Out There* – 'for people who know ... not just teen whimsies', praised Patti Smith and, more courageously, Marc Bolan – proved idiosyncratic enough to allow Morley to shuffle pugnaciously on to the *NME*'s platform. Morley's excess hair was shed at exactly the right time.

Clutching punkiness and Buzzcocks close to his heart, he wrote – if one could forgive the heady pretentiousness of the era's rock journalese – beautifully and evocatively and, just as importantly, could be seen every night in the Ranch, down the Circus and on the late-night buses. Morley skilfully befriended the Manchester bands before most of them were fully formed. Not that it was particularly difficult for a budding rock journalist to ingratiate himself with budding musicians – the sycophancy was equally balanced and, in the end, equally fruitful. He knew where he had to be. A master of timing, he invaded the right dressing rooms and posed in all the right corners. His work appeared in other fanzines: in his own, one-page eccentric word orgy, *Girl Trouble*, in Moss Side zine, *Shy Talk*, and Stockport popzine, *Ghast Up*, in which he adopted the pseudonym, Seven Up. He also managed the

Drones, which is where the 'Best Band In Manchester' boast came into the picture. The Drones, for a while, actually did manage to become the biggest draw on the local punk circuit. Accomplished musicians, they had reincarnated into the punk spotlight after a spell under the name Rockslide.

As Rockslide they were little more than a cynical attempt to emulate Slik and blast into the naff pop market. Thankfully for them, their hasty double A-sided single, embarrassingly entitled 'Rollercoaster b/w Jump, Bump Boogaloo' never threatened to crack the charts. It did re-emerge cruelly, however, as a fierce rumour and then cult disc on the Manchester punk scene. The Drones were speedy popsters who, after nurturing a friendship with the Stranglers, became the epitome of dull, laddish bandwagoning. The worst thing Paul Morley has ever done, quite possibly in his entire life, was produce the band's six-track debut EP, 'Temptations Of A White Collar Worker' which, for a while, shared a stage with Buzzcocks' 'Spiral Scratch'. Soon enough, however, even the most easily guided of the Manchester punks would begin to see through such lines as, 'I wanna see the queen on the end of a beam ... I wanna see the pope on the end of a rope.'

Fleetingly, however, the Drones, who sat very much at the centre of the Ranch crowd, more so than even Buzzcocks, did provide a number of excitable though hardly legendary Manchester gigs. London loathed them. When Morley took them to support XTC at Covent Garden's famous Roxy club, their dulled set ended in riotous disaster, with NME scribe Tony Parsons smashing a chair on the ground in disgust. By the time the band released their tedious debut LP, Further Temptations, Morley had wisely departed. (He reviewed the album, actually, beginning with the line, 'I have a dull ache at the back of my head ... the Drones.') The band's guitarist, Gus Gangrene, threatened to kill him.

It was during an interview/drinking session with the Drones, in the notorious Manchester punk band hangout – the Smithfield pub on Swan Street – that the cracks between Morley and the Drones first began to appear. Morley initially angered the band who, like most musicians of the day, seemed to casually abandon their hastily erected punk ideals whenever they were pitched in conversation against rival bands. These conversations naturally revolved around Buzzcocks ('Have you heard Shelley sing live? It's so-oah embarrassing'), the Dogs ('I'm gonna batter that Wayne Barratt for nicking me act'), the Fall ('God, they are so miserable'). Morley however, would be praising these 'rival' acts. Not that the Drones, one hastens to add, would be any worse in this respect than any of the other bands who no doubt were sitting, probably at that very moment, swapping savage jibes about the Drones ('That cabaret band from Middleton'), etc. Morley, however, seemed particularly interested in a largely unknown new quantity from Salford.

'Have you heard about that new band that Richard Boon has discovered?' he asked, his genuine enthusiasm somewhat lost on the members of the Drones. 'Stiff Kittens, they're called. How are they coming on?'

'Yeah, well,' replied Gus Gangrene, 'one of them came up to me at the Circus last week, kept on asking me to give them a support spot at one of our gigs. I told him that they would have to work at it a bit . . . that it's not that easy. We've been at it for many years, that's what I told him. That's one of the problems with this punk thing. People expecting to just get up on stage after five minutes' practice. Well, it takes a bit of fucking work.'

Intriguingly enough, Gangrene hadn't upset the upstart. Far from it, for Ian Curtis had been struck by the guitarist's unusual measure of honesty.

'I thought I would easily be able to ingratiate myself. I mean, I was very naïve,' stated Curtis. 'I was naïve and in awe. I had no real sense of a band's worth, either. I didn't know whether that particular band was really any good or not, but they were up there, onstage, doing it. I was really in awe of that. It was beginning to dawn on me, I think, that this thing wasn't going to be so easy after all. Things weren't sounding too bad in rehearsals and I was writing all the time. Little notes, here and there. Bits picked up from television programmes, anything that affected me. I was learning how to write and learning, I guess, in a way that far outstripped bands like the Drones. But watching that band I realised that Johnny Rotten was, perhaps, a one-off . . . it wouldn't be such a cinch for us.'

Gangrene wasn't, really, to be blamed for his lack of charity. For the Drones had already started to edge towards paranoia. The fanaticism of their local following might have challenged Buzzcocks in Manchester clubs but had resolutely failed to manifest within the pages of the music press, despite Morley's impassioned pleadings in the *NME* office. It is deeply significant that one new band, an ungigged band at that, should cause such a degree of unrest among the other bands simply by practising in private in Salford and by bumping into a couple of the right people in the right bars.

It has been often written that the name Stiff Kittens came straight from the mind of Richard Boon, in response to Ian Curtis's request for any ideas for a name for the new band (and, indeed, Curtis was genuinely irritated by the suggestion – too close, he felt, to Stiff Little Fingers. Too punky, too downright daft). This may be true, although the name Stiff Kittens had been present on the lips of Pete Shelley three months previously. Shelley fancied, he once gleefully stated, months before meeting Curtis, '. . . having a pet band called Stiff Kittens.'

Curtis, longing to find out just what it was like to be a part of a 'happening band', had met Buzzcocks in the Frederick pub.

It was very much a fan-meets-star occasion, with Curtis asking all the stock questions about the running of a band (rather like a fanzine interview, really). This was the meeting in which Buzzcocks attempted to foist the name Stiff Kittens on Curtis's then unknown Salford band. Other names did fly about during the following weeks – Gdansk or Program, both of which would have surely suited the sound that was beginning to form.

WARSAW – EARLY SIGHTINGS

By April 1977, the young band were almost ready to surface, albeit very tentatively indeed. Since joining, Curtis had brought a freshness and direction into the band, who were all too eager to allow Curtis to take the lead.

'We were pretty hopeless before Ian,' recalled Sumner, 'and although it did take a while for things to settle, there was something about Ian's vision that sparked us off. He seemed to be into extremes. He wanted to make extreme music. He would play us things like Throbbing Gristle and Iggy and God knows what else. He was really into taking the band away from that initial rocky format which was all we knew. We had no better options so we would follow him. It worried me at times. I mean, he was really into madness and insanity. He once said that a member of his family had worked in a mental home and so Ian was full of bizarre stories . . . tragic human stories, really. People with twenty nipples or big heads ... they made a huge impression on him. For a while, while we were forming, he worked in a rehabilitation centre for people with mental and physical difficulties. He was very affected by them.'

Finally settling on the name Warsaw, after the Bowie song 'Warszawa', the band accepted the bottom of the bill spot at the Electric Circus on Sunday 29 May 1977. Above them on the bill were Ferryhill punks, Penetration and, naturally, Buzzcocks.

(Though, much to Ian's annoyance, Buzzcocks had actually advertised the band as Stiff Kittens on the initial poster run.) It was nothing if not an obvious debut. The band would be performing – at least this is how they comforted themselves – before an audience of friends. Strangely enough, this wasn't quite the case. Buzzcocks' small pocket of fame had, much to the chagrin of their most loyal devotees, expanded considerably during the past month or so, and many faces new to the growl and leer of the Electric Circus seemed to be present. To many of these newcomers, their first taste of the Manchester punk scene would be this new band, Warsaw. Unfortunately, due to another typical piece of Electric Circus ineptitude, a number of posters in the city centre had billed the third band as Birmingham's the Prefects. This notion, that the band were in fact the Prefects, prevailed throughout the gig, even to a portion of the audience who had already been exposed to the Prefects, for the two bands did look, if only to the inebriated eye, strikingly similar.

The Electric Circus was half full that night, though in the crowd could be found just about every regular on the local scene. Morley, of course, the omnipresent agitator, haunted the bar. Skulking enigmatically behind him, the striking figure, half-cast, with cropped blond hair, known to the Circus elite as Paul. Paul was the archetypal Mancunian punk character and hardly a gig was allowed to pass by without the curious sight of him sauntering stageward. A daunting sight for many a young band, as Paul's mode of dress would consist of, at its most conservative, shredded denims and leathers. Legend tells us that Paul, a regular at London's Roxy club on his weekends off, was seen hitchhiking on an M6 sliproad, dressed head to toe in bandages, a light bulb dangling from his left ear.

Steve Shy (Burke), from Moss Side, was circulating his fanzine *Shy Talk*, as were the writers of *Ghast Up*. Both fanzines, though only two to three issues old, boasted surprisingly large postbags, a testament, perhaps, to the ferocity of the small scene's blinding enthusiasm. Photographer Kevin Cummins snapped away as ever. The Drones hovered menacingly to the rear, their own gig, three days earlier, proving to be a rousing success. There was also Jon the Postman, who had achieved local fame by making regular, unscheduled onstage appearances, at the dead of the evenings, to unleash a Newcastle Brown-fuelled rant, roughly to the tune of 'Louie Louie'. The Postman – who actually *was* a postman – would often travel back from, say London, with a band, only to walk straight on to his round, unhindered by total lack of sleep. This was the first night that he had been officially, if rather nervously, added to the bill. Eventually he formed his own band, Puerile, regulars in the more ramshackle post-punk venues of the city. There was something unifying about the Postman, though. Those not accustomed to the strange vision of him, straddling the stage, beer bottle clutched tightly in one hand, microphone in the other, would simply stare, aghast. Those 'in the know' whooped and clapped joyously. It was an 'in' joke.

The same, perhaps, can be said of Salford street poet John Cooper Clarke, a supremely gifted writer who, although destined to become the ultimate stand-up cult figure, the inspiration of so many TV starlets of the nineties, would be saved from the rigours of superstardom by his own hedonism. Clarke would also appear, this night, his rhythmic delivery for the first time actually causing sporadic outbreaks of dancing. (Note: They didn't like Clarke in London. Appearing with Buzzcocks at the Vortex, he was subjected to a barrage of jeering. 'Who's this cunt?' one wag shouted. 'He's reading poetry. Fuck off, you posh git.' Such instances were a true indication of just how far the London scene had started to slip away from its original ideas.)

Warsaw shuffled on to the stage, nervously surveying this disparate assembly, and chundered into their set. Curtis, at times freezing to the mike stand, loosened a little as the set continued. Only Pete Hook seemed relaxed, however, his head covered in a peaked leather cap. Bernard Sumner, like Hook, moustached in the juvenile manner, managed only an un-threatening aura of a precocious sixth former. This was seized upon by *Sounds* reviewer, Ian Wood (a bearded tax inspector, mid-twenties and quite the most unlikely spectator let alone authority on the local scene), who noted Sumner's resemblance to 'an ex-public schoolboy'. Though understandably yet to settle into their true musical niche, Warsaw emitted, if nothing else, an air of aloof desperation, a desperation that was born of the knowledge that this, more likely than not, would be their one and only chance to make a name for themselves.

That desperation, enhanced by the 200-mile motorway drive to London, would fuel the best of the Manchester bands during the next six months. It wasn't exactly a camaraderie but the fierce competition did seem to lessen a little as the powers that lay in London became more and more identifiable as the 'enemy'. For Morley's part, with some degree of justification, he saw his weekly battle with the *NME*'s ageing elite as the front line of this battle. At that first Warsaw gig, Morley obviously found a quirkiness within their performance which, frankly, escaped me. Writing in the *NME*, he noted, 'There is a quirky cockiness about the lads that made me think for some reason of the Faces. Twinkling evil charm. Perhaps they play a little obviously but there's an elusive spark of dissimilarity from the newer bands that suggests they have plenty to play around with; time, no doubt, dictating tightness and eliminating odd bouts of monotony.'

Returning the ripples of applause with shy glances, Warsaw apologetically dismantled their equipment, their drummer for the evening – the lofty-eyed Tony Tabac – perhaps beginning to realise that for him the ritual of performing in such decaying dens wasn't quite what he was looking for. Nevertheless, Warsaw were happy ... ish. They had at least made it into the village. The size of this village was perhaps indicated by the fact that, after only one gig, Warsaw would achieve two national reviews, Ian Wood's slightly less enthusiastic appraisal appearing in *Sounds*.

The Electric Circus's legend was intensified one Wednesday night, a quiet Wednesday night, a night when little or nothing was happening elsewhere in the city. These were the nights in which one might trip along to see the Drones – who filled such gaps very effectively – or, on this occasion, Ed Banger And The Nosebleeds. Being ignored or mildly slagged by Paul Morley in the *NME* was, for Vini, a sin that begged redemption. 'AND SO PAUL MORLEY WRITES FOR THE NME ... SO WHAT, SHIT, SHIT, SHIT,' he screamed, before leaping from the stage and chasing the hapless writer behind the fruit machine. Morley would later refer to the incident dismissively during a singles review, writing, 'I haven't been able to dance since that fight I had with Ed Banger.' The incident wasn't quite as trivial as it might at first seem, for the divide between the unhip edge to the city – working-class Wythenshawe – and the hipper, sharper, comparatively intellectual Buzzcocks/Magazine/Morley set was beginning to gape embarrassingly. The Drones, believing themselves to be firmly in the latter category, allegedly attacked Slaughter And The Dogs singer Wayne Barrett on the top deck of a late-night bus.

'They are fucking older and bigger than us,' squealed Barrett, before adding, 'We'll get them back ... one day.' That flimsy camaraderie, which took so long to achieve, seemed to drain away almost overnight.

* * *

Much to the chagrin, not only of the original Ranch Bar clique, but a few other cliques as well, punk in Manchester, buoyed by Morley's increasingly prominent *NME* appraisals, began to swell – at times uncontrollably. Suddenly, spotting 'Half-Cast Paul' or Steve Shy or Morley in a crowd became more and more difficult. The gang-like atmosphere, more prevalent among the audiences than the bands, became inevitably diluted.

On Sundays at the Electric Circus, the scene raged, at times rather dangerously, for no one really knew how 1,000 sweat-dripped, arm-linked manic punks would be able to evict the building should something unforeseeable happen. The gigs flashed by as if in a dream. The Ramones supported by Talking Heads, the Damned supported by the Adverts (with Rat Scabies leering from the upstairs dressing room, showering the outside queue with rocks and badges), Buzzcocks endlessly, Drones endlessly, and perhaps the peak Electric Circus experience, the White Riot Tour featuring the Clash, the Slits, Buzzcocks and Subway Sect on Sunday 8 May 1977 – a seething, rumbling mess of a gig. The full sulphate experience and the furious pace of the bands was countered by the DJ's constant delving into echo chamber dub reggae, which rather suited the circus.

'AWWWWWREGGGAAAARAAAGGAAAA!!!!!!!' scream-ed the Slits' vocalist Ari Up, en route from the stage to the dressing room, this hazardous journey truncated by her swallow dive into the arms and ultimately down to the feet of a group of startled punks, none of whom exactly shared her enthusiasm for the sound of Joe Gibbs. 'There are not enough foookin' black guys in this crowd,' she screamed, at nobody in particular, before rather perceptively adding, 'I bet you lot are a load of middle-class wankers, really.' Many of us were.

The White Riot Tour, more than any other gig, granted the Electric Circus its legendary status. It was just about as big as punk could get without bursting at the seams, without softening to mush. It marked the end, really, and Warsaw were fortunate to have grabbed hold of its grubby shirt-tails at the last possible minute. Any later and they wouldn't really have been a part of the Electric Circus, or indeed the Manchester scene. Any later and merely clambering on to the stage would simply not have been enough.

ROB GRETTON

Back in early 1977, the reputation of Slaughter And The Dogs had spread out of its Wythensharian glam rock shell, and had seriously begun to threaten the precarious supremacy of Buzz-cocks in the city. Many of the people on the band's periphery had started to infiltrate the Manchester punk factions and cliques. The dilution of the scene, which would signify the end of the Circus, probably began at the Ranch, back in February 1977. This was the time when the Ranch clique had started to find themselves lost among an ever-growing influx of new-comers. This, of course, happens in all new trends and cults. It was happening, simultaneously, to the northern soul devotees at Wigan Casino (who, for a while, were bitterly at war with the growing band of Wigan-based punks). Even the Manchester Teds, previously prone to rather mindless outbreaks of punk bashing, had begun to drift into the Ranch, their Brothel creepers matching those of the punks, their drapes mirroring the early Westwood chic of the more glam-conscious locals. The Teds' initial Ranch invasion had been rather brash, however. It came via three noticeable raids on the club, each one displaying a more and more diluted degree of viciousness. By the time the Teds had blasted their way through the doors and down the steps, their clenched fists seemed to soften, and after half an hour of uneasy sarcasm fell into a state of unlikely friendship with the punks. Drink, for once, proved to be a conciliatory force, and by the end of this particular evening, the punks and Teds spilled out, literally, into the centre of Dale Street, arm in arm. The Manchester punk-Ted alliance, as unholy as any alliance on the planet, had been born.

One figure who sauntered more and more down those inglorious steps was Rob Gretton, still looking, it must be said, more like an insurance clerk than punk agitator. One sensed, however, that numerous people regarded him as a Costello figure, a whole brooding mass of subversive thought wrapped up in ultra-conservative packaging. (Only those who had seen him in action at Maine Road, ferociously launching himself at whole groups of opposing fans, or at that Ed Banger Roxy gig, would testify that the apparently gentle shell which enwrapped this man told a dangerous lie.)

Gretton had been a lost figure during 1976. Indeed, an insurance clerk who professed to have never listened to rock music before being lured into Wythenshawe's social whirl, more by curiosity than initial excitement. Nevertheless, as '76 segued so fantastically into '77, Gretton's face could be found, more and more, lurking in darkened corners of Slaughter And The Dogs gigs, a homely antithesis, or so he initially seemed, to the brash bonhomie that surrounded him. True to his image, Gretton really had been a somewhat reactionary character before lapsing into a brief spell of rebellious hippiedom, working on a kibbutz for seven months, accompanied by his girlfriend, before returning to Wythenshawe's bright little punk maelstrom and the dole queue in '76. Gretton was soon part of an inner circle, which included musician-cum-punk entrepreneur Tosh Ryan, Martin Hannett and a plethora of Dogs devotees. Edging closer still to the Dogs themselves, Gretton even began travelling with them in the obligatory battered transit van, more often than not to the punk venues of London. Slaughter And The Dogs, despite gaining affection from the Sex

Pistols and a modicum of excitable music press reviews, most notably from the *NME*'s Neil Spencer, failed to climb into the top league. Their gigs, however, were never less than a furious rush of rant and noise. One remembers singer Wayne Barrett, garbed in chalk-covered teacher's cloak, enticing crowds into near-dangerous frenzy on so many occasions. While Buzzcocks were thrashing around with the kind of Beefheartian learnings so adored by the ever-hovering Paul Morley, Slaughter And The Dogs were the band of the people . . . well, a few people, a few Wythensharian people, anyway.

Gretton, fired by enthusiasm for the Dogs and, perhaps, with a thought to his future, began contributing towards the band's petrol, humping their gear and co-financed their first and best single, 'Cranked Up Really High' – a long-lost, rarely lamented punk classic, full of fire and spirit, slammed down in a couple of hours. 'Cranked Up Really High' would rage proudly from the speakers at every Manchester punk gig, holding its own with the Pistols and the Clash and quite seriously challenging Buzzcocks' more universally adored 'Spiral Scratch'. Gretton provided the band with £200 for the purposes of recording the single, in effect part-financing the whole anarchic little recording empire known to the world – or a tiny, scruffy part of it – as Rabid Records.

Inspired by the local success of 'Cranked Up Really High', Gretton found himself wanting greater involvement, if not in the general Manchester scene, then certainly within the confines of the Dogs. Taking inspiration from the two parallel Manchester punk fanzines of the period, *Shy Talk* and *Ghast Up*, Gretton began piecing together snippets and witticisms which would, eventually, become a fanzine of his own, *Manchester Rains*, wholly dedicated to Slaughter And The Dogs. It was a fanzine in the true sense of the word – dedicated, uncritical, though not lacking in irony. It proved to be nothing more or less than a swiftly xeroxed parody of the era's teen magazines.

In the course of his 'research' in the field of fanzine writing, Gretton tagged along with the *Ghast Up* team – Martin Ryan and yours truly – during an interview session, spent in Manchester's Portland Bar, with Ed Banger And The Nosebleeds. It was an uneasy liaison, to say the least.

Ed Banger, true to his brash, egocentric persona, had failed to inform us that Gretton would be hanging on to our shirt-tails, gleefully holding a tape recorder of his own and intent, it seemed, on inserting his version of the interview into his then unpublished *Manchester Rains*. We met Gretton, as instructed, upstairs in Manchester's HMV record store. Rather like the Virgin shops of the time, HMV was not so much a record store but more a hangout, a latterday coffee bar minus the hiss of steam and rush of caffeine (though a more thorough rush could be gained if one knew the right contacts). Mostly though, people would just hang out and chat about records, aided and abetted by counter assistant Clive Gregson, later to front the musicianly post-punk band, Any Trouble, and later still to gain infamy on the folk circuit. Gretton was immersed in the surrounding chit-chat as we approached, and as we led him from the store uttered the words, 'You two look like real motley characters.' These were the only words he spoke, all afternoon. Mostly he just listened to our naïve questions, blushing once or twice as the conversation honed in on this dark, silent character sitting, huddled, behind us. We had no idea that Rob Gretton was something of a legend at Manchester City's Kippax terrace, nor, at that point, that he was operating in such a forthright role in the running of Slaughter And The Dogs, seen by us and even by Ed Banger at that time, as local superstars.

Ed Banger's rhetoric was unstoppable. 'I'll try anything ... I'll do anything ... I'm not afraid of anyone,' he stated, somewhat threateningly. 'That's why I attacked Paul Morley at the Electric Circus. That guy is just too big for his boots. I'll attack anyone, me, anyone who slags us off. I won't stand for it.'

There was a good deal of bitching amid the beer glasses that day: Ed Banger slagging off the Drones, Ed Banger slagging off Buzzcocks and Sad Cafe, and even Slaughter And The Dogs. Only at this point did Gretton raise his eyes in protest, but even then only meekly. We certainly got the wrong impression of Gretton that night, and even three nights later, when he would ring us up, asking for 'printing tips'. We offered to print *Manchester Rains* for him although we only had green ink. Gretton didn't fancy green ink. Making his apologies, he backed off.

And it was at an Ed Banger gig, at Manchester venue Rafters, where Gretton would flit around the crowd, selling copies of *Manchester Rains* to unwilling punters – 10p for a batch of Dog gossip, complete with, in true fanzine tradition, a batch of darkly printed polaroids, some from the lens of brash socialite, Manchester City-supporting Salfordian photographer, Kevin Cummins, and some not. It was a cheap and cheery kind of fanzine, perhaps well suited to the Dogs who, if the truth be told, would have leapt into the light of teen stardom at the very first given opportunity.

Gretton held great hopes for them though, believing them to be quite the most exciting live band in the country. There was some justification in this claim for, although they were often ragged and showy, their gigs – all of them – carried a certain amount of tension. Maybe it was just the fact that Slaughter And The Dogs, locally at least, had managed to craft a following, many of whom wouldn't be seen at normal punk gigs or any other gigs at all. They were the beginning, in a sense, of Wythenshawe scally chic, and it was no accident that their sub-classic rant, 'Where Have All The Boot Boys Gone' – pre-Sham 69, note – bemoaned the passing of a time before punk, a time of Ben Sherman shirts, two-tone tonic trousers, Crombie overcoats and Barathea blazers.

As stated, and much to Gretton's delight, Slaughter And The Dogs gigs could often be riotous; more riotous than most. One recalls an evening at Salford College when, prior to the Dogs arriving gleefully onstage, two plate-glass windows were unduly smashed as, through them, a string of gatecrashers broke into the common room. On this occasion, as on many others, the cries of, 'It's the Teds . . . It's the Teds . . .' proved to be unduly alarmist.

Gretton became the DJ at Rafters (an ex-folk club, ex-pick-up disco), an elongated cellar on Manchester's Oxford Street which gamely began to house new-wave nights in 1977. He proved to be a knowledgeable, albeit unapproachable DJ who would never succumb to the playing of requests. Not even to the young buck named Steven Patrick Morrissey who requested, at an Ed Banger gig, the playing of the Heartbreakers' 'Chinese Rocks' single. A pity, it would have nicely suited the evening, but Gretton, as I recall, was rather stubbornly sticking to repeated playings of Iggy Pop's 'The Passenger' and Dillinger's flippant reggae classic 'Cocaine In My Brain'. A succession of midweek gigs passed by – Sad Cafe, Buzzcocks, Magazine, Rich Kids twice, XTC several times, Elvis Costello. Tony Wilson, whose air of celebrity was always a menace to him at punk gigs, seemed more relaxed than usual in the venue. One recalls him dancing reservedly while dressed in a white suit topped by white fedora at an Elvis Costello gig. It was during these gigs that Gretton and Wilson became friendly, Wilson being attracted to Gretton's lack of awe and polish.

Warsaw seemed curiously suited to Rafters. Their solid though still rather unadventurous sound gained intensity within those walls whereas even at the Circus, some of the power would evaporate into the surrounding space. In truth, the long, thin shape of Rafters – not at all unlike the Cavern – suited all bands who couldn't pull a sizeable crowd. Just twenty excitable punters were needed to make the attendance seem respectable, especially if they crowded before the stage. The venue was preferable, the band agreed, to the dusty and inelegant confines of the Squat Club, a ramshackle theatre situated next to Manchester's Contact Theatre, slap in the heart of studentland. The Squat gigs – Warsaw played three of them – were wisely used more as a rehearsal than anything else. Well, at least that's what the band told themselves, for the truth was that punk's downbeat anti-aspirational rhetoric, as spouted in a thousand tedious band interviews, was beginning to wear a bit thin. Although Curtis had visited the Squat during a gig by his favourite band at the time, the Fall, and had succeeded in helping the makeshift road crew lug the equipment out and into the waiting van – he couldn't have known it, but his fellow roadies on that occasion were Julian Cope and Ian McCulloch, from Liverpool – he found the gigs at the Squat to be, at best, mildly soul-destroying. Not that Curtis and the band would complain. After their very first performance at the Circus, much to their surprise, they had impressed Martin Hannett and had been rather loosely placed on the books at Music Force. This didn't exactly thrust them into the heart of the action, but a spattering of gigs at the Squat and Rafters would do for the time being. One of these Rafters gigs, a Wednesday night affair in which they shared the bill with Fast Breeder, who strangely enough was managed by actor Alan Erasmus, close friend of Tony Wilson and forthcoming Factory director, followed a fairly sordid little squabble for the 'last on stage' spot. The gig was quite appalling – possibly the band's worst – with Warsaw's sound dipping to a drone and failing to compete even with Fast Breeder's sharp punkiness. It was a late night, too late, and by the time Warsaw had taken the stage, at least half the meagre following had departed. For some reason, our little gang stayed and, reasonably intoxicated by this point, began to heckle, though with no malicious intent, I'm sure. The set was memorable for just one reason. Despite the dour backing, the singer, we noticed, seemed to have a somewhat embarrassing Iggy Pop fixation. Mid-set, a smashed glass in his hand, he erupted into a state of rather dubious frenzy, apparently cutting his legs in the process. This tiny incident would later be catalogued as one of Ian Curtis's most infamous early performances. But, in truth, it seemed rather sad. A stupid act, in fact, which preceded an uncomfortable silence and then a small, sarcastic ripple of applause from the crowd. Apparently, the band's next Rafters gig, supporting Johnny Thunder's Heartbreakers, would provide them with their first ever encore.

During this period, the fledgling band used the services of a number of drummers. Their initial drummer, Tony Tabac, was never suited to downbeat punk venues and inevitably faded away. Bernard's friend from school, Terry Mason, tried his hand also, but after failing to master the sticks was unduly shunted to one side to act as ersatz manager. More infamously came the strange figure of Steve Brotherdale or, as he would later prefer to be known, Steve B'Dale. Steve was wafer thin, in the 'glam' mould. One recalls him attending gigs at, say, the Band on the Wall, garbed in black leather and sporting slicked-back red hair and eye-liner. He was, at various times, a member of a band managed by Rob Gretton, called Panik, whose single, 'It Won't Sell' – produced by Gretton – caused a minor stir in Manchester, mostly because the sleeve featured a parade of strutting 'gays' and the out-and-out glam rock outfit, V2. Brotherdale's egotistical rhetoric became famous in Manchester. He would often be seen at bars, impressing on people dubious facts. 'I'm a superstar in America,' he once told a wholly uninterested punter at the Band on the Wall. This tiresome anecdote, in which he apparently supported Kiss on their American tour, was famously complemented by a mock phone call from the venue to America, during which he allowed such sentences as, 'OHHH yeahh, maaan, see you in Atlanta!' Brotherdale would later claim, and it could conceivably be true, that such conversations were intended as a mere 'wind up'. Whatever the truth, Brotherdale added a somewhat unsettling taste to the Warsaw cocktail and, though a superb drummer, the band decided to literally drive off and leave him stranded one night. It perhaps didn't escape their notice that, throughout their liaison, Steve Brotherdale never actually left Panik. (Indeed, according to Deborah Curtis's *Touching From a Distance*, Brotherdale actually attempted to prise Curtis away from Warsaw and into the vocals spot with Panik.)

When Steve Morris finally took control of the drum seat, all seemed perfect, and indeed it was. For Morris, less of a 'power drummer' than Brotherdale, immediately added finesse to the sound. Morris had been surprised to see an advertisement pinned to the noticeboard at Jones's music store in Macclesfield requesting the services of a drummer for Warsaw. Morris had been flitting to and from Manchester for some time and, though he hadn't seen Warsaw, he had noticed Steve Shy's encouraging write-up of the band's Electric Circus debut in *Shy Talk*. That seemed to signify to him that Warsaw were, unlike the two or three Macclesfield bands he had flirted with, something of a positive force within the Manchester scene. Even more importantly, his personality seemed to suit.

Hooky: 'Steve was the most nervous person I had ever met in my entire life and I was initially worried. He came down to audition at the Abraham Moss Centre in Crumpsall, and seemed so edgy. But when he started to play, it was just fantastic. After all the other jerks, it felt so refreshing. He was also the first drummer I had ever met who was quiet . . . all the others had been assholes.'

Immediately taking a liking to Ian, he slotted neatly into place within the band's often buoyant kinship, and even looked the part – for Morris's sharp hair and dull colours blended superbly with the band's general visual 'darkening'. This wasn't, in any way, a conscious image change on behalf of the band. But, gig by gig, they seemed to be straying away from any noticeable 'punkisms'. It was precisely at this point that Warsaw first began to attract criticism about their apparent 'Nazi Youth' appearance.

It is possible that a few close members of their small audience had started, also, to pick up on Curtis's early lyricism which had yet to seem so unnervingly personal, although in such songs as 'Warsaw', 'At A Later Date' and 'Leaders Of Men' he had clearly started to use his fascination with Fascism. Whether people did pick up on this or not, there is no way of knowing, but there is no doubt that a small and rather vicious rumour was beginning to circulate – a rumour, quite possibly instigated by a rival band or a disgruntled musician, that Warsaw were 'Nazis'. The rumour would surface more fully, more famously, twelve months later, but it began while the band were still in the process of forming some kind of distinctive sound. This may seem, from a 1996 perspective, a particularly ridiculous notion. Indeed it was, but in Britain in 1977, with the National Front riding on a ludicrously disproportionate wave of hype and with pop culture readying itself for a ferocious response, courtesy of the Rock Against Racism movement, Fascistic paranoia was running at an unprecedented high. This was, perhaps, particularly prevalent in the punk sections of Manchester, as already certain members of the Ranch crowd found themselves under attack from a distinctly unlikely radical fringe – right-wing Teddy boys. This didn't amount to much but this young band, Warsaw, could certainly live without any kind of 'Nazi' association, however tenuous.

THE FINAL WEEKEND OF THE ELECTRIC CIRCUS

M.J. Drone (Mike Howells), heftily coiffeured singer with the Drones, took it all to heart. The club's management had been losing the battle to keep the Electric Circus doors open all summer.

The authorities, no doubt bolstered by a stream of puerile anti-punk sentiment in the tabloids – practically all of it made up – closed in on the club and refused to renew the food licence, pushing it towards closure. In retrospect, as the audiences had grown into an absurdly large and generally unpredictable beast, the walls of the Electric Circus seemed fit to burst. (It did reopen in 1978, briefly, but after the bubble had messily burst there was no longer a threat, and no longer a crowd, either.)

News of the closing weekend – the Circus bash to end them all – ripped across the town. The aforementioned Drone sported a customised chef's outfit (his brother, Pete the drummer, was also, and still is, a chef) daubed with the slogans, 'WHY CLOSE THE ELECTRIC CIRCUS' and, more absurdly, 'LIFT OFF THE BANS' – the sentiment of which soon became manifest within one of their seering anthems. Fanzines *Shy Walk* and *Ghast Up*, and indeed *Girl Trouble*, made token gestures in defiance of the closure, although deep down everyone knew that it simply had to be.

There was an air of resignation about the event, in the audience as in the bands, though the divide between the two was still gloriously difficult to define. Nevertheless, the furious camaraderie of the gig, so joyously celebrated in the reviews which followed, was lacking, somewhat, in the unholy band scramble that preceded it. Every band in Manchester, of course, wished not only to perform but to perform at the prime time on the Sunday evening. This was a chance to carve one's way into, if not history, then certainly into the music press. Slaughter And The Dogs found themselves slashing away onstage on the Saturday, but the main action, the true climax, would take place 24 hours later.

In one sense, the spirit had been broken before the doors opened. A queue snaked around the corner, up and on to the rubble at the rear, the attendant punks suddenly seeming like mere punters as the bands, promoters, rock journalists and photographers all filtered timidly through an ambuscade of hateful leers and understandably indignant insults. Even the bands would fight, all scrambling for the best spot. This, in a sense, saved the day and intensified the performances, especially for the smaller bands, Warsaw, V2, and the Fall, who felt as if this really might be their last-ditch attempt to carve a slice of glory. Manchester, courtesy of Morley ... and now, in the audience, Savage from *Sounds*, Parsons from the *NME*, Nicholls, an Altrincham-based wide-boy hack from *Record Mirror*, and every fanzine in the country was there ... or so it seemed. The crowd, anxious to get into the frame, pushed and swelled in the Circus foyer, antagonising the bouncers and the club owners, who had all but given up. No longer concerned with housing an important part of the scene, they attempted, against all odds, to cut the guest list down to a reasonable size.

'No ... no ... I can't pay ... I'm a writer ... I'm from *Record Mirror*,' squealed one young chap, indignance pouring from his stupid head as his manner, let alone his status, failed to impress the towering bouncers.

Inside, of course, it was a nightmare. Pressed solid, like World War One crammed into a telephone box, the riot was prevented only by the sheer impossibility of random movement, or any kind of movement other than a by now rather passé pogo. The Negatives – a joke, a parody, a motley collection of luminaries – bounced hilariously onstage, Kevin Cummins pounding a distinctly unrhythmic drum pattern, Steve Shy plucking a bass, whirling around with considerable aplomb, Paul Morley chopping artlessly away at a guitar, Richard Boon pulling unspeakable ear-splitting squeals from a saxophone and, on vocals, the bearded, unpunky Dave Bent, screaming out such lines as 'MY KIND OF GIRL PAYS FOUR PENCE ON THE BUS,' while gamely accepting the torrents of abuse, and spit, from the front of the audience.

'I seem to remember the Negatives being rather good,' stated Jon Savage, the occasion marking his debut on the Manchester scene. Savage, who had become the leading London writer for *Sounds*, like Morley seemed to find punk the perfect base for intellectual musings, managing to take the very notion of punk – of picking up a guitar and getting onstage – on to a new level of journalese. To some, Savage and Morley were simply unforgivably pretentious. It must be noted, however, that they were never less than entertaining. Pretentious naïveté certainly did creep in, but at the same time they felt it ... meant it. And these were the writers who Ian Curtis most notably warmed to. Morley, perhaps, because he would write about local groups in an indepth, unpatronising manner, and Savage because he grasped the dark side of, say, Throbbing Gristle. At the time, for the punks and bands and writers on the Manchester scene, it seemed rather strange to see the figure of Savage – a lawyer, for Christ's sake – waltzing into the scene, happy to be aloof from insular London. But, in a sense, it was his natural base.

'My first encounter with Manchester,' he now recalls, 'was going to see Buzzcocks at the Roxy, seeing them and being very struck by how good they were. They sang about cars and motorways . . . everyday life in a way that the groups in London didn't. I found that very attractive. I found out about the last night at the Electric Circus and decided to come up to it. I did an interview with Howard Devoto who was just putting Magazine together. That was one of the interviews which helped create the legend . . . it was very cryptic . . . I interviewed him at Birch Service Station. In London, punk had become a fashion and very irritating. It had already gone through the cycle. The Roxy was never really that good. But it was somewhere where you felt you had to be. When the Roxy closed and the focus shifted to the Vortex, the London scene had died. When I came to the last night at the Electric Circus, I was struck by how there was a desperate urge in the bands and a real need to communicate. Especially Warsaw . . . I remember that. I had no idea who they were, but they seemed desperate . . . aloof . . . on the edge in a way that I hadn't seen for a long time. You felt that the bands knew that this was their only chance to pull something off. They weren't very good but they didn't give a fuck. That really made them interesting. I loved the Prefects – from Birmingham but somehow from Manchester also – and the way their singer, Rob Lloyd, would really anger an audience. Immediately I felt at home in Manchester. I met Morley, Buzzcocks, Manicured Noise, that half-cast guy, Paul. It seemed like a wonderful creative collaboration, a place where ideas could become something. Morley had *Girl Trouble* which I thought was a fantastic concept. I felt very akin to Paul and even wrote a couple of *Girl Trouble*s for him . . . doing that seemed more important than *Sounds*, somehow.'

Warsaw's performance at the last night of the Electric Circus is only too well documented in the press and on vinyl, as the song 'At A Later Date' was to feature on the grubby but honest *Live at the Electric Circus* ten-inch album, which finally surfaced, after a good deal of speculation, on the Virgin label. The album was scrappy – perhaps fittingly so – although in no way could an eight-track record, featuring the spirited noises of Buzzcocks, the Drones, Steel Pulse, John Cooper Clarke, the Fall and Warsaw, possibly hope to capture even a small measure of the atmosphere. Nevertheless, the record became infamous for two reasons: Paul Morley's sharp sleeve notes and Ian Curtis screaming, 'DO YOU ALL REMEMBER RUDOLF HESS?' at the moment Warsaw's noise crumbled to a halt. I do remember, standing in the crowd, sweat gushing from every pore, feeling extremely irritated by this foolish remark. More enigmatic, I suggest, was the sight of the Fall's Mark E. Smith planting the base of a mike stand into the balding pate of a particularly vehement heckler. This rather amusing image – well, he *did* deserve it – was topped only by the vision of Big Dave – one of the Manchester Teddy boys who had defected to punk – striding proudly out of the Circus's repulsive Gents, a full toilet bowl held firmly above his head. The evening climaxed, naturally, with Buzzcocks, whose second encore revolved around Jon the Postman's 'Louie Louie', complete, it seemed, with about half the audience looning about the stage beneath the polystyrene tiles, rolling on a bed of cigarette dimps and broken glass.

There are periods, especially when a city's music scene lessens a little, when practically all the young bands suffer from a sense of paranoiac isolation. All the action seems to be happening to someone else – someone undoubtedly undeserving – in another part of town. At the top of this rather messy hierarchy, Buzzcocks had already started to record for United Artists (they had signed the contract on the Electric Circus bar, a reputed £75,000 two-year deal, clinched on the night that Elvis Presley had died). Howard Devoto, after placing an advertisement in

Virgin Records on Newton Street – 'WANTED, MUSICIANS TO PLAY FAST AND SLOW MUSIC' – had formed Magazine and, subsequently, seemed to be walking sweetly into a Virgin recording contract. The Fall, by now heartily pushed along the indie trail by the lovely and rather volcanic personality of manager Kay Carroll ('Hey, put the fuckin' vocals up, you fat cunt,' was one of her standard modes of attack), had settled neatly into place with Mark Perry's Step Forward Records. Slaughter And The Dogs were packing them in at Salford College. Belle Vue's Elizabethan ballroom and Tony Wilson's *What's On* spots on Granada Television were liberally peppered with in-jokes and shameless references to what had become known, in the envious periphery, as 'the Buzzcocks mafia!'

None of which was lost on Ian Curtis. Curtis was fired by a naïveté which, in retrospect, seems quite astonishing, and the solid belief that none of these acts could ever possibly hold a candle to Warsaw. He physically shivered every time he heard Wilson mention another band on the TV. Every time he scanned the reviews and, even worse, the features pages of the music press, he was quite unable to understand why all these bands were getting so much attention. His naïveté surfaced, in its most curious form, in his lack of perspective regarding Bernard's daytime job, at the legendary Chorlton Cum Hardy-based animations factory, Cosgrove Hall. Sumner – bright, sharp, content to be at the bottom of the ladder – deflected Curtis's constant approaches with a noticeable deftness. For Curtis believed that Sumner, with his Cosgrove Hall connections, could have and should have fixed it for Warsaw to appear on Granada Television. In Curtis's eyes, Sumner's reluctance to pull strings which barely existed exhibited a lack of commitment on the guitarist's behalf. Although clearly irritated by Curtis's apparent inability to understand that the cogs and coils of the television industry rarely clanked and revolved in such a simplistic manner, Sumner would later pass it off as commend-able over-eagerness. Curtis just wanted to get on the telly, and for a while this little dream seemed to slip a little further away as the scene weakened and the music press, at least for a short while, lessened their interest.

Priced four pence, here is the one-page fanzine, *Girl Trouble*, issue number eight, written by Jon Savage. Do not blame me; it appears here now, completely unchanged, capturing, I believed, the moment when people began to intellectualise the punk scene. You could have bought this from Rafters.

GUARANTEED NON-STOP ADULT ISSUE/GLAMOUR PREFERRED/THROBBING GRISTLE AND GENESIS P-ORRIDGE/HUMAN BEINZ AND RED KRAYOLA/ MORE LOTHAR/HYPNOTISM/THE REBELLION GENERATION/ATTENTION TIMESPANS-RAMONES-WIRE-ENO/CHARLIE'S ANGELS/GIRL TROUBLE QUICK/DEC/50.

In the beginning there was etc/hey daddio i dont wanna go down to debasement;Interview with Genesis P Orridge about Throbbing Gristle/Image Bank/ICA and Morals. As in fibre . Orridge v. Charming and likeable Savage liking yet unconvinced. Q; Howcum the Death Factory symbol-ism (Belsen Was A Gas etc).and Dean Corll Murder fantasie (Maggot Death)/death obsessions? A; There's so much evil around ... q;Yeah. A;I'd say about 95% thesedays, just like all the NF all around here (Hackney). Q; OK so you reflecting. ... A;yeh. Q;But isn't reflecting, reinforcing it ? And all you seem to relish it. ... Further A&Q@ reveal evasions/tangents. ... s ends by liking o v much but is still worried poor lad about orientation of same. ... tune in next etc.

Testament; (last will) of Human Beinz; Nobody can do the SHINGALONG like I do;

Is it any wonder then with ersatz safety pins & razors that soundtrax here are dippy trippy plain weird/wired psychedelia or the fragmented ? Recommend (tapes done for those who want) any 13th Floor Elevators (The quest for pure sanity is the theme of this album). the Red Krayola, big hit, Hurricane Fighter Plane with free form freak outs . . . liner notes; Silence is conceptual ideology in which sound is published. . . . to the Red Krayola. the Girl Trouble-10-years-ahead-of-their-time-award; Reprise. Limited definitions define limit and one can go just so far. Go deh ! The music of the rebellion generation. . . . .

;Things being wot they are they answer to teh (musical) question posed rhetorical in 7c has turned upin The Negatives set; Lothar & The Hand People emerge as a cult item for positive imitation. Research revealed an lp with the immortal sex-violence . . . and exorcism, restored to its pristine glory, to delight you all. Buzzcox in London-nepotisticircles-play The Negatives during the instrumental break of '16' which to complete The Negatives play the Buzzcox and the last verse. . . . . . .

;And never being a one tp let a good conceptual leap lie I return Love by way of comparison with Red Krayola's Hurricane Fighter Plane which contains also the Feelgood's 'Roxette' bass riff exactement-you read it here first-to Stephanie Red who will now know why. (Rolling Stone Aug 23' 69-from the Savage archive; new Lothar and The Hand People's title track, 'SPACE HYMN'. is an almost exact reduplication of the Harvard Hypnotic Susceptability Test.' In other words, if you play it'll hypnitise you you to thinking you're walking on the moon. Application please to Paul.

;Just want to seminate idea of our post-acid post TV fractured attention timespan which makesconcentrating on anything over 1-1&a half minutes impossible. In step which makes The Ramones/Wire-22trax/Eno Music For Films 27 trax superior to jaunty new one ; Hidden sexual deviations inherent/explicit in 'Charlie's Angles'-just watch i.

Chapter Six

Keep On Keepin' On

To ROMANTICS, AS JOY DIVISION fans so often are, the thought of the solitary figure of Ian Curtis drifting each and every lunchtime through Manchester's dank and cavernous Piccadilly Plaza might seem quite evocative. Was he, perhaps, inspired by the building's enveloping seediness, for it is true that the Plaza has long suffered from having a richly deserved reputation for boasting the most cynical interior in Manchester. Originally designed with the intention of instigating a bustling community of 'young' professional businesses and retail units, it swiftly settled into an area of cold, empty concrete, a place where cigarette dimps and crisp packets would gather, used, alas, by too many drunks on too many nights, for it is a long-standing joke that Piccadilly Plaza is the largest (unofficial) public lavatory in the world. It was, and indeed still is, enlivened at one end by Piccadilly Radio which has, through the years, added a slight spice of celebrity to the building. Ian Curtis, who in 1977 worked at the Manpower Services Commission based in Piccadilly Tower – as did his wife, Deborah – would be drawn into the Plaza, but not because of any romantic attachment he might have perversely nurtured for the building, but simply because just three doors away from Piccadilly Radio sat the (to the mind of Curtis) infinitely fascinating northern promotional offices of RCA Records. To Curtis, this office represented the music business. It was a living, physical contact and he could drift down to it, each and every lunchtime. The office must have seemed like an escape hatch – the door to his dream world – especially as the office manager, Derek Brandwood, was notably fond of using every available square inch of window space to display posters and promotional paraphernalia. And of course, RCA had Iggy Pop, David Bowie and Lou Reed. No wonder the sight of this garish unit caused Curtis's imagination to race away far beyond the meagre scope of his day job.

RCA's Derek Brandwood, a silver-haired, silver-tongued promotional manager with, even then, ten full years' music business experience, had settled cleverly in the building. As it began to dawn on the major record labels, all previously so profoundly London based, that Radio One and *Top of the Pops* would not necessarily continue to hold all the keys to a record's success, they began to reluctantly pay more attention to the provinces. Sensing this new attitude, Brandwood pushed for the revolutionary notion of a northern-based office, a base from which the growing spread of independent radio stations and retail outlets could be effectively serviced. Armed with the full backing of RCA, Brandwood astutely reasoned that to base such an office within staggering distance of Piccadilly Radio's reception would be a logistical masterstroke, and so it proved. Renting the unit for a mere £27 per week, he swiftly transformed its atmosphere of dour austerity into a kind of open-house office, complete with full bar. An unusually welcoming notion for the music industry, traditionally preferring to create offices of an intimidatory nature. Brandwood, however, sat in the centre of the office, on a kind of carpeted podium. It was possibly the most bizarre office in central Manchester. As his assistant Brandwood took on the services of famed northern soul disc jockey, Richard Searling.

This was the atmosphere into which Ian Curtis tentatively wandered, drawn in, despite his natural shyness, by those magnetic posters of Pop and Bowie. Curtis's opening gambit was simple. Like many young kids before him, he would ask if he could have one of the displays, once its shelf-life had finished. Brandwood, not one to discourage such visits, found Curtis to be eloquent and charming – unusually so, for someone so young and so shy.

'It struck me that it must have taken considerable courage for him to actually wander into that office and make conversation,' he states, 'and I soon found that he was blessed with a sound knowledge of rock music, although he didn't really have anything that might be of use to me. I encouraged him to linger and he lingered a lot. Sometimes I had the impression that he was listening in, trying to pick up tips or something. Perhaps he just liked to be around people in the music industry. He was obviously drawn to that kind of glamour. He came back often and I encouraged him.'

Many people, no doubt charmed by Brandwood's all-encompassing bonhomie, would linger in that office. An office of rare if not unique intrigue. Only CBS had ventured into Manchester on a similar level, and *their* office was a comparatively scruffy affair, deep in the heart of a Gothic tower on Newton Street. But at the RCA gaff one could lounge around, watching videos, catching a whiff of celebrity or, if not that, a faint trace of the biz pulsebeat. Piccadilly DJs, more famous in those days of independent infancy than the DJs of today, would drift in, as would various Manchester music luminaries. Martin Hannett, now freed from his punky 'Zero' monicker, would often be found in there. Indeed, it had been Hannett who had alerted Brandwood to Sad Cafe and, subsequently, Sad Cafe scored considerable success with RCA. (This liaison would continue. In 1995, ex-Sad Cafe singer Paul Young would score worldwide recognition as a member of Mike And The Mechanics, his ever-burgeoning solo career being excitedly handled by Derek Brandwood.) It is quite possible that Hannett met Curtis socially in that office, though their professional link as agent and artist was never mentioned in front of Brandwood.

One day Curtis, his shyness finally draining away, casually mentioned to Brandwood that he was in a band. It was obvious to Brandwood that Ian Curtis saw this office as some kind of magic way forward. Warsaw or, as they were becoming known, Joy Division, on the same label as Iggy Pop! It was more than Curtis could have possibly hoped for.

Brandwood: 'I think he found it immensely fascinating that, somehow, there I was, not just some name in a book, not just some label on a record, but someone who worked in the music industry that he could talk to. I wasn't an A&R man. I was in promotions, but that didn't seem to matter to him. It didn't matter to me, either. Deep down I think I was a frustrated talent scout. I wanted to take a band from nowhere and help them develop into something big. It would have made such a nice change from working with established stars all the time. However, I wasn't really equipped to spot talent at such an early stage. I thought I was, but I wasn't. I was looking for another Sad Cafe, I suppose, and then when Ian brought me this record – a low-budget recording the band had done at Pennine Studios, the place we called the Rochdale Cowboys studio – I was disappointed. To me it was just a noise. Badly played, badly produced, no real songs to speak of. I was used to dealing with John Denver, Dolly Parton . . . or at least David Bowie.'

Nevertheless, Brandwood took the record home in an attempt, presumably, to see if it sounded any better through a relatively simple stereo system. It didn't, although to Brandwood's total amazement, his fourteen-year-old son, Howard, immediately warmed to the recording, preferring it to 'the usual soft stuff I would bring home'. Inspired by his son's enthusiasm, Brandwood sent the record to the A&R department, along with a note suggesting that they should, if nothing else, keep tabs on this exciting band. Despite the fact that one young A&R man took the band to his heart, he was swiftly overruled and though his interest would continue during the next year he never managed to persuade the powers that be at RCA that Joy Division were a band worth taking on board. (This was, to Ian Curtis if nobody else, a tragic situation. Throughout his short career, he never lost the desire to climb on to that particular rostrum.)

The record, an EP entitled 'An Ideal For Living', initially surfaced amid minor controversy in January 1978. The band's name change had caused a ripple of indignant comment in the pages of the profoundly liberal *New Manchester Review*. It hadn't escaped their eyes that Joy Division, a name taken from the Nazi concentration camp novel, *House Of Dolls*, was the description of the units where Nazi soldiers would keep female prisoners alive to be used as prostitutes. This wasn't seen as a good way for a band to nurture a small fan base in the Bohemian areas of Didsbury and Chorlton, where simmering political correctness would occasionally paradoxically spill over into displays of negative violence, albeit violence of a green-shoed, rainbow-jumpered nature. And wasn't this a band who, in choosing the name Joy Division, had started to glorify the degradation of women? The band didn't see it that way at all. The name change had been decided upon swiftly in a direct response to the London band, Warsaw Pakt, who in ripple of hype had recorded, packaged and released an album during the course of just one weekend. Joy Division, desperate to get something on to vinyl, probably didn't give as much thought to the new choice of name as perhaps they should have. The situation was hardly eased by the band's choice of sleeve, designed by Sumner during his lunch breaks at Cosgrove Hall. It featured a member of Hitler Youth banging a drum and a German soldier pointing a gun at a small boy. It was an outrageously provocative image which would be tempered only by the short shelf-life of the seven-inch version (the EP would be released in a better, louder, clearer and more tastefully packaged twelve-inch version in June '78). The imagery, unwise and naïve as it was, probably owed much to Curtis's infatuation with the London avant-gardists, Throbbing Gristle, who were similarly fond of flirtations with tastelessness, degradation and Fascistic imagery.

Jon Savage: 'I remember receiving a copy of "An Ideal For Living" in the post, with a little note saying, "This is our band ... here is the new e.p. We don't like it very much because the sound quality isn't very good but we hope you like it."'

It was in the wake of 'An Ideal For Living' and the surrounding press controversy that Brandwood's small empire became entwined with Joy Division. He promised himself that, if nothing else, he would keep an eye on the band and perhaps even venture out to a live gig. His assistant, Richard Searling, was precociously fired with ambition. Searling, peaking in his position as a top northern soul DJ, was furiously pushing in all directions. Forever courting music business contacts, Searling had recently spoken to an infamous American called Bernie Binnick – who had once taken the Beatles Stateside – who ran Swan records. Binnick had been looking, rather perversely, for an English punk band to record a version of N.F. Porter's northern soul classic, 'Keep On Keepin' On'. This still strikes this particular writer, though no expert in the ebbs and flows of singles charts, it must be admitted, as a profoundly stupid idea. At its heart lay a desire to marry the two most exciting music forms in Britain at the time. An odd notion, to say the least.

Nevertheless, Searling seemed interested. He had recently teamed up with John Anderson in creating a label base, funded by RCA, on which to place rare soul records. For some reason the 'Keep On Keepin' On' idea struck a chord with Searling and he demanded of the more rock-orientated Brandwood, 'Do you know anyone who could do it?'

Brandwood knew just one local band – a band desperate for any kind of movement. Joy Division. Whether they would agree to record 'Keep On Keepin' On' or not, Brandwood could only guess.

Brandwood was right – Joy Division were desperate. When the draft notion was presented to the band, they leapt at the chance, and Brandwood arranged a meeting between the band and Searling and Anderson. Apparently, only Peter Hook voiced his unease at the meeting. Mostly, Joy Division just wanted the chance to record. There was, perhaps, a sense of disappointment, certainly with Curtis, that they wouldn't actually be recording for RCA, and it might well have seemed odd that the money for this venture would be coming from a three-way investment from Binnick, Searling and Anderson. As for Searling, much to his partner's chagrin, he used his own holiday fund. Not only this, but he took a week off work to oversee recording, with Anderson taking up production duties.

The sessions were held in Arrow Studios, an unlikely and clinical setting within a flat, cold building at the back of Granada Television. Arrow, a 24 track, had been set up by David Kinson who astutely believed that such a handy location would provide a good deal of Granada Television work, and so it did. Ian Curtis in particular was noticeably awestruck when he discovered that the studio had been used for the recordings of *The Marc Bolan Show*.

Three days into the session, Richard Searling exploded into Brandwood's office, close to tears, his heavy personal investment – time, money and hope – obviously hanging in the balance.

'I just don't know how to handle this,' he told Brandwood. 'There's a situation at the studio . . . you've just got to come and help out.'

Brandwood walked tentatively down to Arrow, intent on placating those involved. Unfortunately, when he arrived, he found an extremely glum-looking Joy Division – if you can imagine such a thing – sitting around the studio. John Anderson, for his part, was sitting silently, staring at the wall. Brandwood attempted, rather pathetically, to break the icy atmosphere by cracking a joke. Although he succeeded in breaking the terrible silence, it was replaced only by a lengthy spell of vitriolic slanging.

'*He*,' Joy Division stated, apparently all of them, 'can't produce shit!'

Anderson swung around in his chair and blankly offered, 'The basic problem here is that the band just can't play. I wanted to get some other guys in. Some session guys . . . and *this* is how they reacted. So I asked them to use synthesizers and they have stated that never, ever, would they lower themselves. They won't touch synthesizers . . . ridiculous . . . ridiculous!'

The huge irony of that refusal, of course, wouldn't be realised for several years. And the stalemate couldn't be broken. Not fully. Whatever would be left of the recording would be fuelled by a certain resentment. Not an artistic resentment, not a frisson, but a kind of dullness which swept across the songs. Far from being a mere one-off stab at a soul classic, an album of sorts would be placed on tape. A half-finished album full of promise – good songs like 'Ice Age', Joy Division's lead song of the time, 'Leaders Of Men' and 'They Walked In Line' – which was full of intrigue too, especially with Curtis's deepening and personal use of Nazi-inspired surrealism. The problem was that this didn't quite square with the band's still fairly traditional sub-Banshees rock – a touch Gothic, but rounded, too bulbous, too familiar to make any real impact on the listener. This truth, the fact that the recordings – some finished, some half-formulated – merged together in a most conventional way, must have irked the band, especially Curtis, who was prone to spending long hours listening to such violent, experimental and, more often than not, wholly unmusical noises made by the aforementioned Throbbing Gristle. Indeed, their *Third Annual Report* album had become Curtis's most treasured possession of the time. As such, convention was the last thing he wished to hear seeping from Joy Division speakers. As it would turn out, his worries would be unfounded, for lurking in the muddy backwaters of the band's naïve sound was something completely, absolutely, unquestionably unique.

Richard Searling, perhaps more than the band themselves, felt saddened by the results of the sessions – not just the recordings but the prevailing air of negativity which followed them. He was also, the holiday money blown, receiving considerable hassle from his partner, which was particularly sad because even Joy Division would forever admit that Richard Searling had entered into the proceedings for all the right reasons. There was, initially, a loose kind of agreement between the band and the so-called company. Searling and Anderson would try to 'pass' the band on to another company. Brandwood advised Searling to try to get some kind of percentage point on some of the material because, in Brandwood's words at the time, 'You never know, Richard, they could become massive. You took a step to further their career. It didn't work but you never know what it might lead to. You have got to cover yourself in this business; that's the whole point.'

Much has been written about the night of 14 April 1978, when the floating 'on tour' talent contest, the Stiff Test/Chiswick

Challenge, went to Rafters. According to so many reports, the early morning Joy Division performance was so inspiring, especially to Tony Wilson and Rob Gretton, who had both gamely survived the barrage of rather tedious outings from earlier acts, that Factory Records was, if only as a wild, inebriated dream, effectively born on that evening. The truth is that Joy Division were far from enthralling. Without doubt, the frustrations of the evening – frustrations that are evident in every band contest – did add a spark to the performance. However, their songs, still muddied, fell from the stage to little effect. The obvious and often neglected fact that neither Stiff nor Chiswick chose to pursue the band with any degree of seriousness seems to have been omitted from accounts that suggest that it was one of the great largely unseen band performances of all time. Actually, Curtis had performed better earlier in the evening, when he had scribbled a frustration-fuelled note, packed with offensive swear words, and handed it to Tony Wilson who was hovering at the rear of the club near the pool table. Two years of frustration went into that scribbled note; two years spent watching a Manchester band scene mushroom around them; two years of feeling aloof, alone. Of seeing bands like the Fall and even the Worst gain immeasurable column inches in the music press while Warsaw and then Joy Division beavered ineffectively (or so it often seemed), slowly getting nowhere. Curtis, ever passionate about his music, admitted to a streak of envious near-loathing every time he saw Tony Wilson introducing another band on television, either at the tail-end of the nightly *Granada Reports* programme, on *So it Goes*, or on the boldly cliquish *What's On*. All sense of objectivity was lost inside that envy. Joy Division's music, the outsider might have noted, was maturing slowly but steadily. To expose them to the spotlight too early would surely have had grave consequences. But Curtis craved, so desperately craved, attention ... stardom, if you like. Mostly he just wanted people to talk about and listen to Joy Division, and found it difficult to understand why people would walk away, following a Joy Division performance, in a less than ecstatic mood. Such feelings fired that scribbled note. Deborah Curtis, standing next to Curtis at the time – she would later recall the incident in her book – blushed noticeably, clearly embarrassed about her husband's rash actions. There he was, all dignity shred, telling Wilson that he was 'a fucking cunt' merely because he had omitted to put the band on television.

'I suppose I should have been a bit offended,' admits Wilson, 'but I wasn't. You could say that Curtis's action lacked a certain dignity as well. I mean, I was used to getting flak from bands that I hadn't put on the telly ... all the time. But, for some reason, I didn't blame Ian at all. In fact, I had a sneaking feeling that he was right to be so indignant.'

Things didn't go too well that evening. Steve Shy, Dave Bentley, Paul Morley, Richard Boon and Kevin Cummins had ushered the Negatives into the event, their joke status amplified by Cummins who had been feverishly inventing bizarre tour dates – Our Lady and the Apostles Social Club, that kind of thing – and had submitted them to the music press who had unquestioningly placed the dates in their news pages. There was, indeed, little to suggest that the Negatives were anything less than a proper band. Curtis, Sumner, Hook and Morris loathed the Negatives. They believed that, as a joke act, they were abusing their position and were taking up column millimetres that could be more effectively occupied by a more deserving cause, i.e. Joy Division (and, on the night of a talent contest, who could blame them for airing such feelings?). Sensing this, however, Morley and Cummins merely chose to taunt the band, and a minor fight broke out backstage. This delighted the Negatives, who believed that their sense of anarchy had been allowed to colour the proceedings. (A tape of the Negatives, which included Dave Bentley counting from one to 350 and 'My Kind Of Girl Pays Fourpence On The Bus' was duly handed to a bemused London A&R man.) In one sense, the Negatives were correct to treat the evening as a sham. It *was* a sham. Such events always are and Joy Division's untainted naïveté seems hard to imagine, in retrospect.

'Nevertheless, it took just twenty seconds of Joy Division's set to convince me that this really would be a band worth investing in,' stated Wilson.

Gretton, for his part, had been given a copy of 'An Ideal For Living' by Peter Hook's girlfriend a couple of weeks prior to the gig. He had quite liked it – non-committal, as always – and had even played it at Rafters. After seeing the band's spirited set, however, he approached Sumner in the dressing room and enquired about the possibility of becoming the band's manager. Barney, taking a curious and immediate liking to Gretton, invited him down to a Joy Division rehearsal.

Peter Hook: 'Well, Barney's always been a bit of a daft sod. He had invited Gretton along to this rehearsal but he had forgotten to tell us about him. He had forgotten to tell us that he had practically invited this guy to become our manager. Can you believe that? So we were all sat around in rehearsals one day and this big, grey-haired man in glasses came in and sat down. We stared at him and launched into another song . . . and then another . . . and then another. While we were playing I thought, "Who is this dick?", and we continued right through our set and he just kept nodding his head. When we finished there was this really awkward moment. Just total silence. I could tell he was embarrassed, because he had been expecting us to know who he was . . . to welcome him, I suppose. And then Barney pipes up with, "Oh aye, lads, I forgot to tell you . . ." Barney hasn't changed. Still as daft as a brush.'

Manchester was, it must be finally admitted, going through something of a musical lull in the summer of 1978. The Electric Circus had long gone, as had the spirit which had fuelled it. Rafters, despite its carpeted warmth, never really produced the same fire. Over on the chip-paper'n'beer-can strewn streets of Ancoats, on Swan Street, stood the true downbeat musicianly heart of Manchester, Band on the Wall. It had changed little since Vini Reilly's attempts to muscle in on the jazz scene. It was still a strange little venue – a pub, a jazz club, a musical hangout with a late bar and a curious 'London' pub feel. It had provided a handy little platform, both for up and coming acts and for those who merely wished to jam. And on Tuesday nights the entire place was handed over to the Manchester Musicians Collective, a motley and expanding gang of strummers and blowers, some immersed in studenthood, although most would scatter about the dole queues of Prestwich, Hulme and Stockport, music being their hope, their passion and, if only for an evening, their form of escape. It was a simple format. Three bands would play each week. In front of them the other bands would assemble as an audience. This did, admittedly, provide a somewhat false atmosphere where the onlookers, uncritical – at least on the night – would clap politely as each and every brash punk song would stagger to a cacophonous climax. It was a curious mixture of insular musical meanderings and stark, half-formulated rock. Mick Hucknall's Frantic Elevators could often be found, noisily employing either the stage or the front row, as could Burnley's hilarious Not Sensibles, the dull, hippyish Manchester Mekon, the Buzzcockian Fast Cars, Blackburn's answer to Devo, IQ Zero, and Joy Division. Joy Division enjoyed the Band on the Wall because it was a world away from the Manchester scene that – at least in their eyes – had so ostracised them. Joy Division, being at least partly working-class, believed that those closer to the centre of the scene (the

Fall, Buzzcocks) tended to look down at them. They felt a kind of existential aloofness. Of course, what Joy Division failed to realise was that every other band in Manchester, including the Fall and Buzzcocks, also felt the same way. While they were sulking in the bedsits of Salford and Hulme, they all believed that a whole mass of lively musicianly camaraderie was taking place somewhere else, in another part of the city. A party – to which they hadn't been invited. Joy Division were very much mistaken in believing the Fall to be middle-class and aloof. Nothing could have been further from the truth. Ironically enough, the unfashionable bands who gathered together under the banner of the Manchester Musicians Collective were in fact the only real multi-band gang of musicians in Manchester. The only party, the only elitist group, the only insular hedonists. They were a paradox.

Joy Division flourished during three low-key Band on the Wall gigs. Though not necessarily on 'Collective' nights, they performed none the less in front of a tight circle of MMC members and displayed a degree of confidence – of arrogance even – that had not thus far been at all apparent, and certainly wasn't apparent with most MMC outfits. Pete Hook, his bass hovering just inches above the floor; Curtis, just beginning to swerve and jerk in an intriguing manner; Sumner, stock-still and nervous; Morris, intense and tightish. Joy Division had become a band.

One week prior to seeing Joy Division at the Band on the Wall – on 29 August 1978, to be precise – Paul Morley beat me to it. He reviewed the earlier gig ecstatically, comparing the band to Siouxsie And The Banshees – a massive tribute from Morley, then hopelessly in love with Siouxsie Sioux (unrequited love, I hasten to add). For my part, I had penned a fairly gloomy little editorial in the rock magazine *Zig Zag*, bemoaning the fact that the Manchester scene, so celebrated twelve months previously, had staggered to a halt ... and it had. The *Manchester Evening News* had picked up on this, and on its Tony Jasper Rock Page had raged in indignant tones. 'How dare this ludicrous man suggest that the Manchester scene is dead?' it screamed, before adding, 'Rob Gretton is the manager of local band Joy Division who are really making waves. Joy Division are the living proof that the Manchester scene is far from dead.'

This, I thought, was amusing. Rob Gretton rang me on 4 September 1978, inviting me to attend the band's second gig at the venue in a week. This I did, and enjoyable though it was, the band certainly lacked any real sense of urgency. Apparently the first gig had been far superior. I wrote a review for *Sounds*. Not a particularly favourable review; not a particularly inspired piece of writing, either. Nevertheless, it did conclude with the line 'Joy Division have a bassist that could eat Jean-Jacques Burnell for breakfast' (JJ being the Stranglers' bassist, a figure simply dripping in Kung Fu machismo).

'You're a cunt for writing that,' Gretton informed me. 'Hooky loved it ... he thinks he's dead 'ard now.'

THE GHOSTS OF LITTLE PETER STREET

Little Peter Street was, and arguably still is, the most curious and ghostly street in central Manchester. In 1978 it had yet to be prettified by an influx of regeneration schemes. Back then, no chrome and glass cafe bars could be found lurking in unlikely corners. Television researchers did not meet for lentil burger lunches on canalside tables. Architects did not scour the area, besuited and hard hatted, searching for the site of their next miraculous, if ultimately pointless, transition, and teams of red-tied officials had yet to drift through in packs, in futile attempts to lift the city into undeserved Olympic status.

As today, though, Little Peter Street was lined with towering red-bricked warehouses, although most had languished emptily, eerily – aside from the odd short lease to dubious businessmen – since their fall from full use 20, 30, possibly 40 years before. The area of Knott Mill, once the very nub of warehouse Manchester, seemed to be crumbling away on the other side of the street. A bombsite appearance prevailed, giving way to an encroaching spread of rough clearances, temporarily in use as car parks. Two pubs perched at either end of the street, and one in particular, The Gaythorn, had been amazed to find itself suddenly flushed with a regular influx of young, downbeat musicians. It was a welcome invasion though, certainly adding colour to the traditional Gaythorn clientele – grease-splattered, tabloid-scouring lunchtime mechanics or ageing, greying men, with wispy chins, brown suits and no apparent vocation beyond the consumption of vast quantities of bitter.

On most evenings, the austere, nicotine-lined tap room would come alive with the gossip, chit-chat, ego clashes and out-and-out backbiting which signified that a music scene, of sorts, was in the process of unfolding. Occasionally, three or four bands would form separate conspiratorial huddles, no doubt fighting over publishing rights yet to be earned or planning to sack the missing bass player or poach a singer from another, marginally more successful band. The bands adhered to no universal dress code. On the contrary, the genres were disparate and often clashed quite strikingly. One remembers Gorton glam rockers V2, for instance, slumped menacingly in one corner, clad in figure-hugging flame-red or marine-blue plastic, bleached hair and make-up, while at the next table sat the darkly-clad Bohemian jazz outfit, Ludus, whose inspiring and beautiful singer, Linder, would at all times be clad head to toe in regulation black.

The reason for this unholy and bewildering invasion was the recent opening of Tony Davidson's rehearsal complex, in truth no more than a web of grey, dusty rooms, all framed by fearsome junctions of industrial piping and all too soon filled with crisp packets, crushed beer cans and cigarette dimps. Quite the perfect setting for the wave of post-punk industrialist bands who would attempt to build a live act around the icy chords produced by a recently purchased synthesizer.

Gretton, who had been involved with Davidson during the Slaughter And The Dogs period, managed to forgive him his Manchester United leanings and negotiated a good deal for Joy Division to use the top-floor rehearsal space. This simple act caused a ripple of consternation among the other bands. V2, for instance, believed themselves to be the number one act on Davidson's TJM label – their elongated, hookless dirge, 'Overture', would open the TJM sample album, *Identity Parade*.

Joy Division's rehearsal room seemed eerily perfect. Ian Curtis in particular fell in love with its dour interior, its romantic austerity, its measure of seediness, even. A tough industrial past had seeped for so many years into the walls and been engrained into the atmosphere. This was a place where tortuous hard work had taken place. You could simply smell it. It was a place of threatening dullness, of foreboding perhaps. It was a room which – I swear this is true – sent a cold shiver through the first-time visitor. Those who view such thoughts with a certain degree of cynicism should cast their eyes across the photographs, taken with the omnipresent camera of Kevin Cummins, of Ian Curtis during this period. Or later, the promo video for 'Love Will Tear Us Apart'. For the prevailing sense of power within the frame of those photographs, within that video, belonged to that room. As the band practised, and practised, and practised, the room slowly became an integral part of the Joy Division image; it darkened the visuals and, some might say, darkened the music also. The entire complex seemed significant, to be fair. Empty, dusty, ex-industrial, lacking in true workman-like purpose, the influx of would-be musicians served only to highlight the curious, prevailing loneliness. Whereas before greatness and horror had inhabited its walls, and riches and poverty had both been sown into its daily function, by this time it all seemed farcical. The bands who came in were merely play-acting; yearning for some kind of industrial focus and yet not really understanding the sense of loss. Most of the musicians, unlike Joy Division, were dole-queue dreamers, their musicianly endeavours providing a sense of purpose but little hope. Joy Division, I believe, allowed that room, that street, that area, to strongly flavour their work.

Joy Division in practice in the early days was little more than the expected orgy of camaraderie. A pit of ambition, hampered only by musicianly shortcomings. With the cluttered sound of Warsaw fading slowly away, Joy Division's noise twisted slightly, though still resembling, in no small way, the Banshees and for a short while, Wire. It was, at its most basic, a light metal noise, conventional rock pushed a little further than normal. Each song would crumble to a close and be followed by – so it always seemed – a swift parade of nervous glances and then, finally, a cackle of laddish laughter, backbiting, sarcasm and, naturally, whole episodes of envy-tinged digs at the bands who were rehearsing beneath and next to them. One band in particular was Mick Hucknall's musically confused Frantic Elevators, who were at that moment halfway on the journey from harsh doomy punkdom to rash r'n'b. They had, in short, yet to peel away the half-baked and underplayed pretensions that dogged their earlier work. There was one song in particular, called 'Every Day I Die', that seemed to exist cornily as the archetypal T.J. Davidson practice-room song, for the song was everywhere. It seeped through the practice-room doors; it travelled along the pipeways.

'God, they're playing that bloody awful song again,' Hooky famously noted. 'The doomy bastards ... can't they play anything else?'

It might be noted that, when Joy Division can be heard complaining about the dour nature of your music, you are in deep, deep trouble.

Joy Division, despite their Brotherdale link with V2, never really mixed with the Davidson crowd. In the pub, for instance, they would huddle alone. They were not, however, adrift on a wave of pretentious introversion. Nothing, absolutely nothing, could have been further from the truth. The talk in the pub was more often than not bright and brash; of football and girls, of other bands and their shortcomings, of venues and venue owners. One remembers them, tumbling into that tap room, joking with the tattooed-armed mechanics and dipping their forks into ketchup-covered potato and meat pies.

Joy Division unfurled themselves into this atmosphere with ease; more at home, it seemed, with the locals than with the other bands. On one occasion though, smarting from the kind of critical slaps one would associate with a much bigger band – for they had yet to cement any relationship with Factory although the plans had been laid – they crowded into a corner, unleashing their venom on any passing soul who might vaguely be associated with the music press, i.e. me.

'Yeah, music press ... er ... we are swiftly learning, are all idiots ... all of them.'

Which is the way in which Barney chose to open an interview. Joy Division's first national inteview as it turned out, hastily – and rather badly, I admit – scribbled down for the readers of *Sounds*. I do recall, actually, two relevant points in regard to the placing of that particular feature. One was Rob Gretton, flushed with alcohol I guessed, unduly haranguing yours truly as I wandered into a gig at the Russell Club in Hulme.

'Go on . . . interview them . . . they're good talkers, damn fine talkers. Great band . . . ask them about the Nazi thing if you like. Ask them anything. It will be a good article . . . won't do you any harm. They're going to be massive . . .' etc. The irony of such a bombardment, of course, wouldn't become relevant for at least a couple of years, when Rob would retreat into a surly 'no comment' stance and remain there, it would seem, for eternity. The second interesting factor was the reaction of the *Sounds* editors, three of them who, after hearing a few scattered rumours about the band, had already pinned them into the 'doomy Nazi' corner. Not that, I hasten to add, *Sounds* was any different from the *NME* – Paul Morley aside – and, in one sense I guess, Barney's initial outburst was truly justified. On the other hand, Joy Division would, surely, only have themselves to blame. To provide a taste of the times, here is a snippet from the question and answer part of the feature, from the pub, from behind the sauce bottles.

On the record 'An Ideal For Living' it says 'songs by Joy Division'. Do you always write collectively? Who comes up with the ideas?

Ian: 'It varies a lot . . . musically, anyway.'

Bernard: 'We usually start with a drum riff, then add bass and guitar on top. Ian supplies the lyrics.'

Ian: 'Yeah . . . you see, I have got this little book here. Full of lyrics, it is. I just pull it out and see if I can fit something in. I have loads of lyrics in reserve . . . all waiting in there. I'll use them when the right tune comes along. Sometimes it's a line from one song mixed with a line from another. Sometimes the original lyric gets completely changed . . . it just gets used as a kind of guide lyric and leads to something else. You never know. But I have to have this reserve . . . this "lyric bank". Some of the songs are two, three years old. "Leaders Of Men", for example.'

And what are these lyrics about?

Ian: 'I don't write about anything in particular. It's all subconscious stuff. Scribble ... sometimes feelings or things that pop into your head. Does that sound pretentious?'

Steve: 'If they were about anything in particular they would become dated.'

Ian: 'Yeah, I leave it open to interpretation.'

So, I suggest, you can't really complain if people take them the wrong way, can you? Like, for instance, this Nazi thing, which has been going on ever since you called yourselves Warsaw.

Bernard: 'We picked Warsaw simply because it was a nothing sort of name. We didn't wish to be called "the" somebody.'

Rob: 'Back to this Nazi thing. It is good if people can jump to conclusions. I think people can be very naïve, sometimes.'

Bernard: 'People tend to take a radical viewpoint on everything, whereas, if they would just think for a change, they would realise that it is absolutely nothing.'

Rob: 'You, for instance, wrote in your review that Joy Division still persist in this Nazi history chic. What does that mean?'

The lyrics ... the way you look onstage ...

Rob: 'They may look dark and mysterious, but why does everyone connect that with Nazis?'

Ian: '*Everyone* calls us Nazis.'

But you do write about Nazi history a lot. More than is good for you, perhaps? ['They Walked In Lines', Ian Curtis 1978, 'All dressed up in uniforms so fine, they drank and killed to pass the time, wearing the shame of their crime, with measured steps they walked in lines.']

Bernard: 'Everyone says that, but compared to Jimmy Pursey who was an out-and-out racist –'

Why?

'You don't think so. That just proves my point. Nobody can remember the beginning of Sham 69 and the things he said then. Now he tries to disconnect himself. Still [heavy sarcasm now] his lyrics are great.' (General laughter.)

Not, perhaps, one of the great rock interviews, and the remainder of it seems far too messy, irrelevant and embarrassing to revive. It was, however, fascinating – even then – to see Joy Division sitting there, clearly very unhappy with their position in the world. It could be argued, of course, that *all* young bands feel the same way – and sure enough, even as we spoke, the odd drifting bass player or vocalist taking a break from rehearsals across the road would cast surly, envious glances in our direction. Joy Division remained completely unaware of these glances, rather endearingly in fact. Nevertheless, Ian Curtis seemed the most open; the most jovial, even. Certainly the only band member who seemed to actually enjoy the process of being interviewed. Pete Hook, by stark contrast, planted his feet on the bench seat, sank his chin thoughtfully between his knees, and declined to answer any questions at all.

'Oh, don't mind him,' said Bernard, 'he's just doing his moody bastard bass player bit … he'll snap out of it soon, won't you, Hooky?'

Some say he never did.

Ian Curtis was a lurker – no, not a member of the dreadful third division London punk band who droned hopelessly across a number of small labels – he really was a lurker. He would lurk in club corners, in the decrepit recesses of Davidson's rehearsal studios, in Manchester city centre on lunch breaks. Now that the appeal of RCA had lessened a little, he would often lurk around the Virgin Records shop or anywhere in Piccadilly. This isn't a flippant observation. He was a lurker; a nice lurker but a lurker all the same.

He lurked, one night, in Devilles cellar bar, next to the cigarette machine, politely purchasing drinks for any passing acquaintances, especially acquaintances of a journalistic nature. His banter was particularly open that night, astonishingly so as he barely knew me and had absolutely no idea who my three accomplices were. (Nor they, he, as it happens. A chartered surveyor, an electrician and a civil servant, none of them reserved any time for popular culture, other than as a backdrop for Friday night disco 'trappings'. They had never heard of Joy Division, nor Buzzcocks.) Upon discovering this fact – that none of them had any pop music interests whatsoever – I expected Curtis to freeze on them, to back away even, or at least allow their waffle – for that's what it probably was – to wash over him. But Ian Curtis did nothing of the sort. In a sense, their lack of interest seemed to intrigue him. When he spoke with great passion about, I seem to remember, Iggy Pop, he was fascinated by their blank stares.

'What kind of music do you guys go for?' he asked, unaware, I suppose, that they didn't really 'go for' any music. Not in that way; not passionately. He respected their reply though; the O'Jays Love Train, the Detroit Emeralds, Tavaris. 'Nothing wrong with that,' he noted, quite correctly, although he did swiftly alter the course of the conversation to take in the rollercoaster fortunes of Manchester United.

THE RUSSELL CLUB AND THE BIRTH OF FACTORY
Wilson's foray into the often rather dubious world of gig promotion had been born not out of a desire to reintroduce an

Electric Circus sense of urgency into the city's club scene – in fact, Wilson does not share my view that the city had died a little during the spring of '78 – but more out of his own, private frustration. He had enjoyed two series of *So it Goes* immensely. For him it had been a dream period; the chance to work not just with rather stuffy TV executives – for Bohemia had yet to encroach into the curious catacombs of Granada – but to work alongside the very best bands of the era. He never really recovered from the fact that, say, Elvis Costello, would meet him in a corridor and utter the words, 'Oh, hi Tony, how are you doin'?' For Wilson, who had still not fully shed his adoration of untouchable American rock stars, this mingling with those who would be heroes – even if, more often than not, the 'heroes' proved numbingly disappointing – still proved magical. It had also become perfectly clear from the mumblings at Granada that there would not be another *So it Goes*. Programme controller Mike Scott, for reasons which never really became apparent to Wilson, had taken exception to the sight of a horse's tail protruding from Iggy Pop's backside during the filming of the Apollo gig. This apparently unacceptable vision was enough, it seemed, for Wilson to be abruptly shunted out, or sideways at least. The chance for Wilson to work as a reporter on the legendary *World in Action* was offered as a substitute. In truth, Wilson, though a little hurt, wasn't too upset. He had been having problems, for instance, in locating a natural direction for a third series. After all, he had showcased all the best talent. The Clash, Costello, Buzzcocks, the Pistols, the Jam, Magazine. He felt, much to the chagrin of no small number of neglected artists, that all the important bands of the era had had their chance.

Nevertheless, the end of *So it Goes* marked a barrier for Wilson. All of a sudden, the show had gone, the bands had gone; the irate phone calls from band managers and agents had vanished also. Although still at Granada, he no longer felt part of the rock industry – and the fire had been lit. Professionally, he knew he would always be first and foremost a television journalist, but deep down he felt a desire to reimmerse himself in rock'n'roll. It was so much more fun. He needed, above all else, exposure to rock characters.

'It dawned on me,' he states, 'that no longer would wonderful and bizarre people be a part of my everyday life. Daft things . . . I remember, for instance, having phone conversations with the old Clash manager, Bernie Rhodes, who was such a wonderful person . . . much forgotten and undervalued as it happens. I'd be on the phone to him and he would be talking about hiring atom bombs . . . absolutely wild, crazy, nuts . . . I loved all that. I first met him at the Music Machine in London. I had gone along with Richard Boon and Rhodes came screaming up shouting, "You fucking bastard, Boon. When you got rid of Garth [oversized, gruff Buzzcocks bassist, replaced rather cynically by comparatively 'pretty boy' Steve Garvey], you severed your connection with the people." Those are the kind of incidents I craved. I knew a lot of brilliant people, in Manchester, and I wished to remain involved with them. Television was work to me . . . still is. I love aspects of it; maybe I love the television industry as a whole, I don't know. But I was always more passionate about music and music-orientated people. Still am.'

This craving would serve to instigate not only the running of a venue but the germ of a rather more obvious idea. In early 1978, Wilson had presented a *Granada Reports* feature about independent record labels. Rather than blandly praise them for their courage and innovation, Wilson probed a little further. Putting his old friend Tosh Ryan from Rabid on the rack, Wilson asked why it had been necessary for Rabid to shunt their one-off comic artist Jilted John on to EMI.

'Why did you do a deal with EMI?' demanded Wilson. 'Why didn't you just keep it on your own label?'

Ryan, perhaps sensibly, decided that such an idea was simply naïve. Jilted John, of course, wouldn't have become a hit without EMI's backing – the moment would have passed. What would be the point? The record, though excellent, was a gimmick hit – and Rabid, naturally, needed to survive.

'You're living in the past, Tony,' said Ryan.

But the state of independent labels had started to worry Wilson. Ryan was absolutely correct. The DIY notion, the 'indie' dream, had long since faded into a kind of unofficial mass scouting agency for major labels. The idea was simple. You began by managing a small band. The Rough Trade network – built out of a reggae base, the true source of the independent dream – allowed you to put your little record out, remain cool, gather in the glowing music press reviews and features, entice a major label or, if you were lucky, a number of majors . . . and sign. The whole point was no longer to bypass the majors, but to feed them. Fair enough, one might say, but it still worried Wilson who, since May 1977, had been quietly harbouring some kind of vague notion about running a record label. A different kind of label.

This little dream had begun exactly one year after he had stumbled across Slaughter And The Dogs in Stockport which, it now seems relevant to point out, also marked his first date with his soon-to-be-fiancée, Lindsay Reade. Twelve months later and Wilson had taken Alberto's singer C.P. Lee and his actor friend Alan Erasmus along on his stag night. Rather disappointingly, this unlikely trio stumbled into a pub in Failsworth, in which a glitzy, punky young band, rather horrendously named Flash-back, were performing. Although Wilson wasn't too impressed, Erasmus soon began to manage the band.

In January 1978, Wilson received a phone call from a thoroughly disgruntled Erasmus. The band, now called Fast

Breeder, had been infiltrated by the aforementioned Didsbury set, and now included such local 'musos' as 'Spider' Mike King and an infamous Didsbury drummer with the somewhat uninspired name of Drummie.

'It's fucking awful ... it's fucking dreadful,' moaned Erasmus, who like so many before him had succumbed to musicianly negativity and been sacked.

That same day, Wilson was to visit his accountant in Prestwich, north Manchester, where accountants are so often based. The accountant was somewhat abashed by the fact that Wilson's TV profile just didn't seem to square with his somewhat modest income.

'Tony,' he stated earnestly, 'I have bus drivers coming to me who earn more money than you. Look, don't you want to be rich?'

Wilson replied that he didn't, particularly, although agreed that something, somewhere, was going wrong.

'My brother,' continued the accountant, by now adopting the kind of semi-patronising tones that seem to be a prerequisite in the accounting profession, 'says that every band you put on the telly, bands who no one has heard of, eventually make it big. If that is true, then why don't you get in on the act? There's big money to be made in the music industry.'

Although this advice was laced with its own particular brand of naïveté, Wilson came away from the meeting in a state of considerable confusion. Driving back into Manchester, his mind began to race wildly. 'What the fuck am I doing?' he screamed to himself and, shunting the car purposefully into gear, altered course and drove directly to Erasmus's Didsbury flat. Wilson found Erasmus in a state of despair. His adept management of Fast Breeder had imploded messily, leaving him with just two musicians sitting idly under his rather non-existent managership – a drummer named Chris Joyce and guitarist David Rowbotham. Not one to allow such pathetic circumstances to swamp his by now uncontrollable enthusiasm, Wilson decided to join forces with Erasmus and build a band around this startled duo. Four days later, Erasmus telephoned with the news that he had found a guitarist named Vini Reilly, the unlikely and strikingly pencil-thin refugee from Ed Banger And The Nosebleeds and, before them, Wild Ram. He ignored a message from Rabid's Tosh Ryan exclaiming, 'Tony, you are fucking bonkers if you take this guy on. Who would employ a guitarist who brings doctors' notes saying that he will not be able to practise next week?'

Wilson, as it happened, was rather taken with Reilly's eccentric illness, incorrectly believing it, at least initially, to be a particularly stylish affectation. Tony Bowers, ex-bass player with the Albertos, who lived in the same Palatine Road flatblock as Erasmus, seemed another logical choice (although Wilson would later state, 'There were a million problems working with Tony Bowers.').

Although a name had been found – Durutti Column, from the situationist comic strip – there soon followed a trickle of wildly varying and wholly unsuitable singers who fronted the band during various rehearsal sessions, all profoundly lacking in the kind of charisma necessary to pin down some kind of visual attack, if not effectively 'lead' the band. This was the unhealthy situation which provided Wilson with his first bitter taste of the heartless downside of the music industry, albeit on the bottom rung. After financing the hire of a scout hut, paid for by selling Wilson's collection of 'freebie' records, attained during his Granada years though rarely played, the band decided, as bands do, that the 'singer would have to go . . . and it's a manager's job to get rid of him'.

'That's fucking great, I thought,' says Wilson. 'Spend my fucking money then get me to do the really horrible jobs . . . I was learning fast.'

Vini Reilly, displaying the kind of disproportionate ego which so often attaches itself to budding musos enjoying their first flush of musicianly control, abruptly declared, 'Tony, I'm leaving the scout hut now and I am not coming back until he has gone.'

That night, Wilson visited the flat of singer Phil Rainford. To make matters worse, Rainford seemed unusually enthusiastic, painfully exclaiming in an increasingly excited tone about his plans for the band and how marvellous the recent rehearsals had been. As every excitable comment passed by, Wilson found himself sinking deeper and deeper into despair. He sat, quietly panicking, preparing to administer the chop while a Bruce Springsteen album filled the room. 'At the end of side one,' thought Wilson, 'I'll tell him then.' Inevitably, side one cluttered to a halt and side two began to spin threateningly. Wilson decided to tell him at the end of side two, and so he did. Feeling profoundly wretched, with Rainford's tones of indignant disbelief ringing in his ears, he strode wretchedly away from the startled singer's flat. Tony Wilson had tasted the dark side of band management.

'I don't know about that,' declares Vini Reilly. 'I mean, Tony tells this tale of him having to deliver the news to Rainford, and maybe he did, but I distinctly remember making a telephone call to the singer and being incredibly rude to him. I mean really, really, really horribly rude to him ... I don't know whether that was before Tony had been to see him or not.'

More singers came and went. One couldn't sing at all, not a note, and so he simply talked his way through the songs. 'He was one of the better ones,' admits Wilson, who also concedes – though he didn't at the time – that, '... that band was fucking crap. We all knew it but nobody dared say anything. There was a kind of, "Oh well, it will all come good in time" mentality. Of course it didn't. That band, as they were at that time, were crap. No direction, no harmony, no fucking idea and yet there was Alan, me and Vini all completely blind to such obvious shortcomings. We thought they would conquer the world.'

Though today, Wilson gasps at his lack of objectivity during the early days of Durutti Column, there was nothing at all unnatural about it. When someone initially begins to manage, play in or become involved with a band, then all objectivity is instantly diffused. Suddenly you just cannot understand why the rest of the world fails to share your warped vision. It is an interesting, not completely negative, condition. For it can fire ambition and determination. For artists, it can summon the muse.

Despite the band's state of confusion, the birth of Durutti Column was one reason why Wilson decided that a new rock venue must be sought.

He contacted local promoter Alan Wise, a Jewish son of a prominent Manchester chemist who had impressed Wilson by his steady running of Rafters, and hatched an idea to 'instigate an Electric Circus-like atmosphere' by joining forces to promote gigs at some already part-established venue. Noticing that the Russell Club wasn't too busy on Friday nights, they enquired about staging a pilot gig with the club having the bar take, Wilson and Wise taking the door. It was a simple, relatively hassle-free deal and the club duly agreed. Then, fired by the pair's liberated enthusiasm, it snowballed slightly. Why just one gig? Why not a series of four or five or, if successful, why not every Friday?

First though, they needed an identity. It has been almost universally reported that Factory merely took its name from Andy Warhol's infamous celebrity-led collective of the same name. This notion, always understandable, would be strengthened further in later years when Alan Wise would manage ex-model and Velvet Underground singer Nico, who by the early eighties would take root in the most unlikely setting of bedsit Prestwich (her presence on the scene severely 'freaking out' no small number of Manchester bands who had elevated the Velvet Underground to near 'God-like' status).

The truth, however, is rather less obvious, and less romantic too. Wise and Wilson were wandering along Manchester's Deansgate, when Wise saw a notice proclaiming, 'FACTORY CLEARANCE'.

'Factory?' snapped Wise. 'Wouldn't that be a good name for our venture? The Russell Club, on Friday nights, could be called the Factory.'

The Russell Club had existed in numerous guises, mainly though as the PSV Club (Public Service Vehicle . . . no, I never understood that, either). It had made its name in later days as a suitably downbeat reggae-oriented venue handily placed, as it was, for nearby Moss Side. Wilson had chanced upon the venue following a meeting with the owner, local 'businessman' Don Tonay.

He was, in the eyes of Wilson, 'an incredible character . . . a civilised gangster'.

Tonay, undoubtedly, had style. He was a tall, commanding, handsome man in his late forties. Each night, after prowling around the club, he would leave at precisely 1 a.m. A van would pull respectfully on to the car park. The rear doors would open to reveal two beautiful prostitutes in reclining poses, between whom Tonay would stylishly flop. The doors would be pulled shut and the van would cruise away into the night. Tonay's style was a throwback, of sorts, to the gangster tradition – he did have links, it was strongly rumoured, with the Kray fraternity – and most people who knew him, and knew him well enough not to cross him, regarded him as a lovely individual. One is tempted, of course, to break into Pythonesque tales of a Piranha brothers nature: 'Oh yeah, Don

... he was a lovely bloke ... ', etc, and such clichés wouldn't be too far from the truth, for Tonay ruled his patch with an iron hand, be it a loving hand or otherwise. This was, perhaps, typified by a conversation overheard at the Russell Club one night when Magazine were performing. The band's van had been cynically and pointlessly broken into in the car park. Two 'drug squad' officers, standing at the bar – drinking Red Stripe – were heard to mutter, 'Whoever broke into that van will be very sorry ... very sorry indeed ... pity for him that it wasn't our precinct. Don will sort them out, poor guys.'

The very notion of 'drug squad' officers inside the Russell Club seems as ludicrous today as it did in 1978. The place was almost a school for 'dealers', most of them, alas, selling packets of Vim, dried privet leaves or dubious blotting paper acid. Nevertheless, in the shadowy corners, on the stairs, in the cafe, at the bar, backstage, little drug deals would be taking place at all times. Even the bands would be approached by a multitudinous array of motley dealers, and would rely on their intuition to sift the main men from the upstarts.

Tonay had a few other quirks. There were signs in the club saying 'NO TAMS ALLOWED'. It was difficult to know quite what this meant. However, one clue could be the time Tonay wandered into the club and, spying three Jamaican guys in woolly hats, screamed 'Haaaaattttts!', following which the offending articles were respectfully removed. On another occasion, Tonay entered the club at 2 a.m., and two or three straggling tables remained – students mainly – only too slowly finishing their Guinnesses, smoking dope, chatting about the evening's gig. 'Don't you know how to clear a club out?' asked Tonay, his question directed at Alan Wise, his sidekick Nigel and Wilson. Wilson answered politely, 'No ... not really Don.' Tonay proceeded to pick a table up, hurl it in the air and, before it crashed to the ground, screamed

'OOOOOUTTTTTTT!!!!' The students, needless to say, filed out respectfully, silently, nervously.

The club's identity was completed, in the manner that would become synonymous with Factory, by a slice of quality, evocative, simplistic artwork. A young design student called Peter Saville had precociously approached Wilson during an extremely poor Patti Smith gig at Manchester's Apollo Theatre. Wilson, though distraught at the sight of one of his greatest heroines performing with such a lack of vigour – she had lost it by then – found himself listening intently to the smart young guy's pleadings.

'I want to design for you,' he stated boldly, and rather oddly, as neither he nor Wilson quite knew just what it was that needed designing. Nevertheless, Wilson agreed to a further meeting with Saville, in Granada's hugely disappointing canteen area. Saville, to his delight and surprise, found his portfolio enthusiastically scrutinised. Wilson, immediately recognising Saville's influences, seemed to warm to the elegant simplicity of the work and immediately commissioned Saville to design the initial Factory Club poster, for 27 May 1978. (Though the poster is now regarded as a classic, due to a portentous printing delay it never actually made it on to the streets.)

Wilson, Saville and Erasmus posed purposefully beneath the Russell Club's angular side elevation, a wall pustulated by ripped posters, missing bricks and sundry stains. They looked smart, the three of them, smiling into the camera of Kevin Cummins who, with one arm outstretched and moving slowly to the right, found the perfect angle – the perfect image for the Russell Club. For, looming large behind the threesome, behind the club, could be seen the vast, daunting semi-circular grey mass of the Hulme Crescents. This was the club that would see the launch of the Factory organisation and become, in spirit and in intent, the true heart of the forthcoming record label. It would be a label for the post-punk industrial age ... and where could be better? If the Electric Circus had suited the slash and thrust of the ragged punk bands, then this place, the Russell Club, would become the perfect manifestation of the late seventies/early eighties raincoated art'n'synth crew. A movement still locked in the independent dream. A movement dressed in old grey suits and brogues, with short back and sides, reading Camus, Sartre or any standard student read.

The Russell Club, and indeed its Friday night transformation, had many problems. From the city centre, it was difficult – and, in a drunken stupor, impossible – to locate. Rather like the Electric Circus, it stood temptingly at the end of a somewhat dangerous trudge or even more dangerous bus ride from the city centre. It was, however, quite perfectly within staggering distance of the largest student university campus in western Europe. This was a fact that didn't escape the attention of Tony Wilson. If they could capture the imagination of the students in the Oxford Road halls of residence, and in Hulme, Whalley Range, Didsbury, Chorlton and Withington, then this strangely situated club, with its sadly and mostly undeserved notorious neighbourhood, could surely become the catalyst for a new and powerful scene. But there were so many problems. Pickpockets flitted, like ghostly shadows, around the downstairs area, preying on wealthy students. The aforementioned drug peddlers remained pushy, irritating, intimidating and, at times, deeply threatening. Few nights at the Factory proved free from some kind of hassle. Upstairs, on the rickety balcony cafe, inedible goat curries would swiftly and infamously become the speciality. Joy Division would debut there on 20 October 1978 although in truth the scene would have begun to settle before their arrival. However, for all its obvious shortcomings, and quite possibly because of them, there was something curiously warm about the

Factory. Essentially, with a capacity of around 800, it was quite the perfect size for a small scene to develop. It was dark enough and intimate enough for a smallish crowd to be able to create a lively atmosphere, while on later bulging, ecstatic nights – who could forget Iggy Pop, the Undertones, UB40? – the entire club would seem to swell and bounce.

'Come down, come down, come down,' pleaded the disembodied voice of Tony Wilson. 'This is the place where it will happen, where everything will happen. This is the perfect venue.'

It was, more than the Circus really, most definitely the place to be seen. Hiding in the darkened corners on any given evening during those early nights, would be the various members of Joy Division, having fun with Echo And The Bunnymen, The Teardrop Explodes – odd escapees from the Fall, and Linder, whose band Ludus, formed by the inimitable Arthur Kadmon, one of Manchester's greatest under-achievers, would debut there. One recalls, in the early days, an eight-piece Durutti Column, complete with Reilly's surging solos, thrashing through a pub rock set, with Alan Erasmus flitting around the crowd, offering free smokes to anyone who looked as though they might be from the music press. And backstage, afterwards, with Erasmus and Wilson injecting the band with boisterous, beery enthusiasm, falling on the floor in an unbecoming fit of giggles, puffing on various cigarettes, and generally screaming about the exaggerated genius of that particular, short-lived version of Durutti Column and claiming that this would be the birth, the true birth, of Factory. Whether they meant the club or the forthcoming label, it was impossible to tell.

JOY DIVISION AND FACTORY

In August 1978, Tony Wilson received a phone call from Roger Eagle, artistically minded booker of Liverpool's Eric Club – a hugely influential cellar club, heavily reminiscent of

London's Roxy, from which, partly under Eagle's guidance, sprouted the entire Liverpool punk scene and, latterly, the very heart and pulse of the city's art societies, a good many rock stars and the parallel label, Eric's Records, which had floundered in the wake of punk. A burst of musical activity in Liverpool had rekindled Eagle's interest in the label although at the back of his mind was a fairly naïve desire to mix the musical activities of Manchester and Liverpool and melt them down to form one, superior record label.

'I wondered if you would be our A&R man,' asked Eagle, rather tentatively. This sounded serious, it sounded like involvement – further involvement – and involvement was Wilson's favourite drug at that moment. Both Wilson and Eagle agreed that Joy Division were hot and getting hotter. Wilson also convinced Eagle that a band he had recently discovered, Durutti Column, featuring ex-Nosebleeds' guitarist Vini Reilly and managed by his close friend, Alan Erasmus, were emerging as an equally potent force; that they were slotting things into place, even though nothing could be further from the truth. Wilson mumbled something about an initial 'sampler' record, intended to establish the new label's credentials, fond as he was of the low-priced samplers of the early seventies. It was an idea which fell straight out of his head. On the Saturday night, with Eagle's rather loose offer swimming around in his head, Wilson decided to add a little spice, a little freedom, to his thoughts. He promptly dropped a tab of acid, which always seemed to help in such situations, and visited the flat of Durutti Column drummer, Chris Joyce. Once inside, Wilson sat cross-legged and engaged in buoyant and rather unpredictable conversation. Observing Joyce's record collection, he noticed a copy of Santana's *Abraxas* album, a personal favourite of his from days of early seventies Cambridge-based reflection. On this day, however, the sleeve –

stunning on the most normal of days – looked spectacular. It was, in fact, an import copy from Thailand or Singapore. In the Eastern way, the psychedelic sleeve had been printed not on card but on paper, and had been sealed in a layer of cheap plastic. Staring intently at the sleeve which, in Wilson's chemically aided condition, simply 'came alive', the notion of the Factory sample sleeve began to stir. Wilson came away from Joyce's flat, his ideas for the proposed 'sampler' multiplying by the second. Driving to Liverpool the next day, he formulated the idea of a plastic bag and a sheet of folded paper housing a double seven-inch format – a lovely format, he believed. The mix of artists would be simple: two Manchester bands, which he had, and Eagle's pick of two Liverpool units.

The meeting in Liverpool was extensive, amiable and, ultimately, fruitless. Eagle's heart had been firmly set on a twelve-inch format while Wilson, lost in his stylistic dream, refused to budge from his eccentric twin seven-inch idea. A friendly argument governed the meeting and, reluctantly, Wilson agreed on the practical advantages and the comparative cheapness of the twelve-inch. He changed his mind, however, during the drive home. His mother had left him £5,000, and there was more lying in a trust fund. Why not, he reasoned, use it. By the time his Peugeot crawled back into Didsbury, his mind had been made up. He would contact Alan Erasmus – they had talked about forming a label for Durutti Column – and they would do it themselves. What's more, they would use his impractical, lovely little format. It would, Eagle had warned him, be a logistical nightmare. It probably wouldn't make money but he was sure it would at least look fantastic. It would be Factory Records. He felt happier, once the decision had been made. Delirious even. They were a record label.

* * *

A month or so after the Arrow recordings, Martin Hannett strode briskly into Brandwood's office, intent as usual in hanging around and watching videos, as well as, on this occasion, talking excitedly about the new label he was setting up with Tony Wilson and Alan Erasmus. Hannett, it transpired, was hoping to be the 'head of A&R and production'.

Brandwood: 'There are a number of versions about how Joy Division came to be involved with Factory. Obviously Wilson had seen them at Rafters and knew Rob well and I know was thinking about the band at the very start of Factory. But, I distinctly remember having a conversation with Hannett about the new label and at that point he had definitely never thought about Joy Division for the label, which still seems a bit odd as he had been acting as their agent. But he was genuinely surprised when I mentioned them. I remember handing the tapes over to him, suggesting that maybe he could work on them. He seemed a bit tentative but a week or two later called me back and in excited tones – rare, for Hannett – exclaimed that, yes, the label was very interested in Joy Division and asked if I could arrange some kind of meeting. I set up the meeting in a hotel . . . probably the Piccadilly. Richard went along, and Rob, Tony Wilson and myself. It was really tricky because Richard had put a lot of time in, and money. But eventually a deal was done . . . I think they agreed to pay a thousand pounds and we handed the tapes over at that meeting. I'm not trying to say that that was the real beginning of the Joy Division/Factory relationship, and I know that they had already been talking, but that is how I remember it happening.'

Despite all that had happened, and the final truth that Ian Curtis could never have become the soul singer required to fulfil the Searling/Anderson requirements, he still spent many lunchtimes drifting through Piccadilly Plaza. Although the Factory dream was beginning to unfold neatly in the pages of the music press, and Curtis was drawn to the DIY notions of the indie scene, there remained a part of him which still longed to record for RCA. Not, however, that such a thing was ever truly on the agenda.

'They would almost certainly have been dropped by RCA,' admits Brandwood today, 'simply because there was no obvious hit among any of their material.' True enough, RCA would, with respect, probably have released a couple of over-produced/under-promoted singles and a glossy rockist album, a million miles away from the spirit which would settle so majestically on *Unknown Pleasures*. Joy Division, had they been snapped up by any predatory A&R character, would almost certainly have failed. What they needed was not the glitz, push and bullshit of a London record company, but the services of the scruffy unassuming genius called Martin Hannett. How fortunate they were.

Joy Division, like all truly great bands, all bands flushed with innovatory freshness, hadn't been able to grasp a smidgeon of interest from the major labels who, to Rob's manic frustration, barely returned a phone call. Nevertheless, musically the band were fast losing their dull edges. The sound hadn't quite tightened into its true mesmerising intensity, for that would soon be achieved via the hedonistic catalyst named Martin Hannett, but they were – *and they knew it* – streets ahead of any of the sounds that seeped through the rehearsal room doors at T.J. Davidson's. The confidence that had started to surface during the Band on the Wall gigs was duly channelled into their new songs and, in rehearsal, Joy Division were pushing further and further into unique territory. A few of the other bands did notice this though most would be loathe to admit it. I recall, however, V2's amiable guitarist, Mark, admitting, 'We can't match them, you know. I was listening to them in rehearsal and they seem to be creating the kind of intensity that we strive for but have only achieved, I reckon, on a couple of fleeting occasions . . . and then when we were drunk. The rest of the band don't like them but . . . well, there is certainly something there.'

The decision to offer Joy Division two tracks on this imaginary sample, and pair them with Martin Hannett, fell nicely into place. Even Rob would admit that Joy Division simply didn't have any other offers. They had little to lose – perhaps, just perhaps, the release might stir the interest of some sleeping corporate giant. Joy Division, though grateful for Wilson's enthusiasm and investment, initially saw Factory Records as a simple step forward, and Wilson seemed more than happy to provide this initial step.

Durutti Column, despite anarchistic internal problems, were of course the natural 'house' band. At least *they* would stay. Cabaret Voltaire – Factory Club regulars, from across the Peak District – seemed another natural choice, despite having opted to record for Rough Trade.

'Well, they had two tracks spare,' says Wilson, 'so we thought we would bang them on . . . they seemed very Factoryish, anyway.' The act that completed the quartet was not so typical. Comedian John Dowie, a friend of Wilson's since working on Granada, had just been unceremoniously 'dropped' from Virgin Records and had wandered back into Wilson's circle with, literally, three tracks under his arm. It is surprising to note that no trace of a 'masterplan' was in evidence here. The record, intended to become a base from which a new label would evolve, was a simple hotch-potch, cobbled together by chance. Martin Hannett, it was decided, would oversee the artistic input.

Hooky: 'We went into Cargo Studios in Rochdale with Martin Hannett, and John Brierely was working the desk.

This was to record "Digital" and "Glass" for the Factory sample. A lot of people were saying that that was the moment when things turned ... that Hannett was the man who changed us, found our secret weapon. I don't see it that way at all. Hannett was OK – we were a bit in awe of him – but he didn't write the songs. We went in and did those build-ups and drop-downs that Joy Division became so good at ... and Brierely was a good engineer. We must not forget that. Hannett was just one aspect. Yes, the result was brilliant. There were actually some dub mixes of "Digital" and "Glass", created by Martin, working alone. They just stayed on tape. I bought Cargo, eventually, and it changed into Suite Sixteen. But when my partner Chris Hewitt finally sold his share, he also sold all the tapes that were just sitting around. Tapes for 50p each, just as blanks. I was so busy at the time that I just forgot. The dub mixes were gone, lost forever. My fault. They should have been released.'

The Factory sample sleeve, the true Factory precedent and if anything, more important than the music, was a study in bold impracticality. Saville's design was slick and minimalist; grey and unobtrusive. As if in an affectionate nod back to the days when Buzzcocks would sit in Boon's front room, folding and packing 'Spiral Scratch', the Factory sample was, similarly, a DIY venture.

Jon Savage: 'I recall sitting in Wilson's house, in Charlesworth, Derbyshire, folding thousands of those things ... it was such a tricky thing to do. There would be a "folding party". Everyone who attended would take five hundred sheets of paper, five hundred plastic bags and five hundred singles.'

The physical trauma of the folding, however, hardly dampened Wilson's enthusiasm, and he would often be seen at gigs – at Manchester Poly, I seem to remember – floating from table to table, opening his briefcase and proudly showing off the completed article to a more often than not bemused gang of local punters, band members and the odd journalist.

Things continued to fall into place, into Wilson's lap. A typical example of this took place while Wilson was sliding his car past Woodhey's restaurant, on the Glossop to Marple road, accompanied by his wife, Lindsay. Slapping tapes into the car cassette had become second nature to him and he wasn't unduly excited by this particular cassette, whisked to him by two heavily frustrated Wirrell boys who, after a full year of flogging the tape around majors and indies alike, were just about reaching the point of giving up. Wilson remembered their name. For, six months previously, they had sent him a distressed plastic reel-to-reel tape, obviously whipped out of one of their fathers' machines, for the name Shirley Bassey had been crossed out, to be replaced by the weird and elongated Orchestral Manoeuvres In The Dark. This time around it was, at least, on a playable format. Two songs swamped the car. 'Play it again . . . play it again!' screamed Lindsay, excitedly. The two songs: an icy synth ballad called 'Almost' and the popping, bubbling, hopelessly catchy 'Electricity'. By the time the car had drifted through Marple, Wilson was convinced. Orchestral Manoeuvres In The Dark would become a Factory band. More than that. They would become a Factory 'pop' band. Under no illusions, he needed something to throw at the charts. He knew, also, that Orchestral Manoeuvres In The Dark, should they prove immediately successful, would also be whisked swiftly away from his meagre resources.

Durutti Column's band membership problems had intensified beyond belief. Indeed, even Chris Joyce and Tony Bowers had departed to form the rhythm section of the untested band, the Mothmen, initially to record for Absurd Records, a Tosh

Ryan-less wing of Rabid. Managed by Manchester Polytechnic social secretary Elliott Rashman, they were eventually to evolve into the foundations of Simply Red. Indeed, everyone had left, leaving just Vini; pale and very ill, awkward and prone to dark, illogical mood swings. Wilson loved him.

Wilson: 'I thought, Let's stick with him. He was the best guitarist I had ever heard. Still is. He was art. He was also either going to die . . . or he was going to live. He was really very, very ill. But I thought, Who needs a fucking band anyway? Vini is the purest talent I had ever come across . . . why not develop that talent? Why should Durutti Column be anyone else other than Vini? It was a really weird concept but I knew that no one else in the music industry would ever attempt such a thing. They would always try to construct some naff band around him. Well, I knew very few bands that were capable of producing work of sheer beauty, and that's what I could hear when Vini was strumming away. I decided to stick with just Vini.'

Well, Vini and Martin Hannett, as it happened. Wilson courageously booked the pair into Cargo Studios, not really knowing what this unstable and quite possibly unworkable partnership might produce.

'Vini played for two days, and Martin twiddled about on the third,' says Wilson, proudly adding, 'and that was the first Durutti Column album. A work of great, great beauty. It was all very smooth.'

Vini's recollections of the session sound rather less easygoing.

'I'll never forget the way that Martin was totally impervious to my, let's say, extreme behaviour. And I was extreme . . . I was completely out of control, totally suicidal, totally stressed out, depressed, and he just didn't seem to notice. I sat in a chair for two whole days and just screamed and screamed at him while he was playing with synthesizers . . .

spending three hours just getting one sound. I mean, I was under intoxication too, so it was all pretty strange. But he just occasionally made comments like, "Well, that's a bit extreme, Vini. I think you are being a bit unreasonable there." I was fascinated by the way he was just completely centred on what he was doing, as if nothing else in the world mattered. Totally focused. He was twiddling around and he found these funny bird noises. I kind of liked them and started to play something. He told me to play it again . . . so I did, and that was "Sketch For Summer". In fact, what you hear on that album is that second play through . . . that was it. Five minutes in all, it took.'

Liberally scattered throughout Manchester music folklore are a million Hannett stories. Some, the merest tip of the iceberg, lie scattered through this book, to be seen, perhaps, as the true anarchic heart of Factory. For Hannett's wayward genius, fuelled and fired by the sheer force of uncontrollable hedonism, would flicker away, on . . . off . . . on . . . off. In his later days, mostly off. This is the reason that Manchester is filled with musicians all too eager to testify against the Hannett legend. The truth is that, perhaps 70, maybe 80 per cent of the time, the irregular methods and off the wall scams which would typify his approach to his craft would act in a thoroughly negative manner, leaving the bands feeling deflated and underwhelmed. Hannett could be expensive and absurdly unproductive. Ask the Stone Roses about Hannett (Ian Brown: 'He didn't have a fucking clue . . .'). Or Easterhouse, or Simply Red, or even, and we will come to this later, A Certain Ratio. So many Hannett sessions failed miserably but that, in a sense, was the nature of the man. When viewed as a whole, Hannett's career was bewilderingly erratic. When one tunes into the subterranean netherworld of Manchester's sound engineers and would-be producers, an ocean of Hannett tales remain in circulation to this day, many gaining in absurdity as they roll along. More often than not, stories that can be viewed in two opposing ways.

'No one who ever worked in a studio had a greater musical vision than Martin Hannett,' one Strawberry-based engineer told me. 'He was absolutely the best. On one session, he never even came to the mixing desk. He lay on his back in the reception area, reading the *Beano*, and every now and again a band member would approach him and await instruction. That is how he chose to produce that particular band.'

But was the end result any good? I further enquired.

'No, it was total shite,' he laughed, before adding, 'but that was the point. On another day it would have reached the highest peaks. He was hit and miss, Martin ... and mostly miss. But you can't doubt his brilliance.'

Brilliant! Idiosyncratic! Erratic! A master technician! A man who squeezed esoteric human endeavour from dull, cold machines. Consider him, for instance, driving his Volvo late at night, up, out and away from the grip of Manchester, to park on the moors of Lancashire and Yorkshire. Once neatly parked, a second car would pull to a halt in front of him, and out of it would step two sombrely besuited representatives – no, not from some dark mafioso, but from a Blackburn-based digital delay company.

A strange and curious meeting would take place, with the intrigued though dumbfounded representatives attempting to catch Hannett's artistic rhetoric and transform it skilfully into a brief for their engineers.

'And that,' Hannett would conclude, 'is the sound I hear in my head. Can you construct it for me? Can you make me something capable of producing such a sound?'

Chapter Seven

Unknown Pleasures

A ND AFTER THE FACTORY SAMPLE, what next? That basic question had been all but evaded by just about everyone, although the Joy Division camp found themselves secretly hoping for the phone calls to trickle if not flood in. But there was no master plan; no plan at all, really. It was more like a void; anti-climactic and quietly shambolic. The Factory sample had sold well, extremely well. It had also created so many blocks of largely superlative-enladen reviews, glowing so bright-ly from the 'singles' pages. It had been an event, of sorts. The spirit of the Factory Club – or at least part of it – but one didn't get mugged, threatened or poisoned by listening to it. The image had been cemented. Hannett's production on 'Digital' and 'Glass' had been truly inspired. The sound was glistening and sharp; so tightly woven, so neat, so crisp. Pared to the bone, with all musicianly wanderings curtailed.

But, as Factory's major band, Joy Division were all set to depart. Excitedly set, especially Curtis, whose dream – could it be RCA? – seemed almost tangible by now. The initial lull which followed the sample eased a little as Rob began to travel to London, falling rather reluctantly into exploratory record company meetings. Martin Rushent's Genetic began to hover close by, heavy in vulturous intent, as did Radar. And then, suddenly, Joy Division were off to Warner Brothers. That was it. The rumours in the town were loud and heavy. Joy Division had all but departed. Tony Wilson, though accepting the inevitable, found himself feeling suddenly lost. For all his good intentions, for all his stylistic notions, Factory had been little more than a handy step forward. There was more to Factory than that, of course, and Wilson's closeness to his new band, A Certain Ratio, who were recording their debut slab of rather shambolic funk, the great 'All Night Party' at Cargo Studios, had certainly fired him with fresh enthusiasm. Nevertheless, there is something profoundly dispiriting about taking a band from nowhere, nurturing their sound and image, and watching them float happily away. It was worse than that. It was 'up' and away. A wholly humbling sense of loss.

Unknown to Wilson, Gretton had been sitting in the rear of the Band on the Wall one night, nursing pints of bitter and thinking. He had been doing a lot of thinking during the previous few days and, in the manager's way, calculating. A slight panic, perhaps, had started to set in, and the huge shadow of a major label commitment began to hang more ominously than he had anticipated. To suggest that Gretton didn't enjoy his journeys to London would be an understatement. He felt, in no uncertain terms, rather lost amid the bland and stupid sycophancy of London.

'To be honest,' he informed Wilson, 'I don't want to spend the next five years travelling to London to talk to cunts.' It was a Gretton generalisation and in time it would become a Gretton cliché, but he meant it all the same. Something had dawned on Gretton that had escaped not only Wilson but most of the independent labels – the obvious fact that the music industry is fuelled by album sales. Singles are promotion; albums are the beef. It had been taken for granted that Joy Division would shift on to a major, and that only a major could possibly finance and correctly promote an album. But did it have to be this way?

Gretton had been doing his sums. They had, in truth, been swilling around his head for some time, and at the Band on the Wall were finally transposed into scribble on a beer mat. He had looked closely at the Factory sample. He knew that 4,700 had been sold, with no promotional budget at all. Indeed, with no promotion. Nobody had really expected a profit from that first release. It was seen as Wilson's investment but nevertheless the money had come straight back to them ... and more ... and then a little more. Not a lot, but it was an unexpected and welcome trickle.

Rob's idea was simple. Nevertheless, he did feel rather nervous as he telephoned Tony Wilson with his proposal. Why couldn't Joy Division stay with Factory for the duration of the first album, and then leave? A 50/50 Factory deal would be better for the band. Admittedly, no large advance would soothe the musicians' egos or pay off their swelling overdrafts, but no gigantic recoupable debt would mount up either. To Rob Gretton, this seemed like mere common sense.

Until *Unknown Pleasures*, Factory Records had been a familiar little beast, for all their individualistic intentions. For all the aforementioned reasons, the company was not at all unlike every other independent record company in the country, i.e. a bubbling mass of ideas and ideology, a hopelessly optimistic and unworkable set of ethics and, most important of all, a good deal of solid enthusiasm. Unfortunately, such admirable qualities are never enough. In effect, Factory Records was little more than an unofficial A&R department; a nursery, a training ground, a scouting agency for the major companies. But the exact point when Factory twisted weirdly, and suddenly found themselves gleefully, dangerously alone, was that moment in the Band on the Wall when Rob Gretton decided to stay with Factory. To Gretton and the band it didn't seem such a revolutionary move at the time, and at a band meeting, the notion that, 'Why don't we let Tony release the album?' failed to cause the merest flicker of protest.

Pete Hook: 'It was a bit of a weird time, when we nearly signed for Genetic. We did do a couple of demos with Martin Rushent, actually, and they went pretty well. But all I can remember about Martin is that he had a huge boil on his bum and had to sleep in his car . . . an XJS . . . brand new!!! Being typical Salford oiks, we were wandering around the car and we tried the car boot. I can't say what was in the boot, but we were stunned. In fact, at one point we thought about nicking a couple of them, but our bottle went. I'll have to leave that to your imagination. But we didn't sign . . . and we didn't object to Rob's idea. Thinking back, it seems crazy. We were all skint. I think if someone offered me sixty grand or whatever it was now, I'd be flattered. But we were funny. I don't remember being excited at all. None of us were. We never really thought about money . . . we honestly didn't. We knew we were in a state of artistic change, and that things were coming together, and that was *all* we were worried about. I remember Joy Division having a full set of songs – five or six songs that would make that first album. And one day we played at the Good Mood Club in Halifax. We borrowed the PA from Gillian's [Gillian Gilbert, later of New Order and future wife of Steve Morris] band. This was before Steve knew Gillian, but they practised at T.J. Davidsons. We had to drag this PA up a circular staircase and set up. We had one person in the audience. And he lasted two numbers. It felt like the end . . . like we were just wasting our time, that nobody wanted to know at all. Then, just three months after that, we played at the Mayflower, and when we were soundchecking we launched into 'Transmission' and all the other musicians, all the sound crew, everyone, just stopped and looked at us. I looked at Barney and Barney was looking at me saying, 'Fuuuuuckin' hell, we have really got

something here.' That's when it really hit me. I never understood that we were special before that ... and I knew it would
be a good album and I couldn't give a damn who would put it
out.'

Staying with Factory seemed like the natural thing to do.
Whether it would prove, in time, a shrewd business move,
remained to be seen. The band did show a high and unusual
degree of intelligence, however, in opting to stay within the cold
confines of near impoverishment and cleverly gamble with their
future. The mathematics was quite simple. With Rushent's
Genetic, for example, the band would get £35,000 plus an eight
per cent royalty rate. Although £35,000 must have seemed like
an absolute fortune to all concerned, that eight per cent figure
undoubtedly appeared diminutive. With Factory there would be
no advance at all but the deal would be a straightforward 50/50
split. It was risky, for the Genetic deal or any other major label
deal would at least provide the band with that comforting initial
sum. Should they drift into pop's sad backwaters and fail to
break through, that amount, at least, would stay with them
(although the debt would forever be recoupable). Like every big
record contract, it would be, initially, a kind of insurance policy
against failure. With Factory there would be no such comforting
insurance. Failure would mean, simply, nothing. On the other
hand, as a confident band with a string of gigs in front of them
and a general feeling that their songwriting was beginning to
blossom into lucrative prolificacy, Joy Division, even Curtis,
could see the sense of the Factory deal.

The 50/50 split – after costs – would soon become part and
parcel of the Factory ethos and would be applied to all Factory
acts. As an antithesis to the general advance system favoured by
the majors who naturally enjoyed seeing the effects that fat
carrot would have on their grateful new acts, it would prove
perfect. Factory acts, with no huge amounts to recoup and a

comparatively massive royalty rate, would only have to secure moderate sales in Britain and across the world to see relatively swift returns – or in the case of Joy Division, a profit, even. In contrast, the same sales would, if achieved by a band signed to a major label, see that band sinking still further into debt. It seemed to make sense although it would, in time, be partly responsible for Factory's constant flirtations with bankruptcy.

There would also be a famous word of mouth 'freedom' clause. 'All Factory acts have freedom,' stated Wilson on one of his more caustic days. 'The freedom to fuck off.' That most unusual, nay, unprecedented freedom, would stay with Joy Division and New Order throughout most of their career. That was the basis on which the Factory/Joy Division contractless deal was struck.

'Fuck!' exclaimed Wilson, when he met Rob Gretton to discuss this new possibility. 'An album ... we must be fucking mad.' Nevertheless, together, on dinner napkins, the extent of the commitment was worked out. They decided that to make the album in Strawberry, with Hannett at the controls, would cost seven or eight grand. Wilson knew that, with the money he still had left and the extras he could raise from his trust funds, he could stretch to about twelve grand. A huge amount for Wilson; a minute amount, however, to spend on the all-important debut album release from the band he regarded, quite rightly, as the finest in the world at that particular moment in time.

Booking a band, any band, into the glossy 24-track world of Strawberry Studios for anything more than a couple of hours, was new to Factory. (They had previously booked it for four hours – two hours to mix the OMD single (both sides), and two hours to give A Certain Ratio equal treatment.) For *Unknown Pleasures*, Strawberry reserved three weeks. Three solid weeks of major studio expense, offset only slightly by Hannett's familiarity with the studio owners. Had Wilson wandered casually into the studio on the third day, however, then regret would have plastered itself across his features. For it was in Strawberry Studios, and in particular during *Unknown Pleasures*, that the Martin Hannett legend would be truly cemented. Joy Division fans would understand this legend to be the innovatory use of the 'digital delay' machine – and the subsequent perfecting of Joy Division's intensifying drum sound. For studio technicians, apparently the world over, Hannett would be the master of in-studio psychology. A thousand stories were told in breathless awe, stretched, tugged and exaggerated by time. And if Hannett's technique would be dimmed into obsolescence by technical advancement, then conversely, his eccentricities would be massively enhanced.

And so, on the third day of *Unknown Pleasures*, Martin Hannett, furious with himself for not quite catching the perfection of that drum sound, infuriated and frustrated the band by telling Steve Morris to dismantle his entire kit – every nut, every screw, everything. Morris was bemused. For Hannett, the drum sound had to be exact. It was the basis of the recording. It is the basis of *all* recordings.

Tony Wilson: 'Martin was particularly interested in echo and digital delay and that the essential concept of what you do as a producer is to take all the sounds into your mixing desk, strip these sounds to their perfect, naked form and then you, the producer, start creating imaginary rooms for each sound. That is how Martin saw it. He had a really visual sense that most people just don't have ... he could *see* sound, shape it, rebuild it. Martin knew that that was the secret of good production ... he told me, just at the point when digital delay was coming in. That early digital delay was his true era. I knew that at the time. What I didn't know was that, with that digital delay, he had found a new, fresh, innovative drum sound. That came as a total surprise to me . . . and probably to the band, also. We were so lucky to stumble across a producer who had just found his true moment in technical evolution. And Joy Division were the perfect band for this. Years later, in 1981 I think, he went to Nashville on holiday and when he came back he was moaning that they had all nicked his drum sound. He came of age with that drum sound, as all great producers come of age linked to a particular piece of equipment. A year later it was Martin Rushent with the early sequencer.'

Vini Reilly: 'Martin used that digital delay not as a repeat echo delay but to make a tiny, tiny milli-second delay that came so close to the drum it was impossible to hear. I would never have thought of doing that. Nobody else would. I don't know how he could have possibly envisaged the final sound. But that is what he did . . . Joy Division, Durutti Column, A Certain Ratio . . . we were all so lucky to benefit from Martin being there just at that moment.'

Tony Wilson: 'The Joy Division drum sound was . . . well . . . Steve Morris would play his drum and then Martin would relay the drum to a speaker in the back toilet room and have a microphone picking that up . . . from the toilet.'

MORE ON HANNETT . . . GENIUS IS A PAIN

During the recording of both *Unknown Pleasures* and Joy Division's second album, *Closer*, Joy Division's relationship with Hannett would be, to say the least, strained. One thinks of the former recording when Hooky, still nurturing a passion for Mark 10 Jaguars, was rationing himself to one gallon of petrol a week. Knowing this, and knowing also that no other member of Joy Division could be reached by phone, Rob would keep Hooky on hold, just in case Hannett decided to get down to Strawberry Studios, intent on mixing the album without the added hindrance of actually having any members of the band present. With this in mind, he would conspire to wrongfoot the entire ensemble.

Typically, Rob's phone would ring at 3 a.m. and the disembodied voice of Martin Hannett would spit, distinctively.

'Rob ... it's Martin ... I'm going into Strawberry to mix, right now.'

'But Martin,' Rob would protest, 'it's three in the fucking morning.'

Instinctively, Gretton would ring Hooky, pray that he still had a gallon in the Jag, and instruct him to get down to Strawberry as quickly as possible.

Upon arrival, Hooky would be treated to the most immense discourtesy, from Hannett and engineer Chris Nagle. Indeed, Hannett would attempt to unhinge the bassist by instructing Nagle to turn the air-conditioning on full blast. This somewhat crude tactic would fail, although Hooky would be rendered into an uncomfortable state, shivering at the rear of the console; ignored, fatigued, attempting to represent the feelings of the entire band.

'In a sense, this worked quite well. I would stay through the recordings, and this continued into New Order and then Barney would come in and then Steve and Gillian at the very end. They would bring a fresh perspective. They would notice things that I had missed because I was always so fucking knackered ... but I would keep things on a level. Odd, but it was a system that stood us well. One has to admit, the whole scene was stupid from the word go. Martin never understood that he was working for us. We were paying him and so he should have done the mixing when we said so ... and he should have done what we wanted at all times. Ridiculous. Of course, the public don't know this. Martin was great in a sense, but he always came up smelling of roses.'

Releasing your own album rather lacks the power of going with a major. The record doesn't, for example, instantly materialise on record racks across the country, to be accompanied by displays, hoardings and television advertising. That kind of magic, so alluring to any young band, would be missing. More romantic, perhaps, is the idea of Rob and Hooky climbing into a crusty Ford Transit and zipping at a tremendous and highly dangerous pace down the M1, where they 'handballed' 10,000 copies of the record into the back of the sadly sinking Ford, a vehicle which, not surprisingly, would groan and trundle and barely make 45 mph on the deadening journey home. Back at Palatine Road, Rob and Hooky would laboriously hump the records, 75 at a time for a while, then 50 at a time.

'Romantic my arse . . . it took hours and hours,' says Hooky, 'and I remember Charles Sturridge, who shared the flat with Alan Erasmus. He crept upstairs, past us, with Margi Clarke. I think they were having a bit of fun. We could hear them! And we were getting more and more knackered. Then they came out and asked us if they could have a copy. We got really angry about that. Rob shouted, "You can fuck right off, both of you, and we know *exactly* how many there are so don't even think about nicking them." We just thought they were poncy TV people.'

JULY 1979, *UNKNOWN PLEASURES* RELEASED

'You can have a white label,' stated Rob Gretton, magic words for any young rock journalist, and all rock journalists believe they have a divine right to be granted pre-release copies of their favourite band's records, for them to soak in the sounds, muse over their importance slowly, and carefully construct a considered, balanced review. Bullshit. Journalists like to think they are special, and hearing an album a month before the public finally manage to get their grubby mitts on the record somehow intensifies this feeling of importance. Gretton, though, had an ulterior motive.

'You can have a white label if you perform a little errand for me. Will you pick up the artwork from Factory's office in Palatine Road, and bring it to the Russell Club tonight? I'll have some copies of the album, but I have got to see the artwork . . . I haven't laid eyes on it yet.'

I enjoyed this little errand. For once, it wasn't much of an inconvenience at all, as Didsbury did lie more or less en route from my base to the Russell Club and – rather more fun, this – it meant that I would be able to cast my eyes across the *Unknown Pleasures* final sleeve artwork *before* Gretton. A minor detail but one that, to the tiny, sycophantic mind that I lived in at that time, seemed little short of glorious. It did seem glorious, too, when I peeked into the brown envelope and saw Peter Saville's black sleeve, graced with a small, white, central Fourier analysis. It was printed, in this instance, on glossy paper, and so the complete linen look would be denied to me until the release. It looked, I swiftly decided while shuffling through Didsbury, fantastically stylish; so stark and severe, so unlike anything else I had ever seen. I didn't know what it was. I had never heard of a 'Fourier analysis'. Indeed, I swiftly concluded that it was a close-up of the grooves on a record. I even asked Bernard Sumner what the image was taken from, that night at the Factory Club, and my question was met with the inevitable shrug accompanied by the words, 'Fucked if I know.' If that was all Sumner had said that night, I probably would have forgotten the incident. But there was more, as Gretton handed out copies of the album, not just to me but to *Record Mirror*'s precocious Altrincham socialite Mike Nicholls, Echo And The Bunnymen's Ian McCulloch and, I think, Paul Morley. Sumner looked abashed; embarrassed even. Confronting him later in the evening, as goat curries were being served all around, he once again shrugged and offered, 'Well, it worries me, seeing that album go out to people. I'm not sure if I like it, you see. I think Ian does, but me and Hooky listened to it the other day and we decided that we hated what Martin had done. The sound seems "drained" . . . weedy. It just sounds so much better live. It's just not really us at the moment.'

This hardly filled me with optimism. Certainly, it didn't sound like the words of a man whose band was about to release the most influential rock album of the era, perhaps – who really knows? – the very album that would lay the foundation for the rock music of the eighties. Sumner though, in his post-recording haze, couldn't possibly hope to retain any kind of objectivity or perspective. Joy Division were, after all, a small indie band at the time. A band who were, at this point, surviving on sub dole-queue wages and happy to be merely living the life. Hannett, too, had been so clever. With the use of the digital delay, he had created the impression of suppressed power; of intensity of the feeling that, at any moment, something might blow. In a live situation, the band could pump and push along with those drums, as they did, the whole image controlled and conducted by the central and improving presence of Curtis. On record, however, the attack had to be more subtle – if Joy Division were to escape the fate suffered by so many rock outfits whose enthusiasm would splatter messily across their initial album recording. The importance of Hannett in controlling this beast cannot be overstated. Had the sound of *Unknown Pleasures* exploded into tasteless epic rock, then the album, the band and the songs would have sunk slowly into obscurity.

Hooky: 'No, we didn't like *Unknown Pleasures*, and I still don't like it. Me and Barney wanted to be much more rocky. Hannett took it right down. And he did it very well. But, yes, we hated it. I think he did us a favour, actually, because when people heard that and later came to see us live, and we gave it all we had got, they were completely blown away. They knew the songs, but only as these stripped-down things.'

(Despite the album's instantly applauded genius, it didn't sell too heavily at first. Only 5,000 would fly from the racks amid the initial rush of release. As they had pressed 10,000, the remaining 5,000 had to be physically lugged into Erasmus's flat, and the Factory office at Palatine Road, Didsbury. During the next six months the album would sell 15,000, netting the new and naïve company some £40,000 to £50,000 profit. At one stage Wilson would turn to Gretton and exclaim, 'God, Rob, this is so easy. No wonder the London labels are so fucking wealthy.')

But, as every Joy Division fan and perhaps everyone reading this book knows already, there was more to it than that. So many writers, and many of them far more eloquent than yours truly, have attempted to pin down that peculiar Joy Division passion in print, and most of them never managed to write their way out of numerous pretentious cul de sacs. Most Joy Division album reviews have been wholly ridiculous. Only the Fall, perhaps – sixteen albums old – could claim to have made more writers make complete and utter fools of themselves. Mostly they are the same writers. Oh yes, and the Smiths, but we won't go into that. But nobody, I sense, has managed to focus on one extremely important point. The very best singers – and I do mean the *very* best singers (Garland, Minnelli, Fitzgerald, Holiday, Redding, Gaye, Robinson). You think I'm exaggerating? You think *I'm* the one making a fool of myself? Let's continue the list: Morrison, Morrison, Morrissey, Plant – manage, somehow, to fade their no doubt considerable egos from their studio performances. They sing one on one, direct to the listener, and the listener, sitting there in some pathetic bedsit, half-drowning in tears and hoping for all the world to find some way out, soaks in the message. More importantly, perhaps, the listener *believes* the message. And the message isn't, 'Oh, look at me, I'm a star, aren't I so great!' (Most modern pop singers, even those blessed with angelic voices and astute songwriting partners, still fail to transcend that shallow norm.)

But Ian Curtis, on *Unknown Pleasures* and, more so on the follow-up, *Closer*, managed it. The pain felt by Curtis, which I believe would have been just as intense *whatever* his social circumstances – some people really are, and will always be, *that* intense – dripped from *Unknown Pleasures* to eerie effect. Now I don't have particularly good rock ears, so many times I have listened, unmoved, as some classic rock song spits through the murk of an early demo tape – the Smiths, the Stone Roses, Oasis – and yet, that night, after returning from the Russell Club, I sat down and listened to *Unknown Pleasures* while I drank my way through a bottle of Fleurie. What stunned me then, and still stuns me now, is how a band and their manager could have created a record of such awesome beauty and, by and large, fail to notice it. Martin Hannett knew it, because I joined him, six pints into a rambunctious evening, in the Wellington pub in Stockport, and for a full twenty minutes he exploded before me, ecstatically pronouncing that *Unknown Pleasures* was the finest thing he had, as he put it, 'ever had the privilege to polish'. For once, I did not have a tape secreted on my person, but the endless pints of bitter did not, as they never did, dim my memory. A works party – civil servants, I guessed – from nearby Heron House took the rise out of Hannett that night. And there he was, dressed like a council road worker fresh from a week on the tarmac, spending his way through a month's wages, hair dripping inelegantly down his ruddy face; his stomach, already, beginning to bulge; his bloodhound eyes dripping down his face. And he sat there, while a crowd of stupid, besuited mediocrities verbally abused him, believing him to be the drunk in the corner. But he was a proud man, Martin Hannett. He *was* the drunk in the corner, as it happened, but he also knew that he had created something of rare beauty. The band would come to know this, also, in time. One can speculate for ever about Ian Curtis's lyrics and the ambiguous suicidal references, but no one can ever know the truth. Curtis dredged to the bottom of his thoughts; selfish thoughts, we have since been led to believe, and I have no reason to doubt it. He was focused, skint, desperate and confused – a perfect combination. *Unknown Pleasures* was, unlike *Closer*, recorded in a state of considerable self-doubt, uncertainty and – it's there, it really is – mounting desperation. Needless to say, had Joy Division been cosseted by a large record company advance, albeit temporary, the magic would possibly have been considerably diluted. When Rob Gretton had sat in the Band on the Wall, musing over the possibility of producing a Factory album rather than opting for the instant glitz of Genetic or Radar, he set out the backcloth for a serious and moving piece of art.

LIFE AT THE FACTORY

Margi Clarke – then merely an aspiring Kirby gal – had planted her feet firmly under Granada's table. She had even brusquely taken control over the presentation duties on Wilson's local listings show, *What's On*, her brash Liverpudlian voice yet to become a national institution, screeching anarchically from the television and causing letters of complaint to flood in from across the region. At the Factory she 'performed', miming to the sound of Kraftwerk's 'The Model'. Few people in the club – and there were only a few people – could understand what on earth was going on, which seemed to please Margi. Margi – named Margox at the time – was presenting herself as the ideal, post-punkette, industrial babe. She did succeed, however, where many people have failed, in rendering the entire membership of

Joy Division, and assorted sundry hangers-on into a state of unlikely silent embarrassment. Arriving in the weirdly thin, triangular dressing room, Margi noticed, somewhat testily, that this tiny area was packed with the aforementioned gang.

'MIND IF I 'AVE A PISS?' she asked, in her Kirby-girlie manner. Accepting the brief shrugs from the assembled and by now rather bemused gathering, she proceeded to saunter through the group, before turning around, leaping backwards on to the sink, dropping her knickers and peeing in the sink . . . immodestly accepting the open-mouthed stares from everyone in the room. It would, surely, have made a particularly evocative scene from some gritty northern drama, with Clarke, perfectly cast in overtly brash mould, as the Scouse mouth, the dressing room pisser. Many were of the opinion that she thoroughly enjoyed the performance.

Factory would, in truth, dominate the scene. Only Tony Davidson's TJM Records, which never quite managed to gain the same degree of kudos, or Rabid who, despite Jilted John, would soon metamorphose into the esoteric, though ubiquitous Absurd Records, could stake any real claims for making any true impact on the new scene. At the heart of this new scene, it may be justifiably argued, lay, not really Joy Division at all, but the pop band, the Distractions – the only band to swing from TJM to Factory and then later on to Island before imploding horribly just as they were expected to break into the charts. The Distractions were lovable and great fun. Their lightweight pop tones actually created much-needed relief in a scene generally occupied by dour raincoated 'arties'. Fronted by the rotund, trendlessly besuited figure of Mike Finney, an ex-soulboy blessed with the kind of voice that would later inspire his TJM labelmate Mick Hucknall on to finer things, the Distractions would, more often than not, be seen happily supporting the Fall in the Manchester satellite college halls of Oldham, Rochdale, Bolton and Bury. When supporting Joy Division, they made the most perfect antithesis. Paul Morley captured this in these two sentences. 'Joy Division are the perfect rock band for the eighties . . . and the Distractions are the perfect pop band.'

For a while, and only for a while, the greatest hopes of Manchester would be perfectly captured by that particular phrase. For while Joy Division were intensifying by the day, the Distractions bopped along with unnerving ease, their support spots at the Factory attracting as many punters as, say, top-of-the-bill Simple Minds. Refreshing, soulful and occasionally joyous, the Distractions waltzed on to Factory Records and into local 'hipness' with consummate ease. Wilson, in particular, had no qualms about the 'signing' of a traditional pop band, a band rather more akin to the Everly Brothers than Throbbing Gristle. Finney's counterpart, and the band's main songwriter, was Steve Perrin, an angular-faced, schoolboy figure blessed with the rare talent of being able to produce sharp, bright, sex-tinged teen anthems straight out of a pub rock r'n'b base – and make them seem important and fun. The TJM EP's lead song, 'It Doesn't Bother Me', for example, was a wonderful slab of indignant angst, Less incisive than, say, the Undertones but maybe just a little more risqué.

The Distractions' Factory single was to become a tragically lost classic, a record that would remain, undoubtedly, close to the hearts of most who would trundle down to the Factory.

Wilson: 'I just think the Distractions were a wonderful moment in time.' Failing to make waves, despite its simmering poppiness, the song, 'Time Goes By So Slow', became as locally anthemic as 'Transmission' later, or the Fall's 'Totally Wired', or Buzzcocks' 'What Do I Get?' or Magazine's 'Shot By Both Sides', but it just couldn't seep into any kind of mainstream. The fault lay, most definitely, with Factory's idiosyncratic approach towards promotion. I recall, just as a typical case, attempting to prise a white label of the song away from Wilson's clutching hands. 'I've only got two copies,' he would scream, and scamper into the Factory Club's appalling 'dining area'. Gretton's statement summed up the event neatly.

'I understand your problem,' he said. 'Here you are . . . about to go to London to write a singles column for a national music paper, and Tony won't even give you a copy of the Distractions' single to review. It will probably go down in the mail, to some skinhead cunt at *Sounds* next week, who will thoroughly slag it off. Tony will then complain and refuse to speak to *Sounds*. It is stupid, I agree with you, but I sense that just about sums Factory up.'

Gretton, it seems important to point out, was just as perplexed by Wilson's behaviour as yours truly – although I did manage to scrounge a copy and make it joint Record of the Week. It was Record of the Week in the *NME* too. Was this a case of Wilson deliberately intensifying the press fervour, or just being cheekily awkward, or dangerously evasive because rock journalists are a pretty stupid and unforgiving bunch?

The Distractions were more than just a group. In Manchester, at least, they represented a central axis of the scene, a scene which flourished in the poorly produced, reduced type which splattered inelegantly across the pages of the Manchester fanzine, *City Fun*. For a full five years, this often libellous and scurrilous rag managed to scoop up the underground gossip swiftly and neatly. Unashamedly crammed with in-jokes and brittle bitchiness, it soaked in the unwise and unguarded bar-room chit-chat, and repeated the stories with ferocious exaggeration. It was also, being a co-operative – for co-operatives *never* work – a pretty stupid little beast. *City Fun* meetings, more often than not held in some godforsaken warehouse-cum-office space in the city centre, would be messy and ultimately rather pointless squabbles. Nobody would agree on anything, and so a little bit of everything made it on to the pages. If *City Fun* had a leader at all, then it must have been the affable, glassy-eyed Andy Zero, who would 'moped' himself around town, the balance of his timid vehicle disturbed to a dangerous degree by the stack of *City Fun*s eternally strapped to the rear and elsewhere. Andy Zero, closely linked to the Fall – he once failed an audition for the drumming spot in the band – would have died for *City Fun*. He revelled in its meagre power, loved it for its parochial warmth and arrogance. He believed, quite rightly, that it could offer an insight into the Manchester scene that would extend way beyond the scope of either nationals or one-dimensional fanzines, of which there were many. Zero's chief cohorts were Cath Carroll and Liz Naylor (or Neer), two female friends who built themselves into an insular world, often sniping rather viciously at any males who strayed too close. Despite this, Carroll and Naylor remained close to Factory, and in particular the Distractions. At one stage, Wilson even paid Naylor a £200 advance to write the script for a film entitled *Too Young to Know, Too Wild to Care* (the cheque even had a Fac number – Fac 22), a kind of cross between *Ferry Across The Mersey* and *The Girl Can't Help It*. The central theme – Wilson's idea – revolved entirely around the Factory roster. Indeed, in the script, A Certain Ratio and the Distractions rampaged around Manchester city centre attempting to blow up Joy Division.

When Liz Naylor recalled the film, for a feature in the magazine *Mojo*, she wrote, rather disloyally, 'In the end the Distractions blew themselves up because they weren't any good.' It remains unclear whether she meant that they were no good as a band, or were simply no good at blowing up other groups, or both. Cath and Liz also performed, messily, in the band the Liggers, a feministic mush of a group. Later on, in a response to a plea from *NME* editor Neil Spencer on Channel Four's *The Tube* television programme for Mancunian writers to come forward, they would be accepted into the heart of the *NME* (Carroll later to surface at the heart of Factory's early nineties decline, and into the later pages of this book).

The Distractions, being quite the antithesis of Factory's undeservedly greyish image, were therefore perversely suited to the label. Joy Division enjoyed performing after them, believing the lightness of the support band to be the perfect precursor to their dark intensity. The prevailing logic, however, was that the Distractions would only gain the pop success they craved by hopping on to a major label, and their managers, Brandon and Bernie Leon, kept a constant rhetoric with the A&R departments on the boil. Wilson, however, displaying a desire to encourage and nurture artists that would not, ultimately, be of benefit to himself, finally and unselfishly managed to secure a deal for the band with Chrysalis. Curiously, Brandon Leon rejected this vigorous and promising offer and instead took the band to Chris Blackwell's Island Records, a move that, despite the lack of serious advance money, pleased Finney and Perrin – for both were staunch reggae fans – and seemed to present them with a reasonable chance of cracking the charts. Unfortunately, the moment the Distractions stepped away from Factory, their power began to diminish. A couple of singles led into an album, *Nobody's Perfect*, which, produced by John Astley, saw a gathering of the Distractions' nugget songs almost completely drained of their innocence, their naïveté, their essential edge. When pushed through the smoothness of hi-tech production, the Distractions sounded depressingly ordinary. How sad, perhaps, that Island Records couldn't understand that the true strength of the band actually lay within those raw edges, within that sense of naïveté. Sensationally – at least within the pages of *City Fun* – Perrin quit the band, to be all too hastily replaced by the hugely talented but unsuitably Bohemian Arthur Kadmon, who had recently departed from Ludus and the rickety umbrella of New Hormones. Inevitably, the band were dropped from the label and, simultaneously it seemed, lost their grip on the Manchester scene. Nevertheless, before their spectacular fall – from playing to local audiences of over 1,000 to enticing just 65 people into Rafters one year later – the Distractions would play an important role in the evolution of the Manchester scene and, as the following pages will testify, would seem to be present at most of Joy Division's more intense performances.

TRANSMISSION

To the music press, Joy Division's 'Transmission' – performed so famously, and with such spirit and fire on BBC2's *Something Else* programme on 15 September 1979, despite the fact that Steve Harley had declared, 'Those guys can't play their instruments' – was a masterpiece. A slab of ultimate independent genius. With Curtis's vocals soaring through the lines, 'Dance DANCE DANCE TO THE RADIO', it initially seemed like it might make a triumphant independent surge on to the hallowed playlist of Radio One. This could, and quite possibly should, have provided the breakthrough; the sharpened tip of the proverbial snow plough.

Tony Wilson thought so. The moment he heard the final mix, his head exploded with promotional expectancy.

'Rob!' he screamed down the phone. 'Rob, it's fucking great ... Dance ... dance dance to the radio ... maan, Radio One will play it to death!'

This was the release with which, at least in Wilson's eyes, Factory would come of age. If the game had to be played then it had to be played properly. Believing 'Transmission' to be 'the most fantastic record he had ever heard', he ordered 10,000 to be initially pressed and duly marched to London, intent on hiring the finest and, of course, most expensive plugger in town (Neil Ferris, one presumes).

However, placing too much faith in the instinctive surges of Hannett's troubled and somewhat fevered mind would always be a Wilson weak spot, and he bowed rather stupidly to Hannett's abject refusal. 'No!' insisted Hannett. 'No way . . . not a plugger . . . complete waste of money, pandering to the London assholes . . .' That kind of thing. Although taking notice of this absurd advice, Wilson nevertheless remained immensely excited about the single. The rave reviews, as stated, bubbled away in the prestigious 'Single of the Week' slot in virtually every music paper, each review spawning a follow-up, triumphant interview. Joy Division took up residence in the all-influential, inky weeklies. One year later, despite Joy Division's march into tragedy-filled legend, Wilson could be found sitting in silent mournful reflection in the warehouse, barely able to comprehend the 'fact' that Joy Division, through what looked like being their prime – they would achieve their true sales position some time later – had only managed to sell 3,000 copies of 'Transmission'. Indeed, less than 3,000, for that number included all the promotional mail-outs. There was no way around it. Seven thousand copies of 'Transmission' remained embarrassingly stacked in the warehouse.

'What the fuck have you got to do?' he asked himself, as he left the warehouse and travelled back to the comparatively stable world of Granada.

Chapter Eight

A Certain Ratio – Adversity Over Triumph

TONY WILSON'S MAROON PEUGEOT estate skidded to an abrupt halt outside Manchester's Royal Exchange Theatre. Beckoning me into the car, he explained that our interview, intended to appear in *Sounds* but destined never to surface, would have to take place, in transit, betwixt Strawberry Studios in Stockport and Rochdale's Cargo Studios. The very point of the twin studio visit was the transporting of an A Certain Ratio master tape, from one to the other. This simple task was performed inexpertly, for nothing was so simple where Tony Wilson, especially at the height of his local TV fame, was concerned. Things . . . complications . . . so often got in the way. On this day, for instance – a Sunday – he had to, first of all, dive headlong into Granada's disappointingly mediocre office block, which meant, naturally, skimming around the small collection of autograph hunters, omnipresent outside those doors (. . . and they are still there).

Flitting in and out of the office, even on a Sunday, proved difficult also, for a plethora of messages greeted him on entry; screaming at him from an in-tray, blinking from an answerphone, stacked in memo format on his crowded desk top. There was only one thing for it. He had to swiftly ring around and appease those who desired his attention. Similarly, once in Strawberry Studios, the chance to grasp Wilson's attention was rarely passed upon.

'It's always like this,' he stated afterwards, surging towards Rochdale on the M61, a burning joint wedged conspicuously between his fingers, relishing his pre-carphone state of isolation. 'Sometimes I think that my life is mad enough . . . without being involved in the running of Factory. I'm always flying about . . . never can stop. I mean, what am I doing today? Delivering a fucking tape for A Certain fuckin' Ratio because the lazy twats can't be bothered to run around for themselves. Oh well . . . I am supposed to be the manager . . . manager and label boss, what a stupid combination. And to make matters worse, here I am talking to a journalist who hates them.'

'No I don't . . .' I aborted my reply.

'Shouldn't I be at home, in Charlesworth, eating steaks with Lindsay?' he continued. 'I'll get a real bollocking off her for doing this stuff on a Sunday. So why do I do this Factory stuff? It keeps me in touch. We don't run the music scene . . . the scene is already there. We just tap into it, maybe ease it along a bit, encourage it. I love transforming an idea, like this Ratio stuff, into a reality. I believe in them . . . they are my favourite band, my very favourites . . . even though I know you hate them . . . and I want to share them with everyone else. I'd love to bask in their success, also, but that is not the main objective. We have already proved that we are crap at business. We don't want to be good at business. Factory has got to survive . . . but I hope we are an antidote to that music business mentality.' The Peugeot swayed onward, the interior slowly filling with blue, intoxicating smoke. 'Don't mention the joint, I'll get sacked . . . It'll get in the papers . . . Wilson the drug addict. I mean, it's all image really, but you have got to consider that I sit there, each night, opposite Bob Greaves, and my job is to be universally amiable, at least to the viewers. They may go out and down ten pints of bitter each night ... but if dear little Tony was caught with a joint in his mouth, then that would obviously be seen as an act of unforgivable criminality ... I would be condemned by permanently pissed journalists.'

'So,' I asked, not unreasonably I thought, 'isn't it rather risky, given your local profile, to be smoking a joint while speeding through Milnrow in a big red Peugeot?'

'Naah ... fuck it,' he replied, and started to chat about sex. Oh, and A Certain Ratio.

TO EACH ...

Those soothed by the sublime, pulsating hi-tech funk punched out by A Certain Ratio in the eighties and nineties (incredibly, as I write, A Certain Ratio, ever the classy under-achievers, are languishing on Rob's Records, allowing themselves to wallow in an entertaining hole of insular musicianship while still hoping ... who would have thought?) might be surprised to discover the loose, jagged, spirited noise that heralded their arrival. There were occasions when Ratio's dipping, chopping, swaying, out of time attack would be pinned down by the finesse of drummer Donald Johnson – a throwback to Vini's Wythenshawe set – and would suddenly click. For the duration of their live set, usually performed in front of, say, eight punks and a disturbed hippy in Hebden Bridge, A Certain Ratio would find themselves producing music of such unlikely intensity.

Tony Wilson: 'I remember, once, standing in the Factory Club, watching a Ratio set ... and the club was almost completely empty ... and, on this occasion, they were so incredibly stunning. I felt so ashamed that I hadn't managed to fill the club, so more people could witness it. In that sense, they inherited their unpredictability from Joy Division. Joy Division could be fucking dreadful – and so could A Certain Ratio – but on this day I looked to one of the tables at the edge of the stage, and Jon Savage was there, looking completely stunned. I think he knew what I was thinking, that A Certain Ratio were one of the truly great bands of the era. Sadly, they never really recaptured that fire ... not the Simon Topping-fronted A Certain Ratio, anyway. But I knew that, if nothing else, Jon Savage would know how great they were that night. That would be something he would never forget.'

Jon Savage: 'I don't recall that at all. Not that specific night ... but there were gigs that were spectacular, but I took my time to get to like them. The first time I met A Certain Ratio they were absolutely foul. Really obnoxious. The most horrid people who seemed to be labouring under the illusion they were some kind of superstars. I just thought they were pathetic as people, and I couldn't understand why Tony kept raving about them. I became quite friendly with Simon Topping later, and I became quite a fan.'

As A Certain Ratio were gathering press – which included a stunning three-page *NME* cover story, penned and conceived by Paul Morley – Tony Wilson had the bright idea that I, a man who had slammed the band for looking and at times sounding just a little too much like Joy Division, should interview each member of the band separately, on the same night, in their own homes. Hence, I would have half an hour with each of them, and each interview would be half an hour apart, beginning with guitarist Martin Moscrop, in his parents' large Withington semi, and finishing up, via Topping's low-tech, high-rise Hulme flat (exactly where you would expect him to live) in Donald Johnson's Wythenshawe kitchen. All that transpired, in fact, was little more than an ill-equipped journalist receiving four separate outbursts of abuse. Obviously, the weight of being compared to Joy Division was hanging very heavily.

Simon Topping: 'That's such a stupid comparison. We are nothing like Joy Division. We don't even like them or what they are doing. It's naff to us . . . all that stuff. We are a funk band, truly . . . I mean, that is why we were formed. We would all be down at the best Manchester clubs, listening to Funkedelic, Parliament, Earth Wind And Fire . . . Bootsy . . . those are our roots. Not Iggy fucking Pop or the Velvet Underground. Can't you fucking well see that? We are made up from completely different sets of influence. It's just insulting to make comparisons like that.'

The comparison wasn't completely redundant. The similarities in look and at times feel would be strikingly obvious. In Manchester, A Certain Ratio became – more so than Joy Division – quite the epitome of the post-punk industrial aesthetic, garbed, as they so often seemed to be, in grey trousers and ill-fitting second-hand jackets and, Topping in particular, sporting increasingly shrinking short back and sides (or indeed, striding the stage dressed in the shorts purchased for them by Tony Wilson who, intent on completing the effect, spent pre-gig time rubbing 'Tanfastic' into those white, Mancunian limbs). In and around the gigs of Manchester, and in particular, the Factory Club, they would be seen . . . and when, finally, their first album, *To Each*, would crawl on to record store fixtures, the music would become a city centre fashion item, a soundtrack in the intimidating atmosphere of the more elitist clothes shops.

HANNETT AND THE RATIOS

Martin Hannett's relationship with A Certain Ratio, if rather less legendary than his liaison with Joy Division, was twice as volatile and, to this day, remains peppered in myth-building rumour. Small things, in the Hannett way, punched into studio drama.

'Give me an E,' demanded Hannett, of a startled Ratio guitarist Martin Moscrop.

'What's an E?' came the punkily brash reply.

Funnier, perhaps, was a further Hannett instruction to the same guitarist. 'Right, I want you to play that again . . . only this time make it faster, but slower.'

Tragedy always plagued A Certain Ratio. The American recording of a Ratio album being a typical example. The band, and Hannett, had travelled to blue-collar Newark, New Jersey, for the session, gleefully grasping the star-struck notion of a Stateside recording. On the penultimate day of the recording, having traversed a number of ego clashes – the usual thing – spirits were running high. An entire day was spent, as Newark swirled grubbily about outside, just sitting and listening to the tracks. A backslapping orgy, perhaps, but a general feeling of satisfaction prevailed. This, they all believed, including the normally hyper-analytical Hannett, would be a classic debut album. The idea was simple. The final day would be spent knocking together a 'monster' final mix – perhaps to be touched up later, back at Strawberry, but nevertheless a fairly sealed and solid album would be pulled out of Newark. Hannett, not wishing to ruin anything, left all the channels open that night, and he and the band returned to Manhattan, where the joyous atmosphere preceded a night on the town. The next day was similarly buoyant, not at all dimmed by collective hangovers. Upon arriving at the studio, they were greeted by a lively engineer called Jeff, who cheerily informed them, 'Oh, guys, you left the desk open . . . so I zero'd everything for you.'

The energy, the optimism, the buoyant spirits, instantly drained away from the Factory crew, relieved only by a bout of furious name slanging. 'YOOOOFUCKING STUPID-DDDYANNNNKCUUUUNT!' That kind of thing. Thoroughly drained, A Certain Ratio and Martin Hannett climbed back into the van, which slid slowly and solemnly back towards the Big Apple.

Things were not that bad. The original rough demo tapes of the album, polished by an irritated Hannett and delivered by November, left the apparently simple task of mixing to be concluded in Strawberry Studios, where the engineers, at least, could be trusted. The studio was booked for one full week. Shortly before the recording, however, Island A&R man Nick Stewart rang Wilson with the news, unlikely as it may seem, that Grace Jones had expressed a desire to record the A Certain Ratio track 'Again'. Flushed with such celebrity interest, Factory and A Certain Ratio dedicated three days to record a backing track for Jones. At one point the liaison managed to capture a straggle of press column inches, even pumping the name A Certain Ratio on to one broadsheet diary page, though it must be noted that the writer surrounded their name with quizzical references (i.e. what is Grace Jones doing hanging around with this bunch of northern no-hopers?).

Needless to say, the track was never used, leaving A Certain Ratio in a state of anti-climactic shambles. A condition that was hardly eased when, come January, they fell back into Strawberry with Hannett. By this time, the relationship between band and producer had dipped to an almost unworkable low.

Strawberry Studios, like all studios, is quite accustomed to acting as a battleground for vicious ego squabbles; bitchiness over the downstairs pool table, snide remarks at the coffee machine, bass player sackings in the Wellington pub opposite, mutinies and reprisals in the reception area. Most of these flashpoints would occur during more serious recordings, and the best producers manage to hone in on the anger, harness the energy if you like, use the conflict in the most positive, possible manner. But when the tension is a fairly straight fight between band and producer, the end result can tend to rely too heavily on luck. Hannett called Moscrop a fucking Fascist. This wasn't, one senses, any kind of deliberate artistic ploy. Hannett actually thought Moscrop *was* a fucking Fascist.

'Getting you to mix the album is like getting a baby to eat its fucking dinner, isn't it?' came the reply.

'It was awful,' admits Wilson. 'And I was in the middle of that lot. I was the manager of the band *and* Martin's partner. Talk about a "no win" situation. From that day onward Ratio hated me because I hadn't sided with them, and Martin always thought that I should have sided with him. All I could do was to say, "Look . . . just get the fucking thing finished!" '

Jon Savage: 'A Certain Ratio recordings were always edgy affairs. It could be because they were a bit musically inept, although that shouldn't have mattered at all. But perhaps they felt intimidated by producers or engineers. I don't know. I remember going to Prestwich, to the Graveyard Studios, where Martin recorded ACR for "The Graveyard And The Ballroom" cassette release. Simon was just getting into all that Nazi bullshit. I remember once seeing him wearing a swastika, and I really told him off about it. I think he just wanted to annoy people with it. I think it would be a great mistake to play it up too much . . . as the press did. It was more like a really stupid affectation really. I can't understand why Simon did that, especially if he was always worried about being associated with Joy Division. I just thought it was stupid to mess around with that stuff.

'But there were good times, in Manchester, and Ratio were a part of those times. I used to go round to Martin Hannett's first-floor flat in Didsbury and get completely stoned. Everybody did. I did that for a year and Martin was always very funny, very intelligent. I never saw the dark side. I never saw any heroin lying around, perhaps because I just didn't take it. But it was a lot of fun . . . Manchester had a very womb-like atmosphere, especially in Didsbury. People would just hang about. A lot of people hung about Martin because, him being a chemist, he always had the best drugs. We used to go for long drives at night; Martin, me and Susannah O'Hara in Martin's Volvo, driving around Trafford Park, completely stoned, listening to Public Image . . . that was a big Manchester record. It was post punk. People said it was grey but it was a good time. A fun time. That first Public Image album, which nobody in London liked, was a big, big dope album in Manchester. I remember having long, drawn-out conversations with Tony about it. Nobody ever smoked dope in London . . . that was another good thing about Manchester. It was such a relief to get to a city which had no hang-ups about using a nice drug. In London it was all cocaine. The dope thing was related to the music in quite a direct way. Especially with things like ACR and the track "Hot Knives".'

27 DECEMBER 1978

'Joy Division came marching into London', exclaimed the *NME*, in a wonderful cover story depicting a smalltime band arriving in the capital for the first time, full of wide-eyed hope and tentative confidence. It was a classic beat-up transit van full of excitable chatter, sliding through Hendon, arriving to play in front of – as they saw it – London. The great adventure. Rob Gretton's mild ploy, to keep the band away from the capital for as long as possible – although they had played at Brunel University, Uxbridge, a month before – had certainly paid off. At least in terms of press attention, if little else. A germ of curiosity, initially implanted by those Morley reviews, had started to grow, and that night, the famous though tiny cellar bar of the Hope and Anchor in Islington was filled more with professional attendees – record company A&R men and journalists – than actual punters. (Apart from a Honda Civic full of excitable Mancunians, including yours truly, who, believing the Hope and Anchor to be a divinely blessed rock venue, had become regulars inside this dowdy interior. Drunk, I suppose, not just on the beer but on the thrill of seeing future superstars. As it turned out, we were wrong with the last band we had seen there, Clayson And The Argonauts, and in luck only when our local band visited the venue. Mind you, it did seem a little weird, seeing them perform on that tiny alien stage.)

Joy Division looked cool, too, their grey trousers and functional, featureless shirts clashing stylishly with the spiky black-haired, leopard-skinned, plastic-jacketed rock crowd who regularly attended the Hope, the true home of London pub rock. A venue more suited, in truth, to sweaty, beer-bellied fags'n'tattoos macho r'n'b than some stark, industrial/romantic bunch, with severe short back and sides.

The Hope and Anchor was actually disappointing for Joy Division, who had yet to learn the sad truth that most so-called 'legendary' rock venues tend to be deeply anti-climactic. This, without doubt, was no exception. It was merely a pub and the fact that Dire Straits, the Stranglers, the Feelgoods et al., had performed regularly on that stage didn't soften the blow of humility felt by Joy Division as they lowered their amplifiers and speakers down through the trap door. Their lacklustre set helped to sprinkle a touch of small band realism into the NME article, but in truth, the emptiness they felt as they hoiked their gear back up through the traps and into the transit van, wiped out, rather than dampened, the final dregs of enthusiasm. Bernard's depression was the more justified. Pulled from his bed in the morning, he had complained about heavy flu symptoms; symptoms which would intensify during the drive south and seem to rise to a hallucinatory flourish during the set. He stood and shivered, his face glowing red then white, with beads of sweat expanding grotesquely on his forehead. He would later state that every time Steve hit the cymbals, the room would turn upside down.

The band drove back in Steve's car, with Bernard huddled in a sleeping bag, clearly in no mood to mess around. The mood was sullen: the worst gig, they all agreed, that they had ever played. For some reason, Ian began tugging at Bernard's sleeping bag; tugging and dragging it across, almost in a childish manner. Bernard, naturally affronted, tugged it back and a scramble ensued. Suddenly Ian, after growling like a dog, began lashing out at the windscreen. After the car pulled on to the hard shoulder, the band dragged Curtis out of it and held him to the floor, casting nervous glances at each other . . . not quite knowing what had happened. They took him to a Bedfordshire hospital where they learned that Ian had had an epileptic fit.

A SMATTERING OF GIGS AND THE MOVEMENT WITH NO NAME

City Fun's Andy Zero deserved a medal, they said. And he did. And more . . . much, much more. Perhaps he should have been allowed to join the Fall on drums – he did audition – after all. Some people wanted, so desperately, for Andy Zero to 'make it'. To make something; to climb on some lucrative rollercoaster. As it was, he was still *City Fun*'s Andy Zero. Still the man on the moped, glassy-eyed and lovable. His failure to surge triumphantly on to the pages of the *NME* seemed, somehow, to keep his image intact. Andy Zero would always apologetically ask if his name was on some far-flung guest list – he was no ligger. For a while, just for a while, he lived it. He *was* the Manchester scene. Far less pretentious than many who clamoured around him, he was difficult to dislike, even in his most speedy, most extreme state. Andy Zero's finest hour came on 24 July 1979. The festival he had all but singlehandedly organised took place at the Mayflower venue, in unlovely Gorton, just a hop away from the Belle Vue Speedway Stadium. A twin-towered venue which nevertheless managed to skulk meekly behind the row of fearsome pubs which resolutely refused to crumble to the ground, on the edge of Stockport Road – a terrifying drag, a terrifying area, especially on Saturday nights.

The Mayflower was, back in 1976, the closest cousin to the Electric Circus. It paralleled the Circus with a series of 'progressive rock' gigs, the best, one remembers, being an incredibly dangerous evening with the Sensational Alex Harvey Band. In latterdays it had doubled as an ultra violent reggae venue. Young white boys, treated with racist scorn, would be charged double entrance fee. Mostly in the months prior to this date, the venue had existed as a poor relation to the Factory, often taking the bands rejected by that far trendier venue. Adam And The Ants, dismissed by Wilson as 'London punk rock crap', played to a seriously antagonistic crowd who, though less than 50 in number, managed to smash every chair and every table into the band's PA stack before the lone bouncer bundled them on to the pavement.

Andy Zero, however, loved the venue, and had organised the 'Stuff the Superstars Festival', a self-explanatory eleven-and-a-half hour furiously paced binge, featuring the Hamsters, Elti Fits, Armed Force, Frantic Elevators (complete with Mick Hucknall), Ludus, the Liggers, the Fall, the Distractions, Joy Division and, of course, Jon the Postman. Now, admittedly, this may not have exactly been a forerunner of Live Aid, but at the time, for those in the know, for those who 'read' their music press and actually believed all that bullshit, it was certainly the place to be. Earlier that morning, five miles away in Stockport, *Sounds* journalist Dave McCullouch had come to blows with

Peter Hook during an interview with Joy Division conducted in the Wellington pub. The confrontation wasn't as ferocious as the article and subsequently, the legend would insist, McCullouch, temporarily at least, lost faith in this young band and went to Gorton intent on hanging around in a spirit of defiance, with his beloved adopted Salfordians, the Fall.

The festival, as it turned out, proved to be just about as hedonistic as it is possible for gigs to be. Also, it wasn't confined to the Mayflower. Far from it. The bands, the audience, the journalists and the road crew spilled, rather dangerously, into the local pubs, staggering along Hyde Road. In the Rock Tavern at 2 p.m., for instance, it was possible to see Mark E. Smith holding court before assembled inebriated hoardes including the *NME*'s Ian Penman who had, in a somewhat strange spirit of musicianly bonhomie, taken his saxophone along for the ride. The intention, all presumed, was that he would make a guest appearance. Unfortunately, his mightiest performance that day was reserved for an admittedly spectacular and profoundly drunken nosedive into a suspiciously sticky backstage carpet.

It was a strangely subdued gig in many respects. The local bands – Armed Force, the Hamsters, Elti Fits, and the Liggers, featuring *City Fun*'s Cath Carroll and Liz Naylor – trudged artlessly and joylessly through their sets, all too eagerly bowing before the three main contenders: the Distractions, whose excitable pop tones lifted the dancefloor into an ecstatic, climactic huddle resembling, at best, a rugby scrum; the Fall, with their new bloated line-up and parade of untested songs, who stretched the audience as always, as well as delighting 'those in the know'; and Joy Division, who turned in one of their finest performances. (It is my belief that Joy Division reached this peak on no more than eight occasions.) That day they sucked the silliness from the event and wiped away the rather seedy amateur ambience. For the duration of their set, it no longer seemed local, small, or even aloof and arrogant. Nothing else mattered. They were simply the best band in the world and, to this day, I have seen none to compare with them. Some, I noted, didn't notice at all. Some – rival band members, mainly – spewed away from the club, no doubt to invade the local pubs again; to refuse to admit their comparative frailties. Only the Fall, eternally beyond comparison, staggered away with their resolve intact. Joy Division simply blew everyone else away. Rob Gretton, strangely, didn't notice.

'Why,' he quizzed, 'were we that good? It's all a blur now . . . were we really *that* good?'

Andy Zero, at the death, joined Ian Penman on the carpet.

That night, as I returned home, refreshed by the Distractions (who were like an after-dinner mint to Joy Division's meaty casserole), I opened a letter. It had been written by Dick Witts, musician, wag, intellect and local TV star at that moment in time. 'The more I see Joy Division,' he wrote, 'the more convinced I am that they fly between the black and the white.' It was pretentious but I knew what he meant.

A MOVEMENT WITH NO NAME . . . AND A FESTIVAL WITH NO PEOPLE

Tony Wilson had green wellies. They suited him, especially on that day; the day being 27 August 1979. It was a featureless field in a featureless town and the strangest of settings for the second of the classic eight Joy Division gigs. One month and five gigs had passed since the Stuff the Superstars Festival and a whole batch of heavy work – beginning with their support spot on Buzzcocks' UK tour, kicking off (in both senses) at Liverpool's Mountford Hall on 2 October – lay before the band, stretching into the spring of 1980, during which America would beckon loudly.

Their idea had been simple enough. The underground acts of Liverpool and Manchester – or, in short, the rosters of Zoo and Factory Records, respectively – would merge in a central location, a field of fun. Tony Wilson had hammered out the details with Zoo's Bill Drummond. The outrage and fervour of punk had long since subsided, to be replaced in part by the intellectually affected, so-called 'movement with no name'. In short, lads in long overcoats and girls in their granddad's suits. Some of them, just a few, pushed by Public Image, had started to cock half an ear towards disco. Joy Division had begun to infiltrate it into their dark noise. There were signs of 'lightness', though not many.

The Leigh Festival will be remembered for all the wrong reasons. First, there was the 'reaction' of the local constabulary and assorted sundry hangers-on. They seemed to believe that some kind of siege of Woodstock proportions was about to take place; that rioting would ensue, as well as mass drug-taking, orgying and general rampant hedonism. Alas, nothing of the sort took place. Second, and for reasons that have never been made clear, few people attended the event at all – and those who did tended to spend much of the day in the local pubs. Whatever, the intellectual demeanour of the 'movement with no name' was lost on the police, who seemed to think it their business to search each and every car, probing into glove compartments, poking under spare tyres, harassing the girls and generally making a complete and utter hash of the whole operation. Those who had arrived in a spirit of calmness wandered on to the field seething in anger. Those who had pledged a day of comparative sobriety headed for the pubs. Most people were simply confused. The locals wandered to the perimeters, gazing in, as if into a particularly exotic wildlife park. Tony Wilson circulated the crowd, an unbecoming air of apology rising across his features, wellied up and suited, throwing forth many sentences beginning with, 'The fucking police . . .' As did we all. The lack of people in attendance served, coincidentally, to damage my own reputation at *Sounds* and weaken the paper's efforts to highlight the careers of Joy Division and cohorts. For a full month I had been hyping the event. 'It's going to be the biggest thing . . . the most important event of the year . . .' I had enthused and, if only for a week, they agreed to push back the encroaching twin horrors of the Oi movement and the New Age of British Heavy Metal which were spreading across their increasingly weakening – though circulation-grabbing – pages. Unfortunately, the Kevin Cummins photographs which accompanied the subsequent review hardly did justice to my superlative enladen prose. 'A staggering event,' I wrote, to the accompaniment of a photograph of five punks dotted around a field.

Nevertheless, a 'staggering event' it was. An embarrassment of riches. A Certain Ratio, The Teardrop Explodes, the Distractions, Elti Fits, Orchestral Manoeuvres In The Dark, Echo And The Bunnymen and, finally, devastatingly, as the night closed in, Joy Division.

Despite being one of the two music press writers – along with Jon Savage of *Melody Maker* – who hyped the event, I admit that I had no idea at the time that controversy raged beneath the calm Wilsonic exterior of the event. Indeed, Jon and I had been sold the notion that this was a one-day event, themed to allow the bands of Factory to meet the bands of Zoo and, as Tony Wilson would be seen striding around in his green wellingtons and Zoo supremo Bill Drummond in his Alpine jersey scurried about in much the same manner, there never seemed any reason to doubt that this was fact. Both reviews, in *Sounds* and *Melody Maker* enforced this myth.

To discover the truth and almost 30 years later, I found myself sliding a car effortlessly along the leafy lanes of Cheshire, through the lush pastures to the immediate north of Northwich, winding through farmlands to a pleasant if wholly non-descript housing estate. There, in the sizeable corner house, deep in an area of suburban sheen, I found Chris Hewitt, owner of Oz It Records.

Hewitt's story remains entwined with Factory, not without controversy in places. Back in the day, as the owner of Rochdale's Tractor Music PA System shop and manager of fave John Peel duo, Tractor, he had been a ferocious scenester, running PA systems in the Electric Circus and the Haçienda.

I visited Hewitt to find out about the strange fact that the Leigh Festival had actually been a three-day affair and, according to Hewitt, a festival 'hijacked by Tony Wilson who used it for his own devices'. The memories of the organisers would appear to support Hewitt's claim.

Chris Hewitt: 'I don't ever remember seeing any Peter Saville posters anywhere. The only publicity I remember is Lewis Knight had some small box trailers like you tow behind a car that he would leave parked around Leigh as free advertising. They normally said "Lewis Knight's Discount Three-Piece Suite Centre" on the side so he changed the poster signs to big sheets of paper saying "Pop Festival". He also hired some goons with walkie-talkies to stop a Woodstock-type breach of the non-existent fence – obviously they just walked up and down the boundaries of the industrial waste grassland and challenged probably one person trying to get in over seventy-two hours! The Factory poster only lists the Monday as it wasn't really a Factory or Zoo Event. The Fac 15 thing to me is the typical Wilson scenario. Factory meets Zoo was one third of a three-day event organised by local Leigh people, and myself providing stage, PA, lights, wiring, mixing tower, etc. Look at the picture of OMD playing and there are just over two people in the crowd – I don't reckon there was ever more than about thirty or forty there and you and Jon Savage had hyped it up in the press! There was a joke amongst the bands that "it's your turn to be the audience now whilst we play".'

22 SEPTEMBER 1979

The gig, that night, at London's Nashville Rooms, would seem to be the perfect Factory blend. The perfect rock band for the eighties supported by the perfect pop band for the eighties, or so we thought. Joy Division and the Distractions, in town for the hippest double bill in the country. Light and dark, entrapped in the tight, pub rock smokiness. Such a tiny event, really, and yet so guaranteed to capture the lead reviews, later that week. Such tangible hipness, however, cut little ice with Ian Curtis's boss at Manpower Services who, despite Curtis's mutinous protestations, wouldn't allow the singer to leave at lunchtime with the rest of the band. In a state that can only be described as as near to panic as it is possible for Rob Gretton to get, the manager rang Wilson, asked if he would attend the gig and, if he would, could he bring Ian with him? This was only a problem for Wilson in so much that it meant he would have to sneak away from Granada at 3 p.m. Not such a big deal, really. Picking Curtis up directly from his work, they found themselves shunting through London's gridlocked nightmare at 8 p.m. The only problem was that both Curtis and Wilson had only a vague idea of the location of the Nashville. This fact came to light during a conversation on the Heathrow roundabout. The problem did, however, resolve itself in, in Wilson's words, 'One of the most satisfying and unbelievable moments of my life.'

Turning a corner, they noticed a queue of people, stretching from the front of a typically decrepid and rather uninviting-looking pub, along a pavement and round the rear corner. Pulling to the side of the queue, Curtis wound down the window and asked where the Nashville was. The response was unnervingly positive and one can only assume that the band's experiences at the Hope and Anchor had dulled their expectations. Wilson and Curtis drove silently away, parked around the corner, and unleashed two simultaneous and mighty screams of delight. 'WE'VE GOT A QUEUE ... OUR OWN FUCKING QUEUE!!!!'

2 OCTOBER 1979

The decision to allow Joy Division the support spot on Buzzcocks' British tour in the autumn of '79 was, as far as Buzzcocks manager Richard Boon was concerned, uncharacteristically misguided. Perhaps he believed that the pop primary colours of the Buzzcocks' music would shine all the more brightly in the wake of Joy Division's stark black and white. Maybe he sought hipness by association. Maybe he just made a mistake. It happens. It was an odd choice for Gretton, too – not a man whose decisions are generally guided by buddy-buddy instincts unless, of course, the idea of a Mancunian on-the-road party seemed too good to pass by.

Buzzcocks, it has to be said, had most definitely lost their glimmer. The razor-sharp licks and lyrics that had kept them truly ahead of the game seemed strangely lacking from their 'difficult' third album, rather aptly titled *A Different Kind of Tension*. It *was* different, too. The band's experimental edge, so effortless a year or so before, now seemed oddly laboured. It wasn't really that the songs, a number of which had been written years before, were particularly bad (indeed, Shelley's lyrical irony was still madly apparent), it was just that, well, the magic had faded. Indeed, it had been dripping away from the band for several months. You could just sense it, and so could the reviewers, who had started to use fewer and fewer superlatives. Suddenly, slapping the new Buzzcocks vinyl on the record player no longer seemed like the *essential* thing to do. The edge had gone and the band knew it.

The magic – which would return, eleven years later – probably faded all the more quickly as Buzzcocks found themselves preparing to tour with a band who were simply bursting with songs, precocity, and sheer unstoppable talent. It was almost as if Buzzcocks had simply handed the magic across, like a relay baton, during the summer of '79. Naturally, Joy Division had grasped the baton with unflinching vigour. This tour, it seemed, would be more than just a travelling party . . . it would be spiced with undeniable, naked competitiveness. A different kind of tension, indeed.

The opening date, at Liverpool's Mountford Hall, only served to deepen Buzzcocks' predicament. As luck would have it, Joy Division, who were quite capable of throwing in hugely sub-standard performances at precisely the moment that they were expected to revel in glory, turned in a scintillating set, more than worthy of the band who were simply the finest in Britain. Liverpool music press stringer Penny Riley rather sensually noted that Joy Division played, '. . . music to surrender to. Only then do you receive maximum excitement.' Admittedly, one wonders if Penny Riley had stolen those lines from a marital aid instruction book, but it was the first time, to my knowledge, that Joy Division's music (normally regarded as starkly asexual), had had such welcome connotations attached to it. By contrast, Riley noted the flatness of Buzzcocks who, perhaps stunned by the brilliance of the support, seemed unusually if not suicidally sullen.

Richard Boon was worried. I could tell he was worried. After learning that I had actually enjoyed the *A Different Kind of Tension* album – I had, I had – he invited me to travel with him to Leeds on the following night to review the proceedings for

Sounds. This proved truly bizarre for a couple of reasons. First, only a panicking manager, surely, would lavish such attention on a mere parochial hack and second, the Joy Division half of the gig was to be reviewed by Yorkshire stringer Nigal Burnham (aka Des Moines), again for *Sounds*. The mere fact that *Sounds* instantly agreed to split the gig in two seemed, in itself, significant. Almost as if Joy Division and Buzzcocks had embarked on separate crusades – and so they had, in a sense.

The Leeds University gig was the strangest thing I ever saw. Joy Division, below par in my estimation and by all accounts completely failing to even echo the perfection of the previous night, still managed to squeeze an ecstatic review from Des Moines.

After the gig, upon noticing our arrival in the dressing room, one member of Joy Division broke deliberately from the pack – a pack which was surrounded by earnest student journalists – dived joyfully into the fridge, grabbed two four-pack Carlsbergs, threw one of them into my chest and, much to my utter amazement, dragged me to the corner. This was Ian Curtis. He seemed quite unfathomably happy.

'Do you think we're good at the moment?' he enquired, more in a state of genuine enthusiasm than mere braggadocio, I thought. 'Do you? Oh, it was pretty good tonight but in Liverpool it felt . . . spectacular. I don't know what it is. We're a strange band . . . I mean, we're not really used to touring like this but I've watched Buzzcocks and I've seen how they perform . . . and they seem to be able to work at it . . . to work themselves into a better performance. Well, it doesn't seem to be like that with us . . . with us it either works or it doesn't. At the moment it is really working, but will it continue? It's like . . . I know this is going to sound pretentious . . . it's like some power just comes or goes. Regardless of how we are feeling. I don't know even if the rest of the lads feel this in the same way. But I'm worried about burning out. Rob will tell you [Gretton, now sidling nervously to meet the conversation, affecting the nervous stance of a manager who finds one of his prize artists drinking and talking wildly to any passing journalists – and I had no illusions about this. I had been recognised and singled out by Ian, as a journalist. I could have been *any* hack from any paper, I guess] about this. I am worried, aren't I, Rob? Aren't I?'

Buzzcocks, conversely, performed with considerably more spirit than I had anticipated. The result was a dogged draw, with none of the inebriated Leeds students noticing the battle at all. Buzzcocks retired to their hotel – the four-star, modernistic Holiday Inn – in a reasonably happy frame of mind, though bassist Steve Garvey, lying flat out on the reception couch, cornily flanked by 'glamour girls', was heard to mutter, 'It's not so much fun, this tour. We seem to be up against it . . . I think if we start having a laugh . . . having more of a mess about with Joy Division, then perhaps things will get better.'

It was difficult, that night, as Buzzcocks sank into the most obvious cliché in rock'n'roll – drunken band running rampant through the hotel, terrorising the travel-weary reps at the bar. Joy Division, by stark comparison, were housed in more modest surroundings and, also by stark comparison, were asleep.

Two days and two dates later, the tension that so clearly fell between the two acts exploded, with inevitable consequences, during the drinks session which followed the typically raucous Glasgow Apollo gig. Both bands had retired to the Central Hotel and, as the night wore on, the camaraderie boiled over into a veritable orgy of juvenilia, with a series of 'dare games' causing all band members to 'hurtle' around the corridors, banging on doors, crashing through chairs and sinking deeper and deeper into alcoholic frenzy. The fact that the hotel's bar had been closed for a couple of hours didn't prevent it from lying in tempting darkness. The bar was duly raided and later, much later, an agitated gaggle of police officers arrived, more in an attempt to placate the hotel owners than anything else. It was Richard Boon who would bear most of the pain the next day, when the gargantuan bill was curtly handed to him. In short, nothing particularly extraordinary for a rock tour, although the evening represented a new set of tricks for the comparatively naïve Joy Division. Later, Buzzcocks Steve Diggle would state: 'I think we understood Joy Division on that tour because they were, personally not musically, just like we had been a couple of years before. When we began we thought we were a bit too cool for all that band-on-the-road stuff; we thought it was hackneyed. But things soon change. You have to live it up a bit. You have to have a bit of a laugh, if only to relieve the boredom . . . and it can be so incredibly boring. I think, in a sense, we helped Joy Division get over that same thing . . . in fact it was probably worse for them because people kept expecting them to be really cool, arty types. And Joy Division weren't really like that at all, were they? They just wanted to have a laugh . . . like us. You have to.'

The tour finished on Saturday 10 November, with two heavily filmed and recorded nights at London's legendary Rainbow Theatre. The final night was one of, on the Buzzcocks side, mild tinkering, and in the Joy Division camp, outrageous tomfoolery. The initial fault lay with Buzzcocks. Assuming their role as touring band tutors, and perhaps allowing their million on-the-road anecdotes, usually delivered late at night and massively under the influence, Buzzcocks had lifted their 'final night' tales into absurd exaggerations. This had, along the way, thrown Joy Division – who had never shared a final night – into a state of unbalanced though painstakingly plotted last-night antics. Perhaps they were expecting a whole barrage of trouble from Buzzcocks, who managed only to remove a battery from Steve Morris's syndrum, and a series of potentially embarrassing screws and bolts from the stage set-up. Joy Division had spent much of that Saturday cheekily scampering around purchasing fishing bait maggots, which they would pour liberally over the mixing desks and six white mice, which they unleashed on to the Buzzcocks' tour bus. After the gig, they covered the windows of the same bus in shaving foam while pelting everyone in sight with largely rotten eggs. None of this, admittedly, seems particularly radical in retrospect, although, according to Deborah Curtis in her book *Touching From A Distance*, Joy Division wrecked a toilet block in Guildford that night, '... removing fluorescent light tubes and smearing the light switch and taps in excrement.'

No one from the New Order or the Factory camp would later own up to this.

'It just wouldn't be a Factory thing to do,' came the official reply.

Chapter Nine

Love Will . . .

4 APRIL 1980

In the shock electric glare of the spotlight, on stage at London's Rainbow Theatre during an unlikely support spot to the Stranglers, Ian Curtis allowed his emotions, clouded and confused as they were, to channel into his performance – arguably, and rather disturbingly, the most intense performance of his career. Nervous glances were passed back and forth among the band, as Curtis's dance steps steadily quickened and the band's deep growl staggered to a number of false finishes, before the musicians, unable to stall things any further, finally crashed to a halt. Curtis was dancing still (it was an uneasy, unrhythmic and fairly chilling 30 seconds), by which time he had broken into an uncontrollable spin before crashing into Steve Morris's drum kit, knocking cymbals almost comically on to the floor. With the audience still clapping and blissfully unaware of the drama – Ian Curtis had suffered a fit before their very eyes – the band coldly, silently, carried Curtis from the stage. Nobody really knew how to handle the situation, though all were relieved when Curtis's movements subsided, to be heartbreakingly replaced by a mass of sobbing. He began to say how ashamed he felt, and the band looked down, deeply sympathetic, silently panic-stricken, not knowing what they could possibly do to help. Two hours later, Curtis – clearly recovered – had taken the stage again, this time at the Moonlight Club in West Hampstead, where the band had practically taken up a three-day residency. This gig, by contrast, was understandably reserved, lacking punch. All four band members were relieved when they finally left the club.

Three days later, Ian Curtis would almost go through with a suicide bid involving a handful of phenobarbitone, though he pulled back after realising that if not enough tablets were taken, the attempt could end in brain damage. With a gig pending the very next day, and with Sumner and Hook pulling him from the grips of a psychiatric hospital, the Factory team decided that extreme measures would be necessary.

8 APRIL 1980

The Derby Hall in Bury, a Lancashire market town hanging on the fringe of the Pennines on the north edge of Greater Manchester, might not seem like the most prestigious of rock venues. It was, however, noted for the honest and unbridled enthusiasm of its audiences, especially in 1980 when an inexplicable dearth of late-night buses to Manchester seemed to all but destroy the weekend nightclubbing sojourns into the city centre, causing Bury town centre, like neighbouring Rochdale, to transform into a particularly fearsome vision of late-night revelry. Joy Division's following in Bury had become intense, and the darkly clad clones of Ian Curtis would drift through the town's pubs, their often severe short back and sides haircuts provoking all manner of unsavoury advances from the pastel-trousered disco bar dwellers. This rather stupid divide was more noticeable in Bury – and in Rochdale, Oldham, Hyde and Stockport – than in Manchester city centre, where the sheer diversity of the nightclubbers tended to confuse any juvenile notions of rivalry.

Bury held an odd devotion to Joy Division; odder perhaps, than the band could possibly have known. For, on numerous walls in the town, the legend 'The movement with no name', meaningless to all whose lives didn't revolve around the weekly scanning of the music press, and meaningless to many whose did, had been liberally spraypainted. One doubts whether such deliquent devotion to the raincoated bands existed anywhere else, for were Joy Division not noted for the general intelligence of their followers?

Having struggled painfully through two mediocre gigs, at London's Rainbow Theatre and Malvern Winter Gardens, Ian had retired – exhausted, defeated, socially confused – to the strange sanctuary of Tony and Lindsay's Charlesworth cottage (much to the understandable angst of Deborah Curtis). Wilson, clearly deeply concerned, insisted on speaking to Ian alone. Ian's condition was clearly worsened by the furious Joy Division schedule and the particularly raucous date which had started to loom heavy, at the aforementioned Derby Hall, seemed just too much to take. Ian simply couldn't do it. In retrospect, all the involved parties would agree that the gig should have been rescheduled. Not, however, that anyone could have truly foreseen the events of the evening. Nevertheless, Factory, placing too much trust in their sense of experimental adventure, opted to present an evening of rotational Factory music.

Tony Wilson: 'We just thought that, if we got everyone on stage in a kind of rotation manner, it would be really groovy . . . an event, in fact.'

In a state of panic, Ian had agreed to perform the two slower numbers, 'Decades' and 'Eternal', while a kind of Factory cocktail, featuring elements of Joy Division, Crispy Ambulance, A Certain Ratio and Section 25, would form the basis of the gig. Elements of the Factory camp, Steve Morris and Pete Hook among them, expressed concern about the gig, but Ian and Rob believed it could be done. It could even be fun.

Speaking later, Steve Morris would admit, 'There was obviously something wrong with Ian and I couldn't see how doing this gig was going to sort it out. I was worried . . . terribly . . . I remember thinking at the time that Ian might do it again . . . that's why I thought we should sort it out.'

From the epicentre of the Joy Division panic, Bernard rang Crispy Ambulance vocalist Alan Hempstall, a good-looking avant-garde funkster. Crispy Ambulance, from their beginnings as Band on the Wall hopefuls, had signed to Factory Benelux, the trendily Belgium-based parallel to Factory, and had forged a friendship with Joy Division after providing several spirited support spots. It was a curious phone call. Bernard simply asked if Alan would step in and sing. He asked him, also, to pick his favourite Joy Division songs and the band would build a set around them. For the confused though delighted Hempstall this was like a call from heaven. He found it difficult to understand exactly what might transpire – some kind of mass Factory get-together, he seemed to believe – but, none the less, proceeded to dive into Joy Division's repertoire.

It was, of course, a huge mistake. For the gig had not only sold out but tickets had started to fly around Bury for £5, £6 and, in one instance, £10. The Joy Division buzz rattled around the pubs of Bury and Heywood in a wave of unofficial hype. It was obvious to anyone in the town that expectations were running high for a classic Joy Division gig – a special one-off fanzine, *JD Live*, was even produced – and anything less would surely seem dangerously anti-climactic.

Hempstall, understandably anxious and ill-equipped, arrived at the Derby Hall to find the backstage in some degree of confusion. Ian was there and seemed to be fine, although Sumner, concern creased across his forehead, ran helpfully though all too swiftly through some of the lyrics with Hempstall.

Section 25 opened the gig, their line-up expanding rapidly before the end of their set, to include Simon Topping, Hooky, Barney, Steve and Alan Hempstall. 'Digital' and the unreleased and, to the audience, unknown 'Love Will Tear Us Apart' stuttered from the PA. A flurry of confusion ran through the crowd. This was tempered, rather, as Curtis's familiar profile sauntered lazily on to the stage to run through 'Decades' and 'The Eternal'. It was obvious, however, that something was amiss, especially as Curtis's drawl was built from an unexpected vocal thinness. The band slurred and chopped their way through the songs which, although tinged with uncertainty and hardly lacking in tension – a nervous glance bounced from face to face, like a pinball – failed to convey any trace of depth. When Hempstall replaced Curtis again, a tawdry version of 'Sister Ray' – a song which Hempstall was woefully unfamiliar with – seemed to ignite the fury of the crowd and bottles began to fly from the rear of the hall, bouncing hideously on to the stage and at one point bringing a huge Victorian chandelier crashing down, scattering across the band in fearsome slivers of glass and causing the musicians to ungauge their instruments and scamper swiftly back to the dressing room. Outside in the hall, fists began to fly and sporadic fighting shuddered through the crowd, finishing with an all-out bottle assault on the stage and, ominously, the dressing room door. One roadie, courageously grasping a mike stand, fell into the dressing room, blood pouring from the side of his head.

Rob Gretton: 'Tony was sitting there with his head in his hands, muttering something. I thought, Well fuck this, I'm not going to let those little bastards ruin our equipment. Hooky was the same: he dived out on to the stage, with Pils bottles in his hands. I remember diving into the crowd, kicking out everywhere . . . it was like going to the football again.'

Actually, it had been Rob and soundman Ozzie who initially

dived into the crowd, to become the centre of a small swirl of hatred.

Tony Wilson: 'I saw Terry Mason standing to the side of the stage, looking absolutely terrified . . . partly about joining in the fighting and partly, I sensed, about wondering what Rob and Ozzie would do to him if he didn't. The wonderful Buddhist guitarist of Section 25 was holding Hooky back, saying, "Violence is not a good thing, Hooky. Calm yourself."

Wilson and Hempstall eventually pulled Hooky back from the edge of the fray. It had been a serious fray, too, with five people, including the roadie, in need of hospital treatment. Barney remained, sullen, head bowed, in the dressing room, muttering something about 'hating violence . . . hating it'.

Similarly Curtis, who, like Sumner, didn't share Hooky and Rob's style of machismo, sat upstairs, tears flooding down his cheeks.

'It's all my fault . . . it's my fault and people have got hurt,' he sobbed. The tears, however, would lessen considerably after Tony Wilson reminded him of the similarities between the evening's riot and the infamous, portentious affray at the Lou Reed Free Trade Hall gig in 1974.

'What kind of a gig was that?' asked Wilson.

'Oh yeah . . . that was a great gig . . . the greatest of gigs . . . legendary!' he concluded, brightness spreading across his features.

(It was Lindsay who eventually took the bleeding roadie to the local hospital. While sitting, coldly, in the waiting room, two injured members of the crowd also sauntered in. One of them, stemming the flow of blood, turned to his friend and stated, 'I don't fucking care . . . I saw that fucking Certain Ratio last week and when I saw Topping coming back onstage again . . . well, I had had just about enough!')

Rob Gretton: 'I was never worried about Ian as a manager – perhaps I should have been; but I wasn't that cynical. I was worried about him as a friend. I don't think we ever had to cancel any gigs . . . oh, maybe three in Scotland. But looking back on it, it seems obvious now . . . the whole thing was getting more and more stressful . . . and Ian's stress was obviously bringing on the fits. Sometimes he was bad but normally he'd be OK. I think that's why we failed to be sufficiently alerted to just how bad things were getting. Because, for weeks and weeks, he'd be perfectly fine, as far as we knew. But it was obviously getting worse and worse towards the end. I remember him coming offstage, having a fit and then going back on. The fit would last for about a minute and he'd get really embarrassed.'

ROB GRETTON THE WEEK BEFORE . . .

Rob Gretton stood, like a welcoming roadside diner on a desert highway, arms outstretched, laughing; a veritable oasis of bonhomie on a cold and heartless Manchester Saturday. He seemed pleased to see me, relieved even, for I'm sure I was the one person who looked even worse than him, weighed down, as we both were, by the burdens of shopping amid the city's weekend orgy of commercialism. Twelve shops perused and no purchases; just a growing feeling of emptiness, pointlessness. Both of us had all but abandoned our tasks – Rob's to seek out clothes to take away on Joy Division's first American tour and mine to find suitable attire for a wedding. My wedding, in seven days time. Both tasks seemed reasonably easy, as we trundled into town, but hardened considerably as the day wore on. Seeing Rob there, lost and dazed, child-like even, his eyes wide and curiously innocent, proved warmly startling. Could this really be the same man whose Saturdays had been more fittingly spent charging around the terraces of Maine Road? More incredibly, could this be the man who was managing the band who were, undoubtedly in my mind, the finest in the world; the most sussed, most intense, most effortlessly cool. Rob didn't look cool that day ... he rarely did. Once prised from his vocation, he seemed as lost as everyone else. More so, on Market Street, in the rain, with the shop lights splattered across the pavement. It didn't take us too long to come to a decision. It was 1 p.m. We had both been shopping for three hours, purchases nil. There were another four hours to go before the city centre truly closed all its purchasing opportunities. Only one thing for it.

Once inside the bar – Shorts, a crass boozy hellhole – we lined the table with Pils bottles. Rob was ecstatic, talking endlessly, delightfully, endearingly, about the glories of managing a band in such ascendancy. Namedrops, understandably, peppered his conversation. Namedrops that, to me, a mere provincial *Sounds* hack, held no small degree of magic.

'You know something, Mick,' he stated, arm around the shoulder at this point, 'I can't believe what has happened. I sent you two copies of that 'Sordide Sentimentale' single simply because I feel that it represents the ultimate Joy Division. Both sides – 'Dead Souls' and 'Atmosphere' – when I play them I cry. Other people do, too, it's not just me failing to be objective. Because I am so involved – I remember sitting down on my own, recently, and playing these songs – I couldn't believe how incredibly, utterly beautiful they are. Now, you have to tell me this right now because I really don't know the answer. Is it because I am so close to it, that I know what the band – all of them – put into it, and because I saw Ian singing that lyric, that 'Walk in Silence' lyric? Is it because I really know Ian and know where those words were coming from ... do all managers feel like that about their acts?'

I didn't know. How could I? Do they? Probably. However, most managers are wrong. In this case, Rob was right – those really are beautiful tracks; two of the most beautiful rock songs ever recorded. Why is this? After all, they were just some dumb young band he happened to fall into at Rafters. When I first met Rob Gretton, he was just some hanger-on with, for God's sake, Slaughter And The Dogs. A second . . . third division punk outfit, and a DJ at Manchester's least enigmatic club, so how did this thing happen? I watched Rob, as the Pils swirled about his mind his glasses slowly slid down his nose, his eyes icing to a still glare, attempting to work out just how this had happened. Without doubt he had employed, famously employed, a considerable degree of Wythensharian suss . . . street suss, really, for Rob Gretton would always play his cards close to his chest.

It is important to point out, not to soothe some bland ego of this writer – who cares, after all? – that Rob then stated something really odd in regard to the wedding bash due to take place just seven days later. 'Hey,' he said, absurdity forming in his words, 'I'll see if I can get the lads to play at your wedding . . . I really will.'

It was, of course, the Pils talking . . . at least I think so. Who, to be honest, would want Joy Division, of all bands, to perform at their wedding? The portents of such a performance would not have been good although, in my case, probably quite fitting. Of course, it didn't happen. One week later, on the Saturday night of 17 March 1980, Rob Gretton was stumbling around a Stockport dancefloor, arm in arm with yours truly, whispering joyfully into my ear, 'We are going to America . . . the world is our oyster.' I, for one, felt quite jealous. An unhealthy emotion, on one's wedding night. (Within hours, Ian Curtis, torn between two lives, two loves . . . between sickness and health, fame and infamy, fired by coffee, whisky and medication, would hang himself at the Macclesfield home he had, until a few weeks previously, shared with Deborah and daughter Natalie. Iggy Pop's album, *The Idiot*, was on the turntable.)

IAN CURTIS

Vini Reilly: 'A week or so before he died, Ian rang me and we spent an hour or so on the phone. This was after his overdose. I listened to him and, frankly, I couldn't see any way for him to get out of his predicament. He kept saying, "So what can I do? What's going to happen, Vini? Am I going to have a pile of pills on the table that just gets larger and larger every week?" I had no answer for him. I think he confided in me because he knew that I had had problems. But, at the end of the conversation, absolutely nothing had been sorted out. So I wasn't surprised at all when it happened. His personality was completely fucked up, anyway. I knew a few things . . . he was taking barbituates for the epilepsy. He couldn't *not* take them. I knew that if you get that black depression, if you are taking barbs you just can't shift it. It just gets worse and worse. I could tell just what his situation was . . . hopeless really.'

There was nothing simplistic, or shallow, or strikingly obvious about the suicide of Ian Curtis. It was a private death, rather than a rock'n'roll death, although the encroaching pressures of fronting the band had obviously caused his emotional distress to intensify. In retrospect, of course, it is all too easy to seek – and find – the clues hidden deep in his lyricism and the poignancy of his voice, which stretches eternally and so hauntingly across Joy Division's small but, still deeply powerful body of work.

Beneath the surface, Curtis's worsening illness was crowded by social and personal pressures. Touring with the band had wrenched him, physically, and perhaps even emotionally, away from his home life; from Deborah and his daughter, Natalie. Encamped in their dour Macclesfield terrace, with financial pressure mounting, Deborah and Natalie would effectively be living in a separate world, where only the briefest hint of distant glamour, via the weekly perusal of the music papers, would alleviate the fairly stifling domesticity. Curtis's world would be torn, quite literally, in two and the fairly arduous pressures of touring without large injections of money would, quite naturally, increase the distance between Ian Curtis the emotive performer and Ian Curtis the family man. In *Touching From A Distance*, Deborah Curtis's frustration would eventually spill into print, castigating Factory, at one point, for openly encouraging the split between the day-to-day mechanics of the band and the home life. Suddenly, Deborah Curtis no longer felt a part of Curtis's vocation. This split had been most strikingly evident when Deborah, heavily pregnant, cheerily attended a Joy Division concert only to find herself cruelly ignored by the Factory inner circle. She accused Factory of adopting a simplistic, image-conscious 'How can we have a rock star with a six months' pregnant wife standing by the stage?' attitude.

Tony Wilson: 'Well, the wives and girlfriends thing was simply blown out of all proportion. The central life of a Manchester band was travelling down to London in a transit. Wives just don't figure in that, do they? No way did we ever say to anyone, "Don't bring your wife." We would never tell anyone to do anything. We would never even dream of doing such a thing. It was never really talked about . . . not ever. The band just made up their own minds. It was just the way things were. I don't think Deborah would have enjoyed trekking across the country. I don't know if Ian wanted her there or not. That was his decision. It had nothing to do with us. But . . . then again, it makes a good story. Adds a touch of darkness that wasn't really there. Obviously, afterwards, it is easy to understand Deborah's frustration, and I can see how she felt ostracised from the Factory situation . . . but she wasn't really. There may have been things going on, with Ian and Deborah, but none of that was anything to do with us.'

Ian's emotional life, intense during the simplest of times, attained an added complexity on the day that Joy Division played at the Plan K arts complex in Brussels on 16 October 1979. It was there that Curtis had first met the young Belgian girl Annik Honoré. Their relationship, initially unknown to Deborah, would develop during the final, furiously disorientating gig-packed six months of Joy Division's existence. Looking on, in retrospect, it is not difficult to see how the pressures would mount.

Dual, contrasting lifestyles, an extra-marital relationship, wearying band workload and, possibly as a result of this, steadily, dangerously worsening health.

'I've been through it as well,' Hooky would state. 'It's easy for even the most level-headed person to become confused, especially when there is a child involved . . . and for him to get up onstage, suffering from epilepsy, performing like that . . . being exposed. It must have been absolutely awful. To some extent, we must accept some of the blame. We rail-roaded him into it. He was in a no-win situation . . . he didn't want to let us down, or let himself down, and it was making him ill. We weren't aware of just how bad it was getting. But to have the brains to realise that if you carry on doing it, one day you are not going to wake up . . . that takes a lot of guts.'

Jon Savage: 'I remember catching a train, from Charlesworth in Derbyshire, near where Tony lived, with Alan Erasmus, just before Ian died. Alan was saying that things weren't going too well for Ian. He alluded to the wife and girlfriend situation . . . I must admit, he seemed unusually forthcoming. It didn't make a lot of impact on me because, at that age, you don't really talk about such things. I also went to their last gig shortly after this and, just to show how seriously I took it, I left before the band played. It was in Birmingham. I went with Susannah O'Hara and we got in on the guest list. I went to say hello to the band

and they were as affable as ever . . . they would come out with the usual Mancunian sarcasm. In fact, I doubt if I had ever seen them seem happier, including Ian. I think we saw the sound-check and watched ACR play before leaving. Obviously we can't have noticed any kind of tension.'

The events on and around the death of Ian Curtis are well documented, perhaps *too* well documented. In many cases, badly documented. The downside of this reportage would begin just ten days later when an article in *Sounds*, penned by Dave McCullouch, would be awash with a famous degree of shallow reverence and, alas, peppered with inaccuracy. The article would stoke the disgust of all involved with Factory and, most probably, all who had been involved with Ian Curtis. In McCullouch's defence, though, it must be said that his task – an impossible task – was to begin to write the account immediately after hearing the shock news. He had but a few days to assemble the article, a few in which he – a mere rock journalist – had to approach people in a state of deep mourning. His use of the line, 'This man died for you . . . ' would, alas, be plucked mercilessly and endlessly from the context, and yet was nothing more than McCullouch leaning on the words of his favourite rock artist, Mark E. Smith of the Fall. It must have seemed, to McCullouch, both poignant and hugely relevant at the time. There was nothing more to it than that.

McCullouch's article, regarded by Wilson as '. . . a really heavy fucking piece . . .', in truth wasn't heavy at all. McCullouch, of course, didn't have any kind of retrospective insight or reflection on his side. As such, perversely perhaps, it survives as an intriguing little account of the initial effect of the shock waves. The ripples of flippancy can be, at last, forgiven.

'Last Tuesday,' he wrote, 'I was filling in an expenses form when somebody told me a joke. They said they had had a phone call from Scotland saying the Teardrop Explodes had dedicated a song onstage the previous evening to Joy Division's Ian Curtis who was dead. I laughed, and half self-consciously compensating for black and industrial jibes, said I wouldn't be surprised if he had. But I was half worried as well. So I phoned Factory's Alan Erasmus to erase the joke from my mind and let me return to my difficult expenses sheet. In a frightening, calm, most probably still shell-shocked voice, Alan Erasmus told me it was true. Ian Curtis was dead. I forgot all about my expenses sheet.'

In this intriguing and much loathed paragraph, McCullouch manages to succinctly transcend the gaping chasm that exists between music press, if not music industry sycophancy and shallowness, and the kind of hardened reality that only seems to come into focus following a personal tragedy.

Deborah Curtis's book, naturally spiced by indignation and wifely defences, recounted the final events of Curtis's life with a sense of warm detachment. When I met her, in her Macclesfield cottage in 1995, she seemed willing to admit that the writing had been an excorcism of sorts.

'Since writing the book,' she admitted, 'I've come to understand more about those pressures. And I have now accepted the things that he did that weren't very nice. Also, it made me understand how manipulative he was. I think he manipulated the band . . . I understood this, later, because of the things they would tell me. I knew how they differed from the things he told me, you see? One of the things that I didn't really put into the book was the full extent of his manipulation. Ian was a different person to each person he would meet. His personality would change when it suited him. He was very clever. To that extent I truly believe that I knew a different Ian to the Ian that the band knew. Or the Ian that you knew. You were a journalist . . . Ian would have been very nice to you. That is the way he was. But for my part . . . one of the reasons that I put pen to paper was to rectify this. This fact that so much crap had been written about him. Ian fooled an awful lot of people. I would see articles stating that Ian had 'marital problems' and all that and feel somehow cheated. I wanted to tell people what it really was like. All those articles . . . and books and things . . . made it sound as if I had packed by bags and walked out. My problem was never the band, or the endless nights he spent away, or his epileptic fits, or his other woman. My problem, and it is a problem I still live with, was the fact that he told me that he didn't love me and he wouldn't let me have a divorce, either. He kept me a prisoner. He was off, all the time, playing live, and I had to stay at home, wash his clothes, pack his case for the next gig. I didn't get anything out of it . . . *and he wouldn't let me go!*'

Deborah's hand clasped tightly around the coffee mug. For a moment, for a few moments actually, her face whitened, a blankness descending over her features. There seemed, even in the wake of the book, some kind of unfinished business.

'If you don't love someone you should let them go. I'm just disappointed that he didn't even love me enough to let me go. I would have been a lot happier if he had gone off and lived with Annik. The fact that when he moved out he didn't go and live with her made it worse. That is what really hurt.'

Ian's death affected many people; at Factory, in Manchester, in music, on the periphery and, of course, and perhaps just as intensely, in the Joy Division fan base. It was a turning point. The point where – delayed a little in the public arena because of the posthumous release of 'Love Will Tear Us Apart' and the *Closer* album – the introspection appeared to stop, for a while. The 'yellowness', vivacity, brashness, second glam era of the early eighties can, if one wishes, be traced back to that point.

For the Factory team, it was, of course, devastating and as in any death the ripples of grief would surface differently, and at different times.

Tony Wilson: 'I often wonder what effect Ian's death had on Simon Topping. ACR were, at the very beginning, potentially one of the great bands. The main reason for this was Simon. I spent the whole of 1980 trying to get a brilliant guitarist who couldn't sing to stop singing – that was Vini – and a brilliant singer to start singing again – that was Simon. I failed miserably on both counts. After Ian's death Simon went into retreat. He moved back into the music, back from the front of the stage. First of all it was the trumpet then all kinds of percussion. He was very close to Ian . . . very influenced by Ian, but also very conscious of not looking as though he was influenced by Ian. I just think that Ian's death affected him deeply . . . and in the end destroyed his music career. He finished up, years later, taking a degree at Loughborough University.'

Hannett, never the most stable of the Factory fraternity, was similarly affected. He wasn't shunted into retreat but, nevertheless, something changed within Hannett's complex mind. He too had been closer to Ian than most people had realised. Topping and Hannett were affected in a surprisingly intense manner, possibly because their closeness to Ian wasn't quite so obvious.

Tony Wilson: 'It didn't dawn on me for a few years just how affected Martin had been. I suppose he had worked with Ian in a unique way . . . shared a vision if you like. I remember Hannett coming round to my house in the mid-eighties . . . and he spent a full two hours just crying. It was very weird.'

Bernard Sumner, amid a natural state of shock, merely explained at the time that, 'I will never be able to cope with Ian's death. It will affect me now . . . forever . . . I will never be able to forget it. Personally, as a friend, it means so much to me, regardless of the group. As a friend. He was a real good friend.'

As far as the running of Factory was concerned, Ian's death just seemed to make everything seem a little more serious; more shadowed, more clouded, darker. A prevailing air of fun had been lifted. The label would have been forgiven for shifting off its axis at this point, losing direction perhaps.

'Perhaps that should have happened,' admits Wilson. 'Perhaps we should have all gone bonkers for a while . . . or just shut up shop, maybe just for a year. But it just never occurred to us at all. It always seemed a shame to me that Ian hadn't made it in America. Had he done so, then his death would have had much more gravitas . . . I don't say that flippantly. I think Ian would have liked to have been of Jim Morrison stature . . . and he would have been, too.'

Maybe he still will be. The truth is that, with Joy Division's most important releases pending, the whole operation was rolling so naturally along that there seemed little point in halting things.

TOUCHED BY THE HAND OF GOD

It was odd, finding Rob Gretton, just three weeks after Curtis's death, standing amid a seething horde of leather'n'black T-shirted heavy metal fans, sweat pumping from their foreheads, fists raised in – one presumed – masculine energy. It was simply not the kind of place one would expect to find him at all. The venue was Denton Youth Centre, on Manchester's eastern fringe, and the occasion, a Yamaha-sponsored gig featuring two up-and-coming heavy metal acts. Witchfynde, from Mansfield, who, as their name implied, sang about dark forces while garbed in all manner of appalling medieval robery, and Tora Tora, a pulsating and rather good metal act, from nearby Ashton-under-Lyne. Being Mancunian based, of course, meant that they couldn't possibly manage to build any kind of local following, for Manchester always remained something of a heavy rock desert. Tora Tora's attempts to kick-start some kind of local metal scene, via their own label, Mancunian Metal, floundered at the outset. So why would Gretton attend such a gig?

'I'm here to watch the sex,' he sniggered. 'Look at these kids ... some serious shagging going on here. You never used to get that at Joy Division gigs.'

True enough, you didn't, although Gretton's reasons for attending this unlikely gig were rather less subversive. His relation, Albert Wright, managed the band Tora Tora. It was as simple as that. Albert had spent many hours attempting to sell Gretton, and Factory, the idea of signing Tora Tora, but such a move would have been ludicrous, but not quite ludicrous enough. Albert, for his part, believed Gretton to be blessed in some way; touched by the hand of God, perhaps. For interesting things happened around his shoulders. And something interesting was to happen again. Albert's son, Simon Wright, was also the drummer with Tora Tora. Nothing particularly special about that. However, something extraordinary was to happen to Simon Wright. One night, his friends in the local Ashton-under-Lyne pub, all heavy rock fans and bikers, noticed that Simon was missing. Someone mentioned that he had answered an advertisement, cornily placed in *Melody Maker*, and had set forth for a London audition. To Wright's utter amazement, and to the numbing astonishment of all his friends, Wright returned home that day, a fully-fledged member of AC/DC. It was a position he held for eight years.

Chapter Ten

In the Wake of Ian

PEOPLE WHO KNOW ONLY a little about Joy Division tend to know that the hit single, 'Love Will Tear Us Apart', and the following album, *Closer*, both crept stealthily into the charts following Curtis's death. Most people know, also, that the death had cast a ghostly frisson to the recordings. The beauty had already been in place, but suddenly, with Curtis no longer around, the beauty seemed positively unbearable. One had to admire Factory's courage in proceeding with the releases, especially as both records were wrapped in tombstone-like design.

For *Closer*, Factory – perhaps in an attempt to keep the momentum flowing across America – piled on the irony by splashing out on an extensive American advertising campaign for the album, needlessly actually, as no band would be accompanying this promotional attack with a subsequent tour. Startled US youngsters had flicked religiously through their copies of *Rolling Stone* to be confronted by a full-page ad for the album. Naturally, the advertisement would be an exercise in divine subtlety . . . stylish, pointless subtlety, as very few *Rolling Stone* readers had ever heard of the band. Even stranger, and delightfully misplaced, was a billboard on Sunset Strip, directly above Butterfields Restaurant, opposite the brash, pink glamour of the Chateau Marmont, bearing the legend, CLOSER – JOY

DIVISION FACTUS 36. Quite what this meant to the touristic legions who cruised 'the Strip' or crammed the sidewalks is anyone's guess, though Factory were determined to make sure that Joy Division's presence was felt, if only fleetingly.

In Britain, the uniting of *Closer* with the expectant fan base was a strange thing indeed. The entire thing sank heavily on to record decks across the country, quite often refusing to budge until the listener could take no more. (And this listener, I pretentiously point out, listened to nothing else for a full month, and couldn't face playing the thing again for near on ten years.) There is no doubt that Curtis's death had added a shadow of mystique to a record that, already, was simply dripping with solemnity. Most people, myself included, had never heard such private music before, or since; at least, not from within the field of rock music. The record was simply the darkest thing you could own; a close friend, perhaps, who understood your deepest moods, your most profound fears. And it was terrifying, too.

SECOND GLAM AGE – POST-INDUSTRIAL MANCHESTER

Ooozits Club sat blackly, somewhere in Manchester's Shude Hill area. It was lost, deep in a maze of intimidating streets, flanked with long thin, evil shadows and grimly beckoning pubs. The Fall's Mark E. Smith loved the area. He would spend afternoons, sitting grimly in brown-carpeted, nicotine-lined tap rooms, testily ignoring the huddle of car mechanics who would gather around the dart board. I guess you had to be a Shude Hill car mechanic, or Mark E. Smith, to find magic in the down-at-heel ambience, or beauty in the beer. It was an area, one of the last-remaining areas in Manchester, where the landlady – Bet Gilroy/Vera Duckworth/Annie Walker style –

would still ferociously dominate the fat, tattooed men who gathered within. Out in the streets, however, freed from such imprisonment, the fat men would transform into menacing lumps, all too happy to prey on the student types, the raincoated hordes who would gravitate once a week towards this club ... Ooozits.

Ooozits was set in a warehouse terrace, and would extend sharply upward through three floors. It had been commandeered, on Wednesday nights, and renamed the Beach Club – God only knows what went on during the rest of the week – by Richard Boon and the New Hormones set. Armed with Linder, for the artwork, and Jon Savage, for the promotional scribbling, he set up the Beach Club as a kind of mid-week hip multi-media centre, with bands performing on one level, cult films flickering away on a level below and a number of places where one could escape from the lure of both. The Beach Club was decadent, short-lived and rather fun. When Ludus played, for instance, Morrissey (besotted by Linder, as were many people) was not only in attendance, but reviewed the event for *Record Mirror*, praising Linder for providing, '... a wide mélange of ill-disciplined and extraneous vocal movements, apparently without effort.'

Personally, not recalling *any* kind of mélange, I made my excuses to Ludus manager, Richard Boon ('They are interesting ... but not really entertaining'), and retired to the bar downstairs, where Tony Wilson, Barney Sumner, Rob Gretton, Kevin Cummins and, still around, the ex-*Sounds* reporter, Ian Wood, were idling away, pretending, at times, to soak in the film (a film about Lenny Bruce). No one, I noted, seemed to be in the kind of buoyant spirits one might normally associate with Joy Division.

This wasn't particularly surprising, as their singer had committed suicide just ten days previously. Having returned from the isolation of honeymoon, however, and as the music press had yet to appear in Manchester that week (normally, they would arrive on Wednesday morning but, due to a railway hiccup in Leamington, they had been delayed for 24 hours) I was unaware of this. This was unfortunate, only for myself, whose cheery manner that night must have annoyed most of the band members. For some reason, mercifully, I never uttered the words, 'Where's Ian?' Remarkably so, actually, until afterwards, when giving Distractions singer Mike Finney a lift home, and his reply left me stunned.

The Beach Club was to become an important part of Joy Division's enforced metamorphosis into a new unit. In a sense it was a perfect microcosm of the underground scene that, fuelled by the music press, had thrived in similarly darkened corners across the country. It was, however, also the kind of place where 'The movement with no name' would finally be laid to rest. Strangely enough, in the wake of Curtis's death, it seemed to lose its essential appeal. The music scene was tipping heavily into the upbeat eighties. Richard Boon's New Hormones label, proudly boasting Ludus and the avant-garde funkists, Biting Tongues, suddenly seemed to lose its magnetism. (Unless your name was Morrissey, of course.) But things were changing, and changing fast. Although the Beach Club would offer multitudinous underground delights – Ludus, A Certain Ratio, Cabaret Voltaire, Diagram Brothers, the Things, Nightingales, Felt – there was a prevailing sense that such acts, at least for a while, lacked the colour, vibrancy, optimism, danceability perhaps, that suddenly seemed more appropriate. We didn't know, in our parochial backwater, that America was readying itself for an explosion of dance music – Elektro, house, hip-hop – that would simply alter everyone's perception of popular music. Equally, how could we have known that that brief but so brilliant coloured 'age of pop' was about to take control in England. (This would be most significantly spelt out by the attitudes of the music press. Within a year, the *NME*'s essential 'singles page', once the true home of the archetypal 'indie' single, suddenly couldn't possibly be seen giving column inches to such low-grade scratchy dirges.) The frustration of the indie labels when faced with this backlash was perhaps neatly summed up by an incident in Manchester when Richard Boon approached Paul Morley – then firmly entrenched in London – with the words, 'Well, Paul, what do you think about the stuff we are releasing on New Hormones now?'

'I just *had* to run away from him . . . I was so embarrassed,' said Morley who, seemingly, couldn't even bring himself to speak to the label that had, in creating the punk-independent deal and providing one of the true classics of the genre, so altered the course of his life. Likewise, Factory would suffer enormously from this change of attitude.

'We went from being the coolest label in the world to being completely, utterly unhip . . . well, at least in the eyes of the music press,' said Wilson, before adding, 'It seemed to happen overnight. It happened to an awful lot of labels, but I think we suffered more than the others. The press became almost violent towards us. There was a level of hatred which came out of nowhere, which, after mulling it over for a few traumatic weeks, we just decided to completely ignore, if not just laugh at. It was just so pathetic. Factory had never been a one-dimensional label and yet we were seen as old hat . . . grey, indie, dull; all those things which I thought, and still believe, were totally the opposite of the Factory ideal. I suppose that period taught us just how stupid journalists can be.'

Nevertheless, things did change, and change fast. One remembers seeing Manchester students, for example, whose previous idea of a thumping good Friday night out would be to

congregate around a stage and stare adoringly at Ian McCulloch, suddenly forego the university gig in favour of a trip into
darkest Oldham Street, into the delightfully seedy Dickens Club
– a gay members bar – where they would dance away to
glorious strobe-led Elektro and the lightest of disco. Village
People – whose glory year had been 1979 – and Ottowan were
particular favourites.

Peter Hook, Barney Sumner and Steve Morris were wholly
aware of this shifting axis. (Indeed, Hooky had even been
spotted in Dickens, though whether he actually shimmied across
the dancefloor to the strains of 'D.I.S.C.O.' remains somehow
rather doubtful. Interesting vision, though.) This was reflected,
if not in the music that had yet to evolve from Joy Division's
profound sound, then in their initial, flippant ideas for a new
band name. Though hopelessly lost for a while – they rehearsed
in rotation, each member providing the vocals which, of course,
would eventually rest with Sumner, after taking a couple of
years to find a way of using his thin voice in a positive manner
– they really did seriously consider calling themselves the
Sunshine Valley Dance Band and, less seriously, Stevie And The
JDs. Both names were indicative, however, of a desire to lighten
the musical load; to relax a little, find a refreshing new
direction. The band knew only too well that Manchester alone
was simply brimming with artless, witless, guileless Joy Division
copyist outfits, many of whom persisted in making their
dispassionate drone, despite being suddenly rendered profoundly unhip. Maybe the music press were not quite as stupid as
Tony Wilson would have us believe.

This would be the hinge moment in the story of these three
extraordinary musicians. It involved an unlikely talent by the
name of Kevin Hewick, whose link with Factory would
strangely grow during the next few decades. Those who
attended many Factory-orientated gigs over the years certainly

knew his name. Often it would appear at the foot of posters, at The Osborne Club, Russell or Beach Clubs. A lonesome troubadour who, in almost every respect, always seemed most unsuited to the Factory roster. A singer/songwriter on an eclectic modernistic label? It never seemed to fit ... still doesn't, although here comes the paradox: in so many ways, Kevin Hewick seems still to typify Factory. He truly loved and loves his association with the label and who is to deny him such a feeling? He also shares an ethos, or so it seems, with the acts languishing in the shadows.

He was almost famous on one occasion ... fleetingly. Like Alan Hempsall, who stood in for Ian Curtis at the infamous Bury gig, Hewick briefly emerged at the front of Joy Division, if only for one rehearsal. As the band struggled to find a focus in the confusing days immediately after the demise of Curtis, it was Hewick who temporarily and nervously shuffled into that front man position. For a few precious days, fate hung over him like some cruel spectre. Almost as soon as the dream arrived it was snatched away ... and New Order drifted into initially uncertain stardom, leaving Hewick wondering what might have been.

Hewick came from Leicester, where he still resides, often appearing in local pubs and festivals, of which there are many, still performing. Still writing. Not too different from his pre-Factory days: making demos and slapping them on cassettes, hopefully whisking them away.

Kevin Hewick: 'I had tried sending packages in a very naïve way to a few labels, the usual majors and the "happening" ones of the time like Stiff and Radar. I'd got no contacts, I had no idea how to go about it really, I was a total unknown, I'd never even played live outside of things at the college I'd attended. My demos were all recorded alone in my bedroom on a reel to reel, I just churned these stark, spiky songs out one after the other.

A friend of mine called Roger Holland had met John Dowie [the comedian who appeared on the first Factory release, 'A Factory Sample'] at a gig and told him about me. Dowie gave him an address so I sent cassettes to John and to the Factory office on Palatine Road in Didsbury. I don't think anything happened via Dowie and a few months passed but then I got a telegram from Tony Wilson in October 1979 saying most tapes Factory received weren't much good but they thought mine was. In those pre-text pre-email days things moved much slower and it was Factory, too, of course, right? Typically of them the plan seemed to be that there was no plan.

'Next I got a Kim Philby Factory Christmas card and then in January 1980, I spoke to Tony on the phone at last and he said about my playing at a gig in February. I only knew the night before it was to be with Joy Division. It turned out that A Certain Ratio and Section 25 were on the bill too. Wilson met me at Piccadilly Station. In 2002, when he spoke at the Royal Festival Hall, Tony claimed that as he saw me "mince" toward him on the platform with my guitar case "slung over my shoulder" (which is funny because it was a hard case with a handle so no way could I have carried it like that) he'd thought "This isn't going to work."

'As it was it wasn't a distinguished debut. The venue was The Osborne Club, a roller disco rink of all places. It was big and crowded. I felt very nervous and out of place both in the club, the dressing room and onstage. However Tony loved it. I walked offstage with my cassette recorder still running and there he is on the tape sounding very young and enthusiastic going "Brilliant . . . thank you."

'I was a lot shyer then. Nobody from Joy Division spoke to me at all, Curtis even stood talking to two girls sat next to me and never acknowledged I was there. I was too much the amazed-to-be-there JD fan, too shy to try to join in with the conversation.'

One question would echo down the years. Did Kevin Hewick audition for the singer's spot once occupied by Ian Curtis?

'Was it an audition?' Hewick thought aloud. 'I wonder if they'd deny it was. I daren't ask Hooky to this day. It never occurred to me that it was at the time but I can be a bit slow on the uptake that way. Tony only asked me if I wanted the JDs to be my "backing band" the night before the session at Graveyard Studios. It had been a month since Ian had died. He said they wanted to carry on as a band and wanted to do something with someone else as a way of easing themselves back in.

'I'd never been in a studio before and I was again too much the fan in awe of them. Less than a year before I'd queued for three hours to get in The Nashville Rooms in London to see them . . . and here I was now recording with the three surviving members. They treated me well but the strain did come to show, in Bernard especially. He left the session a couple of times and stormed out altogether at one point.

'One pinch-myself moment was when Hook and Morris and I played bits of a few Joy Division songs with me all over the place on guitar. I didn't sing on any of it. Peter stopped us after a while saying Bernard might be upset if he heard us doing songs they'd done with Ian.

'The night before they'd decided on the New Order name. Peter said it was Rob Gretton's idea. When I said Ron Asheton of The Stooges had already had a band called The New Order, Hooky retorted that didn't matter as only I had ever heard of them!'

Wilson: 'There are four or five times when Rob Gretton has completely stunned me by making exactly the right decision at the right time. That was a great choice of name but, even more importantly, it was Rob who proved instrumental in getting Gillian Gilbert into the band, who was part of the family really, rather than, say, getting a more accomplished musician in. New Order had to go back into learning mode, so she fitted in naturally; she would learn along with them and, eventually, a new sound would evolve. Brilliant . . . quite brilliant. Rob knew this.'

It was Rob Gretton who initially suggested the name, New Order, after watching a television documentary about Pol Pot. Gretton insists, however, that the name was simply plucked from the programme, and it could have been any programme, before any kind of Fascistic connection had become apparent. This was a band looking for a fresh start. New Order seemed perfect, if, perhaps, initially unwise. Journalist Chris Bohn, writing as Biba Kopf in the *NME*, was the first writer to slam the name.

'It is a stupid choice of name for a group previously steeped in gloomy, magnificent Gothic romanticism. The term New Order is irrevocably associated with Hitler's vision of a racially pure Europe,' he wrote, not without a certain venom, and the venom spread wildly across the pages of the music press. It couldn't have worked better if the band had used 'reverse PR' tactics in a McLarenesque manner, and had orchestrated every little press outrage. Immediately, people were talking about New Order.

'It wasn't like that at all,' insists Wilson, 'although, I admit, the Nazi connection with the term New Order, and the fact that, as in the name Joy Division, they were once again associating themselves with the oppressors rather than the oppressed, seems blatantly obvious. I am genuinely convinced that it never even dawned on the band until they started reading about it in the press. I even worried about this fact for a while and so did the band. Rob did, certainly, although in the end I think we all just decided to sit back and watch people falling over themselves and getting very, very indignant. To maintain a dignified silence seemed the right thing to do.'

Peter Hook: 'I never gave any thought to the name . . . none of us did, really. We just thought it sounded pretty good, seemed fitting. We didn't think anything of the Fascist connections at all. So it stunned us a bit, to suddenly see everyone getting their knickers in a twist. There have been hundreds of occasions over the years when I've been asked that dumb question, "Where did you get the name from?" I always tell them that I can't remember, and I genuinely can't. I don't think any of us can. It was smart, short and it sounded fresh.'

Nevertheless, the choice of name managed – to the band's delight – to grant them coverage within the often awesomely flippant pages of *Private Eye*, who, in an all-too-rare dip into the world of rock music, noted, 'This is New Order, which is the unpleasant new name of an even more unpleasant band called Joy Division.' Even A Certain Ratio, whose album sleeve for *To Each* featured a photograph of Wehrmacht officers, were, again to their delight, given a thorough dressing down and regarded, by the *Private Eye* experts, as having 'Fascistic tendencies'.

New Order began their studio life, tentatively, in Sheffield's Western Works studios where, still as a three-piece, they recorded three of the tracks that would later surface on their debut mini album, *Movement*. The session was awkward, as were the recordings. The escape from Joy Division's majestic low growl into something altogether more optimistic, would obviously be a most difficult transition, but at least the music was beginning to sound 'transitional'. For their debut live performance, they opted for a low-key – in fact unannounced – set within the homely confines of the Beach Club, where the surrounding Bohemian colour, they hoped, might 'lift' their sound a little. It didn't.

WITH HANNETT – THE LAST TIME

Hooky: 'When we got to *Movement*, it was a real low point, for us and for Martin. He would sit at the desk and say, "I'm not working until I get a gram of coke." We didn't even know what coke was. We would say, "Rob, what's he on about?" He definitely started to lose it at that point ... and we were not much better. We were confused, musically ... in a mess. Our songwriting wasn't coming together, we were depressed, and Martin would sod off to the little room at the back and say that he wouldn't come out until he heard something he liked. We just sat there looking at ourselves. It was pretty fucking desperate. I don't know how we pulled out of that one. I actually liked *Movement* but I know why nobody else liked it. It was good for the first two-and-a-half minutes, then it dipped. It was a shame because, as New Order, we had made a good start with the single "Ceremony" but that was really the end of Joy Division rather than the start of something new. I didn't think we stood a cat in hell's chance of getting anywhere without Ian. I really didn't.'

Chapter Eleven

Art is Spain!

THE HAÇIENDA OPENS, FRIDAY 21 MAY 1982

Tippling from the coach, the road-weary London journalists staggered around the corner of Whitworth Street, all black glasses and Levis, shoulder bags and baggy T-shirts – hip, freebie journo T-shirts, of course. Perversely, and perhaps optimistically, the coach had also brought Paul Morley back from London although his willingness, as he looked across to the City Arms, was rather called into question.

'I just can't stand it up here any more,' he announced, 'really, I can't. I don't think there is a scene at all. Down in London everything seems possible all the time. Every time you go out you sense that something might happen. Gigs are sharper, too. There's an atmosphere down there now, not unlike it once was in Manchester, only much bigger. The major record companies are on the ball, too. I'm not impressed with the independent scene . . . it seems so bloody pointless.'

This wasn't, one presumed, quite the response that Factory had hoped for. As if to emphasise the point, standing next to Morley, chirruping in his ear in fact, was the figure of ex-Stockport Grammar boy, Martyn Fry, frontman of ABC, yet to take the poll position with the magnificent Trevor Horn-produced *Lexicon of Love*, but a happening, glitzy, anti-indie campaigner all the same. His lamé suit, someone noticed, reflected the image of local lad and Distractions vocalist, Mike Finney.

Morley's girlfriend, Karen, took hold of the other flank as the three of them marched, for the first time, briskly into the Haçienda, Fry arriving as the guest of ex-fellow member of Vice Versa, and Haçienda booker, Mike Pickering. 'Funny how things turn out,' he noted.

It was an elitist opening, as openings tend to be, and in this case, rather added to the chagrin of the local bands and agitators who found themselves coldly uninvited.

'Well, they can come tomorrow. It's Cabaret Voltaire tomorrow, that'll be great,' stressed Wilson, when pressed on this point.

Most of the journalists fell into stony awe upon entering. It is a feeling that would, in time, hit hundreds of thousands of students and clubbers, many of them 'freshers' and new to club life. Fresh, perhaps, from the villages of Hampshire and Kent. Few people would forget the first time they staggered into the club's enveloping lightness. Haçienda designer Ben Kelly's idea – to create an antithesis to the smoky red den, scampi in a basket'n'little red lampshade idea of a nightclub – seemingly worked to initially stunning effect. And then there would be the smell. Fresh paint and plastic; rubber and cold metal. (The smell, unfathomably, lingers still.) The journalists, almost instantly refreshed, seemed content, though they shivered some-what as they scoured the corners, the balcony, the exquisitely named Gay Traitor cocktail bar – Wilson sharing Jon Savage's fixation with the Kim Philby scenario – once a floating bay for a boat showroom. (I remember it, actually, as a marina. I used to purchase cleats and shackles from there. Overpriced and snooty, some might say, that atmosphere would linger on, at least for the first few years of the Gay Traitor. Not me. I always found it to be a nice place to escape the boom and bustle on the dancefloor above.) The first band to perform, as a result of Wilson's devotion to America, were the all-female New York band, SFG, who plunged rather nervously through their set, presumably not used to performing before so many influential journalists, sundry luminaries and inner-circle sycophants (Jon Savage, rather strangely, missed this initial bash – at least, he thinks he missed it). Everyone wrestled with the 'ticket machine' queuing system at the bar, rather like the kind of scheme which can be found on the deli counters at Sainsbury and Safeway these days – apparently a great success in New York at the Danceteria, where punters are generally polite. It wouldn't take long, however, for such a system to fall foul of the 'gruff, British nightclubber syndrome', and in Britain, no such system could possibly operate successfully. All is fair in love, war and at the bar. After a few tumultuous months, it was duly scrapped. On the first night, Wilson's celebrated sense of the perverse joined forces with his Granada connections to produce, before SFG, north Manchester's crude and proudly unfashionable Bernard Manning who, not surprisingly, found this to be the most unresponsive crowd he had ever faced.

'Some fucking club this is,' he snarled, and when approached by an extremely brave heckler, could only respond with the rather disappointing, 'Listen mate, I'm the one who is travelling home in a Rolls-Royce tonight; have you ever thought about that?' It was, one had to admit, a profoundly stupid remark; a remark not entirely guaranteed to caress the affections of the rock journalists in the audience. Then again, Manning's reactionary stance, wholly intended to offend and irritate all who had built a barrier of political correctness and had yet to see the error of this, was actually quite perceptive.

'Tony, why have you built this club? Who is it for?' One remembers Mr Wilson continually deflecting these questions during the course of the evening. The truth is, once past the obligatory 'for the kids', he didn't have an answer. In the opening pamphlet, the place would be labelled a 'purpose-built club'. But purpose-built for what? This wasn't a rock venue, it was a pristine and hi-tech disco. The kind of place that no lingering Joy Division fan worth his third-hand raincoat would be seen within a mile of. This was Manchester clubland … Manchester disco. The kids … more kids … a new batch of kids … kids not dogged by rockist snobbery; these kids would surely find the place, one day. But on Friday 21 May 1982, these kids would still be sellotaping Duran Duran posters on their bedroom walls.

On the next night, a disturbing light show roamed across the bar and a vicious screeching wrenched itself from the speakers. Cabaret Voltaire had taken the stage. Fifty? Seventy-five people – can't have been more – formed a polite semi-circle while the balcony remained deserted.

This was the first public night at the Haçienda. A Saturday night with a name band. Tony Wilson slumped on the bar – after purchasing his token – and moaned softly. 'I'm not really worried. We have built this place with the intention of creating a scene. You can't suddenly expect things to happen. Still, it is worrying. I know, right now, every second, that we are losing money. We have to get a couple of hundred people in just to pay for the lighting and heating … it will come … it will come.'

IN THE BEGINNING

The Haçienda had begun, as so many things did, as a vague black notion, forming slowly at the back of Rob Gretton's mind. (In fact, it may be traced even further back, to 7 February 1980 and Joy Division's aforementioned gig at the New Osborne Club. Despite *City Fun*'s claim that it would become 'the new Electric Circus', it was perfectly clear to all who attended – including Iggy Pop – and all who performed – including Ian Curtis – that the romance of such enveloping seediness had worn a bit thin. It simply wasn't 1977 any more and, frankly, an ex-rollerdisco patrolled by 'pond life' bouncers was no longer what was required of a rock venue. Not in post-punk Manchester, where a rebuilding process had already begun, in the heads of the public if not on the streets. The New Osborne's shortcomings had a profound effect on a whole mini-generation of seventies gig goers, an effect intensified by the fact that practically every attending car had its side windows smashed that night. Indeed, the old 'movement with no name' had come of age. It decided that it wouldn't go to gigs any more.

Gretton hadn't forgotten the traumas of that night. He had also struggled during 1981 to find a place where he could go to relax and swap ideas. Living in Chorlton Cum Hardy, Gretton was naturally engulfed in a swirling, heady Bohemia. The city centre, however, seemed painfully devoid of places to visit, especially for those not entirely sold on the dubious delights of the standard discos. But, since the Factory's demise, the city's rock scene had spiralled down to a painful trickle of inadequate venues and fewer and fewer bands. More significantly, the energy source seemed to have faded. Had it surged into other areas? Not really. Unless one can trace some kind of worthy aesthetic from the Saturday night white-shirted disco rituals of drinking-'n'trapping (which, admittedly, would rage so intriguingly on Pete Waterman's hi-tech, low-brow, no content early nineties, post-rave 'drongo show', *The Hit Man and Her*). Interestingly enough, 1981 (December actually) also marked the year when the troubled Wigan Casino finally closed its doors, instigating a slow but steady implosion of the most intense youth scene in northern England. To see a band in Manchester in 1980 or 1981 would be to sit in the soulless Apollo, to huddle drunkenly in the shadows of Devilles, to scramble around the dangerous expanses of Hulme, to drift into the twin universities or – the best of the bunch, by far – soak up the ragged atmosphere of Manchester Polytechnic's Cavendish House. A venue noted, not merely for the occasional classic gig – U2, Adam And The Ants – but also for the huge mural of Denis the Menace which lurked behind the stage and, consequently, behind the heads of so many lead singers as they leered out of photographs in the music press. The Poly however, as polys usually are, was a one-dimensional venue. A drinking den with a refectory ambience. Rob Gretton wanted something else . . . somewhere, he later stated, where he could 'ogle women'. (And you certainly couldn't ogle women in the Poly, or in Chorlton for that matter – not without receiving a swift boot from a rainbow-coloured Doc Martin.) He had little idea of what it might be or what it would cost, but he wondered . . . just wondered, if Factory, with money now in the kitty, might be pursuaded to honour his notion.

His initial 'let's build a club' angle was met with blank gazes from both Wilson and Erasmus. Understandable gazes, for they had 'run' a club before. They hadn't forgotten the 'lost' feeling one succumbs to when overpaying a band for playing in front of about twenty paying customers. They hadn't forgotten the hassles, either. Did they need a return to those? Factory, after all, was ticking along nicely, largely without the help of an increasingly hostile music press but nevertheless, things could have been worse. And Rob was standing at the beginning of a bright new future as New Order looked set to unlock the lucrative valve which had been separating the apparently incompatible markets of rock and dancefloor. It didn't make any sense. There wasn't even a scene, for Christ's sake. Who, but a suicidal fool, would plough money into such a venture?

It didn't take long. Wilson and Erasmus would soon find their heads nodding accordingly. Enthusiasm began to trickle into their meetings, then seep, then gush uncontrollably, as is the Factory way. Before long, and to Gretton's delight, the 'future nightclub' had become a 'work in progress'.

Factory have always worked in mysterious, often illogical ways; mysterious and illogical even to themselves at times. There has been a belief, to a certain extent, in the notion that like-minded individuals tend to drift together. Indeed, it was this belief that would play a large part in the label's undoing although, without it, Factory simply wouldn't be Factory. Fate has been allowed to have a free rein . . . for better or, more often than not (and entertainingly), for worse.

Howard 'Ginger' Jones had been running the Comanche students union venue in Manchester – a gruff and difficult to locate alternative to the Poly's Cavendish House – after cutting his teeth on Rafters. When the nervous and disturbingly clumsy young band New Order arrived one day, complete with Tony Wilson and camera crew, Jones found himself encouraged into the Gretton-Wilson circle. It had been only his fifth band promotion and, apparently, he had handled the tricky situation of getting New Order onstage, reasonably intact, with a certain degree of aplomb. This task, difficult at the best of times, obviously impressed Gretton, who asked Jones what his plans in the city – if any – were. Jones's reply was obviously supplied by God, for he told Gretton that he wanted to run a club and, in particular, a club that would break away from the strangulating Manchester raincoat brigade. It was a most perfect answer. New Order, in their heads if not yet in their music, were striving to pull away from the raincoated image that had so tainted the followers of Joy Division and had dulled the edges of a thousand burgeoning local bands. The club – perhaps –

would help accentuate that process; create a freshness, a sense of colour. What was needed, most clearly, was a club that would be the bricks'n'mortar manifestation of New Order's music. It could be Factory artwork that you could walk into, get blasted into, fall in love in, dance in, slump in, perform in or work in. Jones, who soon allowed his own plans for a new venue to be truly swamped by the Factory enthusiasm, found himself duly whisked along. The summer of 1981 was spent seeking out premises. A ghostly marina on the corner of Whitworth Street didn't seem particularly appealing at first, although Howard Jones was duly hired as manager of . . . well . . . of something. One day he would manage the club. It wasn't the tightest agreement. It never was. It never would be.

Ben Kelly, who would carve himself into architectural infamy by his staggeringly innovative work on the Haçienda, had met Pete Saville through Saville's girlfriend, who worked, perhaps not surprisingly, in the office of Lynne Franks PR. It was just after Orchestral Manouevres In The Dark had moved to London's Din Disc (Virgin), and Saville, based more and more in London, had been musing over the band's first major label album sleeve. Saville and Kelly, suitably inspired by some perforated steel panels on a door inside the Lynne Franks PR office, twisted this vision into the album sleeve – an orange inner sleeve showing through a mass of diagonal holes in a blue outer sleeve.

Perhaps because of the strangeness of its source, and Saville and Kelly's skill in capturing the effect, the sleeve immediately leapt from the pack, won a barrage of awards as well as, one might as well note, succinctly capturing the pristine steely synth sound of OMD's early music. Kelly had semi-famously designed the 'Howie' shop in London, which had so impressed Saville, who had suggested that Factory might use his talents for the interior of the mooted nightclub. Arriving in Manchester, rather numbed by Factory's apparent enthusiasm, Kelly was picked up by a buoyant Howard Jones, who, after bundling Kelly into his sports car and careering across town, ushered him into the deserted yacht marina, situated rather clumsily on the corner of Whitworth Street West. Inside stood Rob Gretton and Alan Erasmus, strolling around, rubbing their chins, gazing upwards into the surprising interior shell of the building. Dreaming, but not quite knowing what to do. After providing Kelly with a brief guided tour around what was, once past the showroom area, little more than a dusty, featureless warehouse, they swiftly offered him the job. Kelly had, thankfully, immediately thought the building to be 'fantastic'. In true Factory style, however, Kelly's brief was muddled and the budget impossible to pin down. A whole mass of work dauntingly ahead of him, his task was hardly eased by Factory's disparate mesh of ideas and notions. Gretton's vision for the club included a stage at the far end – where the main bar would eventually be situated – while Wilson saw it stretching across the front elevation. Both Wilson and Gretton had been spending time in America with the first tours of New Order and A Certain Ratio and had been impressed by a new breed of Stateside venues, like New York's Danceteria, run by the inimitable Ruth Polski. Danceteria was a three-storey mix of dancefloors and stages, a melting pot where dance and rock merged together with stunning and unlikely ease, and with energetic, positive results. Such a mix had never occurred in England, despite the efforts of a few brave NME and Sounds journalists. In Manchester, the Death To Disco movement (well, it wasn't really a movement, more a scattering of badges) seemed prevalent. Despite their American-inspired vision, the prospect of building a purpose-built club which would serve as both disco and venue seemed sheer lunacy. No such scene existed. Neither Wilson nor Gretton or indeed Erasmus can, to this day, explain quite how they envisaged this club taking off from a sceneless base.

'It *was* fucking mental,' states Wilson, 'and as it all came together, this bright, glitzy New York disco, I remember being asked just who I expected to come into the club. True enough, the only "kids" I had seen had been in Rafters, six months earlier, huddled in raincoats watching some band. It was the most simple question of all and I had no answer. We had invested such a lot of money and time in this business which would supply ... err, what market exactly? I did sit down at one point and wonder what the hell we were doing.'

Or, for that matter, what the hell New Order were doing. Factory had approached them, with Rob donning two hats, fired with enthusiasm and selling the band the idea. New Order, who played absolutely no part in the club's design, initially agreed to put £70,000 into the 'club fund', only to be approached again and again and again as Kelly's ambitious designs swelled uncontrollably, changing the club into something else entirely. New Order were, quite clearly, expecting the whole thing to finish up little more than another dingy dump, complete with dimp-scorched carpets, darkened corners and very bad beer. They were as surprised as anyone else when they first wandered through those doors.

(Kelly's designs were both intricate and practical. The famous sprung maple dancefloor and numerous kinds of industrial rubber flooring, the granite and concrete bar tops, and even the celebrated 'bollards', all had obvious hard-wearing uses. The bollards positioned, basically, to prevent people tripping on to the dancefloor – if you will excuse the expression – and getting their high heels caught in the cats' eyes, were in fact Allegrini Flexible Verge Posts, supplied as standard issue to local councils for £4.50 each. For a while Kelly became obsessed with this feint 'motorway' theme and attempted to paint lines on the floor with preformed thermoplastic road marking. He failed, perhaps thankfully, for surely it would have been taking things a little too far.)

Of all the Factory elite, only Martin Hannett refused to enter into the rather wild entrepreneurial spirit. He disliked the idea intensely. He disliked discotheques for a start, and thought them useful only as fleeting rock venues. That, in Hannett's eyes, was exactly what a rock venue should be – fleeting. To house a scene for a while, until the scene moved on somewhere else. 'It is impossible,' Hannett reasoned, 'to simply create something by building an empty space.' Hannett, angered by Factory's apparent stupidity, wrenched himself away from the Factory pack. His sulk was intensified, no doubt, by the fact that he had hoped that Factory would sensibly use their cash reserves to purchase a Fairlight (computer synthesizer, used to perfection by Trevor Horn) if not a studio. Investing in sound, to Hannett, seemed a wholly creative thing to do. To invest in bricks and mortar merely served to create a backdrop, a blank canvas.

'Who wants to run a fucking nightclub? It's the most horrible job in the world,' he once screamed over drinks in Stockport's Wellington pub, in front of a bemused local band who had no Factory connections whatsoever, and had merely travelled down to meet Hannett under the impression that he might wish to chat about *their* music. Hannett, ears firmly closed, had no intention of working with them. He merely wished to unleash his irrelevant frustrations upon them.

And the frustrations would fester most horribly. One recalls the sight of Tony Wilson, trendily encamped in a simmeringly hot hotel room in New York. It was the night of the Academy Awards, and a fax rattled into the room. On it was Martin Hannett's lawsuit, attempting to prevent the Haçienda opening and, in effect, to close Factory down. Hannett had found himself at odds with Factory, not merely because of the Haçienda but also because of the natural process that takes the state-of-the-art technology away from any producer. His incredible relationship with both New Order and A Certain Ratio had, in effect, ground to a natural end, with both bands musically stretching further and further away from their base, naturally wishing to move on.

Hannett hadn't been happy with his Factory stake for a couple of years. Effectively, he was one-fifth of Factory, sharing with Tony, Rob, Alan and Pete. It was a fairly simple arrangement. Abroad, a 66/33 deal was put in operation. When a band sold abroad, they took two thirds, Factory took one third. Hannett worked out that his fifth of 33 per cent wasn't as much money as the stake he could have claimed as a producer on two (percentage) points. Factory's argument was that the one-fifth system worked better for everyone. Especially Hannett as, if he hadn't produced the record, he was still entitled to his stake.

'I'll never know why he couldn't accept that,' claims Wilson, adding, 'He got paid as a Factory director . . . it wasn't bad, was it? We kept on saying to him, "Look, Martin, you're getting paid for all this stuff . . . everything we do, you have a stake in. Some people would kill for an arrangement like that." ' Perhaps though, Hannett noticed that the biggest-selling Factory acts – well, Joy Division and New Order – were also his productions. Who knows? It is certainly true that paranoia, some of it arguably justified, some of it fuelled by sheer outrageous hedonism, had started to cloud his thoughts, his dealings, his relationships, his work.

The Haçienda's illustrious 'booker', Mike Pickering, seemed to eerily typify Factory's general attitude. Pickering was a musician and a fan, a man blessed with an uncanny ability to spot talent during the weeks preceding the artiste's initial breakthrough into the charts. Aesthetically speaking, this was a most marvellous gift and Pickering would have slotted so neatly into any major record label A&R department in the country – as he later would prove. However, such devotion to the nuances of his own taste would prove initially disastrous for a club booker, the first year being littered with bands on the verge of a major breakthrough but unable to pull a crowd. Rumour has it that the social secretary of Manchester Polytechnic, Elliott Rashman, who could often be found lurking in the Haçienda's glamorous dressing rooms, would simply book the acts two months after Pickering, and practically clean up. Nevertheless, if one takes a long-term view, such eccentricities provided the club with the essential innovative colour, if not initial money.

Mike Pickering was born, rather ironically as it happens, within spitting distance of Bernard Manning's World Famous Embassy Club, the spiritual home of scampi in a basket and Jack Duckworth-style club singers in Blackley. He spent his teens living in the disarmingly plush suburbs of Bramhall, on the leafy edge of Stockport and, like Wilson, Gretton and Hannett, attended a Catholic grammar school. Not, however, that Pickering would spend time in the halls of academia – his true education was gleaned from drifting penniless and sun-scorched around woefully touristic Mediterranean resorts. Before catching the rush of punk at the Lesser Free Trade Hall, he had latched on to the fading mid-seventies end of northern soul. Too late for Wigan, he would none the less spend wild, carefree nights at the almost equally famous Blackpool Mecca, catching on to such 90-mile-an-hour classics as Yvonne Baker's 'You Didn't Say A Word', Rufus Lumley's 'I'm Standing', Jackie Lee's 'Darkest Days', Sam Dee's 'Lonely For You Baby', Invitations' 'Skiing In The Snow', Major Lance's 'You Don't Want Me No More', Earl Wright's 'Thumb A Ride', Earl Van Dyke's 'Six By Six' . . . all of which, and so many more, would flow from the legendary turntables of Dave Godin. Mike Pickering's soul mate, in his later school days and through punk's surge, was – as previously hinted – none other than

ABC's Martyn Fry. The two would form the Sheffield-based late seventies funk outfit Vice Versa together. Pickering's saxophone complemented Fry's throaty vocals and Mike Finney-esque stage stance. Pickering's first contact with Rob Gretton came, rather bizarrely, at the age of sixteen when the pair of them, both Manchester City fanatics, travelled on their separate raucous buses to see City play at Nottingham Forest. In those days, of course, the police hadn't even started to compress the hooligan problem, and fights, taunts, charges and retreats would swirl around the streets surrounding just about every ground in the country, come match day. On this occasion, Gretton's notoriety faded sensibly in the face of a wall of threatening Forest supporters. Careering in hasty retreat down a side street, Gretton leapt for the comparative safety of a rose garden. Within seconds a fellow City fan had thumped down in the same garden. As the chasing feet rattled past, Rob Gretton and Mike Pickering stared at each other and burst into laughter. It was a fun way to meet.

When asked if this somewhat legendary meeting was actually true, Gretton replies, 'Oh . . . yeah that is true, we used to do a lot of running in those days . . . running and fighting. Great times.'

It was in Holland at the start of the eighties that Pickering began to seriously filter his growing love of American dance music – Chic, Earth, Wind And Fire, Motown, all weirdly mixed down with chunks of Beefheart and Velvet Underground – into a club scene of sorts. The club was called Quando Quango – later to become the name of the Factory band Pickering would lead alongside his Dutch partner, the exotic singer Gonnie Rietveld. The club, in Rotterdam, was little more than a dusty clearing inside a disused water tower. Subsequently, the units surrounding the main hall were used as bases for all kinds of creative, media and design work – an 'arts' complex before such things would glisten from, it often seems, every corner of every northern town. Pickering managed to keep in touch with Gretton during the 'Holland years' and gleefully accepted the opportunity to move back to Manchester to become involved, as booker, with the Haçienda, just two months prior to the club opening. One recalls the frantic enthusiasm of his speech as he rang around every relevant journalist and general ligger stuffed into his already bulging contacts book.

'It's such a great club, this . . . you're not going to believe it . . . you are just not going to believe it.'

By his own admission, he had little idea about how such a club should be run, or the ebbs and flows of UK club culture – in the early eighties a profoundly London-led phenomenon. Despite the continuing success of the dated but intense Roxy Room at Pips, which had picked up a few fairly condescending mentions in the glossy club culture pages of *The Face*, Manchester nightlife was about as innovative and fascinating as an average night in the British Legion.

Pickering knew this and had his doubts. Wandering around the still-to-open club, by the side of maestro Ben Kelly, Pickering would often shrug in distaste, especially as the fantastically expensive sound system was being installed by people who didn't have a clue what they were doing (in his opinion). More than once Pickering was heard to mutter, 'If only we could move this place brick by brick to New York.' He was a booker who didn't really have any desire to book bands, even if he was soon to start one himself. Furthermore, the notion that the Haçienda might be a natural nurturing home for local bands filled him with understandable dread. Like many people, he had spent time standing outside practice room doors, listening sadly to the uninspired drone which seeped wearily into the corridors. Almost always a dire, sparkless, sub-Joy

Division drone, grunging on and on through an all-too-obvious set of musical clichés. Pickering was happier in a disco, where the naff punch-beat would at least seem young, daft and colourful. A true visionary, perhaps, for he believed that club culture could become intense, innovatory, important ... that it could and should be firmly at the cutting edge of youth culture.

During the first, famously disastrous year, the Haçienda was filled only with problems. And these problems, stacked ten high, were all too often transformed into complaints. Complaints that, frankly, were difficult to deal with when you had an empty club which quite literally sucked the resources, the resolve and the vision away from the owners. One recalls Erasmus one Saturday night, with the Haçienda typically cavernous on the inside and freezing on the outside, standing on the Whitworth Street pavement screaming into the club's entrance, 'I'VE HAD IT ... IF ROB WANTS TO WASTE ANOTHER TWENTY FIVE GRAND ON THIS USELESS FUCKIN' CLUB ... THAT'S UP TO HIM. I'VE HAD ENOUGH.'

And on the inside, as stated, came the problems. The famous 'booming' sound. The sound of an endless row of double-decker buses, crashing over a cliff, hitting the rocks at rhythmic half-second intervals. The records may have changed but the sound remained the same. The sound system cost £40,000, and was completely unsuitable for the club's steely ambience. A fundamental mistake. New Order band members could often be seen physically wincing as the sound lolloped around the building like a huge sponge ball, expanding and distorting, here and there. There would be times when, for example, Peter Hook would actually remain entrenched in the downstairs Gay Traitor bar just to escape the sheer embarrassment of having to listen to a run of favourite songs pushed through the Haçienda sound mangle. The sound would surge into the 'open' cafe area, making it absolutely impossible for the waiters to take the orders, or for any kind of conversation to exist at all. People would sit and stare and stare, blankly, chewing on inedible 'greaseburgers' and slimy pyramids of chips. They would huddle into little insular gangs, ruling the alcoves. They would sit on the balcony, gazing at the twin video screens. They would crowd in the main bar, while the seemingly vast dancefloor stretched away from them like a football pitch. Bands would often stand onstage, bemused and lonely, helpless and pathetic, in their attempts to communicate with these distant huddles.

Whatever one may think of Factory, however many failed Factory bands may eternally complain about Factory's legendary meanness, nobody could ever deny that the Haçienda was, at least in its initial years, an artistic folly, a ludicrously gargantuan present to a sundry handful; a place of complaint, of agony and, on Factory's behalf, of generosity. The smaller bands who performed during that first year – bands used to being treated as sub-human by the smalltime club owners of the north-west – will forever tell tales of the supreme and unlikely treatment that awaited them at the Haçienda. A pristine, glimmering dressing room, filled with flowers, beer and peanuts would entice in the starry-eyed hopefuls. Before the performance, booker Mike Pickering would drift down into the dressing room to professionally soothe the nerves. Post-gig, Pickering would crack open the cans with the band, sharing and encouraging the in-jokes, offering steely advice, slagging off rival bands, nurturing the bonhomie. If that, and the most reasonable fee, wasn't enough, Claude Bessey – the video man – would present each and every band with a free video of their entire performance. There was a downside to this. Few bands, let alone young up and coming local acts, enjoy seeing live coverage of their performances in raw, weak, cruelly naked sound and brash tuneless vocals.

It always sounded and looked worse – far, far worse – on video the morning after. An encouraging ripple of applause, warming and kind on the night, would seem painfully, sarcastically thin and distant on the video. The empty spaces on the dancefloor would glare so brightly from the screen, stretching away, it always seemed, into a darkened horizon, peopled by a few tiny shadowy figures.

Despite, and possibly because of, such problems, many of the first year Haçienda gigs became embedded in local folklore. For better or worse, there had never been gigs like this before. Who could forget, for instance, Liaisons Dangereuses, performing in stony embarrassment, in front of a completely empty dancefloor while the hugely embarrassed figure of Steven Morris crisscrossed the floor all evening, wondering where his money was going and dreaming of a packed, seething, sweating dancefloor. Who could forget Simple Minds, at last managing to pull half a crowd; a relieved Tony Wilson taking this writer into the Gay Traitor during the performance to explain, in exasperated tones, 'Well, there is nobody on earth who loathes Simple Minds as much as me. I'm offended by this crap, by the fact that it is taking place in our club, and that this is our fullest night to date. If this is really what the Manchester public want, then we have been completely wasting our time. Still, I'm happy to let this night subsidise a few more important evenings. That's the way it goes. I am happy really. You are one of the people who have been critical of the Haçienda, but I think it will come good one day, provided, of course, that we can last out the bad times. Gigs like this help.'

This was the night that yours truly, as manager of a frivolous offshoot of the Distractions, called Secret 7 (which included a curiously voiceless Mike Finney) attempted to prise the band on to Factory Records. Sensing a hype, Wilson advised that we should approach the major companies, as we did, and we filled the Haçienda with bored A&R men three weeks later.

'Your band were crap,' stated Peter Hook on that night, and, for once, he wasn't joking.

Despite the problems, however, it couldn't be denied that the Haçienda ambience was most unlike any you could experience in any other club in England. As previously stated, a similar venture would have been filled with a bouncing, bopping mass in New York, or an anarchistic punky scrum in, say, Amsterdam. But in Manchester, the clientele would sit, drink and, if the 'boom' of the PA wasn't too cruel or if they were downstairs in the Gay Traitor, talk. From Factory's point of view, it may well have been falling speedily, terrifyingly into debt, but from a punter's point of view, with acres of space to traverse each evening and that clean, intoxicating rubbery smell etching into the memory, early Haçienda regulars would be reminded of Haçienda nights for the rest of their lives. Every time they, for instance, wander into an airport, that enveloping aroma will forever evoke memories of, say, the Pale Fountains, Yazoo, Blancmange, Defunct, Culture Club – literally hours before they cracked the charts and Boy George became a household name – or the Associates, or Orange Juice, all performing to disappointing distant shadows. People freezing in the alcoves, selling six copies of *City Fun* per night. (*City Fun*, very much under the dominance of the Cath'n'Liz set, was still capturing the scene, although the magazine's true era belonged back in the grubby days of the Russell Club.) But there were a few staggeringly successful nights. The bizarre evening of the Final Academy with William Burroughs reading, live and onstage, supported by a couple of video films pretending to be the new Genesis P-Orridge incarnation, Psychic TV. Much to the chagrin of most, the bar had to be closed while Burroughs performed in front of 600 people, sitting cross-legged on the floor, like some secondary school lecture, albeit a very, very strange and subversive secondary school. Naturally, nobody could hear a single word.

Strangely enough – the Final Academy aside – the Haçienda seemed to be more in tune with the feel of the day – a great, brightly coloured era of pop was upon us – than many of its regulars, those darkly clad Joy Division followers, still pursuing the dream of the serious raincoat. But 1982 wasn't like that at all. 1982 wasn't grey. It was, as exemplified by Haircut 100, yellow, young, brash, bright and sexy. Those expecting the Haçienda to be a haven of innovative and obscure music might have been disappointed by the official Haçienda top record chart for 1982, plucked here from the club's end-of-year newsletter.

1. Sexual Healing – Marvin Gaye
2. The Message – Grand Master Flash And The Furious Five
3. Poison Arrow – ABC
4. You're The One For me – D Train
5. Torch – Soft Cell
6. Walking On Sunshine – Rockers Revenge
7. Mama Used To Say – Junior
8. Party Fears Two – The Associates
9. Temptation – New Order
10. Only You/Situation – Yazoo
11. Let It Whip – Dazz Band
12. I'm A Wonderful Thing Baby – Kid Creole And The Coconuts
13. Don't Make Me Wait – The Peech Boys
14. Avalon – Roxy Music
15. I Just Wanna – Alton Edwards
16. Forget Me Nots – Patrice Rushen
17. Get Down On It – Kool And The Gang
18. Instinction – Spandau Ballet
19. Knife Slits Water – A Certain Ratio
20. Planet Rock Soul – Sonic Force

Right Anthony H. Wilson, boldly displaying a love of style, good suits and Jaguars

Below Anthony H. Wilson, the television personality, in unlikely celebrity frolics with Debbie Greenwood, Ted Robbins and local DJ Susie Mathis

Above Ian Curtis, the enigma

Left Vini Reilly, the paradox – amiable and awkward genius of central Factory band, Durutti Column

Top right Little Peter Street, Knott Mill, Manchester. Evocative and fitting home of Joy Division rehearsals, later to become the street where the Boardwalk and Factory Too would be situated

Bottom right The Hacienda, wrapped in silence – as the police would seem to prefer it

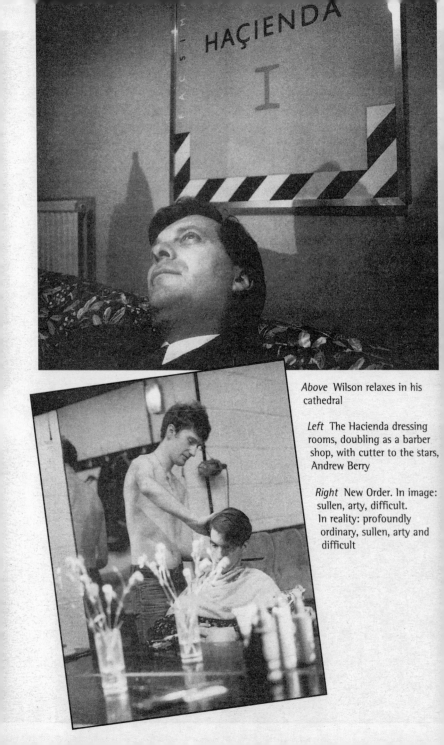

Above Wilson relaxes in his cathedral

Left The Hacienda dressing rooms, doubling as a barber shop, with cutter to the stars, Andrew Berry

Right New Order. In image: sullen, arty, difficult. In reality: profoundly ordinary, sullen, arty and difficult

Above James – Factory folkies escaped to pop star heaven

Left Happy Mondays – 24 hour party people who finally reached their crushing hangover

Above Tony Michaelides.
Independent record plugger
(and Piccadilly Radio DJ) who
pulled Factory into the heart
of the record industry
machinery – eventually to
become a disheartened
creditor

Right Dave Haslam (front)
and Nathan McGough.
Haslam became one of the
pivotal Hacienda DJs but his
Factory association would
end in public acrimony.
McGough – son of the
poet, Roger – managed
bands Kalima and Happy
Mondays. Together they
formed rival indie label,
Play Hard

Left Barney in action

Below The Other Two, destined for a rural idyll on the Cheshire/ Derbyshire border

Chapter Twelve

With New Order in America

NOBODY SMILED IN THE OPEN, in New York. Not in July 1983. Not on the sun-drenched streets, nor in Central Park, where even the lunchtime picnickers, resplendent in their white short-sleeved business shirts, seemed to be anxiously looking around, not for the proverbial mugger, but for an escape of sorts. An entrance to a bar, perhaps, a bar with a fridge. Or an ice-cream seller. Any symbol of coldness would do. The heat – wet, enveloping, strangulating heat – had drained the city's enormous energy reserves. Any kind of physical movement would take an extraordinary amount of human effort. Most people simply didn't bother. People would stand on street corners . . . just stand! The odd street gang down on the romantically hydrant-drenched corners of Brooklyn had submitted also to the levelling, all-consuming heat. They seemed too wrapped in apathy to even attempt menacing leers. All forms of conflict, in the daylight hours at least, had seemingly been relaxed, if they hadn't not ceased altogether. The buildings, so famously huddled, emitted a similar aura of resignation. They silently swayed, and shimmered, weirdly, as wave after wave of heat haze drifted up from the pavements. No city in England – no, not even Leeds – can prepare the first-time visitor for this dramatic sight. Manhattan, standing in heat-dazed silence; dreamy by day, severe and threatening by night.

The twin towers of the World Trade Center winked and swayed with silent menace as we soaked in the sight from the rooftop of Simon Topping's Brooklyn apartment. Topping had semi-famously exited the grip of A Certain Ratio during the previous year, intent (or so he claimed) on studying congas and rhythm in New York. As it turned out, his apartment was exactly the kind of place one might naïvely expect him to inhabit, once ensconced in the city. A metallic lift would surge out of an area of numbing depravity, and deposit you in a loft-like abode. Inside a Bohemian clutter had been transported, en masse, from the rather less romantic Hulme. Topping had found his heaven, or so it seemed. Garbed in the football strip of Brazil 1970, he would spend his days smashing his palms into the twin congas set up by the French windows which opened out, most spectacularly, above the view of a teeming Brooklyn roundabout. Our visit would herald his return, of sorts, into the Factory fold. For he was to perform, on bongos, with Mike Pickering's Quando Quango, during their short stint supporting New Order. Topping proudly claimed to be blissfully ignorant of New Order's rise from the debris of Joy Division, although his claim never to have heard 'Blue Monday' was taken with a noticeable pinch of salt.

'I love that Quando song, "Love Tempo",' he stated, upon our arrival. 'I've been practising like mad.'

Upstairs on the roof, with the aforementioned twin towers winking and swaying, as if standing guard over their fledgling city, the prospect of New Order's imminent arrival fuelled the conversation. It was a curious week for the band to arrive – almost at the end of a short but difficult American tour. Their arrival had already been heralded by a lavish peppering of stark Peter Saville posters which gazed emptily down from a thousand walls in varying degrees of decrepitude. The band would arrive two days into the third New Music Seminar – a three-day orgy of blatant music business sycophancy and hedonism centred by day in and around the New York Hilton and by night in venues scattered across Manhattan. A most 'un-New Order' gathering, one would think. On the other hand, a barrage of free cocktails and the chance to run rampant through a fairly heady cross-section of America's rock biz hierarchy, taking the piss along the way in a truly Salfordian manner, would surely prove too good an opportunity to miss.

Factory's representation at this particular seminar would be strangely lacking the figure of Tony Wilson. This seemed an odd omission, even then, in the days before the annual event would, in part, become the inspiration for the initially local-based In The City seminar which so controversially heralded the beginning of the nineties back in Manchester. Wilson would, during the coming years, spend many hours extolling the virtues of the New Music Seminar. But, in 1983, Factory's thin representation came in the form of Mike Pickering, who had been hoisted on to the clubs and venues panel, New Order tour manageress Ruth Polski (also the promoter of the Danceteria venue, a close New York cousin of the Haçienda, although her Factory credentials seemed tenuous to say the least) and Michael Shamberg, representing Ikon, Factory's video wing in New York.

It was difficult to imagine Mike Pickering falling effortlessly into the music business camaraderie, especially the Mike Pickering who spent most of the evening of 4 July 1983 rolling about Simon Topping's rooftop in an inebriated and rather juvenile bout of mock wrestling with fellow Manchester City fan Kevin Cummins.

It was also difficult to imagine that this unpretentious Mike Pickering would one day become one of the great innovatory forces, both as artist and visionary, in the ocean of dance music that would, as we edged into the nineties, swamp the commercial music world.

However, at 5.30 p.m. the following day, after several tequilas gulped down in a nearby basement bar, Pickering joined the 'Club Management and Promotion' seminar in the Hilton's Mercury Ballroom, and, during his introduction, announced to the world that, 'All cities need a cathedral . . . and we built ours (the Haçienda) and I have to ask, what exactly is New Music?'

Perhaps not surprisingly, nobody answered this query. Perhaps nobody really knew themselves – or really cared – in the wake of a day drifting from record company reception to record company reception, brushing aside endless hovering reps and sycophants, accepting the plethorous freebies and, especially, Toto Coelo cocktails, canapés and bottles of Bud by the dozen. Everyone in the seminar was equally guilty of rampant sycophancy, however; even the apparently blasé Factory-based trio of Pickering, Shamberg and Polski, all of whom would stop in corridors to chat to Bob Geldof, or swap Brit-pop gossip with some blackly bedenimed A&R man over from London, or just to gently take the piss out of the omnipresent American gush.

'Ooohhh my Gawd, have you seen Billy Idol? That guy is soooah hot!' or, 'Toni? Toni Basil? Is that really you? Hey, it's been so long . . . how the hell are you?' or, 'Hey, Jim, guess what? I just shared a lift with Tom Petty . . . maaan, I could have kissed that cat's feet.'

'Hey, I'll tell you something,' stated Pickering, 'these Yanks are fucking mental. They really go for all the showbiz shite . . . it's good fun, though, ain't it? I just hope some of the bastards manage to catch Quando tomorrow night.'

Later, drifting from the Hilton's unholy maelstrom, Pickering and his Quando partner, Rietveld, stopped by the kind of bar one might imagine Tom Waits to be crashed out in – and on this occasion it was quite conceivable that he was – and fell into an intense heart to heart, heavily fuelled by the huge, black, nervous cloud that had darkened their trip so far; the fact that, in 24 hours time, they would be stepping out in front of an intense New York crowd at the legendary nucleus of disco, the Paradise Garage.

'I mean, it's all right for New Order, because people will have come to see them, but nobody knows who we are,' bleated Gonnie, her European accent attracting glances from the blue collar contingent at the bar. 'I'm scared and I'm hot ... that's not a pleasant combination.'

'Don't worry,' consoled Pickering, not entirely convincingly, 'they are just people, and people will latch on to the beat. They'll be there to have a good time – and we have Simon ... it will give us a bit of added depth. It'll be brilliant, Gonnie, honestly ... you'll see.'

There was, perhaps naturally for New York, another dimension to the city's atmosphere, or at least the part of it that enveloped the Factory crew. It came in the form of a constant beat, mainly eminating from the giant beatbox that had been, apparently, welded to the shoulder of a peripheral Factory helper. From these speakers came the omnipresent boom boom boom of the truly magnificent WBLS radio station, a constant smacking disco mix, segueing together all the city's essential noises, cementing the moment. Everywhere he wandered, little black kids would be spinning and worm-wiggling behind him. The sight of those twin towers might forever, at least in my mind, be associated with Freeez's 'IOU', with lesser known noises like 'WICKI WICKI WICKI WOOO ... WICKI WOOO', D. Train's 'Buffalo Bill', Malcolm McLaren's 'Buffalo Gals', Billie Jean's 'Do It Again', and Ashford and Simpson's 'Just Be Good To Me' all thrown in the pot, stirred up by the local DJs, blasted across the beatboxes. The noise, disturbed even further by interference from the owners of these beatboxes mixing in their own recordings, was truly, truly DIY radio. I had never seen it before and I have never seen it since. On the beatbox, and probably only on beatbox, came another record, so close to Freeez's 'IOU' that nobody could ever spot the joins. This strange record turned out to be New Order's 'Confusion', destined to become their least acclaimed single. Some barely regard it as a New Order single at all, believing it to be 90 per cent the work of New York producer Arthur Baker, gargantuan king of hip hop. There is some truth in this belief. After all, its aforementioned close companion, 'IOU', was also the work of Baker. Nevertheless, finding two records so perfectly enmeshed proved to be a gift for those who would mix and match, often with hilarious results. Even greater mixes were predicted, when WBLS managed to get their hands on 'Confusion'. For the duration of our stay, it was the weird rising synth of 'IOU' that seemed to remain in echoey omnipresence around Manhattan's famously thronging streets.

By night, the New Music Seminar changed, in atmosphere and in shape. Even the general public were allowed into the gigs, to swell the numbers in front of the stage, of course, but not to gain admittance to the unashamedly elitist parties. This was the situation at the Danceteria, a strange, three-storey venue where Aztec Camera and Malcolm McLaren would perform, both admirably, although the sport of star-spotting – 'Hey maaan, there's that chick from Haysi Fantayzee' and 'Oh my Gawd, there's Madonna' – would provide the evening's most entertaining activity.

Nobody noticed New Order though, as they crept into the club, slumping before the second-storey bar, Barney's facial features particularly glazed and stony, barely recognising – or so it seemed – quite where he was. Hooky fell from a stool while Steve Morris, at least in an attempt to retain a degree of sobriety, offered, 'It's so weird here . . . this seminar thing. It's like Woodstock. All these people are here and none of them really knows why. You know [the sobriety was fading fast], I'll tell you one thing about New York. It's a fucking shithole. The most horrible town on earth. When we were back in Macclesfield we used to dream of coming here and in Manchester we always said that New York was its twin town. That's an insult to fucking Manchester that is. It's much better out on the west coast . . . we really enjoy it more out there. Which is a bit weird because people say we have a New York sound but, I don't know, I think the west coast kids are better . . . they don't brag so much. They don't claim to have invented anything . . . apart from surfing. And they take you for what you are. It is really odd, but I think they are more into the star trip here than in Hollywood, though maybe it seems worse because of this bloody seminar. All these record company bastards . . . it's a scream, isn't it? Can you imagine such a thing happening in Manchester? I mean, we haven't been to any of the seminars . . . don't need to go really. I've seen these things before. Ruth's all buoyed up by it . . . and all her friends are behind it, really, but we tend to want to get away from all that stuff when we relax.'

By this time, the New Order entourage, led by buoyant birthday boy Gretton, had moved to the elite rooftop garden, where cocktails and badges were handed around, and agents and journalists circled with predatory intent. Gretton held court and, exuding Wythensharian arrogance, proceeded to engulf anyone who approached with a barrage of unwarranted and rather puerile insults.

'Actually, I'm saving the worst for that big Dutch twat, Anton Corbijn [the photographer]. He's coming tomorrow, with Chris Bohn from the *NME*. I'm really going to give him some stick.'

This information wasn't entirely welcome, not to my ears at least. After all, I had just flown, arm in arm with Kevin

Cummins, over from Gatwick, at the expense of *Sounds*, intent on securing an interview that would be spiced by exclusivity. To be informed that the *NME* were also honing in at the band's invitation, presumably intent also on securing exclusivity, was a mite disturbing. With my future at *Sounds* in serious jeopardy – it would become the last piece I was ever given – I tried to contain my disappointment, and approached Gretton with what I believed to be a strangely forgiving amount of reserve.

'Rob, you sneaky, lousy, cheating scumbag!' I eloquently informed him. 'Why have you done this?'

'Oh, relax, maan,' he replied, in his customary conciliatory manner. 'I got you to New York . . . what more do you want?'

Hooky, meanwhile, awash with alcohol, had fallen into a soporific slump at the bar, enough to cause him to miss Gretton's impromptu birthday party, to which all and sundry were invited, in the room below. Barney's face could not be prised from the bar top while Steve Morris, still apparently game for a good night out, purchased bottle after bottle of Budweiser.

Steve Morris: 'This has been the best tour we have ever done. We've enjoyed it so much. It's been really chaotic, though. Totally fucking crazy. We've been driven along by Ruth Polski on this minibus thing . . . all of us completely stoned by this incredible dope that Rob has been handing around. I'm not sure where he got it . . . but it has added a certain paranoia to this trip, I can tell you.'

July 6th began, naturally, at 3 p.m. in the foyer of New Order's hotel. None of the band managed to make it across to the Hilton for the seminar – despite a plethora of invitations, all had completely forgotten about it. Gillian and Steve sat, in stony silence, gazing into two orange juices, cigarettes alight, casting occasional glances towards the besuited sports team – baseball?

– who jostled above them. Ten minutes later, Steve, at the wheel of a hired Buick, was swearing with intent.

'I've been driving five minutes in this fucking city and my bottle has completely gone,' he complained.

'Well, I can't drive, I'm on holiday. I'll navigate,' replied Gretton, his navigational prowess not entirely in convincing evidence, as we jostled through the unholy throng of Chinatown.

Amazingly, Paradise Garage would soon loom before us, giant, dark and intimidating from the outside, light grey and cavernous inside. Fittingly, for the spiritual home of disco – the Paradise Garage was the 'house' venue for Sylvester – a bewildering network of lighting systems sagged from the roof. Soundman Oz Clarke sat cross-legged in the centre of the stage, head held submissively in his hands while the road crew, brimming with mutinous sarcasm, flitted around, poking in the final scattering of plugs. The soundcheck had yet to begin. Barney had gone for an orange juice. Hooky had disappeared. Barney returned. Hooky returned. Gillian and Steve had exited for a nearby diner. Barney had followed. Barney returned. Hooky disappeared. Gillian and Steve returned. Barney disappeared. Hooky returned. Steve disappeared. Gillian went to find Steve. Barney returned. Oz looked at Rob, pleadingly. Rob addressed the situation with calmness and sympathy.

'Sod this, I'm going up on the roof to sunbathe,' he stated, which was not altogether what the situation demanded.

A film crew, sullen and irritable, had arrived, intent on filming the day, the results to be filtered into the promotional video for 'Confusion'. The Paradise Garage seemed, somehow, fitting for New Order's noisy foray into the world of disco. To Oz's amazement, the film crew succeeded in capturing the whole band as they trundled down the steps from dressing room to dancefloor, the entire band immersed in sarcastic, blasé rhetoric.

'The point is,' explained Barney, 'that we stick together this way. It's a gang-like thing. If we can take the piss out of the world, let the rest of the world play our game, then we'll never lose. That's often regarded as arrogant – maybe it is arrogant – but to tell the truth, at the end of a tour like this, I couldn't give a shit about anyone else. It's down to basic survival ... it's fucking hard work, this. People don't realise that and if we start letting everyone have their own way, then we'll just be working for them. Well, fuck them, I say. The rest of the band are not, perhaps, as cold as I am ... but I've just grown enormously cynical. Like these bastards who are filming us ... good guys actually and if they can do their work without treading on our toes, then fine.'

This was a confusing little outburst, delivered in earnest in the shadows behind a speaker stack. A defiant bout of confidence, of self-assertion perhaps, all but belied by his constant nervous twitching; his words spitting forth to unusual and, to some extent, unbecoming percussive intent. Behind him, Steve Morris looked on silently, a crease of concern forming across his forehead.

'Barney is a bit on edge,' he said, as I looked to him for an explanation, before shrugging. 'End of tour blues, and some of that dope ... drink ... the usual things. Gets to us all ... I think we're all a bit nervy about this particular one. I don't really know why ... it has a weird atmosphere, this place, hasn't it?'

'Hey, Pete!' cried a lone voice. 'Will you sign an autograph for this girl out here?'

'Has she got big tits?' came the somewhat juvenile reply. Hooky shrugged apologetically, before clambering onstage, strapping his bass on low ... low ... lower than ever before. A mere six inches or so it seemed, above the ground.

'We'll show these New York cunts how to rock ... We have been to LA, maan,' he groaned mockingly, before blasting into

'Love Will Tear Us Apart', the bass line dipping and rising famously, punched across, perhaps, with a little too much gusto. The rest of the band looked on as Hooky's lone performance echoed around the empty corrugated shell. The soundmen scrambled into position. The soundcheck had seemingly begun. The film crew, equally stunned by this sudden burst of onstage activity and noticeably flustered, also scrambled into position, just failing to catch Hooky in action before his final, climactic flurry.

A clashing mess of sequencers led the band into a firey, funky 'Confusion', the whole chunky affair crashing to an impromptu halt at the request of the panicky film crew.

'Can someone pour water over the band ... over their faces ... make them look sweaty, as if it's the gig proper.'

'Hang on a second, mate,' protested Barney, 'no one is pouring water over me ... what the fuck?'

Nevertheless, he relented, somewhat surprisingly, as a make-up girl flitted before him, flicking specklets of water across his forehead. Hooky, equally submissive, stood stock-still, accepting the flecks without protest. Returning to the soundcheck, the band once again followed the sequencers into 'Confusion's funky growl.

Up on the roof, Gretton's bear-like torso, flat across the tiles, was flanked by an absurd array of umbrellas, tripods, booms and photographic assistants and, sulking angrily by a chimney stack, a *Rolling Stone* photographer. Naturally, he had been promised a sitting by all four band members for this most esteemed of publications. Naturally, they had already kept his understandable degree of sheer 'huffiness' simmering nicely.

Gretton, gloriously nonplussed, wasn't about to ruin a spot of sunbathing for a mere *Rolling Stone* photo shoot.

'Are they here yet?' demanded the photographer.

'Can you see them?' replied Gretton.

'No, I cannot,' conceded the photographer.

'Well then, they're not fuckin' well here, are they?' concluded Gretton, triumphantly.

'Well, will you please go and get them ... You are the manager?'

'No!'

Things were not looking too good. Gretton's apathy after another joint, and then another, became all-consuming, perhaps self-destructively so.

'Rob,' pleaded Ruth Polski, 'this chap from Geffen ... you know ... the publishing guy. He's on the phone again. Will you speak to him? Please ... please, Rob. I think it's really important.' Gretton's face remained upturned, impassive, unflinching. A long, disdainful sigh – the kind of sigh one hones on the terraces of Maine Road – was unleashed, before his growling reply caused Polski's facial features to noticeably darken.

'Listen, Ruth,' he slurred, 'I've said it before and I'll say it again. I'm on holiday. I'm not talking to anyone. I'm not interested.'

As Polski stormed away, Rob smiled. 'Oh, she'll be all right ... typical JAP [Jewish American Princess. A derogatory reference, though in this case, mere harmless banter], always over-reacting. Suppose I had better talk to that Geffen cunt.'

But he didn't. Occasionally, the remainder of the afternoon would be punctuated by the odd band member floating to the roof, grimacing at the sight of the *Rolling Stone* cameras, and drifting away again, arrogantly unconcerned, at least in the view of the photographer.

'Nobody,' he screamed, and then louder still, 'absolutely nobody treats *Rolling Stone* like this. This is the most unprofessional band I have ever encountered. Who the fuck do they think they are, anyway? Just a bunch of snotty Limeys. I tell you what, why don't you [he was pointing to Kevin Cummins and myself] get in the shot, pretend you're New Order. Who would know? I'm serious, maaan, I'm not accustomed to wasting a day's work . . . Well, will you?'

It was, of course, an absurd request. Uncomfortably, we shuffled away from the photographer's glare, fled down the steps and exited the building. The band were to be found, amid much smoke and excitable chatter, in a gawdy local diner, entertaining two eager-eyed young rock journalists, working – they hoped – for two separate American rock periodicals. Some journalists are undoubtedly more experienced than others, some are deftly gifted in the art of making band members talk, some feign knowledge and prowess and yet, when the interview begins, fall back on the standard stock of twenty rock questions, all of which have been answered by the band before in a hundred differing ways . . . all of which are so easily spotted.

'Sometimes,' Hooky admitted earlier, 'we run a little competition among ourselves to see who can come up with the most ludicrous answers . . . but I think we have exhausted all the possibilities by now. Personally I'm sick of people asking me if I would rather be playing in a heavy metal band. That happens a great deal, especially over here where people, perhaps, can't accept that it is possible to mix about musical styles and genres. I usually just take the piss . . . Barney can be a real cruel bastard.'

But not on that occasion. Not with those two, the innocent types. Their questions may have been standard but not one hint of cynicism had been allowed to dent their genuine enthusiasm.

'They're just a couple of young 'uns,' explained Steve. 'They are really still fans. It won't last. A few commissions down the road, after they've scored a dozen bylines or whatever you call them, they'll become as cynical as all the others. They won't give a toss about the music, or the personalities of the band. It'll just be a case of diving in there and getting a story at all costs ... making it up if needs be. So, normally, we'd rather just chat to fans ... but these two are all right.'

'So what is it about Manchester that makes it so special?' one of them asked, his Detroit accent wrapping hilariously around the word 'Maaahhnchester'.

'It's Manchestoh, pal ... that's how we say it. Sounds crap though ... er ... nothing really. It's just another dump, like New York. Sometimes things happen, sometimes they don't. Like Detroit but without guns. Yeah ... dead like that.'

The journalist duo, silent and tentative, soaked it in, as if this new and somewhat startling information had to be allowed to blend slowly with their preconceptions of Manchester – the city, it seemed, they had been daydreaming about throughout their youth.

Paradise Garage filled swiftly to capacity. On the door, poet, socialite, wit, music business agitator, New Music Seminar director and legendary nightclub veteran, Haoui Montaug, employed a bizarre system of choosing just whose name could be placed on the all-important 'guest list'; in this case, a 'willy nilly' affair with little logic or reason. Even Quando Quango, back from their hotel, nerves visibly rising from their shoulders like steam, had to barter their way back into contention, Topping's banter finally winning the excitable Montaug around. Quando Quango would, he decided, indeed be allowed to perform.

Which they did, of course, in front of a dancefloor crammed with those who would, had space allowed, have been moving, spinning, whooping and howling their way across the dancefloor. As it turned out, and as the only available space for dancing seemed to be the air above their heads, a bout of admirably artistic pogoing broke free from the ranks. Most of the crowd simply gave up, the stillness, their silence and their refusal to clap causing understandable consternation among the band. They needn't have worried. New Order's eventual reception would be similarly mooted.

Barney was not in a good mood. When Barney isn't in a good mood, the world around him tends to suffer. He was slight, still schoolboyish and vacant, perhaps not strong enough to add weight to his menace. His lack of power had, perhaps, oozed him into irritability. Most people, upon noticing his tetchiness, politely kept their distance.

New Order, after politely soaking in Quando's set, returned to the flower-strewn dressing room. Hooky sat drinking a pint of wine, his remarks becoming noticeably abusive. Rob slouched on the sofa, staring at the ceiling, accepting and passing on joints, chatting to Oz. During the following half-hour, the club management would burst through the doors three times, with alarming force, gesticulating wildly. It appeared that they were, let us say, somewhat anxious for the band to get onstage. As if in a darker repeat of the afternoon's scenario with the *Rolling Stone* photographer, nobody seemed willing to comply. Mostly they seemed alarmed that Topping, rather than choosing to hang out with New Order or even watch their set, had sneaked away, leaving only the remark, 'There must be some floosies somewhere in this part of town', hanging in the air, serving as a clue to his intentions.

'Miserable bastard,' moaned Oz, his large shoulders slumping, possibly as a result of the enormity of his admittedly familiar task for the evening (keeping the sound in some kind of order), but most probably because of the dope that Rob had been handing around, all too freely, as it happens.

(It seems the perfect point to record an arguably amusing incident involving the writer of this book, at the time rather lost and awash in New York's profoundly unholy metropolis.

Gretton had earlier offered – 'pushed' might be a more fitting word – a sample of this offending substance to the writer (not a dope fiend at all, although having lived near Lancaster University for a while not unfamiliar to such substances either). As Oz, Barney, Hooky and a whole host of sundry hangers-on would testify, this wasn't exactly the kind of substance that woolly-hatted dullards would hand around, at parties in, say, Lewisham, while listening to scratched Henry Cow records. This was the kind of dope that caused the inhaler to melt, speedily, from the head down. A swift, admittedly painless melting, leaving a rubbery torso loosely guided by an intensely paranoid mind. If you had managed to induce somebody into such a state, and in unfamiliar surroundings (in this case, the most dangerous and bewildering city in the Western world), common sense would surely prevail. You would look after them, wouldn't you? You would not sod off back to the hotel on the other side of Manhattan, leaving your poor, bewildered half-hearted toker – me – to wander out into the streets alone – streets which, I hasten to add, were liberally peppered with bars crammed with predatory gay 'leathermen', hookers, pimps, drug addicts and Brit-loathing Irish expatriates. Those people would be my 'comforters' during the time it took for the dope to wear off/return me to something approaching an only marginally altered state – my normal state, as it happens. I recited a blurry description of my adventures during this period to Gretton who, at regular intervals, would roar with infectious laughter, frequently pausing to shout, 'Ooohh, ha, hang on . . . hey, Hooky, have you heard this? Mick wandered into a leather bar, stoned, this evening.' Really funny that Rob Gretton. Real funny guy.)

Things were becoming more than merely threatening in the dressing room. In fact, they were verging on the seriously, knife-wielding nasty. Gretton, whose aura of cool may still be legendary around the Kippax but was in serious danger of deserting him at that moment, was mouthing something along the lines of, 'Look chaps, I think you had better get on that stage or we'll all be murdered here ... I don't think these guys are kidding.'

It was, in fact, becoming very ugly indeed. It would later transpire, and this might not come as such a shock to many people, that New York club owners are not really the kind of folk that one would wish to unduly antagonise. And yet these guys were, indeed, unduly antagonised. One full day of soaking in New Order's blasé attitude and brazen insults and complete lack of respect had taken its toll. These guys were not taking it any more. This band would have to get their fat Limey asses onstage inside five minutes or something very serious would occur. New Order went onstage within five minutes. Just. Gretton, a much relieved man, lit a joint to celebrate. The entire day had whittled down to this one, intense, hour. Barney, however, was in no mood to celebrate. Twice, during two songs, his foot kicked out at no one in particular. Twice it connected. Quite what it connected with – flesh or material – was never fully discovered. 'Ceremony', 'Your Silent Face', 'The Village' flashed by, amid a soaking of lights and dry ice, the tight disco beats diluted by a certain 'looseness'; Hooky's bass almost touching the floor, blasting out the lead-in to 'Age Of Consent', with Oz wrestling with the sound effects. It was weird and superb. The crowd, however, refused to be moved.

'You're just about the most unresponsive audience we have ever played to. Yank bastards!' muttered Barney, between songs, to predictably masochistic cheers. The opening sequencer to 'Blue Monday' brought forth a little more movement, but not enough to prevent Barney from tampering with the famous intro.

'How does it feeeel . . . to stand in front of a bunch of fucking cunts like yoooooo,' he sweetly sang, as the punch and flash of the song washed across the packed dancefloor.

'This is one for all you Funhouse bastards.' This was the way he introduced 'Confusion', the Funhouse being, arguably, the most intense disco in New York in 1983. 'Temptation' closed the set, the band exiting the stage a full five minutes before the music finished.

'Hey . . . did you see that, mannn?' a voice from the crowd exclaimed, more in admiration than complaint. 'The band walked offstage and the music kept right on playing, maaan.'

'Hahaaa . . . that gets them every time,' remarked Steve Morris.

It had been a gig. A good gig? Who knows? It had been another gig. By the time New Order tumbled into the dressing room, they no longer cared. They were a spent, inebriated, irritable beast, with Barney bitching profusely, as musicians so often do, about the monitors. With absolutely no intention of returning to satisfy the obligatory chants of 'Encore!', the band seemed genuinely relieved when the disco kicked back into action and several thousand Americans transformed into a state of nightclub ecstacy, New Order's somewhat arrogant set already a hazy memory.

'I couldn't give a shit what they thought,' grumbled Barney, 'I thought they were a crap audience, anyway . . . probably too many of them music biz bastards. They didn't seem to have any heart. I don't think many of them were New Order fans, and if they were before they certainly fuckin' aren't any more. Who cares?'

His apathy, perhaps understandable, was fuelled by all-encompassing tiredness. For a full five minutes, all the band members remained in an eerie trance-like silence, a sleeping camaraderie, unbroken and impenetrable, especially from the occasional barbed roadie quip or even Mancunian guffaws from Mike Pickering. The silence dissolved slowly, to be replaced by guarded post-gig rhetoric and Barney's infectious cynicism.

'Only two more gigs to go and then at last a rest,' he drawled, sinking slowly across an armchair, his bare legs flopping lazily over one armrest, his outstretched neck arched over the other. As if in parody, a hand reached forward and placed a joint between his welcoming lips, while a bottle of Bud was tightly clutched, somewhat lewdly, between his legs. It was a slightly disturbing sight, this clean-cut vision of dancebeat modernity now fatigued and defeated, stretched in the manner of a post-gig heavy metal drummer or an off-duty roadie. Somebody, somewhere, reminded him that, once back in England, the band had a one-off gig at the Haçienda to perform.

'Shit!' came the expected reply. 'I had completely forgotten about that . . . Oh nooooah! Rob, can't you fucking well do something about that? At the moment I really don't care about the Haç! I just want a rest. I have got to admit that I'm totally wrecked . . . totally, completely, utterly wrecked. I'm not getting to sleep until seven in the morning and waking up at . . . well, this morning I was watching cartoons at eight-thirty . . . so that's how much sleep I'm getting.'

On that somnolent note Barney slid to the floor, stretching messily between the beer bottles and cigarette dimps, the crumpled set lists and seminar programmes. Accustomed to seeing such cries of post-gig weariness, life seemed to continue, unconcerned, up and around him. Seizing some kind of opportunity, though still dulled by the dope and angered by Rob's apparent lack of concern, this writer edged towards Barney. With a lack of sensitivity that would, when recalled, alarm me in later years, I broached the subject of 'Confusion'. It really did seem most odd to me that New Order were currently promoting a single – the final mix of which they had yet to hear – while most of their New York following and, quite possibly, all of their UK fans, had already clutched it to their hearts or dismissed it as a disco cop-out, as the case may have been.

'It does seem odd,' he explained politely, 'but, to be totally honest, I'm just too scared to hear it. I'm scared because, if we all agree, then it will be the next single, and I know that there are white labels just about everywhere, but we haven't fully decided yet. And look at me now. Just look at me. Do I look like a man capable of making any kind of decision? [No, was the most readily available answer to that one.] I can't be objective about anything . . . and *that's* why . . . *that's* the real reason why I have been pretty insulting towards journalists, especially this last week. How can I possibly talk to *Rolling Stone* when I am in this state? Everyone seems to be jealous of us . . . of our success . . . they all think we live these wonderful rock star lives and the reality . . . well, you can see the reality right now. It's right in front of you. Is there any trace of glamour in this stinking shithouse of a room, or going onstage tonight? I just don't get a thrill out of those things any more, and I probably never will again. I'm rambling on now. Please don't put this in your article [I didn't] because I am a pretty pathetic individual right now. That is how I feel. I don't want to play again live . . . not ever!'

It was an interesting though, it must be noted, inebriated and unguarded confession. But Barney seemed to me, that night, like a man in a state of crisis; a man who, if only for a few minutes or days or weeks maybe, had truly lost his grip. He would, during daylight hours, hide behind a barrier of sarcasm. A fairly obvious barrier, actually, though enough to keep journalists at bay and the road crew in a state of nervy devotion.

'Has Barney given you one of his icy stares?' one of them asked a female reporter. And he had, too, although it must be stated that these stares, apparently so terrifying to those who had nervously shuffled towards him, armed with only a tape recorder and the echo of an editor's voice in their heads, merely confirmed the image, and cemented the aloofness. In truth, though, the barrier was only effective on first meeting. When Barney's guard was lowered, or when it fell away or peeled off during the course of a gig – as happened at Paradise Garage – a disturbing bundle of vulnerability began to glow. This, one female colleague informed me, is one of the reasons why Barney was considered – apparently – such a catch for vulturous females. Not, however, that there had been any trace of such distractions during my time with the band. Not in New York or, later, in Washington, or later still, in New Jersey.

New Order, in their own words, 'knackered as fuck', crept away unnoticed from Paradise Garage leaving the club owners to count the takings, rather too excitedly as it turned out. (It was, they stated, the fullest the club had been since they had taken control, though no one seemed willing to state just how long that had been.) Somewhere else in New York that night, a booker from the Roseland venue had been left wondering just why he had turned the band down in the belief that they wouldn't fill the place. Two thousand American kids wondered how instruments could play themselves.

'Confusion', as it turned out, proved to be the music centrepiece of New Order's brief surge through sweltering New York. It had been, despite Barney's protestations, the pivotal moment of the gig and, to be honest, had found its natural level on the ghettoblasters. The band had met Arthur Baker via conversations with the aforementioned Michael Shamberg, the Manhattan-based film and video man, blessed with Factory connections. It had been Shamberg's idea for the band to enter into the insular confines of Baker's New York studio. The band had arrived at the studio with absolutely no song ideas at all – indeed, with the blankness of touring still hanging heavy. As Baker had been working on the Freeez song at exactly the same time, it perhaps cannot be too surprising to see two similar songs emerging from the sessions. Baker even produced his own seamless mix of the two songs together, not back to back, but complex and intermingled although none of the band have, apparently, ever heard this version.

The next day began in the kind of anti-climactic haze that can only follow a gig in a big city. It was the kind of feeling – and it affected everyone – that one might achieve by returning to, say, Stockport after two weeks in Antigua. Somehow, the magic, or whatever magic there was, had all but evaporated and the prospect of a drive away from Manhattan down into the blue-collar abyss of New Jersey and, in particular, Newark Airport, seemed to excite absolutely nobody.

Ruth Polski, buoyant to the point of absurdity, steered the vehicle with expert aplomb. Barney fell asleep. Somewhere else, in another car, perhaps – for nobody seems to have managed to grasp the finer points of the itinerary – Rob and Steve were, we assumed, winding their way in a similar direction. Once at Newark Airport, with the Washington flight impending, Barney fell asleep again, amid the rubble of baggage, dead centre on the concourse. Irate Germans and besuited American businessmen stepped over him as if hurrying past a particularly unsightly Bowery drunk. Hooky appeared, pale and ill, his features sagging beneath the pain of a hangover, his hands visibly shaking, depositing his luggage on and around the crumpled Sumner. Polski fell into understandable panic. With just seven minutes to go before the flight call, Rob and Steve had failed to appear. Showing an admirable, or an alarming, lack of concern, Hooky ignored Polski's gesticulations and sauntered away, seemingly in search of the missing persons. Barney, shrugging himself back on to the planet, yawned and offered the advice, 'Don't worry, Ruth. We're early. Usually we all arrive just one minute before the plane leaves. Boy, do I hate airports . . . this is the twelfth time I've fallen asleep on a concourse during this tour . . .'

For once, the plane was ready to leave on time, on the dot of 2.40 p.m., by which time it contained all but Rob, Steve and Hooky.

'Don't worry, Ruth, don't worry. They'll only be getting outrageously pissed somewhere,' muttered Barney, before falling asleep, an ocean of cornfields drifting beneath his window.

And so they were. Rob, Steve and Hooky sat apparently unconcerned, at the airport bar, surging into the first of the seven melonball cocktails that would carry them away from reality, or at least from the torture of touring; of being part of New Order; of having to face the expectant youth of yet another city . . . Washington.

Outside Washington Dullas airport ('Dullas? Dull-as-fuck!' – Simon Topping), Barney languished, cat-like, on top of a cement wall, slurping on an ice-cream and displaying a surprising degree of merriment. It was the first time I had seen him smile on this tour. I mentioned this to him and he broke into a curious bout of demonic laughter.

'I *can* laugh!' he asserted, as if believing this to be a truly astounding revelation. 'I *can* have fun . . . but this tour, any tour really, isn't that much fun. You probably think I'm nothing but another wingeing pop star and I don't blame you. In fact, it's true . . . how can I deny it? I *am* a wingeing, spoilt brat of a pop star. Not that I am a pop star, but you know what I mean. Here we are living this fucking great life . . . and getting paid really well for it, although not half as well as people think, and you've got to go home and face your gas bill or whatever. But I'm not . . . the *truth* is, that I'm not really cut out for this. I don't do many interviews simply because I'm not very good at them. Yes . . . I know, we always blame the journalists. We always have a laugh at their expense . . . try to get them to ask some really unusual questions but, in fact, there aren't any questions worth asking, are there? I mean, they have got to do their jobs, I realise that, but it becomes a problem when all you find yourself doing is filling in the interviews for them. They need you so they can complete their task. Nothing wrong with that but there is nothing important going on. They don't really care or even know about New Order. It's just a game and so, occasionally, well, quite often actually, we just say tough shit, chaps, go and find some other band to pester. We are pretty self-sufficient and yet, obviously, without them – without the press, people like you – we would be well fucked. We would be back in fucking Salford. So what is the answer?'

There isn't one. New Order don't like doing interviews. New Order hate journalists. New Order don't mind doing interviews. They need journalists. It just depends on the day, depends on how they feel. On how the journalists feel. Perhaps they should just stay silent and let the journalists rave on and on, with whatever degree of pretentiousness they wish. In doing that, New Order would relinquish all control. Also, they would release themselves from any responsibility. On the other hand, would they, by not speaking, merely encourage disinformation? Would it, therefore, be their fault? Or wouldn't it make any difference in the long run? Can New Order win? Can they only lose?

'You see,' observed Barney, warming to the subject by this point, 'if I just sat here now and said nothing, just brooded moodily, you could go away and write all kinds of things. On the other hand, if I opened up you would still write all kinds of things. You would still get it wrong but, then again, maybe your view is the right one . . . the objective view. I still haven't heard "Confusion" and I know that if I leave it any longer then I'll be relying on journalists, on reviewers, to tell me whether it's good or not. Only now, only at this moment, can I possibly be objective because, if I start reading things, then I'll probably believe them. The trouble is, of course, I'm too shit scared to listen to it . . . and I'll probably be too shit scared to read the reviews as well. I'll be honest, right now, for a change. I've spent time opening music papers slowly, absolutely terrified that there would be a bad review. I've been affected by lousy reviews . . . really, really badly if the truth be told. It gets inside of you . . . twists your thoughts, fucks you up. You can pretend to be really cool. You can tell yourself that it is only one person's opinion, that it's all bullshit anyway. Logic tells you that, but it doesn't stop screwing you up. Nobody in the world is cool enough to be able to lift themselves about reviews and things, not even us. Despite what Hooky might say. So it is all dead confusing, isn't it? Maybe "Confusion" is a really good title, good for the moment, as you said. What the fuck am I going on about? Barney, I say to myself sometimes, you are a real boring bastard. Who would want to listen to your half-baked notions, anway? But people do. People are fucking stupid, aren't they?'

Sometimes; some of them. Fans can seem stupid . . . fans and journalists . . . and musicians.

'Yeah . . . musicians can be the most stupid of all,' he concluded, before resting his head back on the sun-scorched concrete, gazing reflectively into Washington's blue haze. He was lying there, with airport buses and taxis and luggage-enladen travellers looking like anxious refugees all flitting past him, for a full fifteen minutes before he spoke again. Fifteen minutes in a half doze, soaking in the sun, inwardly mulling over the absurdities of the US tour. A tour which, he thanked God, was folding neatly into its conclusion.

A minibus, driven again by Polski, took half of New Order, all of Quando Quango, Kevin Cummins and yours truly deep into Washington, depositing us all at the Holiday Inn destination. Rob, Steve and Hooky would arrive, much to Ruth Polski's enormous relief (though nobody else seemed too bothered), within an hour. A poolside lounge doubled, much to the persistence of Cummins, as a photo shoot – just 30 lazy minutes captured on camera; close-up profiles, reddening flesh clashing with the brilliant blue sky. Simple shots which would wind their way out into the world, collecting together for the *Sounds* cover story before splitting up and filtering out and into, it would seem, a thousand periodicals. They would be found, in time, adorning book covers and record sleeves. They would sit modestly on the news pages or would spread arrogantly across numerous centrespreads. It would become one of the few New Order photo sessions that would gel into an essential part of the image. Clean, neat, simple, elegant. New Order, relaxing poolside. A symbol of success. An antithesis to the wintry shots of Joy Division. It wasn't even supposed to be a proper photo shoot; merely a Cummins practice session, a bit of training, a chance to air the camera. Mostly, the band didn't even notice the camera at all which, I later realised, is a testament to the skill of the photographer and quite the opposite of the *Rolling Stone* shenanigans. (Indeed, when the photographs initially appeared, adorning the *Sounds* article, neither Barney nor Hooky could recall the photo shoot at all.)

Lying by the pool, melonballs in hand, ignoring the bundles of holidaying blobs – clad mostly in regulation check shorts – seemed to suit the band.

''Course, it's not all bad,' said Barney.

That evening began weirdly. Chris Bohn from the *NME* had arrived, with celebrated photographer Anton Corbijn in tow. Despite the fact that both Bohn and myself had been promised 'exclusives', and had flown out at very great cost to our respective organs, there was no tension between writers or, more curiously perhaps, photographers. But there was a problem. Be it for sheer devilment, or relief from encroaching boredom, or a desire to agitate or inject tension into the admittedly rather deadening atmosphere, nobody seemed to be able to tell, but Rob Gretton, recalling the darker side of his nature, chose to unleash an unrelenting stream of quite astounding abuse at poor Corbijn who, as is his way, merely smiled shyly, accepting it in the spirit of a joke.

Except that it didn't seem to be a joke.

'Oh, come on, Anton, you big Dutch twat . . . you fucking lanky pillock!' On and on Gretton would taunt, in the minibus travelling to the gig and later backstage, admittedly inebriated.

Even Sumner, not a man noted for sensitivity in such matters, softened into an unlikely conciliatory role at one point.

'Come on, Rob,' he said. 'Can't you give it a rest? What has Anton done wrong, anyway?'

The answer never came . . . and the abuse never faded. Mercifully, several other tensions were to replace it as the evening unfolded.

The venue was a dank, dark ageing cinema, more fleapit than plush. Quando, much to their annoyance, had not been allowed to support on this evening, this task being taken up by some synthesizer-wielding local.

'He's one of them arty bastards,' sneered Sumner, as the dour musician struggled to produce a sound which fell – typically and so, so predictably – somewhere between the strained anguish of Suicide and the precision disco thump of Kraftwerk. This sad affair was, alas, eagerly lapped up by the crowd who didn't appear to own any kind of critical faculties.

Barney: 'Fucking hell . . . what a shithole . . . what a mess.'

It *was* a mess too; not just the venue, nor the inept management, but also the band. Hooky, for reasons he chose to keep to himself, had vanished from the dressing room. He had provided no indication of this sudden departure; none at all. As the appearance time approached . . . and passed by . . . and retreated into the distance, the remaining three members sat in stony silence, their glazed eyes indicating no emotion, not even to the frantic club management who, though less threatening than their counterparts on the previous evening, began to turn rather nasty. Only Anton Corbijn, the heat finally whisked away from his shoulders, appeared relaxed as he jostled with Cummins for the best below-stage position. The band, well aware of the consequences should they dishonour their contract, trooped dutifully down to the stage, minus Hooky but blessed with a new, mysterious fourth member. A member who, for a full three numbers, played no significant musical role other than messing around with a bit of synth and slapping one of Steve Morris's overhead cymbals, apparently in completely unexpected places. (That is, if the pained expression of Sumner was any indication.) Finally, and just as the crowd were beginning to wonder just who this bear-like stage persona actually was, the frantic figure of Hooky could be seen, as if a cartoon shadow, careering down the left-hand aisle, bass guitar in hand.

'HELLO SHITHEADS!' he screamed, joyously accepting the cheers of the crowd, his high-pitched bass immediately lifting the music into another, altogether more suitable dimension.

Gretton took a bow and retreated from view. The gig was easier and somehow rockier than the previous night, and the Washington kids seemed less disco sussed, and more UK in a sense. And in the post-gig analysis, the band agreed.

'I slagged the crowd off last night for being apathetic,' said Barney, 'but they weren't really, they just danced a bit but forgot to applaud. Here they applauded all right, but wouldn't dance . . . like a heavy rock crowd. I liked it, though, especially Rob, who looked such a fucking plonker –'

'What do you think then, Anton?' teased Rob, who by this time was becoming a little wearying. 'Do you think I looked like a plonker, you big Dutch twat?'

Corbijn smiled, in his lovely innocent Euro-man way, and offered a spunky, 'Yes, Rob ... I thought you very much a plonker.'

Gretton fell about, slapped Corbijn on the back, lit a joint and fell into a mock egotistical rant.

'I always was the true fucking star of this band. They used to say I was the fifth member ... I'm the *first* fucking member. Always was and always will be a star ... that's me. Fucking Wythenshawe taking over Washington, that's what this is, miles more suss we have than any of these bastards.'

After a brief stint in a local bar, all retired to the comforts of the Holiday Inn. All, that is, apart from Gretton and his stooge for the night, yours truly. Together we plunged into a 2 a.m. restaurant meal, complete with spritely yuppies on the inside while, on the street, a short but numbingly violent battle briefly raged, as if on a cinema screen or in a dream. Gretton, his glasses sliding slowly down his nose, watched the action over the dessert. The sound of a head banging harshly against the restaurant window interfered somewhat with his enjoyment of the chocolate pudding.

'Is that dope really evil ... or I am really sitting here, eating me chocolate pudding, watching a man get his head bashed in?' asked Gretton.

'You really are watching it,' I said. I couldn't be sure though, but I thought it was real at the time.

The next morning dawned impolitely before it was invited, with that scourge of the rock band, the hotel cleaner, hoovering sadistically down the aisles, offering aggressive little knocks on the doors, dragging the band from their slumbers, despite the 'Do Not Disturb' signs, despite the enormous expense of the rooms.

A long drive was the order of the day – a Polski-guided slide back through Philadelphia, to Trenton, New Jersey. Easy enough, one would have thought, though the trip would be punctuated by Barney constantly leaping from the bottom of a deep, deep sleep. 'Foooking hell!' he would scream. 'It's that fooking dope again ... never been so paranoid in me life ... Jeeeezus!'

'It's called on-the-road paranoia,' corrected Hooky. 'Been getting to me as well. Don't know where you are ... what you are doing ... keep getting flashes ... seeing things. The dope doesn't help though, does it? Nor the melonballs. Nor the –'

The final word was lost, at least to my overloaded tape recorder. Not sure I want to know what it was anyway.

The trip, as such trips are, was uneventful, save for a couple of notable incidents. In a Baltimore diner, which looked for all the world like York Minster converted into a McDonald's, Barney's creeping childishness surfaced as he planted a hair in his lasagne, thus saving him the humiliation of actually having to pay for it. It was a struggle, for sure, and he was forced into verbal embattlement with two waitresses, two floor managers and a voice from on high – from the tannoy system, not from the profound, although looking around the place it wouldn't have surprised me. Finally, he was allowed to keep his precious four dollars sixty.

'It's the principle ... the principle of the thing,' he claimed, somewhat ludicrously, before someone (Rob probably) reminded him that he had actually planted the hair in the first place. 'Oh no, not that. I mean, the principle is, am I still capable of pulling the old Salford tricks? I have saved my money, therefore I have kept in touch with my roots.'

'Therefore, you are still a tight-arsed bastard,' somebody said and nobody, I noted, seemed to argue with that.

Inevitably, in Philadelphia of all places, Polski drew the van to a submissive crawl and then a halt. Five minutes went by; five minutes during which a relentless dance beat punched from someone's ghettoblaster. Street sounds of the day. The Rake. D

Train. Ashford And Simpson. More 'Wicki Wicki Wicki'. On and on and then . . .

'Ruth.'

'Yes.'

'We are not moving.'

'Correct, Rob.'

'We are not moving and we are parked here in what looks like a particularly unsavoury ghetto.'

'Yes, Rob . . . we are lost.'

'We are lost in a Philadephia ghetto. Nine wrecked *white* English tossers in a van. All of whom can barely move or think, let alone defend themselves. They barely know what band they're in . . . or why.'

'Yeah, Rob, that's about the size of it.'

Mercifully, and just as the interest of a small number of not particularly friendly locals had been roused, Ruth began to snake the minibus through the myriad streets. It was the first time that I, for one, had seen ghettoised street gangs congregating on tenement steps, gazing with cat-like curiosity at the drifting minibus and its rather interesting cargo. We slowed to a halt outside a massively decayed diner, a diner which looked as if it had been machine-gunned on the previous night. (And all the indications were that it had been.)

'Well, go on then, Rob,' encouraged Polski. 'Go in and ask for directions. We've got to get to Trenton.'

At that precise moment, with edgy comic timing, ten black faces peered from what was left of the diner's window.

'Do you really think, for one minute, that I am going in there?' enquired Gretton.

'Yes,' replied Polski.

'Listen, no fucking chance. This ain't Wythenshawe. I'm not going in . . . no way . . . er Mick . . . Mick!'

* * *

Trenton, when it eventually came, was a revelation.

It must have been a film. What's more, it must have been some dreadful, post-apocalyptic pseudo punk flic, with rubble stretching bumpily towards the distance, little fires here and there, hooded dwarves flitting to and fro (OK, I made that bit up – and Toyah did not appear dressed in purple rags). The Clash, however, really did blast from the local radio station, captured on the minibus stereo. 'White Riot', I seem to remember. This was followed, absurdly, by Buzzcocks' 'Ever Fallen In Love'. It was as if, all of a sudden, we had been whisked away, back from the hip-hop glory of 1983, back to '77.

'Jeezus,' exclaimed Barney, staring intently at the club which stood, crumbly and sad, before us. It looked for all the world like the Electric Circus. All four band members, plus Kevin Cummins, seemed to share that same, surreal thought. Corbijn and Bohn, unaware of this unexpected foray into time travel, drifted away over the barbed wire and into the vigour and colour of a travelling fairground, itself a surreal vision.

Chapter Thirteen

Subculture – Factory/Manchester/New Order, 1985

BRUCE MITCHELL, 1985 (ex-Alberto Y Lost Trios Paranoias 'drummer', Durutti Column drummer, lighting and interior decor expert, fabulous wearer of fabulous suits, Drambuie drinker, Factory 'character', Didsbury socialite, Orson Welles fanatic, decent chap): 'I think that Factory is very similar to early Stiff, when it was under the guidance of Jake Riviera. They are crackers at Factory. Crackers. I don't think that can be in doubt. It is, though, an honest way of bringing music to the people. They let it grow naturally. They allow it to mature. If music is good then I believe it will get through in the end and I think that Factory take their chances and just stand back. Major companies have to work on a Tuesday to Tuesday basis. They have to push and hype and get rid of stuff ... push it to the limit and then, if it fails, move on to something else. I don't think that Factory is any more, er ... moral than the big companies. In fact, some would say the reverse is true – some might, not necessarily me though. But it is different. There are no rules at Factory. Maybe, in a way, a lot of the people involved, including me, might not know what we are doing half the time, but we do work by instinct.'

Tony Wilson, 1985: 'I think that Factory's most significant achievement to date, after, what, only six years or so, is that it is no longer just a Manchester operation. We are very keen to push the international edge to Factory. We are in New York, Los Angeles, Japan, Australia. That is so important to us – like-minded people across the world, still small but covering the globe. People gravitate towards us in those places. Does that sound stupid? Well, it is true. You can sort of tell who is a Factory person. They are no better, no more intelligent, nothing really unifying, but you can just sort of tell. Instinct. We always did go by the words, "Well, why don't we do that? Why not? Why don't we ..."'

Alan Erasmus, 1985: 'We have had quite a lot of meetings about this ... erm, throughout 1985 in fact. We see the oncoming of the CD age as something very important and an era is about to sweep in which will see people, through the medium of CDs, trying out more and more diverse kinds of music. This will be great news for people like Durutti Column, who will be well suited to the format ... perfect for it. There has been a lot of interest in Durutti lately ... which has kind of got us thinking. We are wondering about classical music, about starting a classical label based on the CD format. There is some incredibly beautiful classical music around at the moment. What's more, it is in desperate need of release. Modern classical music isn't all that unlistenable crap ... it is something that is very close to my heart. May not sell, but certainly worthy of having a go.'

And Factory *did* have a go ... and it *didn't* sell.

(Arguably the most intriguing artist on the tiny Factory Classical wing was Steve Martland, a man who actually managed to transcend the gargantuan and, one would think, unbridgeable gulf between classical and modern dance music. His lavishly packaged classical EP included a dancefloor remix of one piece, 'The World Is In Heaven' which even managed to gain a few plays on Steve Wright's Radio One show. Although the remix proved rather distant from the original, and more like an orchestral backing for a pop song than a symphony (and considerably more commercial), Tony Wilson, typically, opted to place most of Factory's push on the original, which had extremely limited appeal. A video was made, originally intended to be produced by horror writer Clive Barker, but eventually controlled by Keith Jobing – one of the infamous Bailey Brothers who would work on the much-touted, never-filmed Factory movie, *Mad Fuckers*, a sorry script about four crazed kids joyriding from Manchester to Blackpool in a Jaguar. Jobing would eventually work on the Happy Mondays' videos. Martland's music failed to reach any kind of audience although he caused a minor ripple by lashing out at the Nigel Kennedy approach to self-promotion via the classical banner. Further Factory Classical releases included *Flak*, by pianist/composer Graham Fitkin, *Country Music* by pianist Rolf Hind, *The Art of Monteverdi* by Madrigal Singers, *I Fagiolini*, *Songs of Love and Death* by vocal duo Red Byrd and, possibly the most obvious release, a new recording of Erik Satie's *Socrate* by Music Projects, London. If nothing else, the entire batch would highlight Factory's quirkiness and prove a welcome antithesis to the dance beat norm of the late eighties.)

Tony Wilson, 1996: 'I don't care if it didn't sell. Throughout our history we have packaged pop music as if it is classical music . . . as if it is a work of art. With Factory Classical – OK, so no one fucking listened . . . actually, quite a few did but I don't need to argue that point – we decided to package classical music as pop music. Our ideology in reverse. It was a very beautiful concept.'

DURUTTI COLUMN, 1985

Since their messy beginnings, at the point of conception of Factory Records, Durutti Column never surfaced boldly and never sank away feebly. They were just there. An omnipresent whisper. A beautiful and refreshing alternative, buoyed along by feverish pockets of intense fandom – in Japan, of course, but also in Los Angeles, London, Norwich . . . strange little pockets of people drawn towards the increasingly tortured recordings of Vini Reilly. Drawn strangely too, for Vini always received the most curious fan mail. The letters, small in numbers, almost violent in adoration, and thick with praise, would tend to knock the modest, blushing, edgy Vini sideways, or alternatively feed directly into his ego.

'Dear Mr Magic . . .' began one letter from a particularly passionate female fan.

'Mr Magic . . . hah!' scorned his girlfriend of the time, Pauline. For Vini was, and still is, one of the most bewildering paradoxes in popular music. Artistically, he wanders alone, drifting through various phases, picking up snatches of influence, eternally allergic to any trace of 'scene' or movement or 'in' sound. Indeed, rather like the Fall, whenever the call of large record sales began to howl, offering untold riches, Vini would promptly produce something completely contrary to expectations. More often than not, his muse has drawn him away from the expectations of Tony Wilson, too. Their relationship has never been easy. For it has been littered with battles. One recalls one incident when Wilson famously slagged a Reilly demo tape – although those close to the heart of Factory were always aware that such battles were an important part of the process – with the words, 'Have I listened to the tape, Vini? You mean that piece of shit you gave me last week? That thing with you singing and talking on it. Is that the piece of shit you mean?'

'Chairs crashed to the ground,' recalled Bruce Mitchell. 'Doors slammed and Vini left the Factory label again, for at least half an hour.'

For all this aesthetic flirting, and even his legendary illness – for the drugs of Vini Reilly, prescribed and otherwise, are very much entwined into Manchester music folklore – Vini Reilly, in person, has always seemed, at least to me, the most amiable of lost souls. One hesitates to use the words 'down to earth', but that is how he has seemed. Direct and happy to chat about anything, from football to television comedians – indeed, one way into the Vini Reilly psyche is the rarely travelled 'popular route'. Get him talking about Michael Barrymore, or Bernard Manning, or anything at all that reeks of normality, domesticity even, and Vini will chat for hours. One senses that people tend not to chat to him about such things, believing, as they surely do, that Vini is a classic aesthete.

Well, I have news for those affected fans. It may seem disappointing but Vini for all his wonderful quirks and affectations – and he wouldn't really be Vini without them – is pretty down to earth. Most at home, I guess, when in the company of women, be they young and beautiful – yes, Vini always had an eye – or, more interestingly, aged and simmering with memories. Vini Reilly likes old ladies and old ladies, I'm sure, like Vini Reilly.

For all that, Vini would drift alone, in 1985, mentally and physically. You would see him often, shyly sauntering down Manchester's King Street, glancing in the boutiques, nervously avoiding the predatory 'change grabbers', drifting through bookshops and into the hot, teeming, sub-yuppie basement of the Royal Exchange, where he would sit at the same table each day, ordering the same food and drink (apple pie and Appletise), chatting to the same people. For Vini, living a life so gloriously free from workday restrictions has always secretly longed for order, for borders to his days, for structure, repetition, warm boredom, familiarity. Without such things, even Vini Reilly is truly lost. Apple pie and Appletise. (The venue would change during the years – Dry Bar, Gringe, Atlas Bar – as would the menu – decaff coffee and vegetarian breakfast – but the search for order would remain, providing Vini with the reputation of a 'cafe society' dweller, more suited to Paris, perhaps.) For all this, there is a good deal of the 'traditional muso' within Vini Reilly. As recently as November 1995, when the manager of Pete Waterman's Manchester-based Colosseum label, John Barratt, asked if Reilly would play guest guitar on a recording, Reilly replied with a straightforward, 'Yeah . . . I'll play on anything if you just give me a load of draw.' And again, a week later, Vini was attempting to press a new batch of demos on Tony Wilson.

'Have you heard it yet, Tony?' asked Vini. 'It's really, really weird isn't it? Almost like rock music . . . "Fidelity", it's called "Fidelity".'

Wilson: 'I'm coming round to it, Vini. Maybe it's growing on me. Don't like "Fidelity" as a title . . . Jeesus, Vini, you and your fucking titles.'

In the summer of 1985, you would find Vini Reilly pottering through Didsbury on a Honda 70, screaming down leafy streets – well, not 'screaming' exactly, but, helmeted and aloof, he would not notice or wish to notice the hoots of derision from the schoolkids on the corner of Palatine Road. He would park, and skirt past the ancient and crumbly black Morris in the driveway. The Morris and the house, a typical Didsbury Victorian terrace – vast whitened rooms, sun flowing into the hallway through coloured glass – belonged to Bruce Mitchell. Vini was lodging, for a while, in Bruce's house. Conversely, Bruce was lodging in Vini's band. It seemed like a most convenient arrangement. Downstairs, Mitchell could huff and puff, as only he knew how. He could watch his Orson Welles videos – often with Roger Eagle in tow – to his heart's content. In a sense, being just a hop and a skip from the Factory office, Bruce Mitchell's house was exactly where you would expect to find it; slap bang in the centre of Manchester Bohemia, wacky post-student artists and musicians billeted in every bedroom. And upstairs in Bruce's house, in Vini's bedroom, the thin occupant would dry out his photographs – photography being a Reilly passion; check out his intimate portrayals of Morrissey, taken during the recordings of Morrissey's first solo album, *Viva Hate*, which featured extensive Reilly fretwork – and lounging, smoking, on his Futon, or gazing forlornly across the bricks and trees of 'alleyway Didsbury', plucking away at an acoustic. It was in this room in 1985 that I met Vini Reilly for the first time in eight years – indeed, not since the anarchic implosion of Ed Banger And The Nosebleeds – although many times I had sat alone at home draining a bottle or two of Domaine De Tariquet to the strains of Vini's gorgeous guitar. Poor, self-pitying sod that I am. But, then again, aren't Durutti Column fans supposed to be self-pitying sods? I would have thought so. Durutti fans are Joy Division fans who have taken things a step too far.

I asked Reilly, back then, why his fans were so fanatical, as if belonging to a tiny, intimate club.

'I don't know that they are,' he stated, rolling around on a beanbag, joint dangling precariously from his mouth, eyes glazing over in familiar fashion. 'Maybe I can't understand why anyone would want to spend two hours in a smoky club watching us. I just can't see why they don't get bored stiff. I know I would. We are completely self-indulgent, really. No compromise. I think that is why people tend to like us. I don't know why they should take time to listen. I am glad they do . . . but I feel so lucky that I am allowed to make a living just by doing what I want when and where I choose. Complete freedom. But all our records are shit, really. Unlistenable shit.'

LOW LIFE – THE (LACK OF) SPIRIT OF '85

In Manchester, if not elsewhere, the transitional year of 1985 – where rock and dance would clash intriguingly – remains grossly underrated. One recalls a latterday *NME* feature, recalling a Manchester glossy mid-eighties music magazine, displaying the words, '. . . and this was a Manchester music zine before there was a Manchester scene.' No scene in '85? Nonsense. It may be correctly regarded as just about the weakest year in rock's tumultuous history; nobody is looking forward to the day when *The Rock'n'Roll Years* reaches '85. True enough, it was betwixt the second glam age and the dreaded overkill of Acid House and Madchester, but all the Madchester seeds were being liberally sown in '85. That was the year that the new attitude – Manc!, as derogatory Liverpudlians would eternally refer to it – would be born. Manc! A horrid word, a yobbish concept, yet it would, none the less, be the result of a clashing of cultures, where the massive student heartland of Manchester would finally meet, seep into, and celebrate with the vast working-class, football-loving, swearing, spitting, unpretentious, utterly sour heart of the city . . . of Wythenshawe, Salford and, even more significantly, Manchester's hard, cold northside! It may appear churlish now to point this out, but this initially uneasy liaison had never happened before. The furious and time-warped phenomenon of northern soul, which raged from '73 to '79 (although a latterday 'touristic' Wigan Casino didn't stagger to a halt until December 1981), had been a result of an aloof, parochial pride, wholly unhinged from the London fashion spotlight or, for that matter, London-based music weeklies, who would so often openly mock the Wigan faithful. Nevertheless, it had been the Wigan faithful who, unhip as they may have been, would so portentiously parallel the 'rave' scene of the late eighties. There is, indeed, power, innovation, passion in the sticks. One recalls the soul gangs of the mid- to late seventies, in profoundly parochial outposts – Lancaster, Preston, Blackburn, Blackpool, Burnley, Chorley – stop laughing in Chelmsford – revelling in such unhinged celebratory manner. What would it take, we often thought, to bring these people in line with, if not the south then certainly the student-dominated south of Manchester? Well, it would be another couple of years before the two sides would clash, and clash so positively, but no one can deny that it began in 1985 . . . possibly with New Order.

1985 had begun, in earnest, with New Order's *Low Life*. So stylishly packaged, low key, aloof, soft and grey, shrinking from the record racks at Market Street's HMV store; a beautiful Saville creation featuring, for once, the faces of the band members, ironically enlarged and fading to introverted grey. It contained a strange batch of songs which hovered, simultaneously, in the bedsits of studentville and the darkened Saturday night front rooms of profoundly working-class Middleton, Oldham, Rochdale, Bury.

Low Life, much I'm sure to the astonishment of its creators, became a significant part of the soundtrack of the surprisingly vibrant Manchester city centre. It was in the air, omnipresent – albeit intermingled with the Smiths and the Fall – blasting from the record stall speakers in the new heart of market store Bohemia, the Afflecks Palace complex. A curious complex; the place to purchase your third-hand overcoat, your 'dead man's' dark suit, your New Order and Smiths posters, where you could eat houmous and listen to New Order's infectious pulsebeat. *Low Life* was neat (ironically as it turned out), clean, smart, moderne. It was pristine 501s and brown, suede shoes; white

T-shirts beneath clean, faded Wrangler jackets; Doc Martin shoes (Greasys); overcoats (of course); tanned distressed suede jackets; short back and sides that had extended – *à la* Morrissey – into quiffs; second-hand scuffed Italian brogues. It was pints of stout and the Pogues, bitter and pub lunches in Cheshire, or trips across the Pennines to the parallel city of Sheffield, or merely, as with Durutti Column, sinking into an alcoholic haze in a Chorlton Cum Hardy bedsit. There was something different; something rather 'open', naked perhaps, about *Low Life*. Although a fine and undemanding pop album, quite the antithesis of *Movement* and blessed with much more clarity than the patchy *Power, Corruption and Lies*, which had faded in the wake of 'Blue Monday', it would remain, to this day, the most surprising of all New Order records. Most New Order fans will have embedded into their memory the day they first heard track one, 'Love Vigilantes', the lyrics to which were not ambiguous at all, but an open and fragile tale of a soldier perishing on a tour of duty. Perhaps, as has been noted elsewhere, it would be no accident that *Low Life* would be the first, last and only New Order record to date that the band chose to place themselves on the cover, albeit via Saville's misty and distant greyness. Most of the songs seem to contain a most un-New Order-ish strain of 'personalisation', apart, that is, from the lovely hi-energy swirl of 'Sub-Culture', which became a constant delight on the tightly packed dancefloors of Manchester during 1985.

New Order performed live, in Manchester, on numerous occasions during 1985, although their most significant local date took place, bizarrely, not in the city at all, but twenty miles to the south, in Steve and Gillian's hometown of Macclesfield. The unlikeliness of this event was intensified by the venue – the icy, cubic, featureless and difficult to locate Macclesfield Leisure Centre. This most unusual night was hyped locally by the two opposing viewpoints which raged and battled in the reactionary pages of the *Macclesfield Express*, a weekly platform for vehement and often rather wealthy locals to air their entertainingly opinionated views. Many objected to the very notion of a large pop concert taking place, not just in Macclesfield Leisure Centre but, in this case, dangerously between Macclesfield and the plush leafiness of prim and prettily snootish Presbury Village, languishing nearby. The objections were arguably justified, for hugely exaggerated tales of 'crazed, drugged teenagers rampaging through rose gardens' would keep the local tearooms alive with gossip for weeks. Conversely, and to the newspaper's credit, the notion that Macclesfield '. . . should be proud of its world-beating supergroup' was also given a fair airing.

The gig itself, not one of New Order's best but not one of their worst either, was notable mainly because it was the first time many of the northern audience had seen the very strange support band, Happy Mondays, whose ragged demo tape, flipped on to the Factory desk by Arndale Centre shoe salesman and latterday Factory A&R man, Phil Saxe, containing the band's debut Factory single, 'Delightful', had been blasting through the Factory office for some considerable time. The band's name, an antithesis to New Order's biggest hit, caused a ripple of amusement among the Macclesfield crowd and the amusement continued as the band sauntered sullenly onstage before launching into the wildest, loosest, most ramshackle sub-funk any of this crowd had ever encountered. Equally fascinating, Happy Mondays looked like, and indeed probably were, the kind of dubious youths who had trampled through the rose gardens of Prestbury. Afterwards, filtering into the bemused audience, aspects of the Mondays' downbeat personnel would wander around in the manner that would soon become their local trademark, blankly, almost sweetly, posing the question, 'Got any dope, mate?' to numerous, needless to say, dopeless punters.

New Order's encore was late and tentative and anti-climactic, though not as late or tentative or anti-climactic as their previous encore at Birmingham's Tower Ballroom, which had followed the finest date of the tour. This had been typical New Order, for the one thing they had inherited from their Joy Division days was an exasperating ability to produce the very worst gigs at the worst possible time, and produce their finest moments in the most obscure corners. This erratic swaying, simply the infuriating nature of the beast, was often confounded further by the undeniable fact that Joy Division and New Order jointly share the prize for being the most terrible and unpredictable encore band of all time. This was due to one simple reason. They never planned to encore . . . they never planned anything. Therefore, before they could possibly appear back onstage, a consensus had to float around the band's membership and management and, quite often, anyone who happened to be hanging about. This little anti-ritual had reached absurd proportions at the Tower Ballroom after the band had surged through arguably the greatest set of their career. The cheers of appreciation continued for a full twenty minutes before, eventually, the numbing ecstasy subsided and the crowd filtered reluctantly out. At this point, Hooky began to urge the band to go back on . . . and they did, playing through a furious and rocky two-song blast, to be watched by absolutely nobody, apart, that is, from two security guards, Rob Gretton, Tony Wilson and a startled team of mop-wielding cleaners.

'Fucking great that was, lads,' mocked Gretton, 'you really showed Birmingham what you were capable of.'

SHELL SHOCK! DECEMBER 1985

American record producer John Robie collapsed in a heap in the middle of the road, slapping on to the tarmac, his raucous guffaw slicing through the freezing, dead still, Stockport air. He had hit, one presumed, a patch of black ice or a frozen puddle. Whatever it was, it had taken him by surprise, as had the knawing, biting cold. He hadn't expected this, not in England where, he had been led to believe, the winter would be mild. But it was far from mild on that night, the third and final night of the two song recording intended, eventually, to lay down on the soundtrack of the forthcoming brat-pack movie, *Pretty in Pink*. It was 10 p.m. and Robie, chuckling band in tow, had been returning from a Rusholme 'blow out' – a celebration, of sorts. The recording, a complex electronic affair to say the least, had finally settled to await only the vocals of Barney, who couldn't possibly sing, he had stated, on an empty stomach on the soft side of midnight.

Robie, guffaws still spilling from his ample frame, picked himself up from the floor and waddled inelegantly into the Conran-cum-McDonald's interior of Stockport's Yellow Two Studios. Indeed, the studio's interior looked for all the world like a trashed Habitat showroom; a mess of pine and aluminium, carpeted by ashtrays and beer cans, discarded copies of *The Face*, part-nibbled chocolate biscuits, Rizla packets, half-perused synthesizer operation manuals and one rather famous Sunburst Gibson guitar. From a television screen a wild Philip Glass movie blared ineffectively away. Over in the corner, a record turntable was spinning around with equal ineffectiveness, the needle clicking irritatingly around the label, over and over, while the empty album sleeve – Jesus And Mary Chain's *Psychocandy* – glared from the shagpile. It looked, to be fair, like the aftermath of sheer hard work and reckless recreation. Rob Gretton sprawled across a sofa, chunnering away to himself (presumably about the merits of his beloved Manchester City), turning a reefer expertly around his fingers, occasionally breaking from his rhetoric to offer impromptu bouts of rather unbecoming giggles. Steve and Gillian sat by the easy chair, wading through a bottle of champagne, poring over yet another synthesizer manual, the instrument having been delivered earlier in the day. Hooky remained curiously amiable and openly courteous, cracking open beer cans not just for himself but for the odd predatory photographer circling the band, intent on capturing this vision of recreational in-studio chaos. Here were New Order, perhaps the ultimate technical rock band, falling into a mild rock star cliché. They hadn't exactly wrecked the interior, merely caused it to sink into a state of virtually irretrievable chaos. But it was the perfect situation for the band, none of whom had the faintest idea what the film would be called or indeed what it would be about. For New Order, and for Factory, here was a chance to record for free . . . (better still, get paid for it), get a royalty point on a feature film soundtrack (always a lucrative option), *and* get a single out with no recoupable cost, neither to band nor label. On top of that, the chance to work with a top producer and find a fridge stuffed with champagne and smoked salmon. This, Rob Gretton would proudly testify, wasn't such a bad deal, the only problem being the fact that the band didn't really have one song, let alone two, ready for recording. Not that such a problem had prevented 'Confusion' from cracking and popping into existence.

Barney, refreshed, voice presumably intact, had deserted this vision of leisure and had finally entered willingly into the sealed environment of the studio below, with only John Robie and a mixing desk – albeit a famous mixing desk – for company. (Within the insular confines of – our old friend – studio engineer folklore, this desk achieved infamy in the early seventies. Back then, after being electronically constructed by an in-house engineer and cobbled into place by local builders, it had become the nerve centre of Yellow Two's mother studio, Strawberry, just 50 yards away. Its claim to recording innovation stemmed mainly from the session involving two studio owners, two sound engineers, 10cc and the recording of the hit single, 'I'm Not In Love'. Mythology tells us that, in order to overdub the 147 voices apparent on that track, studio workpersons had to stand in each corner of the studio, holding screwdrivers aloft, around which circulated the loop tape. An intriguing tale, and one which New Order, being technophiles, adored. They also adored the fact that *Unknown Pleasures* had been recorded at Strawberry on this desk, manned by Martin Hannett.)

'There's something warm about recording in Stockport,' stated Barney, unaware, I'm sure, of the irony. Outside the studio, Stockport shivered under the grip of an intense, cracking frost. While we are on the subject of Yellow Two, it is worth noting the words of Derek Brandwood, the same Brandwood who ran the Piccadilly RCA office, latterly the studio manager of Yellow Two:

'New Order ... how can I forget that session. The biggest technophiles I have ever come across. The extent of their equipment was ridiculous at that point. Every computer gadget known to man seemed to be delivered, new and in boxes, for that session ... everything ... gadgets here, there and everywhere. Half the time the band didn't have a clue what they were. We had to sweep out the polystyrene padding chips when they left.'

Funnily enough, polystyrene chips were in evidence that night, mingling artistically on the floor with the ashtrays and discarded champagne bottles. At one point, as Hooky lay on his back, plucking an imaginary bass, and Rob smoked, and Steve and Gillian giggled over some newly delivered piece of gadgetry, the whole scene did look a mite clichéd. To accentuate this vision, the Mary Chain album had been slapped back on, pinning the vision neatly down to a point in time.

'This,' stated Gretton, indicating the Mary Chain album, 'is regarded by the *NME* as the hippest, most state-of-the-art plastic in the land . . . and *listen* to it. These guys are trying to recreate bad recordings of old Velvet Underground albums. It is totally stupid. I don't dislike the Mary Chain . . . well, maybe I do a little, but the music press are so fucking gullible, time and time again. Listen to where we are at now. I know we have a massive advantage . . . we have money behind us now and that certainly alienates us from the grassroots but it also opens up a lot of opportunities. Look at these guys [indicating Steve and Gillian] . . . just like kids playing with new toys. I would like to think that, given all this new technological opportunity, we have progressed with a certain amount of credibility. If you listen to that, downstairs, you will see that an immense gulf has been transgressed since "Everything's Gone Green". Since "Confusion" even.'

And downstairs the studio throbbed mercilessly: Barney's newly laid vocals, a little shaky, as always, spinning around the room, keyboards rising and falling all over the place, soon-to-be-famous icy synths, and Hooky's rather understated bass. Off went Barney. What the hell was he singing about? Lyrics, scribbled hastily on the back of a cigarette packet and entrapped instantly, horribly on tape.

'I'VE BEEN GOOD AND I'VE BEEN BAD BUT COMMON SENSE I'VE NEVER HAD, NO MATTER HOW I TRIED AND TRIED, I HIDE THE TRUTH BEHIND OUR LIES.'

Round and round the words would circulate, filling every corner of the studio. How odd to think that, with those introductory synth block chords the pivotal section of *Pretty in Pink* would become cemented – not a bad film, actually, and eventually to evolve into a classic on late-night British post-pub telly, if nowhere else – and there it was, that refreshing sound, bouncing around the studio, drowning out the Mary Chain and Rob's incessant voice. He was attacking me by this point.

Drawing on his Wythensharian armoury, his reserves, he plucked out a reference I had made to him, most probably in *Sounds*.

'You called me a fat man, you fucking bastard,' he snarled, half in jest, thankfully, for my withered and white Stockport frame was no match for his solid girth. 'In that article you called me a fat man in glasses. I have never forgiven you for it, you bastard!' I did think, though only for a moment, that he was being serious – perhaps he was, a bit – and I thought he might, fuelled by alcohol and God knows what else, make a lunge. But he didn't. He just lay there. Smoking. Talking.

Hooky, from nowhere, chirped in. 'I remember from way back, when you called us a bunch of Fascists.'

'Oh, for God's sake,' I replied.

'Yes you did . . . in the old days. I never forgave you for that. You implied that we were Fascists. You can't deny that you implied it . . . you quoted our lyrics.'

This astounded me. It really did. Here was Hooky, a truly international star by now, attacking a poor Stockport hack and occasional acquaintance, for something written, and repeated only in this book, so many moons ago. So they really *did* take notice.

'Of course we did,' replied Hooky. 'We pretended to be cool, to not care . . . but we were just like the next band. We took everything personally and . . . though I was only joking back there, we still do. We may sell millions of records . . . we may be sitting in a hotel in Sydney or somewhere, but if, say, we get a call from home and someone tells us that a local paper has slated us, we would still be devastated. It's a load of bollocks, all this cool, aloof stuff. We have never really been cool, aloof people . . . *you* know that, but the music press has continued that angle, which has been brilliant because *they* created our image and that image worked perfectly. For fuck's sake . . .

though I'm immensely proud of a lot of things we have achieved, especially with Joy Division, I know . . . *you* know . . . and a lot of people know, that the image has been such a lot of bollocks. We have stumbled across things. That has always been our way. We may be innovators but we are also stumblers. We mess about . . . often with no ideas at all and . . . somehow . . . somehow . . . we have chanced upon a formula and that has made for a good sound . . . fuck knows how we did it. I don't know, I really don't. There it is. Some people try all their lives to make an impression and we, somehow, have been touched . . . guided . . . I sometimes think . . .'

At times Hooky thought, and still sometimes thinks, I believe, that a guiding hand had helped along the way. It wouldn't be impossible – and this is mere speculation, but I believe it to be true – that Hooky, if no one else in the band, believes that the hand in question belongs to Ian Curtis. Somewhere, deep down in his psyche, lies that thought that Ian is taking care of business. I am taking a chance here, simply because New Order have never really spoken about this . . . but Ian Curtis remained in the undertone. The successful formula, however, had been discovered well before the sudden demise of Curtis.

Those were my thoughts, that night; that cold Stockport night.

A video was, at some point, slapped in place, and set up for half an hour's highly critical viewing. To my delight this turned out to be an unofficial Japanese New Order video which New Order, with one eye on fiscal possibilities and the other on artistic merit, were considering whether to authorise as a British release.

Steve Morris: 'The trouble with the Japanese is that, although they are technically brilliant, they have no artistic capabilities whatsoever. I mean it. They just haven't got a clue. So we are the worst band they could ever work with. I mean . . . how can they possibly understand us? Impossible. They turned up at our gig with all this incredible colour technology and we told them that we wanted it done in basic black and white. This was impossible for them to comprehend. They had colour equipment and so they simply had to use it. They said that they didn't have a black and white camera. It was an example of two opposite cultures meeting. In a million years they could never understand why we thought that, in this case, a black and white film would be more artistic. In the end we took a couple of surveillance cameras, you know, from the ceiling, and said "use them".'

The finished product turned out to be a disappointingly straightforward, though artistically black and white, documentation of a live gig in Japan. Nice camera angles completely destroyed by over-use of cuts ... and cuts ... and cuts. The soundtrack, similarly, seemed disjointed and frankly unlistenable.

'Oh fuck ... I've seen enough of this,' exclaimed Gretton who, not surprisingly, continued in a mock racist vein. 'Never work with the fookin' Japanese. They haven't got a foookin' clue. We can't authorise this shit ... but the trouble is, we can't do anything about it, either. You can't stop people from making things like this. You can't stop people from writing a book. You don't allow it to become official but you are basically powerless. So as long as something comes along, and it doesn't interfere with our work, we usually lend a hand ... we strive to help these things ... if only to make them better. We have had a few bust-ups, especially with book writers, mainly because we have had such pricks following us around. We had one guy ... Mark Johnson. He pestered us and so we agreed to help him. And at that point his attitude completely changed. He was saying, "Did you or did you not play at the Lyceum on December 8th, 1982 ... I say you did ... you did." I mean, what was the point of all that? He had this stupid mentality. He followed us around on this moped which he had bought with his advance. It was really stupid. So we strung the thing up from a crane outside the Haçienda. Actually, I agreed to go on Radio One – *Saturday Live* with Richard Skinner – with Mark Johnson and I completely slagged him off. Skinner loved it . . . said it made such a change. People normally *like* having books written about them.'

'Look,' screamed Hooky, clearly affronted by the video, still flickering away, though now rather ineffectively, on the screen. 'Look, can we turn this crap off, please?'

It was swiftly replaced by a film of Hooky prancing drunkenly around a radio studio in Ireland, refusing to be interviewed by the increasingly hapless DJ, Dave Fanning. In the end, Hooky, still refusing to answer any questions, began to play his favourite Iggy Pop records.

'This is typical . . . it is how we are these days. We had nothing against Dave Fanning, but when you are doing interview after interview, in radio station after radio station, you have to think of ways to liven things up a bit. So on this occasion . . . yeah . . . yeah, I admit it, I got a little pissed and started messing about . . . it happens . . . it happens a lot these days. It gets more and more boring, doing all the promotional stuff. Dull as fuck, really.'

At 3.35 a.m., Barney staggered out of the studio, a smiling John Robie clearly visible behind him, gloating in the studio, happy that the work had finally slammed to a halt. Two songs, 'Shellshock' and 'State Of The Nation' would bounce around that studio until the morning broke.

Barney: 'There is something that I have been thinking about recently. I feel that we have been undergoing a period of audience transition . . . lately, the crowds have started to look different. They really have. It depends on where we play. The more regional the venue, then the younger the audience. When we played in Preston recently, there were two hundred people all involved in a giant fight. This was purely because of the odd mixture we attracted. I can't put my finger on why. In the old days, it was easy; they were all *NME*-reading types.'

But not now, Barney ... The new New Order audiences come from far-flung places; from lives that the members of the band have absolutely no conception of; from completely separate cultures; from out there in Burnley, Bradford, Preston, Chelmsford ... New Order mean something, obviously, to these people. But what?

Barney looked to the heavens at this point, or at least up to the Habitat lighting which governed Yellow Two Studios. He couldn't answer that one. Not that it was a great question, or observation or anything ... just unanswerable.

'Shit,' he shouted, literally shouted. 'I have never thought of it like that ... but that is true. I have absolutely no idea what New Order are to these people ... we are pumped into their homes, just like any other band. I suppose we line up alongside the bloody Jesus And Mary Chain ... I suppose, to be honest, we mean fuck all ... just another distraction along the way. Not important at all, and I can live with that. Just court jesters, really. We are not part of the real world. I never believed all that "soundtracking the lives of the young" bollocks. Their lives would have been just the same without us. Just different music, so so what? Yeah, I don't have a problem with that. I am happy and I couldn't give a toss as long as I can get through life doing this ... and I would be proud of it even if no fucker ever bought our stuff ... but they do.'

Hence the champagne.

Hence the studio.

Hence the late-night browbeating.

'Last year,' he continued, 'we played "Love Will Tear Us Apart" in America and nobody could understand why we were playing it. They knew the song, they recognised it from their radios, from their record collections probably, but they didn't know it was by us. Some of them had even made a transgression from rock to dance and had, apparently, decided that they could never go back again. Joy Division, it seems, had been cast into the past and it didn't seem possible that a band could evolve into such a different field. We found this quite amusing, in a way. It definitely showed a certain lack of intelligence on their behalf . . . not because they didn't really know who Joy Division were, why should they? JD were never massive in the States, but because they expected you to sit in your little box and never evolve. It struck us that maybe that is what happens in America. Black and white. R'n'b and rock. Opposites . . . So god only knows how they really saw New Order. Oh . . . maybe I'm being a little simplistic . . . it is 4 a.m. and I am a little tired . . . and I don't know whether I like the song we have just finished or not. People keep telling me that it is going to be heard all across America . . . and I just think, Shit, do I like that song? Is it really what we are about? Is it really us?'

Barney shrugged, stretched two feet across and on to the reception desk, took a swig from his can, cocked an ear towards the studio, from which the hiss and pop of 'Shellshock' was seeping through the soundproof doors, and sighed. Exhaustion, one presumed, had rendered him incapable of forming an objective view and, while he waited for the initial mixing to finish, his thoughts were muddying by the second. He should have gone home, really. He should have prised himself away and returned, brighter, fresher, the next day. But something was keeping him there. Something was keeping him awake . . . and he just wanted to talk, to warble, to mumble into the walls and, because I was hovering with intent, he rambled at me. I can't remember whether this was a scheduled part of the interview or not, but he rambled on and on and I just nudged the microcassette beneath his nose. Barney rambling . . . a strange concept.

'Erm, do you think we're underrated? No? Well, I do. I don't think we get anything like the recognition we deserve. We are much better than people give us credit for. We are very underrated. It is really strange at the moment because, in the eyes of some people . . . *NME* readers mainly, we are no longer regarded as fashionable. Yes, there is a kind of "Perry boy" following at the moment, but that will change . . . but if people decide that they want to ignore dance music, which is what we are mainly creating at the moment, then that is their problem. We can't really be blamed for people's narrow-mindedness. A lot of our music isn't exactly dancefloor stuff anyway. What am I talking about?'

I couldn't tell him, but it sounded as if a little insecurity was seeping out of him while he was there, tired, adrift from the camaraderie of the band. He agreed.

'I shouldn't say this . . . I love the band and all that but sometimes, just sometimes, I feel like I am out on my own. As if I should be playing something different. They would go fucking crazy if they heard me saying this, but I don't mean any disrespect . . . there are just occasions when . . . when all this fucking equipment arrives . . . that I want things to be simpler. Well, that's just a thought. I still enjoy the band, but I don't, and never did, enjoy the "celebrity" aspect. I always thought that was just fucking stupid and that's why I got a reputation for being a bit icy. I'm not really icy . . . just can't stand idiots who think you are something that you are not. I mean, look at me. I am hardly Mr Fucking Charisma, am I? I am sorry to winge on like this, right now . . . I'm just a little muddled. There are wonderful aspects to fame, of course. I may not like it when I go in a pub and people start nudging each other. I hate all that, but that is a small price to pay, really. We are so incredibly lucky to be living this lifestyle. I couldn't work to routine . . . I never have been able to work to routine. Even back at Cosgrove Hall I struggled. I am the sort of person who has to do something just when it feels right . . . nothing will stop me from working at that point but, conversely, if I don't want to do something, no matter now advantageous it might be for me, I just will not do it. That makes me seem a bit arrogant. It also makes me very difficult to work with . . . but the others know me very well and they all have their little idiosyncracies. In fact, we're an odd fucking bunch. But what I am saying is that, for all my wingeing, I wouldn't be here if I didn't really enjoy this. Sometimes I feel like laying in bed all day, so I do. But this, even if I'm not sure about this song, is the most satisfying feeling I know – sitting here, right now, waiting to hear the result of our work . . . I love getting that sound, you know. Getting it just how we want it. Getting a song to a perfect conclusion. That is the one important thing. That is success. Much more than how many records you sell. It is about getting the feeling of satisfaction.'

As, by this point, we seemed to be dumped into the centre of some kind of interview, I continued this theme by asking if he was still fascinated by the way people attach their own individual importance to his music. Once a record is released, it has gone, and takes on a thousand different facets. (Listening to this tape now, this 'question' sounds convoluted and dull. Barney, however, warmed instantly to the theme.)

'Oh wow . . . yeah . . . that is what it is all about. Of course. I am endlessly fascinated by that. We have always played on that . . . you know, that was always the plan with Joy Division. To never deal in specifics and let people draw their own conclusions. If you deal in specific situational lyrics, you freeze the music and it dates. My lyrics . . . they may seem stupid to you . . . but they are intensely personal to me, although I change them and play about when we are performing live. I can do what I like. That's my freedom. Great, isn't it? Journalists can't do that; they are tied down by facts ... not me, mate. No one ever ties me down.

'The ethics don't change. It is difficult to stick to them, especially now, with all the new technology, but we try. We never, ever use tapes live. Sequencers, yes ... they continue after we have left the stage and all that ... but not tapes. You can't ignore technology and, more importantly, you have still got to play these newfangled instruments. It doesn't matter if it is a Fairlight or a saw; it's the tune that matters. A strong melody was always the most important thing with any songwriter, and certainly with us, it always will be. However easy it is to play ... and anyone will soon be able to play music ... you've still got to produce the melody. That is the art. We are often called naïve ... people say we are poor musicians ... and that helps us. But it isn't true. We are very polished in some ways. The press was all wrong about "Blue Monday". That was a very polished, professional song. *We* knew we had reached a certain perfection with it. It wasn't naïve, you know. It wasn't an accident. It took a good deal of very hard work.'

Are you still excited, I asked, by music in general ... by what you are doing?

'I'm still excited about what we are doing, yes. When we first started we were excited by punk and the Stooges, now it is a different music ... it is all just as important to me. I haven't grown apathetic or anything. For example, I really love the Smiths. I think what they are doing is wonderful, and I love our music. I mean, really love it. Still. I mean, I know that I said I was unsure about this particular song, but I also know it will turn out fine. Robie in there is a genius. We always work with people who are ... er ... at one with us. He is one of us for the duration. A member of the band. I think what we do is genius ... I really do, you know.'

Lost in his own fatigue, dazed by work and expectancy, Sumner wandered back towards the studio, in which Robie, as if a mad professor in charge of a time machine or spaceship, played the control desk like some kind of bizarre theatre organ. During the playback, Robie danced furiously, ecstatic, spinning and twisting, sliding faders expertly in and out. Like Ken Russell's idea of a pop producer, the whole room swirled with his madness, or so it seemed.

Hooky, though soundly asleep, still managed to beat a steady rhythm on his thigh with a drumstick. The other three gathered around, anxiety creased across their features.

'I think that is a wonderful piece of music,' spluttered Robie, after 'Shellshock' had stuttered to a beaty conclusion.

ORANGE COUNTY, CALIFORNIA, 1986

It was a family affair – a twin family affair – with both Gretton and Wilson choosing to spend their annual holidays just outside the southern fringe of LA. The previous week had been spent in blissful sun soaking in a prestigious Newport Beach hotel and, freed from the day-to-day rigours of Factory and New Order – who had been ploughing across America, on tour with Echo And The Bunnymen – Wilson and Gretton were finally able to spend time sifting spacily through the rather surreal problems of the previous year. It had been the year when Rob Gretton's body and mind had – as at least one theory has it – finally succumbed to the ravages of constant rock'n'roll. That, at least, was the rumour which had lodged in Manchester folklore. The truth was rather more complicated. Nevertheless, Wilson, in his celebrated tradition of affectionate tactlessness, bluntly explains:

'It was a coming together ... first the holiday ... then the New Order gig, which was the final gig on the American tour. It had been a terrible year, really. I had had to deal with all the

New Order stuff that Rob had instructed me to do, just before he went off his head. I had to take over the New Order reins for a while and this wasn't so pleasant. For instance, I had to do the dirty and sack Ruth Polski as tour agent as New Order had decided to go with Triad. That was really hard as Ruth was ... well, close. So close, in fact that she was for a while in love with Hooky. I had to do my consoling trick ... one night, wiping away her tears ... telling her that Hooky, sexually speaking, wasn't fucking worth crying over in those days. Anyway, I had to sack her and I also had to tell Michael Shamberg that he wasn't managing New Order in the States. That wasn't easy, either ... think I gave him a point though, for doing the video.'

The Newport Beach holiday/meeting was, however, the climax of a wonderful Factory family week. Shamberg had flown in from New York. Vini was in town with the Duruttis, Rob seemed to be well again and New Order came in blissfully relieved to have ploughed through to their final gig. They held a Factory meeting in the hotel bar at 2 p.m. By all accounts a lovely meeting, a mess of positive arguing and, mainly, anecdotal monologues about the tour. Suddenly, it seemed, 8 p.m. came and knocked them rather cruelly out of their bar-room heaven and a mass, scrambling, 'Shit, we got to play a gig,' ensued. Nevertheless, in two cars, the party departed for the twenty-mile slide down the San Diego freeway to the gig at Irvine Meadows. Five miles later, the cars stuttered testily to a halt as five lanes of gridlock blocked their route. Eventually reaching their filter, and expecting to be freed from the horrendous jam, they felt their hearts sink as the full five lanes became crushed into their slim fork. What, they thought, could be happening, at 9 p.m. on a dull Thursday night? The answer dawned gloriously on them, rippling through the two cars almost simultaneously. Those people, those cars, those kids, were en route to the New Order gig. Wilson's mind flashed instantly to that day, in 1979, when he had driven Ian Curtis down to London's Nashville Rooms, only to swell with pride as they discovered Joy Division's first real out-of-Manchester queue. On the San Diego freeway that night, the feeling was almost as good. A touch of sadness would creep in, also, not just because the jam had triggered memories of Ian, but also because it had triggered memories of a simpler, fresher, more exuberant, more naïve, more optimistic Factory Records. That feeling had surfaced, temporarily, that afternoon, as they argued in the hotel bar. But it was only temporary. Wilson glanced around at the members of the band – lost really, cynical now, famous, rich, but so happy to reach the end of the tour. And Rob, recovering but not quite the Rob of old. Something had changed. It wasn't just to do with success and money, either. It was merely the passing of time. This gig, thought Wilson, would be fun . . . but it wouldn't be *that* much fun. It wouldn't be Joy Division and the Distractions carving up a fuss on a fag-burnt carpet in London, or giggling schoolishly over large turds at the Leigh Festival, or hitting out at *Sounds* journalist Dave McCullouch in the Wellington pub two hours before the Stuff the Superstars event. Nobody in LA would sit through the entire gig with a broken arm at that New Order gig, so fearful that, should they retire meekly to the local casualty unit, they might miss something truly important. He could glance around at the traffic jam around him and feel the rush of pride. But he couldn't deny it – something had changed. The magic had faded.

JAPAN

New Order's aforementioned problems in Japan are the merest tip of a problematic iceberg which has deeply affected not only

New Order but also Durutti Column – small in Bridlington, unfathomably huge in Japan – and Happy Mondays and, indeed, Factory as a whole. The same problems arise, one would imagine, to a greater or lesser extent, with all British rock visitors. It is simply born from that basic clash of cultures, but the clash, which clangs away every minute of every day in the more central and sober areas of industry and commerce, is accentuated by the sheer belligerence of the British rock industry, and accentuated further still, I suggest, by the sheer daft and blasé attitude often adopted by New Order.

New Order, because they always allowed their instinct to govern their approach to each gig, are too unpredictable to fit into a neat Japanese shell. It has to be said that, despite travelling across there many times, and enjoying quite fantastic success, they know so little about the place. In Tokyo, one of the most fascinating cities on earth, New Order have always remained resolutely within their expected rock-star capacity, rarely venturing out into the streets, moving from limousine to hotel while frequenting, in the main, just one tacky nightclub – a dire place, inhabited by similarly displaced pop stars and (perhaps this is the clue) wave after wave of British models.

Tony Wilson: 'That's true . . . it can be so annoying sometimes. Rock stars are often just plain daft. New Order never, at least to my knowledge, showed the slightest interest in the fantastic culture that surrounded them. It was all a case of, "Where should we go tonight, lads?" And that was it. I never could understand it . . . I am a journalist. I always wanted to get out there. Bruce Mitchell, even more so than me. You would find yourself in, say, Helsinki or somewhere, in some hotel and you would look out of the window at 9 a.m., and you'd see Bruce cycling down the street. He had got up, shown enough guile to hire a bike and off he went exploring. New Order never gave a toss about any foreign culture, not really.'

305

Back to Japan. The lack of repartee between band and promoters often verged on the surreal. If their encores in Britain had, because of their nature (erratic in quality, unpredictable and often very late) gained them a rather comedic reputation, in Japan events often twisted nastily.

Tony Wilson: 'Ahh yes . . . but that is part of the Mancunian attitude. Morrissey is the same, Stone Roses, Happy Mondays . . . they all hate it when audiences *expect* lengthy sets and lengthy encores. And Oasis. Meet, greet and fuck, that is the attitude. New Order were always the worst. They did some awful gigs . . . and even worse encores. They never gave a damn.'

Perhaps the worst situation of all took place in Japan, in Tokyo, in a beautiful, pristine, 4,000-seater stadium. The set had been average and the crowd, in the time-honoured Japanese manner, had remained seated, clapping politely between songs, observing all kinds of ludicrous crowd restrictions. Indeed, the aisles were dotted with security guards – mere kids mostly – physically holding gates in place. After the set, the band retreated for the usual twenty minutes in the dressing room while Hooky, so often the source of the band's enthusiasm, rekindled the band's waning desire to perform. 'Come on . . . come on . . . let's go back on,' he squealed, to be swiftly surrounded by no small number of panicking Japanese screaming, 'NO . . . NO, IT'S IMPOSSIBLE. NO, NO, YOU MUSTN'T, PLEASE . . . NO, NO.'

Ignoring such pleas with such profound rudeness had been long since turned into an art form by New Order and they took the stage in front of, again, an empty arena. Unflinchingly, they strapped on their instruments, to be greeted by the sound of an eery muffled roar. Outside the hall in the foyer, 4,000 Japanese people had been reclaiming their overcoats when the word went out that New Order had arrived back on the stage. Not only that, but New Order had arrived back onstage *and there was no security*! Liberated from their normal restrictions, the crowd hurtled back into the arena, tearing up the seats, smashing through the barriers and engaging, gleefully, in a full-scale and staggeringly violent riot.

Chapter Fourteen

Last Night a DJ Saved My Life . . .

B Y THE CLOSE OF THE EIGHTIES, Haçienda DJs and ex-Haçienda DJs had rippled out across the globe. With the famous club slotted neatly into their CVs, they would traipse from city to city, expanding their reputations, cultivating the DJ myth. Living a nice, if disorientating lifestyle, reaching eternally for the next white label, staying ahead of the pack and then, as the nineties would unfold, tastefully mixing the state of the art with the pure retro, rediscovering elektro, disco, funk and nurturing all manner of specialist niches. It has often been argued, though incorrectly, that the Haçienda was the first club to fully cultivate the club DJ as celebrity. Not an altogether healthy state of affairs, as many of them (and many who 'performed' in the Haçienda) would get a little too big for their black Doc Martins, remixing here and there, gaining royalty percentage points willy-nilly, pushing their status until evolving into record producers if not pop stars in their own right. (Mike Pickering's route to pop stardom would be a little more wholesome and a little more musicianly, as his work, initially with Quando Quango, then with T-Coy (featuring Simon Topping) and then, most famously with M People, would always steer a separate course from his DJing activities.) In

Manchester, if not elsewhere, the best local DJs did, for a short while, attain a 'god-like' status, steering the little clubbers this way and that, literally instigating musical trends.

There have been so many names, of course: Graeme Park, Paul Oakenfold, Hewan Clarke, John McCready, Colin Curtis, Jon Dasilva, Dean Johnson, Dave Booth, Tim Lennox, Peter Robinson. A multitude of guest DJs. But it is, I suggest, the tale of dislodged Brummie Dave Haslam, latterly cast adrift from the Haçienda to run the legendary 'Yellow' nights at the Boardwalk, who most typifies the eighties/nineties DJ phenom-enon and, in particular, runs through the very core of the Haçienda story. It is a tale that would conclude, somewhat messily, with a public rumpus between Wilson and himself, in the Manchester Deansgate branch of Waterstones bookstore during the launch of the Haçienda's in-house book, *The Haçienda Must be Built*, after Haslam had slammed the Wilson-led In The City music convention in the pages of *City Life* magazine.

'You really are an asshole, aren't you, Dave?' sneered Wilson, though his venom would dilute almost immediately. It was a rather crass confrontation. For so many years, Haslam had been omnipresent at the Haçienda, either pushing ground-breaking sounds from the DJ booth or merely drifting around the dancefloor. It seemed strange to imagine the club without the sight of him lurking somewhere.

BRUMMIE ON THE RUN . . .

Dave Haslam came to Manchester, from Birmingham, in 1980. Like so many people involved in the Manchester music scene, he came initially to attain a university degree. He chose Manchester, perhaps unwisely, not because of any syllabus, but because his three favourite bands – Joy Division, A Certain

Ratio and the Fall – all hailed, more or less, from the city. His musical experiences in Birmingham had proved both happy and educational . . . and rather portentous.

'Birmingham was really good in the late seventies,' he states, 'and in a way it was a bit like the Manchester of the early eighties . . . a village atmosphere. It was very involved with Rock Against Racism. The Au Pairs were the top local band. That served to politicise me and give me a music education. Obviously they were crucial years for me . . . late adolescence. I left Birmingham just before the whole Duran Duran thing happened, which I don't think was really me. I was fortunate enough to be at the very last Joy Division gig, with ACR at Birmingham University on May 2nd 1980. ACR played Joy Division offstage, as it happened.'

Despite spending most of his time at college listening to Joy Division, Haslam's spell at Manchester University would prove successful. Upon graduating, however, it dawned on him that he was in danger of losing his state of immersion in local music, which had come to mean so much to him. Determined not to leave Manchester and equally not to sink into the entrapment of a 'proper job', he searched hopelessly for some indication of his true vocation. Loosely, he harboured aspirations to write. He drifted through the city centre, delaying his moment of decision, sauntering into WH Smiths, endlessly perusing the magazines. Frustrated, he noticed that he couldn't seem to find a magazine that suited his mood and soothed his mildly esoteric interests – music, literature, film. He loathed the glossy London fashion stance, typified by *The Face*, almost as much as the gushing inky sycophancy of the then weakening *NME*. Only *City Fun*, at that point stuttering to a meek demise, seemed to suit his mood although, not having even the most tenuous links with the Zero, Carroll and Naylor clique, he felt rather cast adrift. This aloofness, he thought (displaying a positive streak hardly synonymous with post-grad neuroses), might work in his favour. Indeed, he channelled his frustrations into an intelligent fanzine, *Debris*, cited by many in later years as 'the best fanzine in the world'.

Haslam, up until instigating *Debris*, had absolutely no links with music at all. No one knew who he was and, as such, the magazine instantly proved refreshingly free from localised gossip or smug sycophancy. The second issue, in January 1983, carried a Morrissey interview and, coincidentally, the rise of *Debris* coincided with a new smattering of local guitar bands who would follow in the wake of the Smiths; James, Easter-house, Big Flame, the Bodines. In November 1983, a *Debris* party coincided with a James gig at nearby Fagins. While James performed to virtually nobody, the *Debris* party, possibly because 50p admission was preferable to paying £1, attracted over 200 people.

In '85, Haslam, very much in love with the flow and charm of the Smiths and the slowly expanding surrounding scene, spent the entire year in fragile fiscal circumstances, producing and selling *Debris*. It was hardly a vocation although, forever urging involvement, he was thrilled to feel part of 'something'. By the mid-eighties, with the Haçienda becoming his home from home, he noticed that a flow of bands in parallel with James – on Factory, Easterhouse; on Rough Trade, the Railway Children – were struggling to move from demo to vinyl. Intent on filling the gap between the demo tape and the vinyl debut, which could often be painfully large, Haslam instigated the idea of placing these acts on flexi discs, to be given away with *Debris*. This lowly but spirited medium would see the first published recordings of Inspiral Carpets, Laugh and Dub Sex. The quality was erratic but the spirit remained pure. The *Debris* flexis became an integral aspect of the scene which became known as the C 86 generation – the new age of Manchester indie pop.

Dave Haslam: 'When you ask Tony Wilson, he always pretends that everything that happened had rationale and everything could be justified in some long-term plan, which has contributed to the position he now finds himself in. When I look back, I can never see the reasons that certain things happened. I can't think why I started DJing or why I started the flexi discs. I can't work them into any tidy plan and pretend it was all destined to turn me into what I am now. Flexis were an accident. Promoting was an accident. Everything has been accidental, really.'

In 1986, Haslam, forgetting his earlier differences – as fanzine writers invariably do – began writing for the *NME*. At the same time he struck up a partnership with Nathan McGough, then manager of Kalima, later to take control over Happy Mondays and later still to become Head of A&R at WEA. Together they began to promote Saturday night gigs at the Boardwalk. Within six months they had pulled a scene into the club, showcasing such bands as the Mighty Lemondrops, the Wedding Present, the Bodines, Happy Mondays – the Boardwalk 'house' band in both senses of the word – Inspiral Carpets, Sonic Youth, Liabach ... It was a solid base and, four years prior to Madchester, ten years prior to Brit-pop, Manchester was beginning to succumb to a lively circle of heavily fringed guitar slashers. One band in particular seemed to typify the 'look' – the brash Glossopian Creation band, the Bodines, whose great debut single 'Therese' convinced McGough that they were a band truly worthy of his burgeoning managerial capabilities. Though the band would eventually and unfortunately implode in the face of the rising, surrounding dance culture – ironically, as they would have fitted so neatly in line with Stone Roses, Charlatans, Oasis and the Bluetones – McGough firmly schooled himself on the band's contractual, logistical and ego battles, though whether that would sufficiently prepare him for his latterday role as manager of Happy Mondays – bouncing from anarchic, hedonistic band to anarchic, hedonistic record label, and often getting stoned in the process – would remain in some doubt. Nevertheless, McGough's connections, coupled with Haslam's reluctant role as *NME* Manchester correspondent, seemed to be able to fuel the couple's promotional aspirations and their modestly stylish record label, Play Hard. Haslam, however, became increasingly cynical of the whole promotional process.

Haslam: 'When we would put on a group like Big Black or Sonic Youth in a small club like the Boardwalk, we would have to pay them a lot of money. We would have to badger their record label for promotional material, send it out to the *Manchester Evening News*, to Tony Michaelides on Piccadilly Radio, to Bob Dickinson who would write a review in *City Life* . . . or I'd write a review myself, under a pseudonym. I would go into the Haçienda and leaflet the entire place the Thursday before the gig, which was quite bizarre because the club would encourage me to do that. That's how I got to know Mike Pickering and all those people . . . by them letting me promote a night that was in competition with their ailing club. I still can't believe they were as good to us as that, but I think they were intelligent enough to see the overall picture . . . that we, down at the Boardwalk, were helping to build an overall scene and the Haçienda would benefit also. Now, how many club owners would act like that? I think they knew that it was all a labour of love for me and Nathan anyway. We never made any money at all. As for working for the *NME*, that only made me more and more cynical, if not downright angry. As Manchester correspondent in those days, you were never allowed to have any kind of national or international perspective. You were just expected to go to the Manchester leg of any band tour and no kind of feature ideas input was ever encouraged. I was treated like that for two years . . . like a local hack. They seemed to really despise Manchester even though the Smiths were obviously big and James had broken through as well. I tried and tried and eventually persuaded them to let me write little bits about Happy Mondays and the Stone Roses. But I hated the way they thought I was only saying good things about these bands because they were from Manchester. This became hugely ironic later, of course . . . it took me six weeks of solid pestering to get them to actually put a review of the Stone Roses in. But what galled me more was the fact that I wanted to write about things like On-U-Sound and Sonic Youth, but I wasn't supposed to know about things like that. In Manchester we would all listen, on Sunday afternoons, to Steve Barker's fantastic, innovative *On the Wire* programme on Radio Lancashire, probably the most up-to-the-minute music show in the country, and yet the *NME* just thought it was some parochial clog dance . . . that's what made me so angry. We were far hipper than the *NME* . . . and they just wouldn't acknowledge it. I think, through that experience, I understood how the northern soul people felt. I was immensely frustrated. I just carried on with *Debris*.'

The northern soul connection was stronger than Haslam could possibly have known. For his frustration was already boiling into a state of ferocious independence, and it would be this independence that would fuel his new vocation. The role of the sussed vinyl guru. The Haçienda DJ. (Though, since 1985, he had been working as occasional DJ, mainly to cut down the costs of his own promotions.) His cynicism, however, had still to sink to uncharted depths.

'I had grown quite close to the Smiths . . . well, not the Smiths exactly, but close to close friends of the Smiths and I would hear things that, I knew, had yet to reach the *NME*'s ears. When the band split, there was quite a lot of genuine angst and sadness in Manchester. It was like something familiar had suddenly died.

Before the split, people I knew would be openly talking about it . . . the grapevine was alive . . . it was all around the Haçienda, the Boardwalk. And, about three weeks after I first heard the stories, I received a phone call from *NME* editor Danny Kelly. He couldn't believe that my first action, upon hearing the news, hadn't been to ring him and scream, "SMITHS HAVE SPLIT!" When there were people all around me who were genuinely upset. He told me to ring him at the typesetters on the Monday with further news. It was the first time he had phoned me in two years and I had been constantly ringing him with feature suggestions and he was never interested. What I really resented was not the way he treated me, but what this said about the *NME*'s relationship with the Smiths. He even told me that, had I rung him three weeks earlier, I would have made a lot more money. So that started to make me think. Four or five months later, the Haçienda gossip, which was always the worst kind of gossip, was that New Order had split and would never play together again. It was when Barney had first decided to do a solo project, which eventually became Electronic. I thought that my chance had come to earn a few hundred quid. So I phoned Danny Kelly and told him I was sorry about the Smiths mix up, but I had some other news. I told him that Barney had gone solo and New Order had all fallen out. The next week there was a huge banner headline, "NEW ORDER SPLIT", complemented by a ten-column epitaph written by Cath Carroll (rather ironic, to say the least), complete with quotes from bemused Factory employees, all saying, "I know nothing." All of which proved not to be true, of course, but I was intrigued by the way the *NME* handled the Smiths split . . . so I threw them that bit of nothing.'

Significantly, Haslam would duly leave the *NME* because his growing cynicism would finally snap when the paper – and all music papers at the time – split into two; into a wearying and unintelligent 'printhead' argument between the dance and indie journalistic factions. This was simply too much for Haslam to take. In his head, and certainly in the heads of the Mancunians who were just beginning to bustle into the Boardwalk and the Haçienda, it was perfectly acceptable to enjoy, say, both Joyce Simms and the Fall, and Haslam's initial DJing forays at the Haçienda would reflect this diversity.

'According to the *NME*,' continues Haslam, 'this just wasn't happening and they always wanted me to fall on one side of the fence or the other. That's what made me realise that I would be so much happier ignoring them completely, and staying in Manchester ...'

Haslam's DJ career – as DJ Hedd – began, in earnest, at the low-tech and lowly Man Alive Club which, on Thursday nights, transformed into the Wilde Club. Haslam and McGough would put bands on; no small feat, considering the venue's miniscule interior. Back in the summer of 1985, Haslam had also spent time behind the decks at a club just 30 yards along Whitworth Street from the Haçienda – a long, dank, bedraggled basement which would, in later life, attain the dull monicker the Venue, although with archetypal blackened stage and warm beer, the name would be fitting. Haslam had ingratiated himself with a wacky bill post gang from Moss Side. The gang, wild and lovely, some balding, some dreadlocked, worked from a Moss Side Portakabin, and wished to start and run a weekly club. One of them, being a refugee from the r'n'b days at the legendary Twisted Wheel Club, named the venue the Wheel.

Haslam: 'On the very first night, I discovered the magic of DJing to a packed club. It was the most fantastic night of my life. It was like the whole of Moss Side had crowded into the Venue. I felt so proud.'

Arriving at the empty club on the previous evening, Haslam and the poster gang realised that the place lacked a stage. A swift, mysterious and somewhat dubious cruise around the building sites of Hulme was all that was needed to fill their van with wood. The gang stayed up all night, hammering away, creating the most almighty botch-up job ... but the stage remained in the Venue for at least two years.

The regular night at the Wheel lasted three months, although the club owners would allow Haslam to continue, putting on such bands as Big Flame, Age Of Chance and Dub Sex. After Big Flame's performance, the band, impressed by Haslam's innovative and courageously disparate choice of records, asked him to work at the Man Alive Club. The regular Venue crowd duly followed him. It was simply, and heartbreakingly for the Haçienda, who duly took note, the hippest night in town.

Haslam: 'The Haçienda, at that time, had been having an awful lot of problems. They never really had a booking policy. I think that if Mike Pickering was in the office when the phone rang, the band would get the gig; if he wasn't, they'd miss out. They had never thought seriously about booking acts, let alone promoting DJ-only nights. Tony Wilson was certainly considering closing it down. But that was the point when they got Paul Mason in from Nottingham's Rock City and almost immediately the place seemed to have a different atmosphere ... more professional. On Friday nights, Mike Pickering and Andrew Berry had been putting on bands but for some reason they decided to continue the night without bands, playing James Brown, black dance and hip-hop. That is what became known as Nude night ("nothing on" – it seemed like a revolutionary idea at the time), at the end of 1985.'

On Saturday nights, Haslam worked the decks at the Boardwalk, a rather dispiriting affair as Colin Sinclair had yet to secure a late-night licence. As such, the night would build until 11 p.m. and then, just as it should have reached a natural peak, it would instantly dissolve. Haslam and McGough would leave the club and, their natural buzz tempered by anti-climax, wander woefully around the corner, blag their way into the Haçienda, to be confronted by the sight of a cold, empty, soulless shell. Fifteen people, maybe, would gather tentatively at the far bar, perhaps a few sparse gatherings here and there, or a couple eating chips, and downstairs in the cocktail bar, two hairdressers would be swapping chit-chat about their clients, over banana Dacquiris. A bedenimed New Order fan or a bedenimed member of New Order might be standing at the cigarette machine. Tony Wilson would be flapping around, suppressing panic, watching another sackful of money floating away. And the boom would continue. The DJ would be playing 'Ring My Bell' for the fifth time that evening. The club was a graveyard rather than a ballroom. The air was thick with defeat.

Nevertheless, Pickering, impressed by Haslam's work at the Boardwalk, enquired if he would consider running an evening aimed at catching a tiny portion of the largest university campus in western Europe (many of whom would actually wander in and out of town on a Saturday night, passing the Haçienda en route to comparatively dull city centre rock venues or dowdy Knott Mill tap rooms. Bewildered, the bouncers would watch this weekly drift and remark to each other, 'Can't we start throwing them in?' It was a standing joke. The Haçienda was the stylish void at the end of Whitworth Street.) Thursday nights, the student nights, with DJ Hedd at the controls, became the Temperance Club, the dancefloor pounding to the sounds of Mantronix, Eric B, the Railway Children, James . . . a furious and unholy mix of indie rock, hip-hop and funk. Instantly, things improved, with 600 people attending after just a couple of weeks.

'Pickering was ecstatic,' states Haslam. 'He thought the club had finally made it . . . funny, because if I had attracted only 600 in later years, I would have been instantly sacked.'

The first time the Haçienda became full for a bandless disco was in August 1986. Wilson was still weary after successfully promoting the Festival of the Tenth Summer at G-Mex, and had been disappointed to note that the expected 'knock-on effect' had failed to materialise. Thoroughly dispirited, he had departed on a Factory jaunt to China; on his mind, still, even after Mason's injection of professionalism, was the probable closure of the club. Wilson phoned Mason on the Friday morning to enquire about the previous evening. Barely able to contain his glee, Mason explained that the club had been packed solid. That was the moment when Tony Wilson changed his mind. The Haçienda would remain open – at least for yet another trial period.

Unknown to Wilson, perhaps until he reads this, there was another reason why the club was full that night. By chance, it was the night after the 'A' level results had surfaced in the *Manchester Evening News*. Every sixth former in Manchester would throng wildly into the city centre, intent on crazed, inebriated celebration, on sharing their relief, or numbing the pain of failure. Many of them arrived at the Haçienda. As such it was an extraordinary and somewhat freakish night. Haslam knew this: in fact, it was to his immense relief, and considerable surprise, that many of the revellers would return the following week. Madchester had started. Haslam was duly invited to work on Saturday nights and, more slowly perhaps, they too would steadily fill.

To be fair, it was Pickering who simultaneously had picked up on the sudden influx of energy in the curious world of 'house music'. He filtered it, with knowledge gleaned from his not infrequent Stateside sojourns, on to the Haçienda dancefloor. A Manchester nightclub had actually managed to attain an innovatory stance. Kids flocked to the Haç, not to spin and twist to their favourite sounds, but to actually discover new avenues of dance music. This hadn't happened, at least in Manchester, since the earlier days of northern soul. I recall meeting an unusually ecstatic Pickering, on the occasion of the Haçienda's fifth birthday party. He seemed to have sensed that the corner had been turned; that the club was, at last, at long, long last, embarking on an upward curve. He was standing on the balcony, enthusing wildly to me about the young dancers he had found in Moss Side. They would, he said, star in the video for his band T-Coy's single, 'Carino'. When I asked what these kids normally danced to, he looked at me as if astonished by my naïveté. 'Well, "house", of course, these are Moss Side kids,' he replied. Pickering had created, in the Haçienda, a whole focus for house imports. A focus, as it would turn out, for the whole of Britain, for coaches would soon line, nightly, along the Whitworth Street gutter. For a while, Mike Pickering's DJing would touch perfection. That's where it happened, 'acid house', right there on the Haçienda's previously barren dancefloor.

Dave Haslam: 'For me, it wasn't until November 1989 when it all came perfect. Suddenly, one night, I had the Stone Roses' "Fools Gold" and Happy Mondays' "Hallelulah" remix to play. All of a sudden, people had stopped saying, "What are you playing . . . don't play that . . . play some Smiths, not this crap." Now people were coming up and saying, "Play the Fall and Public Enemy." It was the perfect crossover and just the right answer to all that *NME* one-side-or-the-other crap. I had waited for three years for that moment. For the ball to come to me . . . I knew then that the *NME* crowd knew it too . . . we were right at the sharp edge of popular culture. I think that what happened was that the bands I would play would have resonance all over the world and no longer seemed "local". The fact was that I was in Manchester and was getting records two weeks ahead of anyone else . . . absolutely anyone. No radio stations, no clubs . . . certainly no London clubs, no music papers, no matter how specialised . . . none of these people were getting there before us. It didn't last for that long – a year or so, I guess, but the Haçienda was the place where everything would get played first. I had, without trying really, become the right DJ, playing the right music, in the right club in the right city in the world. I felt like a god. It wasn't entirely by accident, but it wasn't entirely planned, either. It wasn't an explosion, the Madchester thing. It had been building for two years. The Mondays had released two great and strange albums and the Roses couldn't find a venue big enough to play. They had lost a lot of the musical things which had previously held them back . . . they were not so retro. They had really grown up since "Sally Cinnamon" and were writing great songs . . . Things were on the change . . . the Haçienda wasn't suddenly full, it grew slowly. It was never even a scene . . . not like the old days. All the groups didn't meet in the same pubs and swap guitar licks. Madchester was never like that, and it was terribly reported in the press. Like, if you were to buy a car magazine and every article would be about the colour of the car, you wouldn't know how to judge which car to buy. You wouldn't know about the engine, about the power, how to drive it, or where to buy it. We had all this press, across the world. *Newsweek* in America . . . a thousand lengthy articles, all filled with superficial descriptions.'

Chapter Fifteen

Gunchester

THE HAÇIENDA, AS A VIBRANT, fluctuating, musical base for a sussed, hungry, vivacious clientele, peaked during '88/'89 when Mike Pickering and Graeme Park – the latter DJ discovered and poached from Nottingham's Garage – pulled Chicago 'house' into their innovative Nude nights, providing a template, of sorts, for the feverish boom times of acid house and Madchester. But it was acid house, such a ferocious musical 'magnet', which arrived as a double-edged sword. Initially filling the club to capacity, Factory (displaying rare entrepreneurial suss) transformed the outside queues which snaked for 30 optimistic yards into a separate event, by employing various 'street entertainers', including Manchester's celebrated Little Big Band – a punchy bundle of street r'n'b in the form of one man, Rob Grey, close friend of Vini Reilly and latterday Factory recording artist.

But inside, at its peak, the Haçienda was a mesmerising sight, especially for those who had suffered during those early cavernous years. A huge, playable beast of youthful sweat, piercing eyes, wide grins, clenched fists, pounding feet. There were times when even the DJs would just stand and watch, open-mouthed in disbelief as the party momentum carried the night along and people, many of whom would transform from a natural state of shy intelligent reservation into a somersaulting, swirling, dipping, clapping, grinning frenzy. The building would pound, the heat would rise; you had to take the pace or get out. On the best nights, there was simply no escape. The most striking parallel, of course, was always with Wigan Casino – the music had changed and twisted weirdly, and had been spliced together from a hundred disparate strands of dance beat, rock and world beats, but the collective energy and the unsteadying sense that the whole thing had taken on a life of its own, like a runaway rollercoaster, remained heavily reminiscent of northern soul. At the Haçienda, the beast had been let out. It was easy for Factory to sit back and count the takings – no one could deny they deserved every penny – but, in truth, someone, somewhere, should have noticed that disaster, of sorts, was wholly inevitable.

As hinted, rather strongly by Dave Haslam in the previous chapter, the true currency of the Haçienda changed, and changed swiftly. The central importance of the music lessened, to be replaced by the rapid encroachment of drugs and drug dealers. An early hint lay within those piercing eyes – fun for a while and then, all of a sudden it seemed, the party atmosphere changed. The intensity remained but it was to be replaced by a certain strangeness, an unholy tenseness; a sense of slowly building paranoia.

It was a perfectly natural process, of course. The Haçienda's swelling numbers, boosted further by the swirling media attention as 'Madchester' (initially just a wholly daft Factory marketing ploy, optimistically intended to boost interest in Happy Mondays), would gain an international media attention and would be a natural market for the worst kind of drug-dealing predators. This swelling of demand for drugs changed the lives of the city's minor drug dealers overnight. Before long, the almighty cliché of the mobile phone-wielding, BMW-driving 22-year-old, flushed with cash, orders and rivals wishing to blast him away and take over his ground, was a stark reality on the streets of Manchester.

'It's dead risky . . . like, everyone knows that,' one young dealer stated at the time, 'but at last, for kids like me, there has been some hope. We had fuck all to do for years and years . . . now we are all running around, covering ourselves, smelling the money, doing the stuff! Life is dangerous . . . but it's exciting.'

This dangerous scenario became apparent on the streets within weeks. With the police rather helplessly trailing after archaic leads, drugs flooded into the city centre. Drugs, tension and, before long, guns. The pattern, as numerous American reporters would perceptively note, was strikingly familiar. Before we knew it, the pages of the *Manchester Evening News* were filled with a new phenomenon which, although empty, filled the schoolyards and the teen-scattered gutters with misplaced though vibrant gossip and awe. Gang warfare.

In the darkened background of street culture, it had actually been slowly swelling for some considerable time. Just a couple of miles from the Haçienda stands the flat, myriad of brick terraces known as Moss Side. Despite a positive surface community, and a good deal of conciliatory social work, nobody ever denied that, lurking in the undercurrent of Moss Side, was a thriving, gang-controlled drug culture. A culture that would spread through neighbouring Hulme and into the city centre where, inevitably, it would be met by forces from the north of the city and, in particular, the stark, Gothic area of Cheetham Hill, very much a parallel dark force to 'the Moss'. Before long tit-for-tat shootings, distressingly and inevitably, made regular headlines in the local media. Reports vary, but a conservative estimate, provided by a team of investigative TV journalists from Granada, stated that 35 shootings occurred in a six-month period in 1991. Such attacks failed to make more than a small dent in the local media, while the headlines were reserved for a small but chilling outburst of gangland killings. Outside a pub in Cheetham Hill, 'White' Tony Johnson – apparently a 'notorious trouble maker at the Haçienda' – was slain at point-blank range. This was, arguably, the incident which led to Manchester briefly attaining the appalling post-Madchester tag, Gunchester.

The Haçienda, as the centre of Manchester youth culture, couldn't possibly hope to survive the blast of surrounding controversy. Back in 1987, a tabloid press hack, hungry for any kind of 'shock' angle, had seized upon the fact that he had witnessed the consumption of cannabis on the premises. Hardly a shock horror tale, but the seeds of outrage had been sown. Unfortunately, these initially misinformed protesters seemed justified when, in 1989, in the heart of the acid house era, nineteen-year-old Clare Leighton collapsed in the club and later died in a rare reaction to the central acid drug, Ecstasy. Overnight, acid house became noted as a 'force of evil'. The surrounding furore was hugely ironic, for it was to precede the influx of the true menace. Nevertheless, the tragedy would serve to instigate a lengthy and costly battle between the Factory directors and the Greater Manchester police authorities. In February 1990, following a 'hurried' piece of legislation – presumably in the wake of anti-acid house tabloid frenzy – the police were gifted greater 'discretionary' powers to object to the granting of licences to nightclubs by local magistrates. The Haçienda had been closely scrutinised and cleverly infiltrated by the police for some time.

Wilson: 'There were all kinds of undercover operations going on in the club just prior to that period. It was a bit bewildering, to say the least. We wanted, very much, to work with the police to help prevent the flow of drugs, but it seemed to be very much an us-against-them situation, which we didn't, and still don't, understand.'

In May 1990, Greater Manchester police informed general manager Paul Mason that they intended to apply to revoke the Haçienda's licence at the magistrates' sessions because of alleged drug abuse on the premises. This 'action' would form part of a police attempt to cure the drug problem by attempting to 'squeeze down' city centre nightclub activity. A fairly pointless exercise, one might suggest. The Haçienda responded swiftly though, and in a typical piece of Factory bravado, hired top barrister George Carman QC, himself coming into the story direct from the tabloid headlines (Carman was famous for defending, among others, Ken Dodd and Jeremy Thorpe). For all his flash and high profile, it was Carman who injected a modicum of common sense into the proceedings, by pledging, at a licensing hearing, that '. . . the club would work closely with the police to "declare war" on drug abuse and drug dealing in the Haçienda'. Significantly, Manchester's Labour leader of the city council, Graham Stringer, had written letters in support, stating that the club had made a 'significant contribution to the active use of the city centre core'.

After attaining an adjournment until 3 January 1991, the Haçienda triumphantly circulated a 'licences update' flyer, duly handed out to club revellers across the city centre:

The Haçienda licence hearing on July 23 resulted in the case being adjourned until January 3 1991. This means that the Haçienda will remain open until this date. Fac 51, the Haçienda, now wishes to redouble its efforts to keep the club open. This must involve the complete elimination of controlled drugs on the premises. In this we continue to rely on your help and co-operation. Please do not buy or take drugs in the club. Please make sure everyone understands how important this message is. Thank you for your support.

'We were fighting to survive,' says Wilson, 'and it is true that we were all pretty depressed by the apparent "darkening" of the scene during that period. Nobody enjoyed the fact that a drug culture had infiltrated the scene so effectively.'

Though sincerely meant, the paradox of Factory's war on drugs seemed to be laid glaringly open for a while. And no tabloid, it must be noted, managed to jump in there at the right time and make the most of the fairly blatant hypocrisy. For hadn't Factory always relished a somewhat subversive and free attitude towards drugs? And hadn't their major band of the time, Happy Mondays, openly embraced drug culture? A fact typified by Mondays' singer, Shaun Ryder, in a soon-to-become infamous article in *The Face*.

Ryder: '. . . 'cos, like, two years ago we 'ad to 'ave drugs on our person because we were sellin' em, right? So, if you got caught then it were a bigger problem. 'Cos it were bigger amounts we were carryin'. But, like, now, we always carry the name of a good solicitor around with us. I've got this card, right, and I just show it to them, the filth, when they come pryin'. Whereas before when they'd search me they'd always find like, forty-seven plastic bags and no solicitor's card . . . Foookin' hassles, y'knowwwharramean?'

As much as one may admire Happy Mondays, it is difficult, and perhaps near impossible, to square such a stance with a Factory organisation dedicated to wiping away the drug threat in their very own club.

Tony Wilson, 1991: 'That is a very good criticism and one that is extremely difficult to defend, though I have to say we are not responsible for the backgrounds of our artists. We certainly wouldn't ever attempt to censor their behaviour either. No, Factory isn't a drug-free zone but, one day, I'd like to think the Hacienda might be. We certainly have never advocated the peddling or pushing of drugs but we do believe that people should take an intelligent attitude towards them. It is like the old cliché, where fathers who drink ten pints of bitter on Friday nights disassociate themselves with their offsprings who might get caught with a tiny bit of dope. We have to be sensible about it. What I am not into, and am, in fact appalled by, is the violence that sometimes comes with drugs and has caused problems at the Haçienda. What people take or smoke or drink is up to them until the point where they might harm other people. Then it becomes an issue and we would have no truck with that.'

On 3 January 1991, the magistrates, impressed by the improved atmosphere within the club, decided that the Haçienda should be allowed to stay open, '... because there has been a positive change of direction.'

Paul Mason stated: 'The directors of the Haçienda are delighted with the opportunity to maintain better standards at the club. The problems we have experienced at the club are part of a wider problem which affects licensed premises within the city.'

As such the Haçienda remained open, albeit under a fragile truce with police, and an even more fragile dependence on the non-reoccurrence of violent or drug-related incidents. To celebrate, Electronic, featuring Barney and Johnny Marr, performed on a 'Thanksgiving' evening, on which the decks were manned by the mighty DJ trio of Pickering, Park and Dasilva. It was difficult, perhaps impossible, to judge whether or not the optimism of the club owners prevailed deeply among the crowd, but a party ambience did, if only superficially, remain in place. Sensing that there was still an undesirable element who would still try to infiltrate the club, the next Pickering and Park 'Nude night', on 19 January, would see the introduction of a membership scheme, aimed at retaining the 'old' atmosphere.

Wilson: 'I don't know. Something didn't feel right. We knew that there were gangs in the city who were still at war, and that it would be a miracle if the Haçienda could have escaped some kind of involvement. I never felt really happy with the optimism that January.'

MANCHESTER EVENING NEWS, 30 JANUARY 1991

The Haçienda has closed because of gang violence, it was announced today. The thriving Manchester club, recently described as 'the best of British venues', has fought a losing battle to bar gun-toting gangsters. It is understood that club management blame the police. Co-founder, Anthony H. Wilson said, 'It is with great sadness that we close the Haçienda to protect our employees and our clients. We are sick of violence and until we can run the club in a safe manner, it will be closed.'

Cheetham Hill and Moss Side gangs are the root of the problem.

The last straw came on Saturday when there was an incident involving a gun which was not fired. The club will close for two to four weeks while discussions are held with the police.

The cataclysmic incident involved a doorman, new to the club, who was threatened with a gun on the second of the 'membership' Nude nights. It wasn't a major incident, but it was enough to convince the Haçienda directors that their club was, in its present form, simply lying in wait for tragedy to take place.

Wilson: 'The only way forward at that point was to have extensive negotiations with the police . . . and it worked. There was simply no point in just shutting the club down for good, everyone agreed that that would just shunt the problem elsewhere. The Haçienda wasn't the cause of the problem . . . it was never that, it was just a central point for that kind of activity, and we felt extremely uncomfortable with that. As it turned out, we shut down for twelve weeks. During that time, we sorted out an awful lot of problems . . . Factory, simultaneously, was having a horrendous time [as the next chapter will testify] and so there were times when I would sit down, at the end of the day, and refuse to understand why everything that could be happening, in a negative manner, was actually happening. Our whole world was falling apart. But we weren't going to let gangsters beat us. That was one thing that we could sort out.'

During the twelve-week closure, the Haçienda team remained busy, installing £12,000-worth of new security measures – an 'airport' style metal detector, external video surveillence cameras on swivel mountings, infra-red cameras to peep into the darkened club corners where drug deals had always taken place, and a new, thoroughly professional security team. The measures may have seemed a little cold, and the risk was that the clientele would tire of being treated in such a way. As it turned out, and strangely, the measures served to instigate a new wave of 'post-Gunchester culture', in which passing through such measures was seen, bizarrely, in a romantic light. Living proof, perhaps, of the toughness of the times.

'Yeah, it was cool to be searched,' stated one student in the *Manchester Evening News*. 'It makes the whole thing seem like LA. That may sound stupid, but it has become part of the culture and most people are intelligent enough to know that, ultimately, it is in their best interests. Tough security kind of suits the club, you know. The security guards are not meat-heads. They know what they are doing.'

There was a ripple of reverse gun culture too. It wasn't a case of glorification of gang violence; indeed, it was quite the opposite. It was the drawing of strength from opposing such forces. This weird, unexpected subculture, which flavoured all the evenings in the spring of 1991, would surface almost five years later in the form of a novel, *Acid Casuals*, by Nicholas Blincoe. The book, a crazed tale of a transsexual assassin wandering through Manchester and, naturally, through a thinly disguised Haçienda, was the best rather than the first of a trickle of 'Gunchester novels'. Ironically, Blincoe had, as a member of the Rochdale rap outfit, Meatmouth, been signed to Factory Records, their hugely ignored twelve-inch disc being recorded in the 'in-house' studio of Lisa Stansfield. There were other references. Down at Pete Waterman's northern-based PWL Records, the Johnny Jay-led dance band, Family Foundation, included the track, 'Gunchester', on their critically acclaimed album which, though failing to break through to any unexpected audiences, became a fixed noise in Manchester's hippest dance clubs. *The Face* magazine similarly paid distant homage to this strange new spirit.

The Haçienda reopened on Friday 10 May 1991, complete with a new Ben Kelly colour scheme and the aforementioned security measures. The new optimism would last until the fateful night of Friday 1 June, when 1,200 revellers, partly dazed, wholly unaware of what had transpired, accepted the fact that the doors had been locked and danced away until 4 a.m. On the silent, eerie streets and canalsides, the full force of Manchester's Tactical Aid Group to police officers was making its presence felt. Roadblocks halted the traffic rather pointlessly on Whitworth Street, trapping bewildered casino dwellers attempting to drive swifly away from the city and out into the comforts of their native Cheshire. Above them, while officers smirked as the scantily clad female companions were forced to step out on to the kerbside, Manchester's irritating police helicopter whirled around in ever-decreasing circles. Inside the club, the dancing continued.

'It was the oddest of nights,' says clubber Matt Peacock. 'We just seemed to keep going, getting higher and higher . . . I still don't, to this day, know what had happened. We were all led out at about 5 a.m., I think ... police everywhere, like the miners' strike. It didn't matter 'cos we'd had a great time ... then someone said that a doorman had been stabbed. I still don't know the truth about that. But my mates all keep talking about that one crazed night, when the police forced us to party. Fucking wild it was.'

The 'incident', though serious – a doorman had been stabbed following a fracas involving five frustrated 'men' who had been faced with a 'house full' sign – became all the more notorious because of the police overreaction. It was, simply, a nasty, isolated incident; an incident which affected and involved absolutely none of the club's revellers that night. Nor had it any connection with the 'drugs war', or Gunchester. The Haçienda, being the Haçienda, would naturally command yet another barrage of hysterical headlines. Ironically, that same night, in a seedy, unglamorous late-night drinking den, a man was stabbed to death. That incident achieved the standard two column inches in the local press, while the media debate about the Haçienda raged on.

'We had won the battle ... and yet the headlines were still against us,' moaned Tony Wilson, resigned to the fact that notoriety, though not without its bonuses, would forever plague his beloved club.

Chapter Sixteen

Sex, Lies, Videotapes, Lost Bands, Ex-Wives, Daft Gigs and Football

SEX

Like all record companies, and all offices, building societies, bakeries, car garages, department stores, newspaper offices and, most probably, all tax departments too, Factory has always been awash with sexual intent, sexual gossip, sexual tension, infidelity and, almost certainly, sexual harassment. Unlike most other offices, however, this bewildering maze of sexual energy has never been ignored or swept under the carpet. It has been allowed to seep openly into Factory folklore, if not Factory art (though Factory recordings are littered with rather dubious in-jokes, many of a sexual nature).

'Isn't it funny,' quipped Wilson one day, while curled up on Factory Too's gigantic couch, his Travel Fox trainers tucked beneath his besuited torso, his mind racing wildly, perhaps recklessly. 'It's funny how no writer has ever picked up on the Factory sexual thing . . . I don't recall that ever being covered.'

Was this, I wondered, slipping the Pearlcorder next to the vase of lillies, the celebrated 'dark side' of Tony Wilson rising to the fore? Smiling, I checked my 'record' button.

'Do you want me to switch this off?' I asked him, genuinely concerned, though hoping he might, just possibly, say no.

'No!' he stated adamantly, casually adding, 'No ... keep it on the tape ... that's the whole point. Put it in the book ... it's about fucking time.'

It is? Is it? I shuffled nervously as Wilson passed the 'cigarette' across to the eager hands of Vini Reilly, sending a 'do not disturb – in a meeting' message to the amiable Bridget, who, phone clasped to her ear, churned out a standard, 'He is busy just now ... in a meeting ... can I get him to call you back?' message in parody, like a Valley Girl on speed which, as it happened, was one of the images which flickered into view during the following half an hour.

Wilson, happily on tape, continued, 'Yeah, the Factory sex angle. I do want to talk about that ... but where do I begin? I remember that I was once talking to the wonderful Mark Williams, from London Records, who has just A&R'd the Joy Division compilation album. He once said to me, straight out of the blue, "What is this sex thing with Factory?" I must have looked puzzled, and he said, "You know, the reputation that you lot have in the industry ... that you are a load of fucking sex maniacs. The entire company ... *everyone*!" It dawned on me at that point that that is how we really are perceived. A bunch of sexually overactive, lunatic Marxists ... and I realised that, yeah, that was just about spot on. And it is true ... and it began with ... oh, it probably began with me and my first wife, Lindsay, because we were always shagging people to get back at each other. I remember shagging this girlfriend of a singer with an early Factory band. I remember it well because she had sellotape on her breasts. I still shagged her ... with difficulty ... out of politeness, actually. I was only getting my own back on Lindsay who had run off with Howard Devoto. Well, it is all true. God, there's so much. Every member of Factory has a

dubious sexual reputation ... apart from Rob. He was always
the exception. Even people in our New York office ... then
there was all that with Hooky and Barney –'

Hooky and Barney?

'Yeah ... oh no, not with each other! When they were on
tour. Hooky's famous comment about Ian's death ... that 24
hours later he would have got on that plane and would have
fucked his way across America and would have never looked
back. If they could just have got him there he would have had
such a sexual adventure, he would have forgotten his worries.
That is true. But Barney and Hooky were appalling on tour.
They always were. And Vini's appalling. I was never forgiven
for arranging a *Smash Hits* interview with New Order in Santa
Barbara and, two months later, in *Smash Hits*, was this
photograph of a girl walking out of Barney's room holding up
his underpants. That's what caused his divorce. My fault, of
course. I have a strange view on this ... a lot of my friends have
been hurt by girls but I say well, if you play with fire ... They
always come running to me but I say, if any of my friends get
fucked over by women then they deserve it. That's my feminist
streak talking ... all this really did start with me and Lindsay.
It really did. She would watch me on *What's On*, and Debbie
Harry threw me a rose during X Offender [incidentally, Wilson
wrote a feature-cum-love letter to Debbie, in *New Manchester
Review*. "Some women make me melt ... look at me, a pool of
water," I seem to remember it concluding] and Lindsay
immediately thought, Oh, that's really done it, he's fucking
Blondie. So that's why she went off with Devoto ... and we
were at the Factory Club, on one of the two really bad nights,
when nobody turned up. The Pop Group and, in this case,
Patrick Fitzgerald ... and we had paid them £500 or something.
I remember feeling really depressed, feeling as if nobody is
coming to your party, looking towards the door. Suddenly I saw

a queue forming ... a *fucking queue*! I was ecstatic, so I smiled. Lindsay thought I was smiling at some girl so she followed Devoto into the toilet. That's how stupid we were. Did I ever tell you about me and Linder?'

No, I thought, and I don't, we don't, this book doesn't want to know. Shut up, please, I told him, genuinely concerned. Nevertheless, this alleged Factory attitude towards sex could be the reason why Deborah Curtis, in *Touching From A Distance*, in this book, and in a number of press interviews, openly complained about Factory discouraging her, as a wife, from hanging around the band at gigs. In one incident, described by Jon Savage as 'chilling', a heavily pregnant Deborah Curtis found herself 'frozen out' by a Factory associate because she wasn't deemed glamorous enough. In her words, 'How can we have a rock star with a six-month pregnant wife standing by the stage?'

The accusation sits as a heavy central core of that book, difficult to ignore. Deborah Curtis so obviously believed herself to be on the cold end of a distinctively cruel record company operation; the kind of cruelty one might associate with some corporate monster rather than a precocious, intelligent leading independent.

As I passed Deborah Curtis's accusation over to Wilson, Vini Reilly, sitting opposite, all but collapsed in a rather unbecoming fit of giggles.

Wilson, at this point, cast his eyes skywards and, in a shrug which in itself ridiculed the accusation, provided the answer.

'When Debbie's book came out all kinds of accusations were flying around in the press and yet nobody ever came to me to ask my point of view,' he stated, not unreasonably, as it happened, for *Q* magazine writer and Granada employee Len Brown expressed a certain regret about his penning a feature about the book and yet not bothering to approach Wilson. Even

I am guilty of the same crime, after writing a piece for the *Mail on Sunday*, similarly lacking in Wilson quotes. 'There are so many bogus myths about Factory. There was the idea that me and Nathan [McGough, Happy Mondays manager] conceived the drug angle of the Happy Mondays. Can you imagine? The Mondays were simply like that, true to their image . . . in fact, far, far worse in many respects. People believe what they want. Malcolm McLaren is a hero of mine . . . but a lot of the things he later claimed to have planned weren't planned at all. They all happened by accident. That is the same with Factory, really, except that I wouldn't ever claim to have been an integral aspect of the situations . . . well, maybe the sex situations . . . maybe not.'

Sex and Factory? Sex and Manchester music? Sex and punk? Well, from the start, it was always there, although it often did seem to lurk in the undertone and one had to squint pretty hard to see it (literally, in my case, being short-sighted, and never finding glasses to be a particularly fearsome punk accessory, I was reduced to leering like an Afghan rebel in a sandstorm at the punkettes who would wander into the Electric Circus, alluringly garbed in fishnets topped by stripy work shirts nicked from their dads' bedroom wardrobe).

Unlike London, where McLaren's template for punk fashion had been the flirting with the more comedic fringes of fetish wear, Manchester never really warmed to such a theme. Indeed, I cannot recall seeing a single Mancunian punk wearing bondage trousers in 1976 or '77. Such apparel only became visible much later, after the impetus had long gone and punk had become little more than a rallying fashion for a few parochial stragglers. I remember feeling shocked when, in 1994, I met up with the partially reformed Buzzcocks and found Pete Shelley waddling towards me in bondage trousers! Buzzcocks would never have worn such things in 1976.

But sex was there all right . . . in the songs. In fact, sex, of one form or another, was the fuel for every Buzzcocks song ever written. Magazine, I always liked to think, used a rather more subtle, perhaps more feminine sexual approach. Slaughter And The Dogs were a backstreet gang bang. The Drones talked about it, very loudly, while the Distractions were a charming mix of sexual naïveté and ambiguity. They would hardly dare to steal a kiss and yet would ultimately steal other people's wives . . . in image, that is. Ludus's Linder was – far more than Margox – the most potent post-punk sexual figure in Manchester. She toyed with this in her artwork, and in her music and, eventually, even became the muse for Morrissey. Back to Factory. A Certain Ratio, initially regarded as the 'greyest' of all Wilson's acts were, in fact, stacked with sexual references. It was in the funk, in the lyrics, in the lifestyles. It is no secret that Tony Wilson, at one point attempting to nurture a little ACR sexual ambiguity, purchased khaki shorts for the entire band and – switching from fact to rumour now – rubbed 'Tanfastic' into their pre-gig thighs. Durutti Column were a bottle of wine, a night in and a little gentle, mature seduction. Vini Reilly's aforementioned fan letter was just the tip of the iceberg. There was something, apparently, sexually powerful about a man who, though not exactly blessed with obvious bulging machismo, could filter strong sexual emotions through his guitar virtuosity. As for Joy Division, it has been written that Curtis's stark, though empassioned lyrics were shot through with a savage sexual streak, though, for what it's worth I remain unconvinced about that. Their music as a whole, however, with its constant build ups and drop downs, retains a darkly mysterious sexual potency. Compared to Joy Division, New Order were just a dance around a handbag.

THE FESTIVAL OF THE TENTH SUMMER, 1986

Manchester's G-Mex Centre, massive and dominant, even though eternally pushed to the rear of the magnificent Midland Hotel, was originally the most evocative, smoke-stacked railway station in Manchester. Cheekily semi-cylindrical, it pumped trains out to the west, to Liverpool, to Wales even, the railway parallel to the Manchester Ship Canal. Throughout the seventies, while humbly serving as a car park, it found an unofficial vocation as a location for no small number of rock photographers – though, chiefly, Kevin Cummins – who would drag hopeful young bands into its expansive interior, a perfect decaying industrial backdrop. Or outside even. A hundred bands and a thousand fashion models, whipped into place by *Manchester Evening News* photographers, based just around the corner, would attempt to ignore the biting cold while, behind their shoulders, Central Station arched away in one direction and the words 'Great Northern Railway Warehouse' would scream from the building in the other corner, now also a car park.

As a concert hall, as an exhibition centre, as G-Mex – no Mancunian could ever stand that name – it proved only half successful. An acoustic impossibility, it did, none the less, provide a much needed pristine venue for the larger rock acts who wished not to perform in the horrors of a football stadium.

It was Tony Wilson's idea to hold a celebratory festival (the Festival of the Tenth Summer, intended to pay homage to a decade of post-punk musical activity) in G-Mex, the most 'Mancunian' of all venues and, despite the fact that most of the attendees wouldn't normally be seen dead in such a place (Torville and Dean, Spandau Ballet, Simply Red; these were archetypal G-Mex artists), it seem oddly fitting. Especially as it happened to be a mere 50 yards away from the Free Trade Hall and, more importantly, the Lesser Free Trade Hall.

The event was dogged rather by the ludicrous hierarchical backstage pass system – easy to cheat, as it turned out – and sporadic outbreaks of egotistical inter-band bickering. Nothing, however, at all out of the ordinary.

Wilson's greatest coup was his success in prising an ageing, bearded, massively curmudgeonly Bill Grundy – once the tormentor of the Sex Pistols on Thames Television – out of his Marple Bridge home in order to make a guest appearance on the G-Mex stage. Grundy, unwittingly the catalyst that sparked the Sex Pistols, was a television legend, especially within the bowels of Granada, and Wilson had always adored the man's intolerance, not only of fools, but of just about all who swarmed around him.

'Well, the truth of the Grundy/Sex Pistols thing isn't quite how it has been recorded,' states Wilson. 'Much as I admire Malcolm McLaren, it cannot be said that he, in any way, orchestrated the Grundy incident. In fact, McLaren was absolutely astonished to discover that the television presenter was even more drunk and more bolshy that his band could ever be. This fact didn't surprise any of us who knew Grundy, for there are a million stories about him. But this was the spirit in which we invited him to G-Mex ... and wasn't it wonderful? Bill Grundy turned out to be the biggest punk in the place.'

He did, too, at one point swiping a somewhat over-zealous Paul Morley with his walking stick and generally handing out a verbal lashing to all who hovered near. As the day wore on, so Grundy became more and more intoxicated. By the time he staggered on to the stage, the world and Bill Grundy were well and truly at war.

'Seldom have I seen so many scruffy, lazy ***** in one place at one time,' he spluttered, perhaps half in jest.

The gig itself was shrouded in problems, most of which were impossible to overcome. G-Mex, at this point being the only concert hall of stadium size (11,000) in Manchester, was the only possible venue in which to house a day-long event featuring New Order, the Smiths, the Fall, A Certain Ratio, Wayne Fontana And The Mindbenders, Pete Shelley, John Cale, the Worst, OMD and Cabaret Voltaire. All the acts would wrestle to overcome G-Mex's intimidating coldness.

New Order closed the proceedings, at least as far as G-Mex was concerned, for the entire, unholy mess was duly transferred to a number of Manchester hotels, in which assorted Mancunian pop musicians of note would duly skulk in darkened corners, ignoring their peers and scowling at endless approaching fans.

EMPLOYEES – FAC PEOPLE

It is interesting to note that Factory, as one might expect, always used entertainingly off-centre methods in regard to choosing their employees. For many years, of course, this would be profoundly to their detriment. It is no secret that the notion of 'employing friends' was the main reason why the Haçienda's former years were shrouded in strangulatory inefficiency which resulted, at various times, in sheer logistical lunacy and fiscal anarchy. Nevertheless, there were many occasions when the right people, even if plucked from wholly irrelevant careers, or even mercifully from the dole queue, would slot effortlessly and professionally into place (a prime example, perhaps, being Leroy Richardson, initially employed as 'glass collector' in the early days of the Haçienda, eventually to become the highly visible, somewhat idiosyncratic manager of Factory's controversial Oldham Road establishment, Dry Bar).

By contrast, ex-Factory general manager Tina Simmons's first contact with Factory came in 1979 when she worked as label representative at the distribution company, Pinnacle. Though impressed with Factory's sheer belligerence, she had no plans to approach the company as she departed Pinnacle for Carrere, taking her contacts book with her. Factory's sense of timing was typified when they unexpectedly asked her to run their 'international licensing', just 48 hours before she was about to depart her London flat, already sold, and make the precarious plunge of a move, albeit temporary, to Australia. Factory's offer changed her mind, and Tina promptly chose Didsbury over the arguably more romantic Sydney, becoming an omnipresent stabilising force in the Factory office. Indeed, as a locally based journalist who often had to prise records from the company's needlessly greedy clutches, I can certainly vouch for the fact that, if one wished to attain any degree of sense, one had to speak to Tina. Though enjoying the prevailing 'looseness', odd even for the music industry, even the unflappable Simmons would occasionally find the Factory 'non-system' hugely irritating, as this statement delivered in a celebratory 'Factorial' to mark the company's tenth anniversary, in the music industry trade mag, *Music Week*, implied:

'Factory still manufacture their own product and supply it, finished, to Pinnacle. It's down to the fact that we have more control over, in particular, our sleeves and design side, and the type of material used, which can be really expensive. Anyone who took that on would probably get a bit worried, like our licensees occasionally do. I used to find it a little frustrating at times, when, and it still happens, Factory would announce a release date and then, two months later, it still hadn't arrived, but I can understand now, a little more, how that problem occurs. We have a design consultant, Peter Saville, who is an integral part of Factory and comes up with incredible designs and materials. But he will sometimes change his mind at the last minute, so occasionally there is a question mark about the release schedule with regard to Peter. But we do supply Pinnacle with proofs now . . . back when I worked there, you were lucky if you got the track titles. You certainly didn't get a sleeve or a white label. The first one I ever saw was for "Blue Monday" and Alan still took it away with him because he was going to give it to John Peel in person. The first white label I could keep was New Order's "Confusion", in 1983. But times have changed because – at last – Factory have realised that these are good things to have for pre-selling.' Simmons was made a director in 1986, but not a shareholder. 'That's typical Factory, too. They say, "We are going to make you a shareholder and we'll discuss it at the next meeting." But they never get round to the next meeting . . . it's generally a healthy environment, though. If you have an idea, then you are encouraged to pursue it without anyone telling you it's a waste of time. Just as long as you don't break down the original philosophy.'

MID-TERM GRETTON – DECEMBER 1987

Like a sixth former forced to endure the juvenile horrors of a first-year maths class, Rob Gretton looked truly abashed and hugely misplaced as he huddled in the corner of the bar at Manchester Apollo, his partner, Lesley, helping him to 'melt' into the kind of crowds that assemble at Alison Moyet gigs. 'It is not that I have anything against Alison Moyet,' he would announce, 'but . . . well, I wouldn't really choose to be here, among this lot.' 'This lot' were, in fact, grossly innocuous, often bearded and corduroy clad; the kind, perhaps, who might normally assemble over pasta lunches in chrome cafe bars. Architects? Tax inspectors? Who knows? Not, it seemed, the kind of people who would normally share Rob Gretton's evening hours.

'I'm normally down the Haçienda, working . . . but I tend to enjoy the kind of people who go in there. They may seem young to me these days ... or, rather, I may seem incredibly old to them, but I feel at home. I suppose these people are my peer group really, but I'd rather be at Maine Road. I think I need a bit of edge ... too dull, all this.'

It took just two numbers from Moyet to fully irritate Gretton and, as if a member of the taste police, he pulled me from my seat and forced me, albeit uncomplainingly, to slip away from the grip of the concert and scamper mischievously around the side and the rear of the venue and into the familiar and welcoming Apsley Cottage pub. Lesley would, he swiftly concluded, be more than happy to remain in the hall and would be accompanied by my partner, Karen. This gig 'truancy' was more than familiar to me. For I had spent nine years reviewing gigs for *Sounds* and, believe me, sitting alone at the kind of concerts one would not normally be seen dead at is rather like gate-crashing a 'works' Christmas party alone; an absurd situation and more often than not I would scamper away, mid-set, and sink into the famously welcoming bonhomie of the Apsley Cottage. This wasn't quite as unprofessional as it may seem, for the Cottage would be filled with 'off-duty' roadies snatching a quick pint, friends of the artists, record company personnel. Band managers would often sneak a few minutes in there; fellow rock journalists would be slumped guiltily in the corners and all peripheral liggers of the Manchester scene would be milling and tanking up before, either, pugnaciously shunting backstage for the encore or simply floating back into town, to the band's hotel and the subsequent party. The Apsley Cottage was the perfect place to pick up guest passes and ingratiate oneself with the true on-the-road powers that be.

None of which, of course, was lost on Rob Gretton who, I must say, I had found skulking in that bar on no small number of occasions. On this night, however, before walking into the bar, he chose to take me to his beloved Audi 200 Quattro, the only purpose of this brief excursion being his insistence on showing me the car's central locking system, something which, apparently, had attained near Masonic status within the membership of New Order. (A fact which, admittedly, had already been cheekily recorded in Dave Hill's excellent analytical article in the November '86 issue of *The Face*.) Quite why this central locking phenomenon had attained such a degree of importance was, however, missing from the article ... and from Rob's explanation on this strange occasion. 'Look at that,' he stated. 'Fantastic, isn't it?'

Recalling that Gretton had pulled the very same, somewhat underwhelming stunt, a couple of months previously with the ex-manager of Easterhouse, John Barratt, I could merely shrug in mock appreciation.

'That's really interesting, Rob.' I shrugged, attempting to sound impressed and, although I surely failed, Gretton seemed curiously satisfied.

Smugly, he added, 'Yeah ... it's great ... it's a perfect car this. I just love it ... it's my pride and joy.'

In the Apsley Cottage, Gretton would expand on the car theme.

'Hooky loves my car too, 'cos he is into speed, with his motorbike and his Toyota. I took Hooky across Europe in it ... we were travelling at full pelt, burning off cops along the way, like some kind of road movie. Hooky reckons it is the best road car in the world for that. No police can keep up with it. We *really* pushed it, you know ... it would be really dangerous at times. But Hooky drove it too; pushed the pedal through the floor he did, it was fantastic.'

The image of Gretton and Hook, tear-arsing romantically across Europe, as if taking part in some *Vanishing Point/Dirty Mary Crazy Larry/Easy Rider* excursion is endlessly intriguing, if not particularly pleasant. One imagines the car to be filled with all manner of jingoistic nonsense, about Brits smashing through European bylaw red tape. Crazy rock guys, terrorising French/German/Italian highways. It is a corny dream, perhaps, but one which quite obviously appealed to Gretton's sense of materialistic adventure, and that, perhaps, was the rub. Rob's car, and the subsequent vehicles of Barney (Mazda), Steve (Volvo) and Gillian (with typical modesty, a Fiat) – the New Order car ownership situation – attained symbolic importance; a band moving into areas of materialistic elegance ... and materialistic elegance, strangely, being a strong by-product of Factory's artistic stance.

'We like our cars ... our houses,' stated Gretton, whose 'housing' situation had become in itself something of a local legend. Gretton had, since leaving Wythenshawe, encamped in a flat in Bohemian Chorlton Cum Hardy. I remember visiting him, in the early days, days spent in typical rock-orientated post-studentism (i.e. stacks of records and videos and music papers). Slowly, as the wealth of Joy Division and New Order had slowly amassed, Gretton's ownership of the flat had extended, again slowly, to the whole house. Years would pass by and builders would encamp in the premises, scanning their teatime *Daily Stars*, unaware of their role in Gretton's encroaching empire.

MARCH 1988

Before you could blink, and before Factory knew what had quite hit them, *Substance* – the New Order greatest hits package – became New Order's largest-selling album, effectively ushering both band and label well and truly into the CD market. This might have seemed an obvious move, for surely all New Order devotees loved the idea of seeing the band's brightest moments shunted stylishly together and filtered, so fittingly, through their pristine new CD-based systems. And what band, given their electronically innovative heart, could possibly be better suited to CD? Simple. Nothing, of course, with Factory, is ever so simple. When *Substance* first hit the shops, gathering a willing, new, young audience together with the equally willing devotees, one had to search long and hard to see any trace of commercial perversity. After all, wasn't this the most perfect New Order product? Well, naturally, there was an irony, although on this occasion it lurked darkly. It could, however, be found in the record shops but not, alas, on the CD racks. For the most interesting remixes and the glorious chunks of witty dub and alternative musical angles – some of them quite insane – missed the CD release entirely and could only be found on the lesser-selling double cassette version. Hence, New Order's most extreme musical statement seemed to be allowed only into the private and unsociable world of those who liked to have their heads plugged eternally into Sony Walkmans. Dub New Order became the sound of the streets rather than the hi-fi buff's bedroom.

The success of *Substance* surprised everyone and managed to kick-start a few Factory minds along the way. Surely, they reasoned, this new consumer thirst for 'repackagement' would suit, well, not only New Order but Joy Division also. The ghostly cult could be stirred, rekindled, sold perhaps to the millions of young U2 fans, who just maybe had thus far failed to see the obvious musical link. This rather cynical, though excitingly bankable notion, caused a fairly gaping rift at Factory. Neither Gretton nor Wilson, initially at least, would hear of it. Both had insisted that the repackaging should rest with New Order; that to re-sell Joy Division in such a manner would be, as they used to say in studentland, and possibly still do, 'selling out'. The more Wilson and Gretton thought about it, the more absurd their reluctance to entertain the idea of a Joy Division repackage seemed.

Nothing, after all, could be construed as more of a sell-out than New Order's *Substance*. The crime had already been committed. This, at least, was the line taken by Peter Hook. Joy Division's back catalogue was as dear to him as to any man alive, and for this very reason he wanted to see it '. . . back out there, on the streets', soaking into the listening habits of new-found fans.

'A good deal of the old Joy Division stuff just isn't available any more,' he argued, 'so we will be fulfilling a function more than anything else. The demand is there, so it would be stupid, really stupid, if we didn't listen to it and act on it. If we don't it might become too late.'

It was a convincing argument. Gretton, after all, had always reasoned that if the Doors could become truly massive after their demise, then so too could Joy Division.

'Wouldn't it be nice if Joy Division could break big in America?' concluded Hook, rather happy to see Wilson and Gretton's view slowly changing to fall in line with his.

Hook's passion for Joy Division was plain for all to see. One only had to visit him at the studio he co-owned – with Chris Hewitt, a musician veteran from mid-seventies prog rock success story, at least in Europe, Tractor – in Rochdale. Even the studio, Suite Sixteen, was steeped in Factory history, and there it stood, in 1988, a coolly revamped if not state-of-the-art reminder of former glories. On the wall of the clear white recreation area, the majestic and rather regal figure of Ian Curtis reclined in glorious black and white.

'There he is . . . the old master,' sighed Hooky, as I sauntered into the room. 'Every time I walk into here,' he continued, 'I find myself wondering what might have been. Everything in this studio is, in a way, down to him. Everything we have achieved is because of him. We have lived on, had a great . . . a magnificent lifestyle, and it goes on and on . . . and the further we get from Ian, the closer, in a sense, it seems.'

Ushering me into the control room, Hooky's reflective mood continued and, if anything, grew more intense.

'It never stops feeling weird. I think that is probably why I own half of this . . . why I hang around here . . . because I can still feel it. I stand here, sometimes, and find it so difficult to come to terms with the fact that this is the same studio where we came, as Joy Division, all those years ago. It is really weird . . . really weird . . . echoes . . . ghosts . . . you know what I mean?'

For a moment, and *only* a moment, Hooky's celebrated machismo melted – I swear it did, it did – and the mood of reflection came near to a tearful climax. I had been summoned, as it were, to write a dutifully reflective article to publicise the rekindling of the Joy Division ghost. It wasn't something that even I, someone from the far peripheral reaches of the band's acquaintance, found particularly inviting. As a fan, and as someone who hadn't placed a Joy Division record on the turntable for six years, I rather wished it would all stay in the past. I sensed, in a rather more intense manner, Peter Hook was feeling the same emotion.

'There is part of me,' he continued, 'that probably feels that Rob and Tony's initial instincts, to lay the whole thing to rest, were correct. It is painful, it really is, just listening to that old stuff . . . all the more painful because, as New Order, we had made such a clean break, we had embarked on a completely separate voyage and, I think, it was the fact that we were doing something so different that made it possible for us to keep going. We weren't continually going over all the old ground. Everything felt refreshing . . . well, we have had our jaded moments but, in general, the fact that we have been moving forward has kind of helped us deal with the past . . . does that make sense?'

The new release, again called *Substance*, though the songs were crushed on to just one album, would be accompanied by the single release of 'Atmosphere' – which, rather disappointingly, only charted at UK number 34, thus failing to hurtle the defunct band fully into the limelight – would at least help latterday fans of New Order to understand the connection.

'It has always been very difficult to get Joy Division across to the New Order audience,' continued Hook, 'especially in America. Many times we would play "Love Will Tear Us Apart" and people just wouldn't be able to understand quite why we were playing it. They would have it in their collection . . . but wouldn't have a clue that it was anything to do with us. It was always very different in Europe because Joy Division were much bigger over there. Then the opposite would happen, at least for the first couple of years as New Order. People would turn up expecting a fairly heavy rock band . . . and the divide between rock and dance music was still unbridgeable over there. We played Italy for a while . . . oh, about 1983, and we couldn't understand why we were getting such large audiences . . . and then it dawned on us that they were largely made up of Joy Division fans. There would be rows and rows of placards pronouncing, "IAN CURTIS. REST IN PEACE". It was a bit disconcerting, trying to play "Blue Monday" with a sight like that in front of you, I can tell you.'

TECHNIQUE, 1989

In February 1989, the New Order album *Technique* debuted at number one in the UK, thus ushering Factory into its tenth year on a wave of barely containable optimism. Indeed, more than that, it seemed that at last the label's bizarre and often self-destructive business notions had been sensibly blunted.

'My joy at this particular moment is the moment we are poised at now,' said Wilson at the time, somewhat confusingly. He was referring, however, to the doors that *Technique* seemed to be opening. 'New Order's album is about to become a very significant world force, to actually fulfil – at last – in terms of sales and power, what I've always thought was the best group around. I used to say two years ago, that when the next revolution happened, my big question would be whether we would go platinum, double or triple platinum, and whether we were going to know that the revolution was happening and we were going to be involved with it with groups on Factory.'

The 'revolution', of course, had been dance music – acid house if you like – and, being owners of the Haçienda, Factory, even if hit by one of their periods of bewildering paradox, could hardly have failed to have soared with any resultant revolution.

KICKER CONSPIRACY – E FOR ENGLAND! 1990

Wilson's influence obviously extended beyond the scope of music, for when the Football Association desired a 'decent' World Cup song for the England 1990 squad, PR man David Bloomfield duly telephoned Wilson, intent on securing the services of New Order. Such a move doesn't seem so bizarre in post *Fever Pitch* '96, when soccer, flushed by Fantasy Football League devotees, is encased in a trendy sheen. Indeed, even the writer of this book is currently working as a football reporter for a broadsheet. But back in 1990, the notion of a New Order football song, seemed, to say the least, extraordinary.

At this point, strange and diverse projects were being planned at Factory. Michael Shamberg had pieced together a £315,000 ground-plan for a film based on an old English poem, 'The Sands of Dee' by Charles Kingsley, and, with the help of director Michael Powell, intended to utilise an original soundtrack by New Order. (Michael Powell, legendary British film writer/producer/director, then an octogenarian, is responsible for a huge and innovative body of work, most notably in collaboration with Emeric Pressburger (*The Archers*, '42–'57), though critics often remarked that this was usually marred by a streak of tastelessness. Nevertheless, with *The Red Shoes*, *Gone to Earth*, *Tales of Hoffman*, *Age of Consent* and *The Life and Times Of Colonel Blimp* among his credits, his work attained a timeless quality. His genius was perhaps brought back into focus by the influence his work, especially *The Red Shoes*, held over his close friend, Martin Scorsese. Indeed, Scorsese attempted to persuade Robert De Niro to succumb to an old Powell technique used to bloat the face of Roger Livesey for *Colonel Blimp* for the latter scenes of *Raging Bull*. De Niro famously refused, choosing the more direct method of eating mountains of pasta.)

Wilson liked the idea. He thought it would be wonderful, though ultimately would surely remain largely unseen. Though not opposed to such a courageous, uncommercial venture, he put forward the far more exciting prospect of a Factory England World Cup single. During a lengthy and tumultuous meeting, Wilson managed to turn the enthusiasm away from the Powell film and towards the football single. It was a pivotal Factory moment.

And, naturally, there were unexpected problems. Rob Gretton, despite being a football fan, seemed less than enthusiastic about the idea. Furthermore, as Wilson was driving through Milton Keynes one day, with Barney in the passenger seat, the New Order musician duly noted, 'You stopped me working with Powell. He was my hero. You killed that project. Why?'

Nevertheless, Wilson was convinced about the potential greatness of the notion of a football single, and alerted his friends in the sporting media and pestered producer Stephen Hague, generally hoping that things might begin to fall into place. And so they did. Unknown to Wilson, Barney had contacted the comedian and anarchic television presenter, actor

Keith Allen, who immediately expressed a desire to 'write some lyrics'. Steve and Gillian, having written a melody for BBC2's *Reportage*, duly pushed the same melody into the project and, after an initial week at New World Studios, a further week at Jimmy Page's Mill Studios was expensively booked.

Despite all manner of negotiations with MCA, the recording passed by reasonably effortlessly, with three England players – Des Walker, Peter Beardsley and John Barnes – singled out to attempt the rap. Although, of course, it was Barnes who featured on the record – which immediately hit the number one spot – there still exists, somewhere, a version of 'World In Motion' which features a bewildering and wholly unintelligible Beardsley rap.

On the Sunday lunchtime, mid-recording, Wilson and Stephen Hague travelled through Surrey with the simple intention of awakening Barney from his hotel slumber. As they drove, Hague kept on puzzling over the final lyric, and together Hague and Wilson attempted to prise a three syllable line to follow the words, 'We're singing for England.' Suddenly Wilson screamed, 'ENG-ER-LAND!' and the pair duly fell into hysterics. The three syllable Eng-er-land was subsequently born although, of course, it had been alive, on the terraces, for many years. They were still excitedly musing about this when, unthinkingly, they wandered into Barney's room and forced him from his bed. It was Wilson's fault, for he should have warned Hague that Barney, famously, before re-entering the human race following a slumber, spends two whole minutes physically wretching in the bathroom.

'It is the most disgusting noise imaginable,' says Wilson, 'but you get used to it after a while.'

(The 'World In Motion' single, technically by ENGLAND-NEWORDER, provided just one internal downside at Factory. Wilson and Saville, both claiming to have thought of the 'global football' emblem that embellished the subsequent T-shirts, failed to agree over royalty rights. 'Peter kept saying that we should pay him royalties ... yet I thought up the thing ... shouldn't I have claimed fucking royalties? We didn't speak for a year, which was very silly ... Peter and I shouldn't fall out over such things.')

IN THE CITY – THE MUSIC BUSINESS COMES TO MANCHESTER

It began in Cannes. Rather poetically, perhaps, in January of 1990. Three Mancunians of note – of musical note, at least – were wandering through the town. The occasion was the annual Midem music business gathering, a fantastically well-attended affair during which the movers and shakers of the world music industry gather in dusty seminar rooms or, more often than not, in oceanside bars, gossiping like crazy, sinking deeper and deeper into drunken hazes, perhaps, just occasionally managing to tie up the odd business loose end while running up gargantuan expenses accounts. Much the same, in fact, as every type of business convention and, while my cynicism and sheer unbridled jealousy might well be tainting this opening paragraph, I have to suggest that the social element, which in most cases is a blatant orgy of furious hedonism and sycophancy, is just as important as the business side. More so, in fact. If it adds a touch of glamour and if the South of France milks it for every penny, in the true tradition of the South of France then, well, why not? People want to work in the music business. They want to sniff the glamour, live the fantasy. Where better?

Well, Manchester, perhaps? The three Mancunians – Tony Wilson, his partner (the bright as a button former Miss Great Britain, Piccadilly Radio reporter, Yvette Livesey), and co-manager of Simply Red, Elliott Rashman – began wondering, after Livesey's initial out-of-the-blue verbal explosion, 'Why couldn't we do this in Manchester?'

On the face of it it would seem to be, and Livesey would agree, a pretty stupid suggestion. The principal music industry objection would be simple. After all, it is very nice, very nice indeed, to drift down to the South of France in a post-Christmas haze, or, equally, flit trendily across the Atlantic in July for the ever-improving New Music Seminar. Why would anyone wish to travel to and stay in Manchester?

The answer seemed overtly obvious. The Madchester explosion had embarrassed the capital. Things can explode and unfold in Manchester, in a way which just couldn't happen in London. It could happen – once did – in Liverpool or Glasgow or Sheffield or Dublin, but not in London. It was parochial power that had fuelled the innovatory edges of the music industry since . . . well, since the Beatles, really. The notion of holding a music industry seminar annually in Manchester was, in part, rather a glorious fulfilment of the Factory dream. Maybe later it would move onwards to Dublin, perhaps? (As it did.)

The Holiday Inn Crowne Plaza ostentatiously decorates the Peter Street corner of Manchester's St Peter's Square. For many years, as Manchester's Midland Hotel, it operated proudly as the most classic hotel in the city, an ornate architectural gem, a genuine manifestation of the city's former prosperity. It did fall from grace in later years, at least until the late eighties when the Holiday Inn group rescued it from heartbreaking decay and undertook lengthy and costly renovation, providing it with one of the largest and most stunning reception areas to be found in any hotel in Britain. Since opening in 1981, it gained a reputation as the natural fleeting home of top businessmen and Olympian officials who were dourly scrutinising the city centre and assessing the chances of Manchester hosting the Olympic

Games. Despite a fair peppering of four-star hotels in the city centre, it was the Holiday Inn Crowne Plaza which best captured the spirit of early-nineties Manchester, making pivotal appearances in Tony Warren's weighty tome, *The Lights of Manchester*, and providing temporary refuge for many visiting rock stars. More than any other Manchester hotel, the old Midland – as it became locally known – seemed to become a precious manifestation of the old and the new; old architectural power and bluster and new, smartly besuited flash. It was also the hotel which most resembled the big hotels of New York, specifically the New York Hilton, and, with its subterranean conference suites, seemed to be the perfect venue to hold an international music business seminar. Yvette Livesey, spurred on by Wilson and Simply Red managers Rashman and Andy Dodd, moved into an uninspiring office in Manchester's town hall and took on the daunting task of organising and squeezing music business craziness into a three-day extravaganza to be held, mainly, within the Holiday Inn's walls. Livesey attended meeting after meeting with the Holiday Inn management, seeing at times the project verging on disaster.

'Of course it might be a disaster,' she suggested, before brashly admitting, 'and, this being a rock convention, some of our delegates might smoke.'

'But Yvette,' came the reply, 'lots of our guests smoke, there's nothing wrong with that.'

'No, I didn't mean cigarettes . . . they might smoke . . . you know!'

The blank stares with which this remark was met signified the scale of Livesey's problem. Only the rather pleasing fact that the delegates would be staying, eating and drinking within their walls managed to overcome the hotel's possible objections.

Livesey and by association Wilson, Rashman and Dodd had to soak up immense criticism during the run up to 'In The City', as the project was to be called, and it was to her credit that she didn't crack under the full weight of the verbal attacks. Furthermore, the appearance of Rashman and Dodd alongside Wilson and Livesey in the local press shots which preceded the event certainly caused a few, largely understandable ripples throughout Manchester. The shots – as local press shots so often do – depicted the subjects rather smugly, rather self-satisfied, as if finally cashing in on their capitalistic positions at the top of the Manchester music hierarchy. As if pushing for power, more power; an undemocratic infiltrating of the mysterious, the dusty and the ever-controversial corridors of Manchester Town Hall. In truth it wasn't like that at all, but Wilson, Livesey, Rashman and Dodd displayed either an outrageous degree of bare-faced cheek or a stunning and possibly significant degree of naïveté during the In The City run in. However well meaning their intentions, how could they have been surprised about the well of cynicism which bubbled so furiously during those days? A cynicism quite possibly born of jealousy – how many Manchester musicians had, at some time or another, been turned down by Factory? How many believed themselves to be of far more musical value than the million-selling Simply Red? Practically all of them. Furthermore, In The City's arguably courageous attempt to underpin the main event, with a week-long series of showcase gigs featuring all manner of unsigned hopefuls, was absolutely guaranteed to cause no amount of intense resentment, musicians being what they are. (And, true enough, during the first three years of In The City, the undercurrent of resentment would rage with, at times, somewhat entertaining vehemence.)

Before the first In The City, Manchester was effectively split in half. *City Life* magazine reported that Manchester City Council had subsidised the event to the tune of £25,000. Naturally, such a statement didn't serve to make effortless PR,

357

especially as the council was, and will forever be, in apologetic mode, as local service cutbacks would pustulate in the local news pages.

I do not know, and it probably cannot possibly be calculated, whether In The City actually succeeded in suitably oiling the wheels of the music industry, and whether it has any practical importance at all other than strengthening industry bonhomie, intensifying the rivalry and highlighting the illusion of glamour. Who can tell?

Tony Wilson: 'It has been important for the city ... if for no other reason than to get those stupid London bastards off their arses. It might as well happen up here ... though it is sure to travel to other provincial cities, if only to show the industry fat cats what a truly innovative musical city is like just for three days. It is only right ... we have produced so much more than London. I remember, I think it was before the second In The City, meeting some delegation or other at Manchester Airport. I can't remember what it was about but these guys, who had come from all over the world, were saying things like, "Oh we hear that Madchester is dead ... isn't it a shame?" We said, "Well, yeah, Madchester is dead, but that was just a phase of Manchester." But look at us now. The best teen pop group in the world is Take That. The biggest adult pop band in the world is Simply Red ... and since then we have had Oasis. Not bad for a spent town. Of course it is only natural that In The City should be held here.'

And it has been fun, too. What better than a sycophantic orgy, filled with eccentrics, egomaniacs, subversives, drunks, rampant capitalists, ardent Marxists, self-publicists of every description, leeches, and worse still perhaps, all manner of rock artists. From New Order, only Pete Hook would make regular and often very memorable forays into the seminar rooms, taking every opportunity to leap into the heart of whatever debate was raging. One recalls him, staggering through the Holiday Inn foyer, distinctly garbed in frayed cut-off jeans and cowboy boots, his golden hair flowing down his back, Holsten Pils bottle wedged between his teeth, accepting the looks of disdain from the hotel sub-management with good grace. This was the beginning of 'Public Hooky', a curious social and party animal, who would be seen, during the lengthy periods of New Order inactivity, pugnaciously invading all the right gigs, lurking in the corners of all the trendier cafes, quaffing free white wine at all the most notable functions. To his credit, perhaps, Hooky seemed to be powered more by genuine enthusiasm for the scene than any desire to enhance his night-time presence. Pointless, anyway, for New Order's state of enigma can only be lessened by such public displays. Hooky never seemed to care about this. While Gillian and Steve would be ingloriously 'holed up' in their Macclesfield farm, and Barney would be flitting around the world with Johnny Marr in Electronic, Pete Hook would be tripping down the unlovely stairs of the Roadhouse, a post-rave punk cellar venue, hugely reminiscent of the late seventies, where guitar bands, good and mostly dreadful, would bang away to often rather pointless effect. But Hooky would still be in there, still prepared to take on board quantities of poor quality beer, still lacking any trace of jaded cynicism.

One had to admire him, even if he did take to wearing designer safari suits. People became used to the sight of him. No longer did it seem odd to see a wealthy international rock star staggering down Dale Street at 2 a.m., arguing with some circulatory female, stepping over drunks and mingling, generally, with those who regarded him, quite hilariously, as some kind of cowboy-booted demi-god.

Things changed for Hooky as the nineties evolved. The main reason for this would be his unlikely early liaison and eventual marriage to the universally loved comedian Caroline Aherne –

aka Mrs Merton. Their affair began, at least in the local folklore, in whispered gossip, although before long encroached naturally into the local gossip pages previously occupied by Hooky alone. Before long they became a kind of localised Rod'n'Brit couple, spreading their socialising – though their appearances were always greatly exaggerated – between rock and television events.

Hooky would, in the wake of any noticeable New Order activity, famously front Mrs Merton's house band, Hooky And The Boys, allowing himself to bear the force of Merton's gentle, though barbed sarcasm. (This newfound, semi-serious role for Hooky would have strange consequences, especially as the fame ratio of the couple's marriage would even out as Merton gained more and more exposure.)

Rob Gretton: 'Oh yeah . . . he is a changed man. Completely. He always used to be a bit wild but now . . . right back down to earth. Actually, I think it has done him a lot of good. He is a real family man now . . . really straight down the line . . . and he is dead happy.'

Wilson: 'I never see him now . . . used to be good mates, we did . . . I don't think she'll let him out!'

'89/'90/'91 – GOOD YEARS FOR THE MONDAYS

It was almost impossible to write a boring feature about Happy Mondays. A few tried. One even succeeded after, I sense, a gargantuan effort, her journalese drained of all trace of wit and incident from her encounter with the band. The Mondays were, in effect, the easiest rock interview since the Sex Pistols. Quotable lunacy gushed from their mouths like water from a broken main. When in public, they appeared, at all times, to be completely impervious to the embarrassment which seemed to gather, like storm clouds, all around them. Faces would redden, eyes would glance to the floor, sweat would drip over shirt collars. When Happy Mondays swore, which was all the time, they swore profoundly. In a quiet place they could hurtle swear words like javelins. Despite this, they also had about them a certain sweetness, a lovability perhaps.

One remembers them at early gigs, at the International – playing to fifteen people – or the Boardwalk, circulating around the crowd post-set, all pleading eyes and pained expressions.

'Excuse me, mate,' they would say (just as at Macclesfield Leisure Centre), genuinely surprised as you backed away a little, for they all but typified the mugger look, the crazed drug-boy look – until, that is, they opened their mouths and something warmer, softer, came out.

'Hey mate,' one of them said to me. It could have been Bez. It could have been Shaun. ' 'Ave you got any draw, mate? Please 'ave some, I'm fuckin' desperate, me.' Invariably the answer would be negative and you would feel so sorry for them as their expressions saddened before you and their air of menace – completely unintended – would simply drip away, leaving them somehow lost, drifting dopeless back to the dressing room. Of course, things would soon change, when fame and money rushed in like a whistle-hooting express train and carried them away. By then their image fled before them, alerting eager journalists. They were easy pickings really. Especially to someone like the seasoned and oft-celebrated ex-*NME* stalwart, Nick Kent.

It was Kent who, in *The Face*, chose to grab the story/spill the beans/collect the attention-grasping quotes which, surely, would be lying in huge piles around the *Top of the Pops* studio, for the article was based around the infamous day that Happy Mondays and Stone Roses met, in a state of wild camaraderie, to perform separately on the same edition of *Top of the Pops*, just one month shy of 1990. What a feature this would be! Two great bands. A mad scene. A brilliant journalist. *Face* editor

Sheryl Garrett held great hopes. Perhaps, like Kent's portrayal of Miles Davis, or his latterday Iggy Pop, or his sycophantic Smiths piece, it would be regarded as a classic.

It was a strange article, a rather unsteady blending of the hilarious (being the statements which flowed from the bands' mouths) and the dubious (being Kent's unholy angle, to accentuate the darkness and the weaknesses and finish the piece with a superfluous and numbing slap, so sharp that – most unlike Kent, this – the whole thing would leave a particularly nasty aftertaste).

The article began neatly enough, with a couple of genuinely hilarious tales, of the dangers of hashish and hotel bedroom fires and just of drugs in general. When asked why he took drugs, Ryder replied, 'Illumination, pal, Yeah! Well, like, illumination half the time anyway, 'cos t'other half we just like to get fookin' roarin' shit-faced, y'knowwharrammsayin'.'

Nothing wrong with that, of course. Just about as succinct a summary of the Happy Mondays' view on life as one could wish for.

Things darkened considerably, however, when Tony Wilson was ushered into the article. When asked whether he had any problem with any of the Happy Mondays dying on him, Wilson's alleged reply was, 'I have absolutely no problem whatsoever with any of these guys dying on me. Listen, Ian Curtis dying on *me* was the greatest thing that has ever happened to my life. Death sells.'

This extraordinary quote simply leapt from the page, snatching the attention clean away from any positive noises the article might have been making. It was, of course, designed to make people look twice – to stop reading and gasp in disbelief. As it turned out, it was a sub-tabloid fabrication.

Tony Wilson read it twice ... three times, before quietly placing the magazine on the coffee table and looking towards the heavens.

'I was really fucking shocked,' he says. 'It just seemed totally fucking ridiculous to me. And then I picked it up again and got to the end of the piece where Nick Kent shits on Gary Wheeldon (Mondays drummer), summarising that the band are really just a bunch of wimps. My God!!! This was from a Rolling Stones fan! A band who once sang 'Let's Spend Some Time Together' on American TV. The Happy Mondays, by contrast, were the real thing . . . but that quote . . . that Ian Curtis quote, I had to go back and read it again. I thought I had somehow misread it . . . because I had absolutely no recollection of ever saying such a thing.'

Wilson immediately telephoned *Face* editor Sheryl Garrett to enquire just where the quote had come from.

'Yeah, Tony,' replied Garrett. 'We knew it was dodgy so we triple checked. It is on the tape . . . you *did* say it.'

Wilson was unconvinced by this. For a start, he didn't remember there being a tape at all.

'Oh yes, Tony, Nick taped it,' insisted Garrett, in an almost indignant tone. Wilson shrugged, and concluded that, if they sent him a copy of the tape then, well, what could he say?

'Yes, Tony, no problem, I'll get a copy to you,' came Garrett's reply.

Two weeks later, after no tape had arrived, Wilson phoned again.

'Don't worry, Nick's getting it to you,' insisted Garrett, so forcedly that Wilson was tempted to believe her.

Two months passed by, during which time Wilson had learned that the article had caused considerable and understandable upset to both Deborah and Natalie Curtis. Once again he seemed to have been darkly cast as some kind of Machiavellian guru. Relaying the Curtis upset to Garrett, he was told, 'We have got the tape, Tony. It's with our lawyers but we will get it to you.'

Needless to say, no tape ever arrived. Five years later, Wilson, who by this time found himself forever chairing media conferences, talk fests and seminars, was asked to oversee a small convention dedicated to the 'safe drugs policy'. On the panel, he was rather distressed to note, was Sheryl Garrett. True enough, the meeting between the two remained frosty, until about halfway through the event, when Garrett uttered the words, 'Well, if you actually *read The Face* . . .'

This was simply too much for Wilson, who responded with a firm, 'Well, Sheryl, I don't read *The Face* and we fucking well know why, don't we?' It was a rather clumsy outburst, even Wilson would admit, although his anger would dissolve into disbelief afterwards when Garrett pulled him to one side and offered a full apology.

'I have only made two major mistakes in my time as *Face* editor,' she admitted – presumably, the 'other' one revolved around Jason Donovon – 'and sending Nick Kent to write that piece was one of them. There was no tape, Tony. You were absolutely correct. You never said it. It was made up. When it became clear that no tape existed, I was taken before the board who informed me that under no circumstances could I apologise to you for at least five years. I was to have no contact with you until the five-year libel law had run its course. When I knew I was coming up here, I checked my diary . . . it's five years and three months since we ran it.'

Chapter Seventeen

When It All Comes Down

Tuesday 24 November 1992, Manchester Evening News

FACTORY MUSIC IN 2M CRASH

The factory records empire has crashed with debts of more than 2m, it was announced today. Factory Communications Limited was the flagship of Manchester music for fourteen years, but now the firm is being run by receivers called in by a bank at the request of Factory directors. Anthony H. Wilson said, 'I'm numb. I don't have any feelings except for the staff I have had to lay off.'

Receivers Leonard Curtis and Partners will now try to find a buyer for Factory. 'The best hope,' said Wilson, 'is if it is bought by a record company and preserved in its current form . . . more or less. The worst scenario would be Factory's assets and the bands contracted to it offered up to the other record companies.'

Joint receiver Dermot Power said, 'Unless someone comes up with an awful lot of money, I don't see any prospect of Factory continuing trading in its current form.' He said the Factory 'fall' was due to three reasons. A decline in demand in the record industry, the effect of interest rates on property owned by F.C.L. and the late arrival of some specific records. Throughout the year, Factory has tried to 'sell off' part of the company to London Records in order to provide much needed cash injections.

'A survival deal has been in place during the past year,' said Wilson. 'It had been thought to have been sorted out but every time the quicksand has shifted.'

Three directors and five staff have lost their jobs. But the Haçienda, and Dry Bar, part-owned by Factory, are continuing to trade as normal. Wilson said he hoped these would play a role in the future life of Factory. Creditors include Nat West Bank, Customs And Excise, Inland Revenue and the artists themselves.

Wednesday 25 November, Manchester Evening News

MONDAYS UP FOR GRABS

Happy Mondays are ready to negotiate a new deal within hours of the collapse of their Manchester-based record label, Factory. Happy Mondays revealed the collapse would rid them of all contractual obligation. 'We are looking forward to a new start,' stated manager Nathan McGough. 'We will negotiate a worldwide deal. It is not the end of an era, it's just business and, in this climate, everyone has to be ready for things like this.'

Today, Nathan McGough scoffed at claims that delays in the completing of the new Happy Mondays album could be blamed for Factory's collapse.

'I think it made very little difference, if any contribution, to the collapse. I know how much money is outstanding and even if the record had sold three million copies, it would have made very little difference.'

The band state, 'It is with regret that we received the news with regard to Factory being placed in receivership.

We are sorry for those who have lost their jobs, some of whom have given great support to Happy Mondays. We realise this will cause hardship for creditors, some of whom we have worked very closely with and regard as friends. For those who are concerned, we wish to make it clear that the closure will cause very few problems for Happy Mondays. It will free the band. We hope that Factory could be sold as a going concern and we would be happy to discuss the possibility of working with Factory again, should that be the case.'

Factory director and New Order manager Rob Gretton had 'nothing to say'. Matt, from Factory band the Adventure Babies, was said to be 'gutted'. Local record promoter Tony Michaelides, was amongst those owed several thousand pounds.

FACTORY CLOSURE

Factory had existed, for too long really, within the restrictive confines of the Palatine Road flat, initially rented by *Brideshead Revisited* creator Charlie Sturridge and Alan Erasmus. The flat, blessed with a sweet though, for visitors expecting the hub and bustle of a burgeoning, albeit small record label, profoundly disappointing interior, consisted of a small front room, the Factory office, a tiny central room which, by the late eighties, had proudly become the 'overseas office', and a dank 'bottom' room, which existed as the packaging and mailing-out area. Later, the two upstairs rooms, noticeably sinking into decrepitude, became the infamous Factory accounts department. By the time that Madchester had started to explode all around, and Happy Mondays had pushed the company straight back into the limelight and intensified the Factory workload tenfold, Factory was simply bursting from the building. There just wasn't enough space.

Wilson, flushed with success and fired with realistic hope, began looking at alternative office spaces. Romantic connections led him, naturally, to think about renting somewhere in the massively revamped area of Old Trafford. It was Erasmus, however, who seemed unusually excited upon discovering the dark, damp, forbidding, ramshackle building which lurked on Charles Street, behind the BBC. Enquiries revealed that the building was on sale for £100,000. Initially, Wilson and Erasmus dismissed this as an outrageous amount for a mere vision of decaying grandeur. One day, however, as Wilson was driving out of Granada, past the Museum of Science and Industry, he noticed a 'For Sale' sign flickering from the edge of an ex-Methodist church, latterly an architect's office on Bridge Street. Curiosity forced him to seek out the price. Stunned, he discovered that the developers rationally expected £850,000. Immediately, the £100,000 price-tag on the Charles Street building began to shrink in his thoughts.

It seemed quite perfect. This was, after all, slap-bang in the centre of the great eighties property boom. Wilson's eyes had been alerted to the glittering jewel of property speculation at a large business conference he had attended in 1987, which featured a good deal of excitable though solidly based rhetoric from a big-wig speculator.

'RIGHT!' the speculator had screamed to the audience, like a headmaster installing basic virtues into a set of unruly first years. 'Hands up all those people in the audience who think that the best business deal you have ever done in your entire business career was to buy the house you are now living in.' After a couple of seconds, practically everyone in the audience raised their hands.

'OK,' continued the speaker, 'how many people think that the second best deal you could have done was to buy the house next door at exactly the same time.'

It took a little thought but, soon enough, everybody raised their arms once more.

This rather vulgar display affected Wilson. He looked to his own life and it didn't take long to discover that, indeed, his property dealings far outweighed anything he had personally achieved via the music industry or television. Property had, of course, been booming for 30 or 40 years. His parents had bought their house, on Strines Road in Marple, for £11,000 in 1950. Before the eighties had dawned, it had been worth over £250,000. Wilson himself had bought his Charlesworth cottage, in 1974, for £10,500, selling it five years later for £27,000 before spending a mere £41,000 on his large Victorian home in Didsbury . . . and that seemed a minute amount by the time the booming mid-eighties came around. It was common sense. Every expert in the country was vehemently stating that property couldn't fail, and nobody expected them to be wrong. (Except Peter Saville, who, rather smugly, claims to have foreseen the impending collapse.)

Factory's property ambitions, as outlined earlier by Rob Gretton, seemed to be slotting neatly and wisely into place. Their Ben Kelly-designed Dry Bar was up and stylishly running from 1990, outrageously injecting a slice of much-needed architectural glamour on unlovely though lively Oldham Street. And, by 1990, things were on the change at the Haçienda.

When opening the Haçienda, Factory had attempted to purchase the entire building for £200,000. Unfortunately, the owner (perhaps sensing that Factory's revamp might cause him to justifiably 'up the rent') doubled that estimate, refusing to budge below an enormous £400,000. Factory made repeatedly unsuccessful offers throughout the eighties. Eventually, after apparently getting into difficulties, the owner agreed to sell, and Factory, believing in the inevitability of owning the Haçienda building, put forth the second highest of five bids and to their delight succeeded. Around the same time, the Charles Street property was purchased, by Factory, for £100,000. At a run-of-the-mill meeting at Palatine Road, Factory found themselves discussing how many posters for the Happy Mondays' *Bummed* album they could pepper around town. This was, for Factory, always a big problem, for Factory posters, from the old Peter Saville designs through to this new, stunning Central Station design – the eerie, colour-flushed face – were eminently collectable and would all too often be flatteringly peeled away before the glue had set. Erasmus, glowing with confidence, suggested that they should simply plaster the Charles Street building with Happy Mondays posters. Hence the commuters of Manchester, surging out from their King Street banks and building societies, would be treated to the strikingly surreal vision of a hundred gaudy faces, leering brilliantly from the shape of the previously blackened building.

Soon enough, the plans for the new building would excitedly unfold. Unflinchingly, the bank gave Factory £750,000, secured against the building, for the purpose of development.

'There was a bit of madness in there,' admits Wilson. 'I mean, we were this big anarchic family and we had this mad, genius designer, Ben, who was part of the family . . . and so, what should have cost about £300,000 actually cost over £750,000, for a building that, unlike Dry and the Haçienda, wasn't going to actually earn anything.'

Nevertheless, flushed by the new loan and flushed further by the sudden influx of the money from sales of the Happy Mondays' *Bummed* album, Factory began transforming the poster-clad monstrosity into a shimmering, pristine Factory artefact.

Meanwhile, cleverly – or so they believed – Factory had attempted an unusual 'manipulation' of normal mortgage procedures. They decided – and boy, did it seem like a great idea

– that, if they got a mortgage in Germany, which they could do under their German earnings, then they would be paying a much lower interest rate. Unfortunately, before being able to approach the German banks, they needed to establish a six-month 'stop gap' mortgage. Alas, the next six months – from autumn 1990 to January 1991 – as previously mentioned, just happened to be the most tumultuous in Manchester's nightclubbing history, as the drug gangs from Moss Side and Cheetham Hill moved in on the city centre in general and most notoriously on the Haçienda, capturing along the way a smattering of gloatingly savage worldwide headlines, all furiously screaming the 'end of Madchester' angle. Simultaneously, the German idea disintegrated following Factory's split with Rough Trade and nobody in England would grant a long-term mortgage in this notorious gangland 'hot spot'. What this in effect meant was that Factory would continue to pay the stop gap rate – 8 per cent over the base rate – which meant that, when mortgages peaked at a terrifying 15 per cent base rate, Factory would be paying a whopping 23 per cent – and still are.

'This, I want to tell you,' states Wilson today. 'This is *still* a complete nightmare . . . we are seriously going to try to wriggle out of it during 1996.'

And then, of course, much to the stunned disbelief of every property owner in the country, the property boom collapsed. In the space of three months, the value of the Haçienda building plummeted from £1 million to £300,000, leaving Factory swimming frantically in negative equity, and a 23 per cent repayment schedule stripping away at their already rapidly emptying purse.

Wilson: 'I have taken so much flak for this . . . from the media in particular. They never blame Rob or Alan or New Order . . . but it's always me. The banks blamed, and still blame, me. Yet I'm just some guy who understands bands. I'm not a financial expert ... it was the banks who were the financial experts ... outrageous, isn't it? Everyone in the country who spent a lot of money on buildings just before the collapse would be fucked. There is no way out of that one ... it was just bad luck. If the people who built Canary Wharf can be fucked in such a way, then there is no reason why a bunch of financial idiots like Factory could escape.

'To be honest,' he continues, 'we would have survived even that if we hadn't been so stupid with our acts. We lost James quite early on, which was a real blow ... we knew they would be huge and we thought we might, at least, get an album out with them. And then, on a smaller scale, the Railway Children looked like breaking back in 1988, and they went to Virgin. We just thought, Enough is enough. It was ridiculous. That's when we first started thinking and talking about making some kind of alliance with a major company. We realised that there was just no other way ... the real problem ... the eternal indie label problem is that, when a band starts to happen, even after the label has ploughed lots of money, time and effort into them, their manager invariably gets a hard-on. He wants to fuck someone, or something ... he senses money ... and what does he or she do? Goes to fuck a major label. That is his or her job, except that in the long term I believe James, the Railway Children ... all the bands we lost, would have been better off with us ... with the exception of OMD, who did the right thing. In that sense, those managers who took bands away, eventually let their acts down because, like Rob, they should have taken the long-term view rather than just go for the big advance ... but that is just my opinion. I *would* say that, wouldn't I? It happens to be true, though.'

In the end, the Factory ethic, the unprecedented and commendable idea of 'not owning the artist', would swing heavily, destructively, inevitably against them. This was particularly evident at one of the multitude of meetings between Factory and Polygram (London) that took place between 1989 and 1993. It was one of the more serious and infamously pointless little get-togethers, during which the swallowing of Factory would appear to be the basic goal. Lawyers and accountants from both sides were lined up along the table in Polygram Tower, the general topic of the morning's discussion being Polygram's lighthearted disbelief that Factory had operated for so long with no contracts at all.

'Well,' one of the Factory team – Rob, probably – noted, 'there *is* a contract, of sorts . . . we did sort of draw something up back in 1979. We thought we had lost it, to be honest, but I think someone unearthed it last week. It was just a bit of paper.'

Intrigued, the Polygram elite asked if they could see it and Rebecca Boulton, from New Order's company, Gainwest, duly faxed the innocuous little sheet of scrawl from the Factory office.

When the fax arrived, it was passed around the Polygram side of the room, all of whom fell into stony silence, open-mouthed disbelief clouding over their previous joviality. As it turned out, the piece of paper wasn't the end of the affair, but it could so easily have been.

'The thing is,' stated the Polygram spokesperson, 'that when we heard that you didn't have any contracts, we weren't that concerned. You may not own the bands but you have always got the back catalogue . . . well, you have *always* got the back catalogue *unless*, that is, you have a piece of paper like this . . . which specifically states that ". . . the musicians own all the music and we own nothing! Signed A.H. Wilson, A. Erasmus." At the moment, we don't know what it is we are supposed to be buying here. You don't seem to be worth a single penny.'

The meeting immediately evaporated and for a while at least – the two sides would reconvene – Factory realised that they were a financially worthless company sitting in a new office building that was worth about a third of the money they had ploughed into it, with two other buildings, both of which seemed to be diminishing in value on a daily basis, armed with a roster and a back catalogue which they didn't even own, and no money to break the new acts, who were becoming increasingly, understandably, restless, and with a predatory media gathering on the horizon.

(There was a cruel irony, savagely celebrated in the northwest, though mercifully lost on the rest of England: Wilson had, for some considerable time, been the host of the hugely successful Granada programme, *Flying Start*, in which a weekly selection of small businesses set out to impress a panel of surly 'experts' in an attempt to secure, as a prize, a valuable cash injection. Wilson had been chosen for the role for three reasons. His effortless presentation style had matured beyond the youthfully stylistic and he had attained a level of commanding acceptability. He was seen as a perfect link between the cold, sharp, distant professionalism of the experts, the nervy optimism of the contestants and the warmth of the studio audience. Thirdly, he had attained, in the north-west, a general reputation as successful music business entrepreneur. Granada, to their credit, refused to pull Wilson from the show as Factory began, very publicly, to fall apart.)

For a while, albeit superficially, things looked good at Factory. The new office arrogantly and stylishly surveyed the traffic which endlessly surged past. The building even seemed to accept the derogatory graffiti which, appertaining to Wilson, had been sprayed artlessly across the front door, with good grace. For visitors, however, it always seemed a beautiful though rather distant affair – soulless, clinical and, perhaps, intimidating; quite the antithesis of the Palatine flat. Personally, I only entered the building on one occasion but felt rather like

I was being shunted through some elitist art complex or a cold, wealthy, modern house on Malibu Beach. It was most unwelcoming, suspicious of any casual visitor and held an aura, most paradoxically, of great wealth.

'I loved the building,' defends Wilson. 'I mean, it was stupid and absurd . . . it even had a zinc roof, which you couldn't see. But just think of the satisfaction of sitting under a zinc roof! But maybe it was a little cold . . . Jon Savage said that as well. I think that, perhaps this was because it was built during a comparative 'up cycle', when the Madchester thing was raging, and yet, by the time we got into it, Factory was very much in a down cycle, with all the mounting debt. That probably affected the mood of the place. We were badly staffed as well. Two of the seven main staff were mistakes . . . not Factory people.'

Factory mistakes were rebounding, amassing, ganging up.

Peter Saville: 'It was a time of absolutely incredible bad luck. For Factory to go under, practically everything that could possibly go wrong would have to go wrong . . . and everything did.'

Some of the mistakes, however, would be glaring and seemingly pointless. Factory had famously poured over £100,000 into the Cath Carroll album, *England Made Me*, which came complete with hyper-expensive photo shoots and, for the artist, an utterly superfluous recording trip to Brazil.

'It seemed bizarre but we believed in her, though fuck knows why,' states Wilson, who had originally picked Carroll up as the driving force behind Meiow, a mid-eighties indie outfit, not without a tuneful allure or a certain amount of intrigue, and pre-dating, as they did, the jagged female perspective of bands like Sleeper, Elastica and Echobelly by a good seven years. Nevertheless, Meiow, and latterly Cath Carroll, were always quite obviously never destined for major stardom. So why all the money?

'I'm the only person who can answer that,' admits Wilson. 'Now that was fucking crazy. Cath Carroll actually did me over on three occasions. The first time was back in 1979 when Cath and Liz were working on *City Fun*. They wanted to do a one-off colour special. They said that if I gave them three hundred quid, they would make the mags, sell seven hundred of them and get my money back. OK, I thought, great, yeah! So I gave them £300 of my own money and they just fucked off with it. That little incident should have taught me a great deal. Why didn't I learn? What a portentous and shoddy piece of crap that was. The next time I saw them they were on this New Order documentary, on Channel Four in 1984, and they were screaming, "Oh Tony, he had such bad taste in clothes . . . he even wore COOOOWBOOOOY BOOOTS YEAAAAURGH!" So I just thought, Fuck you. You know, you had ploughed your own money into people, really believed in what they were doing, and they would just shit on you like that. Then, in the late eighties, I picked up again with Cath Carroll. Ask me why? I have no idea. Now this really was, I fully admit, totally crazy, but I believed in her . . . sending her off to Brazil to record her album, arranging mega expensive photo shoots. It might have worked . . . she did have talent . . . if the artist had just shown a bit of commitment, but Cath upped and left and went to live in Chicago. So. I ask you, how the hell do you promote an indie act that lives in fucking Chicago? Then, after all that, Cath turns round and says that we didn't promote her very well. How ironic can you get?'

In the *NME*, in *Melody Maker* and in a 'mad, crazy article in *GQ*', Wilson would receive a heavy bombardment of critical flak for the Cath Carroll expenditure, some of it justified – for, a number of 'lesser' Factory acts were duly horrified to discover such excess – although the paradox of his public image, veering from Machiavellian cynical entrepreneur to artistically guided business buffoon, was at times entertainingly ludicrous and perhaps even true to the Factory ethic, which lingers still.

As 1991 waned into winter, and as Factory's teetering fiscal position began to shudder through the somewhat suspicious and disbelieving Manchester grapevine ('How can they be skint? They made a mint from Madchester and the Mondays', etc.), it became clear to the clearly ruffled Wilson and Erasmus that for the company to remain in parallel financial status while the stop/start negotiations with London staggered to some kind of conclusion, the next two albums from their two big-selling acts, New Order and Happy Mondays, would have to be pulled into the imminent future. Both bands professed to understand the Factory situation, and both acts knew that they had massively overspent during their last album recordings. Wilson received assurances from both bands that the recordings would not topple over the heady £150,000 mark. As it would turn out, the Mondays' album would cost £380,000 and New Order £430,000. Throughout these increasingly expensive recordings, the Factory office would become more and more fraught. A&R man Phil Saxe, on three separate occasions, found himself racing down the M4 in the direction of Peter Gabriel's Real World Studios, where New Order were encamped, armed with a bankers' draft, successfully intercepting a car which was simultaneously speeding towards the studio, intent on picking up the digital delay equipment because Factory, yet again, hadn't paid the rental.

Cath Carroll aside, the most glaring and frankly ludicrous error surely had to be the decision to record the Happy Mondays' album in Barbados. To send Happy Mondays, of all bands, to Barbados, of all places, truly defies logic, and as if to keep their reputation intact, the band duly responded by treating the island to an excessive and elongated hedonistic orgy. What more could Factory have expected?

Ironically enough, contrary to popular rumour, the financial stability of Happy Mondays as a working unit wasn't as healthy, especially in the wake of the mighty *Pills Thrills and Bellyaches*, as it should have been. Manager Nathan McGough showed no hesitation in informing Wilson that it would be hugely advantageous if the next album was recorded, completed and released as soon as possible. In short, both the band and the label needed an album out during the course of 1992. This is not, in defence of the Mondays, the kind of pressure that sits easily on the shoulders of even the most prolific and stable artists, let alone a thoroughly loose arrangement like the Mondays. Nevertheless, McGough, fuelled by an unexpected burst of Shaun Ryder creativity, saw no reason why the band couldn't record the album in, say, March 1992. The original intention had been to re-use the production formula that had so successfully garnished the rough edges of *Pills* ... Once again they hoped to retain the services of Oakenfold and Osborne. After calling the duo, and being told that the producers were fully booked until June, and with fiscal pressure mounting dangerously, McGough and Wilson decided that Happy Mondays simply couldn't wait. Unfortunately, this decision marked a souring of the relationship between Factory and Oakenfold and Osborne, who believed that they had been deliberately overlooked. This wasn't the case at all – the decision to approach ex-Talking Heads Chris Frantz and Tina Weymouth as alternative producers was initially instigated by mere financial pressures. That album had to be in the shops before the end of the year.

NEW ORDER – POWER, CORRUPTION AND LIES?

Tony Wilson: 'The wonderful thing for me was always how New Order saw the collapse of Factory. If you watched the second New Order television documentary, *Neworderstory*, directed by Paul Morley, you would have got the impression that New Order had lost money, wouldn't you? That is because New Order, to this day I think, actually believe that they did lose money. Do you think they did? They were, and probably still are, quite ignorant of the facts. Rob agrees with me, but he says, "Well, what can you do? Musicians will always be like that!" '

As Factory crashed messily, there were, of course, multitudinous creditors. In theory, at the head of this list would be their major artists. Joy Division, for instance, were owed around £150,000 and similar amounts were left outstanding to New Order and Electronic. Nobody can deny that, to those three interlinked entities, approximately £450,000 remained dangerously unpaid. However, when Polygram finally decided to buy Factory back from the receiver, the very first item on the agenda would be the honouring of the New Order/Joy Division and Electronic debts. As it turned out, every single penny returned to the artists.

Happy Mondays, despite Shaun Ryder's insistence that he only recorded the final and critically loathed *Yes Please* in Barbados because he could get some of the money that Factory owed him back by taking it as a holiday, were actually indebted to Factory to a fully recoupable tune of £380,000 (hence McGough's nervousness – had Happy Mondays sold another one million records, then not a penny would have reached them until the £380,000 had been recouped). In addition to this, there were two other bands: Steve and Gillian's the Other Two and Pete Hook's Revenge, managed by Tony Michaelides, both of whom owed Factory considerable amounts (the Other Two owed £180,000 and Revenge £360,000). Hence, a strange little vortex of debt was duly swirling as Factory stood, poised above the plughole. (Factory, in total, owed Barney around £450,000 while the other members of his band owed Factory approx £540,000.) The ever-perceptive Phil Saxe, initially Mondays' 'nurturer' and Factory A&R man, was to point out at the time that Factory had literally gone down the road keeping the Other Two happy, keeping Revenge happy, keeping New Order happy, keeping Happy Mondays . . . well, you get the picture.

(Even 'Blue Monday', partly due to Factory's absurdity, had been weighted heavily in favour of the band. The Factory/New Order deal, which still languished naïvely on the back of a table napkin, was the aforementioned, groundbreaking 50/50 split. This, however, did not include the publishing, which Factory had to pay. This proved to be the most perfect example of Factory's supposedly 'dubious' business practice. The 'Blue Monday' plastic cost 35p. The label cost 2p. Sleeves, 'cut outs' and production would raise the cost to 77p per unit. After the distribution company, Pinnacle, had taken their cut, they would pay Factory 79p per unit. 1p to Factory and 1p to New Order. Out of Factory's 1p, they then had to pay New Order 3.7p publishing costs. 'It doesn't add up, does it?' says Wilson, pondering this little financial disaster. 'My God, that's true, isn't it? It is a wonder, really, that we lasted as long as we did.')

PUSHING, PLUGGING AND PROMOTING

In truth, Wilson had always loathed and loved the music industry, his venom – shared so entertainingly by Alan, Rob, New Order and Vini – balancing paradoxically with his desire to belong; to live the life; to relish the glamour. This balance had existed since his days spent presenting, and to all intents and purposes producing *So it Goes*, a period when he found himself battling against the full surge of record company promotional trickery, and in '76, '77, such trickery was the stuff of tacky legend. Wilson's punkiness, naturally, rallied strongly against such forces and, for many years, the heart of Factory Records would be constructed from this rebellious stance.

It was essential at first, of course. Factory's very identity had been based on a sheer, arrogant, seemingly self-destructive aloofness. Without such belligerence, Factory would have been another meaningless offshoot, a mere platform. In truth, though, such a stance would weaken the very moment that Joy Division first enjoyed fleeting though welcome chart success and, whether Wilson noticed it or not, the industry would encroach and entwine until, quite late in the game, Factory's aloofness would suddenly seem rather petty, pointlessly self-destructive and, on occasions, just plain dumb.

The rot began, arguably, during the time of 'Blue Monday', and was highlighted by Factory's hilariously perverse insistence on the record remaining on twelve-inch format. This was the period when local, regional industry plugger, Tony Michaelides, first became involved with Factory. Michaelides, initially, would act as a bridge between Factory and the industry machine, and would prove instrumental in strengthening the link and drawing the company closer and closer to the main promotional thrust and push; closer to the central power. Things began, typically, in an unnervingly casual manner. At the time, Michaelides was working for Island Records. Though resolutely – to this day – based in Manchester, he had 'paid his industry dues' by ferociously pushing, plugging and placing the early products of U2, whose subsequent and massive success would reflect more than favourably on those who had, as Michaelides might say, 'worked the product' (even if his eventual reward was to see the band snatched away from his grasp, never to look back, as they evolved on to a higher plateau). Naturally, he had befriended Wilson during the preceding years and Wilson, allergic to any trace of 'in-yer-face' promotional tactics, found Michaelides's laidback amiability a pleasant and rewarding alternative. Using this technique – Michaelides readily admits that a hustling nature simmers threateningly behind his affable sheen – Michaelides had secured, among other things, a prime-time slot on *Granada Reports* for U2, though such a coup seems positively absurd in the wake of U2's global dominance in later years. Though a friend of Michaelides, Wilson – still backed by the industry-loathing presence of Martin Hannett – resisted the lure of the industry, refusing point-blank to even consider such vulgar operations as promotional 'task forces', the units dedicated to securing records on radio playlists. Michaelides was persistent, however, and after often calling socially into Factory's Palatine headquarters, soon became accepted – to a point – within Factory's inner circle.

But it wasn't until the initial release of 'Blue Monday' that Michaelides truly began to believe that the Factory operation had become needlessly absurd. On his weekly rounds, flitting in and out of the still burgeoning independent radio stations in the provinces, he even began to be asked by DJs where they could get hold of this record – this record that had actually entered the charts.

'It was easy for the DJs in the know,' he states. 'People like Mark Radcliffe, then at Piccadilly, but all he did was pick up the phone and ring Tina [Simmons] at Factory . . . and Tina would drop him a copy off and that was the extent of Factory's promotional technique. Well, I thought this was ludicrous . . . especially as they were putting out records with such huge commercial potential. I mean, what is the point? Who were Factory attempting to impress? Did they have some artistic notions about running up against the industry? With respect to them, I always thought this side of it was just bullshit. But Factory had never understood the promotions side at all, and as I came in and, in their eyes, represented the record industry, I became a kind of a link. Tony was worried about using "strike forces" and doing things the normal way. But I convinced him. I just said, "Tony, this is ridiculous ... you have got to do something. You don't have to plead with people to put your records on their playlists but at the moment you are trying to compete with companies putting big money into promoting 'priority acts'." I told him that, as a record company mogul, he had a responsibility to his artists. Quality product needs quality promotion ... I think he began to alter his views at that point.'

Despite Michaelides's lone attempt to politely 'shoulder charge' the Factory beast into the wicked world of mainstream promotion, this new outlook resulted in little more than Wilson allowing Michaelides to take a couple of boxes of the 'Blue Monday' twelve inch, and to leave copies with independent radio DJs across the country, simply dropping them off on his rounds for Island Records. The line, 'I'm not being paid for this, but it's really good', genuine as it happened, seemed to work very well indeed, preserving, at least for a while, Factory's precious anti-business ethic.

'I taught Wilson how to promote without using those old in-yer-face tactics,' states Michaelides, 'and to be honest, for a guy who has a reputation for liking the sound of his own voice, he did an awful lot of listening. I think he knew that I respected Factory, as I did, for ploughing their money into high standard product, classy sleeves ... but my point was that these quality records deserved quality promotion. It was the same with New Order. I had them all in my office at one point, all open-mouthed and eager to learn, while I was discussing high-level record company strategy. It was really strange. Here were these guys ... superstars in my eyes, at least musically, and yet, on a worldwide record industry level, they were just beginning to learn. I hate saying this, but I think I introduced them to a new style of promotion, a mixing of big and small. New Order listened. I mean it was obvious ... back in Joy Division they were competing with Buzzcocks, the Clash, the Stranglers, all on major labels. They may have got much better music press but in real terms they didn't stand a chance.'

Michaelides's unofficial and unpaid role as Factory plugger lasted, in that loose and friendly state, for about twelve months, during which time New Order, perhaps coincidentally, found themselves operating on higher and higher levels. For most of this spell, the subject of money was not mentioned by Factory, or Michaelides, who with his Island retainer wasn't too bothered and, frankly, rather enjoyed the kudos granted to him as an insider to the Factory empire.

After a while, and the advance came from Factory, it was decided that Michaelides should, naturally, be placed on a retainer. This coincided neatly with Michaelides's move away from the comforting umbrella of Island and setting up in Manchester city centre as the only truly independent plugger in northern England. This liaison would stretch, famously and fruitfully, through the next ten years, including, of course, the wild times of Madchester. Infamously, however, the name Tony Michaelides would float to the top of perhaps far too many press reports during the depressing days following the Factory collapse. His name would be gathered in a sad though disparate list of creditors, some bitter, some resigned to their penniless cul de sac. Tony Michaelides, or TM Promotions as the company became known, suffered to the tune of £15,000. A mighty smack for an independent, unsubsidised operation. Like many creditors, their friendship would be severely tested, if not destroyed, by understandable, simmering bitterness. But could Michaelides, after all, the most record company-minded person in the entire Factory operation, sense the impending doom?

Michaelides: 'To be fair to Tony, he was convinced that the deal was done with London Records and the bail-out was going to happen. Everyone would get paid . . . and he firmly believed it because he was repeatedly reassured at that point. But, in retrospect, it must be said that it was surely in the interests of the Polygram organisation to allow Factory to get weaker and weaker, so in the end they could say, "Thank you Factory . . . you are fucked. We will take New Order. Fuck Cath Carroll! We'll take Steve and Gillian." London didn't have to break New Order. It was all so easy for them. The band, and Factory, had done all the hard work. All the building up. And they had done it all in a very Factory, Rob Gretton, very individualistic way. It would be impossible to do that now. Look at Oasis. They have Sony behind them; Factory just had Tina picking up the phone. I honestly think that, although that independent stance was important at first, the Factory epitaph was written by London Records. They knew what they wanted. I may be wrong, but in my opinion I don't think they were straight with Tony.

'Factory taught me more about this business than anything else . . . because it taught me to separate business from pleasure. I was naïve, really. I remember when all the talk was of an impending collapse, and creditors would be going around the Haçienda, collecting bits of money here and there. And people were serving "wind-up orders". Well, I wasn't putting pressure on my mates. But I suppose I was the easy target, when push came to shove, and I really needed the money. I remember having lunch with Tony, Allen and Rob in Chinatown . . . and I was looking at the three of them . . . three mates. And yet, I wasn't a funded company. I was desperate for the money they owed me at that point. I was becoming aware that you can't just sit there and be matey, that you don't get any less respect by being treated seriously. I knew, as I was sitting there, that my invoices were being pushed to the bottom of their pile because I was a mate. They knew I wouldn't inflict winding-up orders on them. But I was sitting there, at that meal, saying, "Look,

I'm sorry but I have had ten cheques bounce on me, and it's costing me a lot of money." I knew they were in a state and were paying people off in dribs and drabs, but I had to say something. And Rob said to the others, "Don't you think we should pay our friends?"

'It was my girlfriend at the time, Liz, who still works with me, who helped me see sense. It was she who saw the end coming. I was round at her house . . . and I'll never forget this. I was probably moaning on and on . . . and we were drinking champagne in her kitchen. She just said, "Look Tony, they are your friends, but they are taking the piss. You have got to do something, before it's too late." '

Wilson would dispute Michaelides's suggestion that London took a step back and simply allowed Factory to fold. It wasn't so simple. In fact, the long haul to eventual survival – of sorts – would begin way back in 1988, when Wilson met London Records chief, Roger Ames, in a Japanese restaurant in Kensington. Ames advised Wilson that, 'Your overseas system is crap, Tony. You have all these conflicting labels – Virgin in France, Rough Trade in Germany, God knows who in Holland – and it's all very silly. You have got to get the synergy working.'

Wilson was impressed by this, for from close range he had seen Elliot Rashman and Andy Dodd take Simply Red – whose membership, of course, was so heavily flavoured by the aged and out of favour 'musos' who languished in the initial version of Durutti Column – on to a world stage, precisely by understanding such global networking notions. Wilson knew, back then, as Manchester unfolded spectacularly, that Ames would be interested in buying into, if not swamping, Factory Communications. He agreed with Ames, although with Factory on one of the peaks of their thoroughly disorientating two-year cycles, he decided to wait a while. Nevertheless, during constant conversations with Ames during the following twelve months, the London/Factory deal was beginning to shape into a foggy reality.

The deal began at a painfully slow pace, and slowed even further as time progressed. Factory's long-standing lawyer at one point abruptly left for the comparative safety of LA and recommended that Factory employ the esteemed services of Tony Russell, later to take control of the George Michael affair. Unfortunately, Russell and Ames would tend to, in Wilson's words, constantly 'wind each other up . . . it went back and forth so many times . . . the deal kept being worked on but went further and further down the road. I couldn't see an end to it.'

Things were getting worse and worse. Ames's lawyer, John Kennedy, adding to Wilson's simmering anxiety, was openly nervous about the deal. On five separate occasions, the London/Factory deal seemed to have been sealed and, while the two parties retreated to 'sort out the details', London would pull back, and negotiations would have to restart. At one point, Ames asked his junior accountant, 'Can we really afford to do this?' The initial answer was affirmative although, six months down the line, with Factory's position steadily weakening, the same accountant would advise Ames, 'We are making a terrible mistake. We can't afford to do this.'

Maurice Levy, who had been instrumental in securing Palace Pictures into the grip of Phonogram, with disastrous eventual results, kept informing Ames, 'This is your Palace . . . you are making a big mistake, Roger . . . you'll never live this Factory deal down.'

Wilson: 'In retrospect, I think that the doubters of Polygram – Levy, John Kennedy – were right . . . we were so obviously in real trouble; we were clinging on desperately, and they were edging away.'

Not a particularly healthy base for negotiation. If London had deliberately edged backwards, could anyone blame them?

Wilson: 'No . . . but if the deal had been done at the original time, before Roger started backing away, then they would have bought a fairly healthy company . . . more than that, actually. Phil Saxe wanted to sign Oasis to Factory, when no one else wanted to know them . . . they would have come into the whole package. I may be getting carried away here, but there was also talk of signing Pulp as well but, well, we just didn't have the money. But, as I would later point out to Roger, if London hadn't messed about with lawyers and things, they would have had Factory, Oasis and the people who would become Black Grape . . . it would have been a great deal for them.'

In the end, things would twist even more messily. Roger Ames had assured Wilson that Factory going into receivership didn't matter. It was common practice for a multinational to buy such companies back from the receivers. John Kennedy drove to Manchester, intent on going to the bank, with Factory, to set the 'buy back' deal in place.

'The only thing on the agenda at this point,' claims Wilson, 'was getting New Order's money back . . . it was all going to happen, and happen before Christmas.'

After two years of serious negotiations with Factory, Polygram had finally met with New Order in person, in what had been intended to be a run of the mill, ingratiating meeting. As far as Polygram had been concerned, their previous, multitudinous meetings with Wilson, Erasmus and, of course, Gretton, had also, by proxy, been with New Order. Unfortunately Barney, for reasons he still won't disclose, chose the moment to, in Wilson's words, '. . . fly into a strop . . . he told them that he never wanted to see fucking Wilson again.'

Naturally, this action split the entire issue in two. Stunned, the Polygram representatives immediately decided to proceed with New Order as a singular deal, and they would still purchase Factory, but as an entirely separate entity. Wilson would spend a further eighteen months in a state of fevered anxiety, faxing and phoning every day, desperately attempting to get the deal off the ground. At one point this deal included, 'little bits of money ... enough to sort out all the individuals we owed.' It wasn't to be. John Kennedy asked for a guarantee from the receivers that what they were buying – Factory – were legally able to sell. 'What guarantee!' came the indignant reply. 'Tony, we are receivers ... receivers don't ever give guarantees.'

Wilson: 'John Kennedy wouldn't allow Roger to buy Factory without that initial guarantee ... and then it was a case of London needing a guarantee that we hadn't or couldn't sell the name to anyone else. We spent a year arguing about that. In the end it was all pointless because London bought the Factory back catalogue without any guarantees ... we could have cut two years of crap out of it all, two years in which only the lawyers made money ... and I felt, and still feel, personally responsible for the creditors and the people who lost their jobs. Lawyers made money and people suffered ... and it all fell down because of a lot of stupid, irrelevant hot air. It was all so fucking unnecessary. But, in the end, we were able to get Factory Too up and running, under London's patronage. I went into this second phase in two minds. I remember Ames once saying to me, "Tony, do you want to go through all that crap again?" I nodded my head. I had to reply in the affirmative because the setting up of Factory Too was part of the whole deal ... if it had broken down at that point there would have been a five-year mess, writs flying everywhere. Secretly I was absolutely dreading running Factory again ... but, as it has turned out, things are now terrific. We are smaller and much, much happier ... and we have great artists, too.'

Tony Michaelides: 'There was a certain loyalty that always seemed present in Rob Gretton. And he showed it again, as soon as he could, when New Order signed to London. London, naturally, wanted their guys to take over and start running round, calling New Order "their act". But they had done fuck all to break New Order. No one at London had anything to do with New Order's success. And Rob insisted, under considerable pressure, that London use the same pluggers – that Jeff Bennett did the press and Tony Michaelides Promotions did the regional. They said, "We'll do it all." Rob said, "Fuck off! *They* do it." He was incredibly loyal to keep us and we were put on a retainer, of which he paid half and London paid half. It was just that "goes around comes around thing". Rob acted very strongly and very honestly – a rare thing – and I love him dearly for it.'

Chapter Eighteen

Factory Too

THE COUNTRY FOLK

Halfway up a hill, rising steeply above Macclesfield, with the Cheshire plain stretching out to touch the distant grey shadows of North Wales to the west, and with the Derbyshire hills gathering ominously to the rear, a faintly familiar figure with an angular face and sharp, business-like haircut, watches his neighbours shuffling to and from work. He wonders, if only for a minute, just what it would be like to don the grey suit, clamber into the obligatory BMW, or board the city-bound train; to spend each day embroiled in the battles of office life. Just for a moment he feels a twinge of envy. Ordinariness for Steve Morris and his partner, in life and in work, Gillian Gilbert, remains something to be coveted, something to be cherished. Gillian and Steve might not be utterly normal people – who is, really? – but their extraordinary history lies hidden behind a domestic completeness. This, itself, is extraordinary. New Order might still be 'superstars' two miles away in Macclesfield town centre, but that hasn't stopped Gillian and Steve from effectively 'melting' into the populace. And up here, where rock and dance music count for very little, if anything at all, Gillian and Steve are well known in their locality; well known and well liked. Are they, asked one villager in the local pub, 'That nice couple, with labradors and a studio, or something?'

'It's true that I do envy people their ordinary lives,' admits Steve, a little stressed, perhaps, his Coca-cola shaking in his hand. 'Sometimes, quite often I suppose, I would just like to forget the whole business of being in a successful band, and get on with life just like everyone else, but maybe that's being selfish?'

Some people might think so. Some people might take that as typical pop-star bullshit. After all, farm studios in Cheshire are beyond the means of most. Some people, even, might suggest that Gillian and Steve are actually squandering their celebrity status. It is wasted on them. Shouldn't they, after all, be opening nightclubs in Miami with Sean Penn, or some similarly over-photographed prat?

Gillian Gilbert smiles while absorbing these, frankly, rather daft sentiments. 'Well, are you saying that I'm a pop star?' she quizzes, as if the notion had never been put to her before. 'Well ... about that nightclub business ... I'd love to open a nightclub in Miami – I have *always* wanted to do that kind of thing. It's just that that is not how it happens. Not with us, anyway.' She glances towards Steve, as if in mild complaint, as if to say, 'Nothing like that *ever* happens to us.'

Their kind of fame – a controlled fame, really – is not, surely, a fame of an unpalatable nature. As huge as they may be, the general public do not know them; do not probe into their privacy. One wonders, however, if being adored by a sundry mixture of students and yobs for a full fifteen years has had any adverse effects.

'I often get asked if I am pregnant,' states Gillian. 'On trains ... when I am sitting on a train, some guy will come up to me and ask me that. I don't know why. Do I look pregnant? Do people think that, if a girl hasn't been working for some time, then she is automatically pregnant?'

'I got recognised in Boots once,' states Steve, without realising that he has just made the kind of statement one would normally associate with some third-rate pub outfit in Accrington, or somewhere quite dreadful.

He seems happy, to a point. He shares, with Gillian, a Range Rover'n'labrador lifestyle which might well be the ultimate goal of any self-respecting insurance broker, and yet he remains lost in paradox. So, one might ask, where's the glamour? What was the point of it all? Money? Do they want it or not? These two became pop stars. Once, they so desperately longed to be pop stars, but is that all there is? Two labs and a living gas fire?

'I like getting recognised sometimes,' admits Gillian. 'Sometimes it is nice to walk into a club and hear people saying, "Look, there's so and so." I would be lying if I said that I hated that happening. But it became so stupid at one point. People would walk up to Barney and tell him that they had spent years studying his lyrics . . . even Barney doesn't know half his lyrics.'

But what about the process of making music?

'When you get to this level,' adds Steve, 'making music is often the one thing that you hardly ever seem to get around to doing. New Order became 95 per cent meetings. That's why we haven't existed as a band for ages . . . we may or may not work together again . . . but we can't ever be a band, really. It is all meetings in the end, whatever business you get tied up in. Perversely, I suppose, that answers the original line of enquiry here. New Order and the offshoots could be a nine-to-five job . . . if I wished.'

They have, during recent times, been involved in 'other stuff'. In the main, television soundtracks. For a while, of course, they surfaced under the guise of the Other Two, a reaction, of sorts, to Electronic and Revenge. The Other Two arrived too late, too timidly, on London Records at the death of 1993, and one senses, listening to the album, that it was a result of a set of studio tinkerings from the early nineties; a not entirely successful gathering of songs – poppy, floaty, essentially feminine, the antithesis, perhaps, of the macho driving beat of New Order.

'We had always worked together producing television soundtracks,' states Gillian, 'and the trouble with those is that you would put tons of work in and then the programme would be shown and nobody would see it, and that would be that. So we always pestered Factory to let us work on some poppy stuff but they would always say, "We don't release poppy stuff, go away." That angered us a bit; well, it angered us a lot actually. We became so frustrated, so annoyed ... it was part of the problem. Our relationship with London seemed so much more productive. It was odd though ... when we did the recordings for the Other Two. We had Steven Hague come up to Macclesfield to produce us, and it was a case of, "Oh no, Steven Hague is coming up. We must tidy up the studio ... we must sweep the floor ... do the dusting." '

I tell them that, at the risk of sounding patronising, the whole thing sounded like the thoughts of a young girl, wandering around. Dark thoughts, too. The single, 'Selfish', for example, was about the guilt factor in proposed abortion.

'Yes ... it could be seen like that,' agrees Gillian. 'It is full of things that never could be said within the confines of New Order.'

It is Steve Morris, I believe, who has always been the perfect manifestation of New Order's hilarious paradox. I recall, in particular, a 1983 cover of style mag *The Face*, famously displaying a close-up of Steve's sharp side parting. It was a powerful, lasting image and seen by many as a symbol of hip, young, smart, eighties ... yuppiedom even. And yet Steve Morris, being nothing if not a technocrat, never cared much for clothes or personal style.

'Ha, that's true,' laughs Gillian. 'Yes, that haircut ... the irony is that, before that photo, his hair had just been cut by my sister. At the end of the day, we are not special people at all. Nobody could be more normal than us.'

And yet languishing in their farm garage is the Christmas present that Gillian bought Steve in 1993. It is an army tank. Steve sits in it, sometimes, and plays. The pair had seen it, sitting conspicuously on a used car forecourt in Handforth, a proud, green mass among a sea of Metros. Following Steve's excited outburst, 'Wow ... a tank! I want it ... and I know just where I would like to drive it!', Gillian crept back to the garage and purchased it. That is the kind of thing one can do, when a pop-star background lurks behind the soft normality. But where, one is hugely tempted to ask, exactly would Steve like to drive the tank? It's a question that brings a cheeky smirk to his face. There is a fondness and a bitterness lurking deep within the Morris make-up, and Steve and Gillian, for all their 'nice couple' appeal, nurture a fading fondness and a growing bitterness for their days spent on Factory.

'We lost so much money ... all down the drain to support Factory quirks and stupid buildings. Our history is littered with irony. Tony even asked us, once, to write some music to commemorate the opening of that fucking HQ building! How ironic can you get ... we were asked to write the music to celebrate throwing another huge bundle of money away.'

Gillian: 'When my mum first met him [Wilson], she told him, "I can't understand why a lot of people don't like you." I should have listened to her. Steve reckons Tony should have sold timeshares.'

'I never want to go through anything like that again,' says Steve. 'I prefer things cold and professional now. Factory got very petty and childish ... it was very laddish in that office – everyone going on about who has got the biggest Jag. Horrible. I never want anything to do with Factory again.'

GETTING AWAY WITH IT

Barney, meanwhile, remains, typically, the least visible of the four. The days when he would often be spotted, tripping down the steps of the Haçienda, heading for intense alcoholic indulgence in the Gay Traitor, have long gone. And indeed, of the four, it was Barney who least enjoyed the rigmarole of touring, his celebrated onstage aloofness often being the result of genuine indifference, exhaustion and alcohol. At the time of writing, like the other three, he was wholly immersed in non-New Order activity. Indeed, he was holed up in the studio with Johnny Marr, apparently putting the finishing touches on the long-awaited second Electronic album, for the EMI subsidiary, Parlophone. Not surprisingly, absolutely no information on this recording was forthcoming from the somewhat bewildered record company, perhaps due to a previous hiccup! It had been largely rumoured that the album was ready for release, and, indeed, some tapes were circulating, in October 1995. Not that it necessarily matters. There was always a certain 'looseness' about Electronic, that Barney – and probably Johnny Marr and part-time member, Pet Shop Boy Neil Tennant, as well – found so refreshing. The pressure of producing music for the solid, swelling and identifiable fan base of New Order always seemed artistically repressive. With Electronic, Barney and Marr could make individualistic light pop singles, and albums! And if the albums would be sandwiched by five years of apparent inactivity . . . who cared? Certainly not Barney and Johnny! Electronic would be a fluttering little beast with no real notion of a fan base at all. No intended target.

'. . . and no good music; I don't like anything Barney does away from New Order,' Wilson stated, and re-stated, although 1990's massive selling 'Getting Away With It' single can't exactly have damaged Factory's finances.

'I think that Barney needs controlling,' offered Hooky. '. . . I don't think that his Electronic manager [Marcus Russell] has the kind of personal hold over him, like Gretton. It may seem odd, considering how untogether we often were, and how laidback Rob sometimes seemed, but he could always get Barney working . . . get the old New Order cocktail shaking. I like Electronic . . . but it's not the same.'

Ironically enough, Electronic, instigated as a musical body free of the normal restrictions of group life, was conceived in the Haçienda toilets, with Barney asking Marr if he fancied making an album, while the pair of them stood before the toilet pans. Electronic had been duly born as, in Marr's words, 'two mates enjoying playing music together'. The obvious paradox to this seven-year – although most of it was blank – idyll is that Electronic, at their 1990 peak, began to resemble a dreaded musicianly 'supergroup', an inevitability that has been avoided only by the lack of recent activity.

Meanwhile, it was through the Electronic connection that their aforementioned manager, Marcus Russell (Ignition Management) came to find himself in charge of the biggest story in British pop in the nineties. In 1992, after being handed a scruffy demo tape via his brother Ian, Johnny Marr latched on to the early sound of Oasis, befriended Noel Gallagher and duly brought the band to the attention of Russell, presumably grateful ever after.

THE TOWNIES

Somewhere in East Didsbury, tucked neatly, shyly, mercifully away at the rear of an adjacent house, stands a large, pretty, warmly inviting Victorian detached home, resplendent in an ivy coat, simply the kind of house most people would long for. Quietly large, rather than flash. It is filled with the precocious noise of two bright, bubbling children running rampant and happy. And there in the kitchen, sit Caroline and Peter Hook, television star and rock star, loving the comforts allowed them by their bizarre professions, but apparently free from any trace of affectation. Caroline's fame, one presumes, will not always be dispatched neatly to her alter-ego, Mrs Merton, but it would be a great shame if her affability – and natural comic talent – was touched by the darker forces of fame. But the house is happy, and Hooky happier than anyone can remember. Tomorrow will mark his 40th birthday. In the garage lurks the gift-wrapped Harley Davidson that Caroline will present to him in the morning. He sits, grinning, softly chatting away, quaffing Rioja from a large goblet.

'I am probably the only member of New Order who misses playing live. I do miss that,' he sighs, before cautiously adding, 'but, then again, I have still got Revenge. I record now, just down the road in my own studio. I have learnt a lot of lessons ... I would never want to go through all that again. I don't know. I find it hard to talk about it. Especially Tony. I love Tony dearly, but I would never go through all that shit again. If you were to sum Factory up, you could say that nobody could possibly waste so many opportunities in one lifetime than that. We could all have achieved so much more. But, I suppose we never had to work our bollocks off, touring the US extensively ... we never wanted to. *We* were always very lazy, painfully slow. We didn't do interviews for ages. Some people reckon that's great ... that we never lost our integrity. Others suggest that, had we not been so stupid and so lazy, we would be living in castles, like Bono. It's swings and roundabouts. I am quite happy with everything we have done. I wouldn't want it any different.

'We were never business people ... we would never even talk about business, right up until the Haçienda. For eight whole years we would just tell Rob to sort out the business while we just carried on writing songs like the complete plonkers we were. It was only after the Haç had nearly crippled us that me and Barney went berserk. It was always our choice, though, and that is what, I believe, kept the music so good throughout all those years. It was pure . . . it just dripped out of us. We were always very focused on the music but we never made any real money until about 1985/86. I can remember really struggling to pay my gas bill – and I mean *really* struggling. I was so close to being cut off, *after* "Blue Monday" had been a massive hit all around the world. The biggest selling twelve-inch single of all time and I couldn't pay my fucking gas bill. That is when it really hit me . . . I was thinking about this, standing in the Haçienda, which was full for a change, wondering why all the students could afford to go and drink there and I couldn't . . . and I owned the fucking place. Yeah, me and Barney had a real change of attitude. We went fucking crazy. We will never know how much money we lost through Factory's ineptness.

'I am still a sucker for Tony's patter. This was proven when he went down owing me God knows how much. Then he asked me to produce a band for Factory Too. I said to him, "All right Tony, but I'm only going to do it if you are not going to piss me about with the money." He was paying me £750 for producing Italian Love Party for Factory Sample Too. That was eighteen months ago and I still haven't been paid. What a mug I am.'

Caroline, drifting into the kitchen like a mischievous ghost, slaps a second bottle of wine on the table, uncorks it, and lovingly fills Hooky's glass. She laughs a lot, disappears and sends the kids in to ask questions like, 'Daddy, when are you going back to prison?' or, worse, to drag the conversation down into shameless toilet humour.

'Never marry a comedienne,' advises Hooky, too late as it happens. It's an unlikely partnership, although the two have rather more in common than most people might think. Caroline's initial television break, as the innuendo-based personality of Mrs Merton, came when she was offered a tension-busting comedic spot on the north-west debate programme, *Granada Upfront*, co-hosted by Tony Wilson, who proved, as he so often does, instrumental in securing the gig for her.

'He [Wilson] is such a fantastic presenter,' she admits. 'He is so utterly professional, so in control, that I find it hard to imagine that he could run such a shambolic record company . . . all that money! I like him but I wouldn't trust him to go and fetch my newspaper from the shops!'

But New Order, I insist, did rather well in the end – they got all the money back. I launch into the facts surrounding the money owed to Factory by Revenge and the Other Two.

Hooky: 'I get the gist of that. It is true in a sense. But that's just one side of the story. What happened with Revenge was that I was booked into my own Studio, Suite Sixteen, in Rochdale. Sharn the studio manager just kept sending our recording bills to Factory and Sharn was happy because they kept being paid. And we, as Revenge, made the album slowly. Then I had one monumental meeting with Factory and they told me how much that recording cost. I just said, "Whaaaat!" How ironic. In my own studio I had run up those costs. Tony always says that we owed Factory so much, but he neglects to mention one little fact. Revenge got £300,000 advance from Capitol in America, for the USA and Canada. And Factory got half of that back plus they licensed it to every other country. We sold 88,000 in the States which was, to my delight, more than Ian McCulloch, who sold about 72,000 of his album. I was dead chuffed with that. If Tony is trying to infer that it was Revenge and the Other Two who got Factory into trouble, then that is ridiculous. It was Happy fucking Mondays who caused far more problems. They spent an unbelievable amount . . . stupid bastards. And Tony sent us to Ibiza to record and that was a seriously stupid thing to do. An absolutely unmitigated error. He gave us the biggest bollocking of our lives for that, but it was his idea!

'I will admit to anyone that Revenge was a mistake on my part because I was trying to do it all myself. Unfortunately, the people I picked up with weren't as established as I was so they couldn't teach me anything. It was a very difficult learning process. I needed someone to come to me and say, "Pete, let's have a chat. You are in a mess." That is what record companies are for. But Tony was more of a hindrance than anything. Once past all that, I thought Revenge did quite well. The stuff wasn't bad at all. On a catalogue of errors, Tony was next to me. He should, perhaps, have sent Vini in to help me. I think he was so stuck up his own arse, running a successful record company with the Mondays and all that, that he just didn't bother about Revenge or the Other Two. We needed some A&R help. Factory didn't have a clue. Barney fared a lot better when he went with Johnny Marr. He was lucky because Marr was as experienced as him, so they bounced off each other. It was easier for Barney. Me and Gillian and Steve were left out in the cold.'

Reflectively now, the wine shrinking away in the second bottle, he continues:

'This is what I love about Factory. To this day, up until 1996, I can tell you that neither Joy Division nor New Order have ever been accounted to, by Factory, for sales outside of England. We have been paid but we have never seen any accounts whatsoever. Two international big-selling acts, and we have never been given any accounts at all. Does that seem incredible? Rough Trade in America? In Germany? I have absolutely no idea how many records we have sold. I know about other bands. I can tell you to the last sale, how many discs, say, the Stone Roses sold in Singapore, but not us, and Tony likes to appear completely virginal. Like he was running it all properly. We were all as bad as one another, really. But the downfall of Factory was due to Factory directors . . . and certainly not New Order. We were just musicians. We did our job. They failed us.

'I do miss New Order. Terribly. I have no idea if we will ever play together again. It does get me down. I am very happy with what I am doing these days and, of course, my family life is fantastic, but I long to perform live. The trouble is, me and Barney are so slow. We need pushing and, believe it or not, Rob did that. He did push us. Barney is not being pushed now, in Electronic, and he needs to be. Some people said that after New Order left Factory it could never be the same again. That is true. I still think, and Johnny Marr agrees, that whatever we all do outside New Order, it never quite has that same chemistry. It never could have. Part of the chemistry was the fact that we were all so exasperated by Factory . . . Factory made us so angry and that definitely gave the music a real edge. That was the magic.'

FACTORY TOO

The circle seems complete now, with the tiny new label, Factory Too, operating from a cubic room inside the building owned by Chris Joyce, once the lynchpin drummer of the embryonic Durutti Column. And Factory, for so long, so resolutely aloof, profoundly Mancunian, now operating under the umbrella of London Records, of all people. There is no Rob Gretton now, of course – and it is no coincidence that one of Rob's little labels is called Manchester Records, still, after all these years, refusing to 'talk to cunts', it seems.

It could never be the same though, could it? Factory Too is, surely, just another cog in the machinery now. A cosy niche for

Wilson and his partner, Yvette Livesey, and Erasmus, Saville, Kelly and ... just three bands! Good fun but, well, worth writing about? No one could blame Wilson for opting for safety, for normality. Surely the madness isn't still lingering?

Wilson: 'I presumed that when Factory Too began we would be able to do what we wanted with the music. London, after all, is a dance pop label. They would leave us alone to do our own thing. And so it proved. But I thought that would be it. I thought that all the mad ideas, buildings, etc., would be a thing of the past. But that is not necessarily so. We need success first ... but there is no reason why we can't start spending on diverse things ... like a commercial art gallery! Factory Too is still loads of wacky people. Just the same. A whole lot of molecules swilling around. Making things happen. Good things ... crap things, not always young things. I mean, we even have Kim Fowley in our stable now. He's recording the band, Space Monkeys.'

Factory Too is different. It has to be. For a start, the new bands actually have contracts. A revelation! Nevertheless, there still remains a touch of the Maverick about the place. Contracts for burgeoning Factory Too bands are mercifully simplistic, as if a reflection of the company's scouting policy. If there is to be a bidding war, much the trend in nineties' music industry, much to the detriment of genuine talent, then Factory Too would simply turn away. Indeed, Factory Too are not interested in even going to see a band who have attracted a dozen A&R men. There is no point ... the whole thing escalates out of all proportion and, from such a situation, the only winners are the absolute failure bands, who, once dropped and forgotten, don't have to pay back their bloated advances. Factory Too, allergic to a bidding war, lost the brash, young Stockport band, Northern Uproar, in this way, who were pushed to £80 ... £90 ... £100,000 advance. By contrast, Factory Too deals remain, though not as simplistic as Gretton's Band on the Wall napkin, still fairly straightforward and modest. They will offer a band £40,000 or, if the manager proves sharp enough, £50,000 tops. The breakdown is simple. This means £15,000 on signature, £15,000 on commencement of the album and £10,000 on delivery. Add to this £45,000 to £55,000 recording costs, and the recoupable advance still barely tops £100,000 – not enough for high-powered record company executives from London Records to storm through the Factory Too doors screaming, 'Where are the hits?' It isn't Grettonesque simplicity. That dream died, though elements remain. It is a compromise.

Wilson: 'We have just three acts: Durutti Column, Space Monkeys and Hopper. It is quite weird because, although Manchester has remained at the top of the music industry, in terms of artistic success, down at grass-roots level there really hasn't been much happening. We put out four bands on the initial Factory Too sample – Italian Love Party, East West Coast, the Orch and . . . you know, I can't even remember the other one. None of them were very special. But, in contrast to the old Factory, we are keeping a low roster. We are keeping a space for the moment something really wonderful turns up . . . as it will. I can never forget Phil Saxe turning up with tapes of Oasis and Pulp, and we just didn't have any space. I'm not going to miss out on that kind of act again. Next time around, when it happens . . . and it will . . . I want to make a pile . . . a pile for everyone. I want to create more buildings.'

Chapter Nineteen

Factory Closure. Loose Ends.The Energy Remains

JULY 2008

Through the dense drizzle of summer: through Salford's steaming streets. Through Collyhurst – skirting the old site of the Electric Circus – avoiding big black slug vehicles called 'Animal' and 'Warrior', avoiding glances, cranking up the car stereo. Partly because of this book, and the DJ's fleeting though respectful appearance in it, I had been asked to visit the studio, to chat loosely about old times. Nothing remarkable there although I had been somewhat lost for some time. I didn't know it but this evening would rekindle my enthusiasm for music in general and Manchester in particular. The DJ and, indeed, this book, would reach out and drag me back.

The entrance to the radio station was unconventional. It was situated – somewhere – above a stark, crumbling public house. Upon entering I was met with a barrage of glares from the locals, not hostile perhaps, merely unsure. A new man in their midst; another geezer asking the whereabouts of the studio. The landlord politely smiled, before leading me up creakingly evocative stairs, through darkness, doors and dust. The door gaped open, revealing the blackness of the studio, the dull glimmer of lights red and green, the cheery bonhomie and offers of coffee.

I felt distanced from it all. From everything. Temporarily homeless, I had been skimming across spare beds and sofas from Warrington to Wigan, flirting with bad thoughts in Wales, clutching to the kindnesses of friends, crashing through a personal meltdown. It was the most unsettling period of my life. A week earlier, urged on by a national tabloid newspaper who had wanted to use my little story as a symbol of the underside of the 'credit crunch', I couldn't see any way that I could survive, let alone rediscover my love for music. But this would be the evening when everything changed.

Why is this relevant to this book? I'm not sure. I guess the importance of friends and the importance of music seemed to collide on this dank night in Salford.

The preceding twelve months had been strange indeed and famously included the death of Tony Wilson, the chief protagonist of this much-told tale. It was a year when something changed. Wilson had posthumously emerged as some kind of saviour to the twin cities. It was a situation that, in truth, had little to do with me although, as the Tony Wilson myth spiralled into orbit, I had found it difficult to retain a sense of perspective.

The DJ gave me a look of horror when I told him that he was catching me at a bad time, a real bad time, and he feared the worst. Would I clam up on his show?

The DJ's name was Dermo Northside. One-time leader of his namesake band, Northside, faves of Factory and Tony Wilson. Northside: funked-up casuals of football television, music for the marching Mods, of the latterday category, anyway. Music of the Man U resurgence. Music of a new glory, blasting into living rooms from *Granada Reports* at teatime in the north-west. Northside! One of the great lost bands of Manchester, beautiful in their pomp, later to be filed alongside The Distractions, Section 25, even A Certain Ratio. Factory bands of distinction; Factory bands unable to achieve much beyond a cult status. These were the great eclectic acts that were the heart of the record label.

That night at the radio station, evocative in the intense weather, proved a tremendous success. Fun, great fun. I somehow eclipsed the depression of the preceding months.

I put this down to one simple fact: the effervescent enthusiasm of Dermo Northside. Three records in and we were mates. No doubt about that. The music tripped by. Twisted Wheel, Echo And The Bunnymen, Stiff Little Fingers, New Order. It was pure, simple, full-on banter radio. A joy to hear; a joy to be there. It was a long time since the distraction of music had seemed so profound. Dermo's questioning was simplistic. He'd mention a book title and off I went, spinning into anecdotal nostalgia. I had forgotten about the unabashed simplicity of this. This is what it always was, back then. Banter and rant. Heady emotions dissolving in the underground. How it was, back then, when something as seemingly trivial as music could mean so much.

Factory Records was never intended to be about real life, it's just that real life started to get in the way. People died, famously, and the label became part of a great many real lives. Not many labels have achieved this. Some – Rough Trade, Creation, Stiff, Cherry Red, perhaps – but not many.

The evening carried me back to a better time, a worse place. The blackened, silent Manchester that flavoured the early stirrings of Factory, 30 years previously.

Steamy little joints. Small dense clubs blessed with a bunker mentality. That had always been the point. Any small club, any 'scene' would produce an inspiring camaraderie. The Factory

Records story that would one day be documented in cinematic glory was, in truth, a tiny dark affair. A few mates chancing their luck. A Manchester that believed it was the centre of the universe. A belief so strong that, bizarrely, it eventually became reality.

Boy oh boy, was it such fun back then, when things were so small.

That feeling still occurs, I am sure, though it is now scattered through the multitudinous city venues of today or dispersed in the grassy whiff of festivals, lost beneath the leaden skies of Somerset.

I thanked Dermo Northside for rekindling my own enthusiasm. I left the studio feeling happy . . . hadn't felt that way in years.

Although not strictly relevant, my own personal change really did appear to begin on that night. Three months later, as I type this, I am ensconced in my own lovely residence again. Life is good. Music plays.

This book was written in the mid-nineties, slap bang in the centre of a Brit Pop that I hated. As such it was tainted by nostalgia. Even then, meeting Tony Wilson weekly within the industrial chic of the Factory Too offices in Knott Mill, it seemed so late, so lost. That stumbling late-in-the-day label, clutching to former glories, pushing new acts that, obviously now, would falter in the mists of apathy. Tony's big hopes of the era: Hopper, Space Monkeys and, further down the line, the flickering excellence of Raw T on Factory's final fluttering, Factory 4 (I preferred the short-lived label name, Red Cellars) later in the day. And, later still, his lust for Lostprophets. Not his band, though a favourite of his. Kinda apt, I thought. For Tony Wilson became very famous towards the end of his life. Famous and lost. Not a prophet, really. A big-hearted flash of intelligence. Complex – one of the most complex people I have ever met.

In the early stages of this book, Tony Wilson appears as an inspiring, warmly fired man. Like Dermo, offering the full force of a love and lust of music. Later, less so, I thought. He didn't really like me so much, towards the end. I wasn't entirely sure why. But it wasn't a problem.

And afterwards, after his demise in 2007, the character 'Tony Wilson' in the popular imagination changed, almost beyond recognition. I had spent 30 years defending Tony Wilson to people who felt distanced by the affectation of his television persona. Now, in the afterglow of his life, those same people were informing me of his saintly status. Not Tony. Not that.

But, although this is a personal book in a way, it isn't biographical in regard to Wilson. Other people, who genuinely knew Tony Wilson from up close, rather than some encircling journo, will write those books. And, I strongly sense, they will all be both valid and varied.

Nor was this book ever intended to be an exhaustive scrutiny of Factory Records. From its outset in 1995 I believed and still believe, such a book would be a deadening trawl. I admit I suffered some flak surrounding the original subtitle: 'The Factory Records Story'. I had fought hard to alter one small word: 'A Factory Records Story'. The problem with the 'The', as it were, was that it promised the kind of song-by-song trainspotter text that might please many Factory devotees but would not be the kind of book I would like to read – or write. I apologise therefore, if I offended, say, the bass player of The Royal Family for not providing copious name checks. I apologise for the non-appearance of the Thick Pigeon section. It was simply never meant to fulfil that particular function.

In 2008, as I write, music still thrives in Manchester and surrounding towns even if no artists of true longevity appear to have emerged since Oasis. The breakthrough acts of 2008, The Ting Tings and The Courteeners, while excellent artists, certainly don't appear to be life-changing phenomena, well, not for anyone other than themselves. Beyond them, dozens of artists hammer away in every satellite town. Most are locked in optimism. Most can play and write to a level that might technically seem beyond the early forms of Buzzcocks and Joy Division. Gigs pepper Manchester city centre nightly. A typical example might see Stiff Little Fingers in Academy One, Pere Ubu in Academy Two and Country Joe and the Fish in Academy Three. Thirty years of disparate music gathered in a couple of adjacent buildings on a nightly basis. Back in 1977 we were lucky to discover two or three gigs per week, and everyone on the scene would attend every gig, encouraging a village atmosphere, creating a scene, as it were.

How curious though, to note the one truly breakthrough act of the past two years: not The Courteeners or Fraser King or Exile Parade or The Ting Tings but Joy Division.

Largely due to three films and a thunderous barrage of resultant hype, Joy Division and, beyond them, Factory Records have resurfaced to profound effect. Despite the fact that they no longer exist – or maybe because of that – Joy Division and all things Factory have never seemed so healthy. In Manchester, Factory is positively omnipresent.

The films about Factory had been mooted for several years. A number of good ideas, such as The Bailey Brothers' Factory-centred 'Madfuckers' film and various notions from Icon, Factory's video wing, never managed to successfully locate funding. It seemed that they never would.

The first that I had heard of *24 Hour Party People* came via a phone call from Factory founder Alan Erasmus, who spoke energetically about 'these people who are making a film about Factory Records.'

I must admit that I couldn't see the appeal at the time. How on earth could you make a successful film about an independent record label? How would that work?

When it became clear that Blackburn filmmaker Michael Winterbottom would take up direction duties, it certainly became rather more interesting. A script soon started to circulate in Manchester and, in typical Factory style, caused immediate controversy. The initial script featured inaccurate scenes largely involving Lindsay Reade, Tony Wilson's first wife, which were later dropped. I recall accompanying Lindsay to a rather tense meeting with Winterbottom in London at this time. One could sense the filmmaker was starting to worry about the blurring of fact and fiction that always occurred with Factory.

24 Hour Party People, an orgy of hip name dropping and in jokes eventually screamed entertainingly from the fringes of the mainstream. Pacy and often dizzying, self-depreciating and, in places, extremely funny, it was a film that would be gazed upon with increasing fondness as time past. *24 Hour Party People* was colourful and exuberant. By stark contrast, five years later in 2007 came Anton Corbijn's Ian Curtis biopic, *Control*, which presented the story in a stark monochrome vision of late-seventies Mancunia. Perfect, perhaps, for the presentation of a beautiful and evocative tale, but not entirely honest, not entirely truthful. Ian Curtis emerged from a Macclesfield and a Manchester that regarded itself as filled with colour and fizz, culture and vibe. Even Macclesfield, which has its dour moments, lies bordered by the richest, greenest county in Britain, Cheshire, and, arguably, the prettiest, Derbyshire. The young Ian Curtis would drift down to plush Prestbury, the epicentre of Cheshire's golden triangle, a picture-postcard village gifted with ostentatious riches. Where did that feature in Anton's stark flick? Where was Ian's beautiful, romantic grammar school? Or the

Manchester of post-George Best glamour? Kitchen-sink drama? Not really. *Control* is a beautiful myth and, as Tony Wilson often stated, 'We go with the myth.' Fair enough. Nevertheless, the myth still irks, at times.

Immense hype surrounded *Control*, mainly as a result of over-enthusiastic broadsheet editors happy to tug the lost soul of Ian Curtis firmly into the spotlight and present, largely unchallenged, the supportive writings of Paul Morley and Jon Savage. What became lost in this unholy scramble, however, was the character of Ian Curtis himself, who had been portrayed with the lack of objectivity that came naturally in a film based on the writings of his estranged wife.

For what it's worth I wasn't a fan of *Control*. Elements of it were undoubtedly excellent and, in particular, the shots of the band's performance were highly evocative and generally realistic. The Squat Club event seemed unerringly accurate to me. By contrast, I couldn't understand the inclusion of skinheads in the audience at the infamous Bury gig where a riot ensued simply due to a lack of Ian Curtis on the stage, and not because of some meathead locals.

The film is beautifully shot, albeit in the tradition of the director. For he has passed this way many times before. Corbijn painted grimy, starkly monochrome imagery on Propaganda's 'Dr Mabuse' promo video in 1984. More famously, Joy Division's 1988 'Atmosphere' video was full of typical Corbijn quasi-religious imagery and blackly surreal humour. So it came as no surprise to find him utilising the same effects in *Control*, reducing Macclesfield to a kitchen-sink grime-pit, stereotyping many of the characters, also, to a state of Northern naïveté. The film became a museum, locking the characters into cliché, in part it was a state of cliché they deserved. Yes, Joy Division really were so strikingly, unpretentiously laddish. Yes, Rob Gretton really could stoop to a state of bland machismo. I had seen this many times, but these were also multifaceted, highly talented people. As for the portrayal of Tony Wilson as a grimacing, sexless gorp, lost to the streetwise wit of the band: inaccurate and disturbing. The moment he faints after his blood had burned into the Joy Division contract was pure farce.

Despite these misgivings, it is impossible to argue with the fact that *Control* introduced Joy Division to an entire new audience. Even the soundtrack achieved sales beyond what one might have reasonably expected. And, in terms of soundtrack, *Control* is just one of a lengthening series of movies that have used the music of Joy Division and New Order. It's interesting to note that both bands seem particularly poignant within the cinematic frame. As noted in David Nolan's biography of Bernard Sumner, numerous films have benefited from the use of the bands' music, including *Donnie Darko*, *American Psycho*, *Trainspotting* and *Pretty in Pink* (detailed in this book), and not in the perfunctory manner that has been the prevailing trend in recent years. Added to this might be Steve and Gillian's work for Granada Television and beyond. As I write, in late 2008, talk is in the air of further film work that might involve all members of the band, although not necessarily together, not necessarily in the same room, or even the same country. While this may have fizzled out to nothing by the time this book re-emerges, it's worthy to note that, once again, more than one film producer has been hovering with intent. Maybe films are the way forward after all. In an age when John Lydon agrees to sell Country Life butter on British television, anything is possible.

One thing that unified both *Control* and *24 Hour Party People* was the rather dangerous way in which they flitted in and out of historical accuracy. An incident that featured within the pages of the first edition of this book was repeated – in hugely exaggerated form – in a particularly memorable and controversial scene in *24 Hour Party People*, which involved

Tony's wife, Lindsay Reade and Magazine's Howard Devoto. (Both parties enforced disclaimers in the film and, in the original script, the depiction was appallingly warped.)

'Well, I certainly did *not* go in the toilets with Howard Devoto or anybody else for that matter,' said Lindsay. 'I was sitting at a table when Howard came over, placed his drink on the table and sat talking to me.'

Not, perhaps, an event that would have made a startling cinematic moment, but that's how it often is with Factory. Myths are continually warping all over the place. Smaller myths also. Like this one, which has surfaced in a number of articles and is hotly contested. It centres on the moment that Orchestral Manouvres in the Dark effectively became a Factory band.

Lindsay Reade: 'The part in your book when Tony plays me the demo of Orchestral Manoeuvres in the Dark in the car – and I can hear Tony telling you this is how it was – but I didn't start screaming, "play it again ... play it again". Ha ha. I just told him that I liked it. I did have more mainstream tastes than Tony but I wasn't thinking commercially or anything. I just thought it was the kind of music more people might like.'

And so it proved, with that very track, 'Electricity' becoming a hit and transferring the band to the more commercially weighty Virgin Records.

Arguably the most successful of the three films is Grant Gee's long-awaited Joy Division documentary. Written, for the most part, by Jon Savage and fortunate to have the inclusion of Tony Wilson before his terribly sad demise, the documentary was built firmly on the template provided by two DVDs, James Nice's similarly paced *Shadowplayers* and the unofficial, *Joy Division: Under Review*.

Without the inclusion of Deborah Curtis the documentary was set free from the shadow of her memoir, *Touching From A*

Distance. As a tower of anecdote, the film certainly covers the story in a pedantic, factual manner. Furthermore, footage of Manchester in the late seventies seemed genuinely shocking. Unlike the romantic, stylised vision of *Control*, it displayed images of the city in a blackened state of regeneration. The story arose skilfully from this soot-blackened template and was softened by genuinely loving memories of the time delivered by the usual array of Factory illuminati. At least here the filmmaker allowed the tale to unfold naturally, to tell itself and, to that end, it is difficult to criticise. For Grant Gee and, to some extent, Jon Savage allowed themselves to be guided by anecdote. Nevertheless, it was impossible to leave the cinema without revisiting ancient thoughts of Ian Curtis.

Incredibly, there may be even more films, perhaps with Curtis as less of a central character. But all three of the recent films, even if unwillingly, served to heap a larger celebrity status on the now mythical figure of Ian Curtis.

In relation to this, there was one other result of the films, also rather damning of the times, I am afraid. Ian Curtis had seemingly finally achieved a celebrity status, three decades after his life ended so tragically. Whether he would have enjoyed such crass attention or not – there was an Ian Curtis-inspired mac-wearing photo fashion spread in one of the glossies – we can only speculate. However, a low point was surely reached with the stealing of his headstone from Macclesfield Cemetery. This was truly shocking, partly for the pain such an act would surely cause the family and, also, because of how utterly indicative of today's celebrity culture this act seemed to be.

Another headstone affair, over at Chorlton Cum Hardy's Southern Cemetery, where Tony Wilson was buried, also seemed to verge on the darkly bizarre. It was Lindsay Reade who, after visiting her ex-husband's grave, decided to locate and pay homage to Martin Hannett, another resident of the

415

cemetery. To her horror, Hannett, arguably the true genius of this story, lay unmarked except for a discarded beer can. It was only through contacting Factory personnel and some of Hannett's family that this appalling oversight was eventually rectified. Out of sight, it seemed, out of mind, apart from Colin Sharpe's stylish book about part of the life of the producer. The book, *Who Killed Martin Hannett?* (Aurum), was written as a mock murder mystery and could have been seen as flippant, though I felt that Hannett would have applauded the lightness of touch. A headstone ceremony held by the grave in December 2008 served to seal the end of the affair.

As to Factory, I sense there are people out there who are more concerned with the more obscure quirks of the label. People, and this is fine by me, who like to scrutinise every release and, more importantly, constantly unearth Factory's darkest, most eccentric and loneliest moments. This is not a bad place to search. There is sunken treasure within Factory's back catalogue. I should refer you here, now, to James Nice's exceptional, if occasionally controversial, LTM Records, based in East Anglia, which specialises in ploughing eclectic furrows from the late seventies and eighties. In particular, much unearthing of lost Factory echoes takes place in remastered glory. James and Tony didn't always see eye to eye but, well, much water and many bridges.

On LTM you will find such idiosyncratic talents as Blurt, Section 25, Crispy Ambulance, Thick Pigeon, Kevin Hewick, The Names, The Royal Family and the Poor and other ghostly echoes. James writes well about them, both in his sleeve notes and in book form. Indeed, there are many voices currently talking openly about Factory Records. They're increasing rapidly in number too, from the swell of Haçienda DJs to those who spent years pulling strings behind the scenes, and often for little or no recompense. Mike Eastwood might be such a voice. Also known as Moist, the name he chooses when posting knowledgeable quips on the earnest websites at Cerysmatic Factory and Joy Division Central as well as New Order's own World in Motion. Moist became well known because of his technical work for A Certain Ratio, Intastella and many others. Mike worked tirelessly in the technical background of Factory, where he was fondly known as 'Mikey'. He is an ever-fascinating character and always remained close to the initial Factory ethos: follow the art, don't change it. As such he remains intriguingly opposed to much of the new Factory activity. He is a likeable cynic these days and at one point physically pulled me away from a punk talk at Manchester's Central Library, dragging me to the classic Peveril of the Peak pub because, in his words, 'It was all getting a bit too trainspottery.'

'But Mike, with respect, aren't you known as something of a Factory guru to these people?' I asked him.

'I always left when it got boring,' he replied. 'People do tend to get very boring about Factory, which is perfectly natural, I suppose but I was never into that side of things. I always wanted the label to stay alive . . . to remain fun.'

Mike's eloquence spills into a number of articles he has written – and threatens more – within the pages of *Scream City* magazine, where it files him alongside other worthy notes from such people as David Nolan and Elliot Eastwick. I urge you to tune in.

It is tempting to paraphrase a Dylan quote here: 'I used to care but things have changed.' Well, I still care, but everything has changed.

Manchester, the framework of the story, has enjoyed one of the most extensive regeneration programmes of any city in Europe, emerging – post-bombing – as a giant thoroughbred city in the modern context. Pristine architecture echoes its industrial heritage. We know the past glories. The birthplace of the computer, of liberalism. It has been Cottonopolis, Madchester, Gunchester and Sport City. The glorious structures of Alfred Waterhouse fight for prominence with the pseudo-industrial flat blocks, an inner city of duplexes that rose amid a mess of construction crunching, thumping and whirring. For a while, back then, new buildings would seem to rise on a weekly basis, soon to be filled with Chino-clad people on balconies, drinking Sancerre and talking about their BMWs. I generalise horribly, I know, but suddenly Manchester didn't quite seem like our city anymore.

Tony Wilson would have disagreed. He adored progress, architectural vision, smart post-industrial style, the dumb thrust of youth and the disaffecting nature of rapid change. Put all that together and the ethos of Factory Records begins to emerge. There are many who believe that the high visual style of Factory, set into being by Peter Saville, is powerfully reflected in the regeneration of Manchester. This is stated in this book, though I am no longer entirely convinced. I have seen similar ventures in Newcastle, Liverpool, Leeds, vast chunks of London, Cardiff. They can't all claim a Factoryesque background.

As to Manchester. We oldies of the punk wars tend to bump into one another, every now and again, at suitably themed events at, say, Manchester's stylish city centre museum, the Urbis building, where we wallow in a Haçienda exhibition or a talk by Peter Saville or a 24-hour seminar under the guise of 'The Tony Wilson Experience', where old heads are encouraged to spout wisdom and anecdote in front of an awestruck audience of youngsters and the merely curious. They don't really work for me, well, not beyond the fleeting thrill of involvement. In 2005, when Tony Wilson and Paul Morley took to the Urbis stage to unleash torrents of often rather dodgy punk anecdotes it was good to see them together, although as they honed the past, gathering under the umbrella of their own personal experience – and selective memories at that – I felt a slight chill as I thought of all the exceptional talents who had been left in the cold as these two mapped out a peculiar history. I don't know. Maybe the real story was taking place that night somewhere else, at a place where youngsters gathered.

There have been other sadnesses. The sight of an ageing New Order on tour in 2006 will forever haunt me as I balance such enforced tedium against the great band that took technical naïveté to the USA in 1981 and 1983 and gloriously ransacked the disco scene. I am not suggesting that New Order could have aged more gracefully, it's just that they were playing after the spark had died, and they knew it.

I caught New Order live at Blackpool's Empress Ballroom in October 2006. I don't blame the band – exactly my age – for getting old and becoming rather flabby around the edges. But the camaraderie that once saw them challenge the world in such a precocious manner became lost in a blasé performance that spoke volumes about just how far these people had grown apart. Again, fair enough, but to subject the great songs of Joy Division to such tepid treatment was little short of harrowing. That is possibly why their final spat, between a vengeful Hooky and a defensive Barney, was so deflating, all the more so because it seemed to take place over the Internet, from Hooky's rather good and still active MySpace blog. But, who knows? They may reform next year in a state of renewed curmudgeonly stubbornness. One would like to hope so.

In Blackpool they were usurped by the spirited revival of one-time Factory stablemates, Section 25, whose return, incidentally, after all manner of personal tragedy and trauma seemed little short of triumphant. This would become evident in LTM's release of new Section 25 material in 2008 and, even more intriguingly, the presence of the band at the December 2007 One Night in Brussels event which celebrated the old marriage of Factory and Belgium's Les Disques du Crépuscule, the label named by Ian Curtis's close friend, Annik Honore.

During the autumn of 2008, the Section 25 link would continue into a curious New Order/Joy Division hybrid offshoot with Section 25/Hooky/Kevin Hewick coming together to perform various gig-DJ solo sets which would include a number of Joy Division and New Order songs, side by side with chunks of Section 25.

Meanwhile, singer Bernard Sumner, adrift from anything remotely New Order – literally, on his yacht at times – recorded a single in Berlin with the Germany-based Mark Reeder. To some extent, this recording came full-circle, as in Manchester Reeder was a close friend of the pre-Joy Division Ian Curtis before, briefly, taking up bass guitar duties in the Mick Hucknall-fronted Frantic Elevators. However, Germanic in all but birthplace, Reeder soon skipped the UK to work within the German record industry (he was instrumental in causing Nina's '99 Red Balloons' to surface at the head of the charts in the early eighties). Reeder's role within the influential shadows of Joy Division shouldn't be understated. It was Reeder's fascination with German history that helped fire the imagination of Curtis, and he also promoted their 1979 tour of Europe, literally driving the van. Joy Division's first manager, Terry Mason, even recalled how Reeder once stole Nazi paraphernalia across the borders to hand to the grateful Curtis.

Like many people living in Manchester during the Factory heyday, I didn't really notice or appreciate the internationalisation of Factory. It always seemed like it was our town, our people if not always, our bands. Connected labels, such as Les Disques du Crépuscule and its comparative neighbour Factory

Benelux, naturally pulled a strand of Factory across Europe. To Mancunian Factory-ites, these strange-sounding labels seemed little more than idiosyncratic offshoots, all well and good if it meant the label was able to provide further release to some of the more eclectic acts.

Nevertheless, from that distance, Brussels seemed unlikely as a hot bed of precocious aesthetes and burgeoning eclectic combos. (We had been wrong-footed by the surprise and horrible hit 'Ça Plan Pour Moi' by Plastic Bertrand. That's Belgium getting new wave all wrong, we understandably believed.) But we should have known better. The great Brussels venue Plan K, every bit as influential as The Factory Club or the Electric Circus, had attracted the most influential artists of the post-punk era, including Echo And The Bunnymen, Spizzenergi, The Slits and, most famously, Joy Division. Elsewhere in the city Magazine, PIL, Suicide, The Pop Group, Patti Smith and The Cure had all found themselves surprised by the level of sheer cultural suss and enthusiasm of the city.

As for Plan K, in short, it was pretty much on the same circuit as The Factory Club and its bookings were made by two intelligent scenesters, namely Michel Duval and Siouxsie and the Banshees look-alike, Annik Honore. It was Annik who brought Joy Division to Brussels in October 1979, the event signifying the opening of Plan K, more multimedia art space than venue. Joy Division played twice at Plan K and these two events have perhaps overshadowed another evening in April 1980 when Tony Wilson visited Brussels to witness the Plan K appearances of A Certain Ratio, Section 25 and Eric Random. This was the hinge moment when Honore, Duval and Wilson agreed to instigate the Factory offshoot label, Les Disques du Crépuscule.

In true Factory style, this was utterly confusing. After all, wasn't Factory Benelux supposedly the Euro-wing of Factory?

Joy Division manager Rob Gretton certainly thought so and made it plain – at least to the three founder members of Les Disques du Crépuscule – that Factory in Europe was to be represented by Benelux alone. Despite this set-back, it was Les Disques du Crépuscule that captured most of the attention, it's very first release being the cassette compilation *From Brussels with Love*, which contained such disparate acts as Durutti Column, Brian Eno, John Foxx and Richard Jobson. Gaining lavish praise in the English music press, most people naturally assumed it was simply a Factory release in disguise. In a sense, it was. Then again, it wasn't. Who really cared? It had the verve and flavour and youthful enthusiasm that had been similarly in evidence at the start of Factory. There is a great interview with the young Honore, on the LTM DVD *One Night in Brussels*, which goes some way to proving just how exciting it all seemed.

The legacy of Factory remains strong but rather eclectic in Brussels, and latterday Factory-related events seem to reinforce this. That December 2007 event, *One Night In Brussels*, featured Hook performing the New Order classic 'Temptation' backed by Section 25, Crispy Ambulance, The Names and Kevin Hewick. While this might seem a modest affair, it did signify a continuing fondness between the two cities.

Annik found a largely unwanted degree of fame in the wake of *Control*. Indeed, she had maintained a 25-year silence on the subject of Ian Curtis until speaking to the authors of *Torn Apart* (me and Lindsay Reade). Mysterious, enigmatic, playful, clearly intelligent, it was easy to see why Ian Curtis had found her so engrossing. Easy too, to see why Tony Wilson had wanted to use Annik's youthful energy to further the cause of his label.

Because of *Torn Apart*, this writer knows and likes the Annik Honore of 2008. A genuine character still fired by the freshness of young enthusiasm, still feverishly attending a tumble of gigs, still seeking the next stage while enjoying the nostalgia. In 2005, at the invitation of Lindsay Reade, Annik briefly revisited Manchester, staying at a hotel close to Ian's hometown of Macclesfield. Lindsay and I took her to one of the Urbis punk events, which featured a great deal of talk and rant from Buzzcock Pete Shelley, Howard Devoto, Richard Boon and John Robb. Annik was genuinely non-plussed.

'What, are they just talking?' she demanded. 'Why are they not performing? Is this what it is about now, talking about the past? I can't even hear them.'

She had a point. As I looked around, I could see at least three writers – Clinton Heylin among them – taping the whole event for future publications of their own.

Half-wishing I had taken my tape machine along, I exited with Annik and joined a curious nostalgic get-together at the Urbis bar which included Section 25's Larry Cassidy (who had never forgiven me for a short review, written 27 years earlier), ex-Joy Division manager/technician Terry Mason, CP Lee (of whom more in a mo) and several other folk from the fringes of Factory who suddenly realised that the girl sitting on the left was, indeed, the legendary Annik Honore.

But you can pick any comparable night at Urbis and you'd come across a similar crowd. Could be any Factory-related evening. Could be the Tony Wilson Experience in 2008 which, despite the sight of an altercation between Shaun Ryder and Stella Grundy, actress, writer and one-time Intastella front-girl, was a great success. The event, intended as a one-off tribute to Wilson, brought a wide range of experts into the city – Pete Saville, Pete Hook, Jon Robb – and encouraged young people to circulate Urbis, listen to the talks and interact with the experts. Largely hailed as a success, it was marred only by a typical Factory VIP system that protected the inner circle from the masses.

Or could it be the opening night of The Haçienda Exhibition at Urbis? A museum space dedicated to a nightclub? The cynics would immediately seize on the obvious. Why not just open a new club? Surely that would be closer to the ragged Factory ethos? Closer to Tony Wilson, perhaps? Tony did not attend that particular event, which took place in August 2007. He may not have been well enough. He may have found the idea rather bizarre, as indeed it was. I recall queuing in 'stream two' (it seemed to me a kind of half-VIP section, while those in the first stream – Haçienda DJs and, well, God knows who most of them were, were hurriedly shunted through to the bar. Chatting aimlessly with sundry luminaries like CP Lee, now a professor of pop at Salford University and leader of the rag-taggle Salford Sheiks, dedicated to growing old disgracefully in the most blissfully oldie venues (like the Poynton British Legion). This was a man whose innate sense of anarchy fired Alberto Y Lost Trios Paranoias, the Pythonesque loons of Manc punk and inspiration on many levels for one Tony Wilson. Tony Wilson once told me that CP Lee was his inspiration to delve into the absurd . . . something that he always wanted Factory to achieve, though it never did.

There are, incidentally, two members of The Salford Sheiks, CP Lee and John Scott, supremely talented musos both of them, who, under the guise of a band called Gerry and the Holograms, released a single called 'Meet the Dissidents' in 1978. It was a local DJ hit and appeared on Tosh Ryan's post-Rabid Records label, Absurd. This is interesting because – note the release date – it sounded so intriguingly similar to a later song of note: 'Blue Monday'.

'So sue me,' stated a belligerent Wilson when presented with this coincidence.

Of course, nobody did. Deep down though, deep down, Scott and Lee may still have a twinge of resentment.

This historical snippet was rolling around my thoughts as I stood there, at the Urbis Haçienda launch, chatting to CP Lee, John Scott, Durutti Column's Bruce Mitchell and a number of Factory illuminati. All those old passions. All those battles and mini-wars seemingly forgotten as we drank bad wine and toasted the art of wrapping the past in such thematic convenience. Later, as I wandered through the rather good exhibition with Lindsay Reade, I asked her if she was enjoying the experience.

'It's a nice night out . . . nice to meet people but I do feel a bit weird about it all,' she told me. 'Seeing Tony's photo there made me feel really strange.'

She was referring to the classic Kevin Cummins photo of a smiling Tony. Sweet indeed but I also recall gazing at that photograph as it graced the entrance to the Haçienda and feeling a sense of disbelief. Who on earth would put a picture of themselves at the entrance to their own club? Who? Tony Wilson, of course.

I asked him this simple question on three occasions. I received, of course, three completely contrasting answers. Was it mere ego, as bland as that? Was this Tony's power and Tony's weakness? He looked like some dictator with features chiselled in stone. I remember when I first saw it, I nearly fainted. Tony – how could one be so vain?

I'm asking an unpopular question here because, as we have seen, Tony Wilson is now preserved in myth: Mr Manchester. And I am asking the question despite the fact that my closest friend was his ex-wife. This is tricky. But the photo left me feeling unsure about everything Factory even stood for. It was a label born in the hub of what the great Simon Reynolds dubbed 'post punk'. Fine. But in precisely doing that, in being there, Factory had a duty to present the scene as it was. In truth. *Truth*. Was Factory representing the artistic growth of a small

Manchester scene or was it, one has to ask, merely a way in which its chief protagonist could etch himself into the history books? Was it an ego thing and, if so, was that bad?

As previously stated, the simple truth is that Tony was a complex man. Perhaps he was several people, several different characters. I can only speak of my personal encounters with him. He was often extremely courteous and helpful to me. He attempted to get me a job at the *NME* once and then, in 1986, he was instrumental in getting me on to the then influential *Manchester Evening News*. He also gave me over twelve solid hours of interviews for this book. It is only the cynic within me that occasionally questions the energy and time he afforded me. Yes, it is true that, in 1986, from the moment I started working for them, Factory Records started to feature heavily in the Manchester paper's pages. Yes, it is also true that Factory had fallen out with the *NME* at the time he attempted to prise me in via an endorsement he gave to the *NME*'s Tony Stewart – in fact the *NME* had just suggested, in their endearing journalistic manner that 'why doesn't somebody shut the fucking place up?' The place being Factory, of course. Surely a Manchester-based correspondent would write in a rather more supportive manner? Tony knew this but, as he would openly admit, he was no stranger to the unholy ramifications of PR. I once managed to get him to review Mary Harron's film *I Shot Andy Warhol* for the *Express* (he hated it). He wasn't remotely interested in seeing his own review but he did wish to know one thing. 'Did it go in? Did it? That's all that matters.'

The extraordinary, somewhat unbelievable 2006 Manchester Passion event, which unfolded in Albert Square beneath the gothic shadows of Alfred Waterhouse's beautiful Manchester Town Hall, saw Wilson in ebullient mood, despite the news that his beloved United had, in failing to beat the upstart elves of Sunderland, pretty much declared themselves out of the title race. Manchester Passion, screened live on television, was the effective retelling of the Easter story fused into songs from Manchester's musical legacy – Smiths, James, M People, etc. – and performances from Tim Booth of James and M People's Heather Small. Odd indeed. Nevertheless, and despite the oddness of the entire event, there was a genuine sense of history in the city centre that night. Miraculously, and miracles being very much on the agenda, a balmy spring evening had dawned, causing the café bar clientele to spill out on to the sidewalks, reminiscing heavily while sipping Sancerre and nibbling houmous. Tony Wilson had a dream job that night, earning himself £3,000 as stand in for the event's compere, Keith Allen. Despite the slight chance that Allen might not turn up (his wife was pregnant), Wilson had had to learn the entire script . . . or more or less. Still, he certainly showed no sign of nerves on the night, meeting and greeting the great, the good and the hangers on – of whom I suppose I was one – inside the town hall. Bizarrely, although the live event was unfolding outside the window, most people in the hall preferred to view the television coverage.

Wilson's star certainly seemed to be in the ascendancy once again. He had switched formats from television to the art of radio, supremely presenting two separate shows, XFM's Sunday Roast and a slightly more topical affair on BBC Radio Manchester. The former show would allow him to pull many of his intriguing old friends in for an in-studio natter. Never less than fascinating, Sunday Roast featured such luminaries as New Order's Steve Morris, M People, ex-Haçienda booker, now A&R man Mike Pickering and, in a glorious chunk of ex-marital banter, Lindsay Reade. Throughout all these shows, the history of Manchester music and, in particular, Factory Records loomed large. It was part of a slight warping of Manchester music history that would pull Factory towards occupying a central role that it didn't entirely deserve. There was a significant moment, during the Lindsay Reade interview, when Wilson steadfastly denied watching and learning from the pre-Factory Manchester record company Rabid Records.

'I most certainly did not,' claimed Wilson.

'Well, we did used to go down to Cotton Lane [the Rabid HQ],' stated Reade levelly.

It was a small but classic example of how impossible it is to write a singular truth with this story. There are many truths. Tony himself, believed in several of them.

By contrast to Wilson's rising star, New Order were defunct when the first edition of this book was written and their subsequent resurrection occurred after publication. They are defunct again, as I mentioned before, but, then again, who knows what may happen next. Factory Records doesn't exist, as such, as I write. Yet it is paradoxically bigger than back in the days when it had an office with people working in it, a roster of bands and was regularly releasing records as well as running a nightclub and wine bar. Ah hah! I have just committed a mortal sin. When Factory opened Dry Bar on Manchester's Oldham Street, I recall gently teasing them about moving into the wine-bar scene. I knew full well that it wasn't a wine bar as such – though it was a bar that served wine – but, alas, my gentle comments encouraged the wrath of Bernard Sumner who seemingly never forgave me. I felt well and truly flattered when Tony informed Lindsay of this curious and obscure fact in 2007. I also couldn't believe my ears.

Many of the post-Factory Factory artefacts that have flooded eBay in recent years feed the sense that Factory is bigger than it ever was. The most intriguing, perhaps, of the objects being auctioned off are the Martin Hannett 'Personal Mixes' of Joy Division that have appeared in a variety of lavish formats, from a plushly packaged CD, to gate-folded vinyl, to dubious 'test pressings' and God knows what else. These are bootlegs, of course and I know precisely from where they came. However, it was intriguing to note that the very people who complained were in fact, the people who purchased them. For the uninitiated, they are a clunky gathering of Hannett's sound experiments from Strawberry Studios coupled with alternative versions of the odd song and intriguing snippets of in-studio conversation. Something good did come of this. It was Chris Hewitt's ex-business partner Peter Hook, with whom he was co-owner of Rochdale's Suite Sixteen Studios (so named by Tony Wilson), who openly attacked the release in 2007, again in his brilliant blog. The pair fell out profoundly, only falling back in league together in the autumn of 2008 when Hooky purchased a number of Joy Division master tapes from Hewitt.

Many people who purchased the CDs, vinyl or both have a curious artefact to add to their collection even if, I concede, the price was a little on the high side. I must also add that those recordings are merely the tip of the iceberg. There is hardly any unreleased Joy Division material – as Hooky and Steve Morris stated at the screening of the Joy Division documentary at Salford Quays in 2007. But there are many more curiosities and secrets trapped dustily on tapes stored under beds in Anglesey and, I strongly sense, elsewhere.

But further ironies cloud the story. Tony Wilson's own favourite band, although losing favour with the man himself, always took their principal inspiration from funkbeats and world beats . . . as indeed, did Happy Mondays who, perhaps, enjoyed the fruition of the ACR dream. Manchester funk! It was Haçienda booker Mike Pickering who, almost immediately upon the club's launch, started importing Chicago house into the club . . . and at once the initial failure of the Haçienda set sail for a much brighter future. With a future as one of the world's leading clubs or, for want of another word, discos, the rise of the Haçienda initiated the downfall of Factory. It was a hell of a mess for a while but, as so often happened, the mess would turn to romance. After the ball was over, that is. Even now, at the end of 2008, tourists drift daily into Manchester, searching for hints of the golden days of the Haçienda. For a while they found it with the Haçienda exhibition at Urbis. Even following this, it was possible to dip a toe in Manchester past by purchasing a Factory mug, or Tony Wilson T-shirt, or a set of Pete Saville postcards or that dreary photograph of The Smiths outside Salford Lads' Club. Rather like purchasing a postcard pic of a punk at Piccadilly Circus. A whole attitude etched safely into nostalgia. For the most part, people appear to celebrate this fact. People seem happy with it.

The Haçienda – the REAL Haçienda – seems distant now, lost in some nostalgic fog. I guess I think more fondly of the more 'live music' based International Club of the mid-eighties, or certainly The Factory Club or our punk home, the Electric Circus.

As to Happy Mondays, perhaps that ACR comparison is rather lazy; for the Mondays were famously broad of influence, snipping wit and melody not just from the likes of George Clinton and Bootsy Collins but mixing with the colourful mess of sixties' and seventies' pop, shards of punk, hints of cartoon. Their central force was undoubtedly Paul Ryder, whose driving bass, so underrated perhaps due to his brother's sheer front, pulled the band clear of the many rival acts that clambered on to the Haçienda's talent nights. Happy Mondays were never really a band in the first instance, more a state of party, and a sense of intelligent, if brash, hedonism. Although never bad boys – pussycats, the lot of them – they surged honestly from the streets of Salford, providing Factory with an act that could immediately connect with the knots of embryonic hoodyism (Chav, for want of a finer description) that had started to gather on street corners of inner Manchester. The Ryder lads' showbiz roots came from their father, Derek, one-time pub comic/ entertainer, some-time postman and then sound man and manager. While I was hanging around the offices of Factory Too while researching this book, Derek would often pop by, swapping lovely scurrilous gossip with Tony and Yvette. By this time, of course, the Mondays' crazy dream had splintered into all manner of fall-out . . . and Black Grape, itself a rather controversial unit. I interviewed Derek at length, later, for another book, and he proved to be a most approachable character, blessed with a terrific musical knowledge and a sense of music hall-style comedy. He was fun and believable . . . the two attributes that made Happy Mondays so endearing even if their latterday re-emergence was not only without Paul Ryder, but without any of the musical elements that existed in the initial band at all.

Tony Wilson's infamous championing of Sean Ryder would see the frontman dubbed 'the greatest poet since Milton'. Even Sean Ryder found this absurd – 'Who the fuck is Milton, man?' – and, although no Dylan or Morrissey or Mark E. Smith he did have an endearing knack of hurtling Salfordian streetisms into the mix and making them sound almost Beefheartian. The film title, 24 Hour Party People is, of course, a line from the elongated title of the first Mondays' album and the later single. To Wilson's delight and, perhaps also to his angst, Happy Mondays were everything he wasn't.

While Sean continued to surf celebrity and enjoy the Mondays' second coming, Paul Ryder purchased vast properties in France, married a high-ranking television producer and re-emerged on the low-key though excellent, Big Arm.

'So what do you know about Happy Mondays, as people?' a researcher from Salford Museum asked me in August 2008.

Only then did it dawn on me that I didn't know Happy Mondays at all. Indeed, the only time I had conversed with them was when they wandered into the sparse crowd in a vain attempt to scrounge chunks of dope. First (and last) band I have even known do such a thing. I guess that said a great deal about them. Dickensian oiks to a lad, back then: grubby, desperate, startle-eyed and wholly lovable. Not at all like ACR, when you come to think of it.

The demise of Factory Records, mostly documented in this book through the eyes of Tony Wilson, has itself settled into myth. Indeed, I claim it myself, there is some kind of romantic notion even in the chaotic mismanagement that caused the label to implode. But not everybody saw it that way. Even now, some resentment does linger, as James Nice notes: 'When Factory collapsed in November 1992 there was a good deal of anger and resentment. That tends to be forgotten now. People lost their jobs, and artists and creditors lost money. Peter Hook ended up retrieving a master tape of *Unknown Pleasures* from a skip. In the years since there's been a tendency to spin the collapse of Factory as some kind of heroic failure, or "brilliantly fucked" as Tony put it in his book, but there's nothing big or clever about a company going under with debts of £2 million. The failings were systemic. Factory's collapse was brought about by general internal mismanagement, not just external factors such as high interest rates and a fall in property values. The company was not being run competently; there was a lack of financial control. Add to that too many drugs washing about. Factory invested about £250,000 in the *Revenge* album, but even in 1990 they couldn't even get it together to dispatch a complete set of production parts for the Benelux licence.'

This was indeed a difficult period in Factory's history and one that has been largely ignored by films, books and press alike. Many people were left bewildered and empty-pocketed by the Factory collapse, a fact that has become more poignant as the years have passed. A hinge moment that perhaps shouldn't be ignored.

James Nice, speaking to the author in October 2008, continued: 'By 1987 CDs were becoming commonplace on independent labels, and Factory was certainly not slow to introduce the format for new releases. Joy Division and New Order aside, however, they had no real interest in digitising their back catalogue. I think Tony considered it retrograde, particularly after "Madchester" broke big. It's a point of view, and all well and good for a self-confessed "revolutionary" label, but less helpful for the musicians. From Brussels we began putting out a series of remastered Factory Benelux CDs with extra tracks, including Crispy Ambulance, The Names, and a Durutti Column compilation, but Factory didn't seem inclined to follow suit. In the end I licensed the Section 25 catalogue from Factory for release through LTM, although even then the group supplied most of the master tapes. I then proposed a series of expanded reissues by Durutti Column, Stockholm Monsters and The Wake, which lead to a meeting with Tony and Phil Saxe at the Charles Street office in June 1992. Tony was by then keen to go ahead with the Durutti project on Factory, although he still wasn't too keen on extra tracks. Not long afterwards Factory collapsed, and the Durutti CDs later came out via Factory Too. I'm not suggesting that by keeping their back catalogue in print the label would have survived – that would have been like rearranging deck chairs on the *Titanic* – but it would have been slightly more constructive than spending £30,000 on a fancy floating table.

'In 1995 the receivers concluded a rather nebulous agreement with London Records by which they purported to transfer certain ill-defined Factory assets, including the entire back catalogue. This was plainly incorrect, as most of the artists owned their own music, meaning the copyright in the sound recordings. The result was a prolonged legal exchange, which was eventually resolved in favour of the groups. Tony found himself caught between a rock and a hard place. On the one hand he'd always maintained that the bands owned their music, and went so far as to say so in the clearest possible language on BBC radio shortly after Factory collapsed; but on the other hand he wanted London to fund Factory Too. If it had gone to court he would have had to give evidence, possibly against his will, and it wasn't a threat I enjoyed having to make. Thankfully we didn't need to go that far, and I was glad that there didn't appear to be any hard feelings by 2006, when I filmed an interview with him for the *Shadowplayers* DVD. I think he approved of LTM, up to a point.'

Several people have contributed to and enjoyed talking head infamy by inhabiting the many Factory documentaries that have regularly flickered on the more aesthetic television channels. I don't blame them for this at all, although the predictability carried by a new film containing contributions from, say, Paul Morley and Jon Savage has certainly helped dilute the message. Both have been eloquent, as one would expect, but the circle of anecdote has been ever decreasing, largely due to a lack of inspiration from the many filmmakers. That stated, Paul Morley's *Joy Division: Piece by Piece* (published December 2007 by Plexus), largely the collection of old articles, did prove particularly rewarding.

TONY WILSON: THIS IS THE END, BEAUTIFUL FRIEND

It is with sadness, great sadness, of course, that I state the obvious here ... that this entire story is overshadowed by the untimely death of Tony Wilson in 2007. I recall the exact moment I heard the not altogether unexpected news. Oddly enough I was sitting in a hotel room in the Midlands, immediately after interviewing, of all people, Status Quo, who would later take the stage at the extraordinary biker festival The Bulldog Bash. It was Lindsay Reade, naturally, who broke the news to me, via a text message that carried immense emotion. Lindsay had, in the later stages of Tony's life, once again grown close to him, often caring for him in the most difficult of circumstances.

While obviously heartbreaking for Lindsay and everyone else associated with Tony, there did seem to be something special happening here. They were always the perfect imperfect couple, prone to near violent arguments – and often not so near. Impossible to be with each other; impossible to be apart. I will not delve any further into what I believe to be one of the greatest rock'n'roll love affairs of recent years – merely hinted at in *24 Hour Party People* – because I feel it is a story only Lindsay can tell, if she wishes to do so.

I must admit to a feeling of greyness on hearing the news, rather akin to the way I felt on the extraordinary day that Princess Diana died. The colour seemed to drain away from the day. Even during Status Quo's excellent set, in fact, many times during that performance, I secretly thought to myself, 'Tony will not approve of this . . . bloody Status Quo?' I felt that I should have been watching Kraftwerk, if not Can, if not Faust or The Fall on such an occasion. I couldn't imagine a Manchester without Tony Wilson. I thought of a great many people who had been touched and angered by him, for it is totally false to suggest that he was loved by the entire city. Tony was loathed as much as loved. His onscreen affectation didn't always connect with the average Joe, back from the pub.

Soon after Tony's death I managed to chat to Lucy Meacock, his long-time co-presenter on *Granada Reports* and the late-night debate show, *Granada Upfront*. I had known Lucy for many years. I met her while reporting for the *Manchester*

Evening News at the start of her remarkable career. Lucy is a brilliant journalist, first and foremost, as well as being – for twenty years – the reasoned, affable front-piece of Granada television. In addition to her intelligence, she also has great beauty and there is no doubt that an onscreen sexual tension existed between her and Tony Wilson.

'Without Tony I would have been lost,' she admitted. 'His sheer presence and intelligence was so inspirational to me. I feel so privileged in being able to work with one of the great Maverick presenters of television history.'

Kevin Hewick also spoke to me about how Tony's death affected him.

'I was due to do some comparing and performance during the weekend-long Summer Sundae festival in Leicester. While I was amongst thousands of people watching a brilliant set by The Divine Comedy on the Friday night I felt my phone vibrate, it was a text from Vin Cassidy of Section 25. It said Tony had died.

'My mum had passed away only eighteen days before, we'd just had her funeral on the Monday. I was doing what I had planned to do at the festival as a way of coping and proving to myself that life was going to go on. I still did just that but as well as my mother I couldn't get Tony out of my head. I hadn't seen him since 1982 and we'd last spoken on cordial terms on the phone in 1991. For all that I was still deeply saddened by his death, I still am.'

Tony's death didn't come as a shock and, contrary to some of the optimistic reports in the media, I had realised some time before that the situation was not improving. In February 2007, six months before his death, Tony wrote a heartfelt article for the *Manchester Evening News*, praising the institution that is the health service. It wasn't an easy read. Even the sight of a bearded Wilson seemed somewhat significant, an act of rebellion perhaps, as if Tony had now moved into a world beyond the frippery of the music business, to a more celestial place. By all accounts he was courageous to the end.

His funeral, in Manchester, was apparently surreal, perhaps all funerals are. The crowds, the tributes ... a floral banner bearing the name 'TONY' placed near the old site of the Haçienda, now identically named flatblocks. There were personal reasons why I chose not to attend on that day, although I devoured every news bulletin as endlessly, endlessly the man referred to as 'Mr Manchester' was laid to rest. While the assembled gathering – with Lindsay Reade curiously banished upstairs – were listening to the unlikely sounds of Happy Mondays' 'Bob's Yer Uncle', of all songs, in Manchester's Little Gem church, I lit a candle and played, for some reason, Bruce Springsteen's 'Born to Run'. This might seem an odd, perhaps even inappropriate choice. But it made sense to me. The first time I noticed Tony Wilson on *Granada Reports*, the first time he stood out from the pack, was back in 1975, when his clear love of music – American music at that point – surfaced so forcibly within an otherwise mundane television feature. He transmitted a passion that evening, albeit for Springsteen, that remained with him throughout his career. I had also never seen a regional television presenter air his passion so openly. It wasn't long before he managed to convince the bosses of Granada to allow him to interview the likes of Leonard Cohen, Iggy Pop and John Lydon on the magazine programme. This was a tremendous breakthrough. But there was something about Tony Wilson that always seemed utterly convincing.

So I stared at the candle and, though Tony wasn't my closest friend towards the end, shed a tear. I knew Lindsay was at the funeral. I knew there was genuine pain.

During the week prior to the funeral, numerous London-based PR people informed me of their intention to be at the event. I didn't know them and wondered if they had ever really

437

met Tony, other than at run-of-the-mill conversations about north-west developments and such like.

I let the candle burn to a flat goo. Turned off the lights and went to bed. The following day saw reports in every national broadsheet, *The Times* disgracing itself by referring to Wilson's business partner, Yvette Livesay, as 'his wife'. But, whatever. The *Manchester Evening News* seemed to sum things up with succinct grandeur.

It seemed to me that Wilson's achievement would echo through the city streets for many years ... perhaps it was already contained within that aforementioned modernistic architecture, perhaps he would always be there, somewhere, at the heart of the sheer energy that continues to run through the city. That would be the greatest tribute. Greater than Tony Wilson events at Urbis, greater than gigs carrying his name is the notion that he would be present whenever the city of Manchester showed its true colours – red or blue – the colour of youth, intelligence, aesthetic awareness and, more than all this, unbridled enthusiasm and a pure understanding of how great such a city can be. Small enough to retain camaraderie, large enough to literally change the world, by industry, technology, literature, politics and music.

Mr Manchester might be a crass title and, in truth, it belonged to an old-school journalist – Duncan Measor – who, for many years penned the influential 'Mr Manchester's Diary' in the *Manchester Evening News*. Tony was more than Mr Manchester, really. More than Mr North-West. He understood greatness and knew, also, that greatness was just as alive in the tower blocks and large estates of Salford – more so, perhaps – than the leafy pastures of Cheshire.

Today Manchester is full of echoes. The proud new buildings may serve to disguise them but this angular architecture doesn't hold them – echoes, ghosts, call them what you will. They are still there. It remains difficult to wander through Peter Street, alongside the Radisson Edwardian hotel without feeling a strange chill, a brittle feeling, the sense that things have happened there. Memories flood that street. The hotel was once the Free Trade Hall – how to not recall the angry mob scenes at *that* Lou Reed gig. How not to hear the strains of a hundred bands, the Led Zeppelins, Black Sabbaths, Deep Purples . . . and upwards to the left, deeper in the building, where the Lesser Free Trade Hall so famously housed The Sex Pistols. You may think beyond that, to 16 August 1816 when eleven people died and four hundred lay injured following one of the most infamous events in British political history, the massacre of Peterloo. It was one of several demonstrations in the area against the corrupt nature of the British government. It was a rising against injustice. It was anarchy in the UK.

There is your history. It has left an energy in the area. An energy that, one might say, at least provided an added frisson to those Sex Pistols concerts . . . and to so much else. Manchester is full of history and Factory Records always reflected that fact. Now Factory itself lies embedded in the city's past and it continues to reflect, to echo and to inspire.

Discography

JOY DIVISION

EPs

Enigma PSS 139, *An Ideal For Living EP*, 7″ (Warsaw/No Love Lost/Leaders Of Men/Failures) (June 1978)

Anonymous Records ANON 1, *An Ideal For Living EP*, 12″ (October 1978)

Factory Singles

FAC 13, Transmission/Novelty, 7″ (September 1979)

FAC 13-12, Transmission/Novelty, 12″ (September 1980)

FAC 28, Komakino/Incubation/And Then Again (Flexi) (April 1980)

FAC 23/23-12, Love Will Tear Us Apart/These Days/Love Will Tear Us Apart (Remix), 7″/12″ (May 1980)

FACUS 2, She's Lost Control (Version)/Atmosphere, 12″ only (October 1980)

Sordide Sentimentale 33002, Atmosphere/Dead Souls, 7″ (March 1980)

Samplers/Compilations

Virgin VCL 5003, *Short Circuit/Live at the Electric Circus*, Joy Division track At A Later Date (June 1978)

FAC 2, *A Factory Sample*, 2 × 7" EP, Joy Division tracks Digital/Glass

Earcom 2, *Contradiction*, Joy Division tracks Auto Suggestion/ From Safety to Where . . .? (October 1979)

Factory Albums

FACT 10, *Unknown Pleasures* (June 1979)

FACT 25, *Closer* (June 1980)

FACT 40, *Still* (Double) (October 1981)

NEW ORDER

Factory Singles

Factory FAC 33, Ceremony/In A Lonely Place (February 1981)

Factory FAC 33-12, Ceremony/In A Lonely Place, 12" (March 1981)

Factory FAC 33-12, Ceremony (New Version)/In A Lonely Place (Extended), 12" remix (July 1981)

Factory FAC 53, Everything's Gone Green/Procession (September 1981)

Factory Benelux FBNL 8, Everything's Gone Green (Extended)/Mesh/Cries And Whispers (Belgian pressing), 12" (December 1981)

Factory FAC 63, Temptation/Hurt, 7" at 33 rpm (April 1982)

Factory FAC 63-12, Temptation/Hurt, 12"

Factory FAC 51 B, The Haçienda Christmas Flexi: We Will Rock You/Ode To Joy (limited edition of 4000, given away free at Haçienda, December 1982)

Factory FAC 73, Blue Monday/The Beach, 12" only (March 1983)

Factory FAC 93, Confusion/Confused Beats/Confused (Instrumental)/Confusion (Rough Mix), 12" (August 1983)

Factory FAC 103, Thieves Like Us/Lonesome Tonight, 12" (May 1984)

Factory Benelux FBN 22, Murder/Thieves Like Us (Instrumental, Belgian pressing) (July 1984)

Factory Benelux FBNL 22, Murder/Thieves Like Us (Instrumental), 12″ (July 1984)

Factory FAC 123, The Perfect Kiss/Kiss Of Death/The Perfect Pit, 12″ (May 1985)

Factory 7 FAC 93, Confusion/Confusion (Rough Mix) (1985)

Factory 7 FAC 103, Thieves Like Us/Lonesome Tonight (1985)

Factory 7 FBN 123, The Perfect Kiss/Kiss Of Death (1985)

Factory FAC 133, Subculture/Dub Vulture, 12″ (November 1985)

Factory 7 FAC 133, Subculture/Dub Vulture (1986)

Factory FAC 133-7, Subculture/Dub Vulture (1986)

Factory FAC 143-7, Shellshock/Shellcock (March 1986)

Factory FAC 143-12, Shellshock/Shellcock, 12″ (March 1986)

Factory FAC 153-7, State Of The Nation/Shame Of The Nation (August 1986)

Factory FAC 153-12, State Of The Nation/Shame Of The Nation, 12″ (August 1986)

Factory FAC 163-7, Bizarre Love Triangle/Bizarre Dub Triangle (November 1986)

Factory FAC 163-12, Bizarre Love Triangle (Extended)/Bizarre Dub Triangle, 12″ (November 1986)

Factory FAC 183-7, True Faith/1963 (July 1987)

Factory FAC 183-12, True Faith/1963, 12″ (July 1987)

Factory FAC 183R, True Faith (Remix)/1963/True Dub, 12″ (July 1987)

Factory FAC 193-7, Touched By The Hand Of God/Touched By The Hand Of God (Dub) (December 1987)

Factory FAC 193, Touched By The Hand Of God/Touched By The Hand Of God, 12″ (Dub) (December 1987)

Factory FACD 193, Touched By The Hand Of God/Touched By The Hand Of God (Dub)/Confusion (CD single) (December 1987)

Factory FAC 73-7, Blue Monday 1988/Beach Buggy (April 1988)

Factory FAC 73-12, Blue Monday 1988/Beach Buggy (Version)

Factory FAC 223-7, Fine Time/Don't Do It (December 1988)

Factory FAC 223-12, Fine Time/Don't Do It/Fine Line, 12"

Factory FAC 223-12, Fine Time (Edit) (Messed Around Mix)/ Don't Do It

Factory FAC 263-7, Round And Round/Best And Marsh (March 1989)

Factory FAC 263-12, Round And Round (Extended)/Best And Marsh (Extended)

Factory FAC 263R, Round And Round (Club Mix)/Round And Round (Detroit Mix)/Best And Marsh

Factory FAC 293/7, World In Motion/The B Side (May 1990)

Factory FAC 293/12, World In Motion (Subbutteo Mix) (Subbutteo Dub)

Factory FAC 293CD, World In Motion/World In Motion (Subbutteo Mix)/The B Side

EPs

Strange Fruit, SFPS 001, *The Peel Sessions*, Turn The Heater On/We All Stand/Too Late/586, 12" (September 1986)

Strange Fruit, SFPSC 001, *The Peel Sessions*, Turn The Heater On/We All Stand/Too Late/586 (Cassette)

Factory Albums

FACT 50, *Movement* (November 1981)

FACTUS 8, *1981–1982 A Compilation of Singles* (December 1982)

FACT 75, *Power, Corruption and Lies* (May 1983)

FACT 100, *Low Life* (May 1985)

FACT 150, *Brotherhood* (September 1986)

FACT 200, *Substance* (August 1987)

FACT 275, *Technique* (January 1989)

London Records Singles

NOU1, Regret/(New Order Mix), 7″ (April 1993)

NOUX1, Regret/(Fire Island Mix)/(Junior's Dub Mix)/(Sabre's Slow And Slow)/(Sabre's Fast and Throb), 12″ (April 1993)

NOUX1, Regret/(7″ Version)/(New Order mix)/(Fire Island Mix)/(Junior's Dub Mix) CD (April 1993)

NOUX2, Ruined In A Day (The Bogle Mix)/(Live Mix)/(Reunited In A Day Remix) 12″ (June 1993)

NOUCD2, Ruined In A Day (Radio Edit)/(Ambient Mix)/(Mike Haas Mix) (London) CD (June 1993)

NOUCDP2, Ruined In A Day (Sly And Robbie Radio Edit)/(12″ Bogle Mix)/(Dance Hall Groove)/(Rhythm Twins Dub)/(Live Mix) (London) CD (June 1993)

NOUX3, World (Perfecto Mix)/(Sexy Disco Dub Mix)/(Brothers In Rhythm Mix)/(World In Action Mix) 12″ (August 1993)

NUCD3, World (Perfecto Edit)/(Radio Edit)/Perfecto (Mix)/(Sexy Disco dub mix) CD (August 1993)

NUCDP3, World (Brothers In Rhythm Mix)/(Brothers Dub-stumental Mix)/(World In Action Mix)/(Phatmacy Dub) CD (August 1993)

NOUX4, Spooky (Magmix)/(Moulimix)/(Album Version), 12″ (December 1993)

NOUCD4, Spooky (Minimix)/(Magmix)/(Moulimix)/(Album version) CD (December 1993)

NOUCDP4, Spooky (Out Of Order Mix)/(Stadium Mix)/(New Order In Heaven)/(Boo Dub Mix)/(Stadium Instrumental) CD (December 1993)

NOU5, True Faith 94/(Perfecto Radio edit), 7″ (November 1994)

NOUX5, True Faith 94 (Perfecto Mix)/(Sexy Disco Dub)/ (TWA Grim Up North Mix)/(94 Remix), 12" (November 1994)

NOUCD5, True Faith 94 (Radio Edit)/(Perfecto Radio Edit)/ (Perfecto Mix) (94)/(TWO Grim Up North Mix) CD (November 1994)

NOUCD6, 1963 (Arthur Baker Remix)/(94 Album Version)/ (Lionrock Full Throttle Mix)/(Joe T Vanelli Mix) CD (January 1995)

NUCDP6, 1963 (Arthur Baker Remix)/Let's Go/Spooky (Nightstripper Mix)/(True Faith 87 Shep Pettobone Mix) CD (January 1995)

NOUX6, 1963 (Lionrock Full Throttle Mix)/(Joe T Vanelli Remix)/True Faith (Eschreamer Mix)/(Eschreamer Dub), 12" (January 1995)

LC7654, Blue Monday 95 (Hardfloor Mix)/(Original 12" Mix)/(Manuella mix)/(Andrea Mix)/(Plutotone Mix) CD (July 1995)

LC7654, Blue Monday 95 (Hardfloor Mix)/(Andre Mix)/ (Manuella Mix)/(Original Remix), 12" (July 1995)

London Records Albums

LP 828413-1, CD 828413-2, *Republic* (May 1993)

LP 8285801, CD 8285802, *The Best of New Order* (November 1994)

LP 8286571, CD 8286572, *The Rest of New Order* (August 1995)

London Records released the complete Joy Division and New Order album back catalogues on 5 July 1996:

Joy Division

520016.2.4, *Unknown Pleasures*

520015.2.4, *Closer*
520017.2.4, *Still*
520014.2.4, *Substance*

New Order

520018.2.4, *Movement*
520019.2.4, *Power, Corruption and Lies*
520020.2.4, *Low Life*
520021.2.4, *Brotherhood*
520008.2.4, *Substance*
520011.2.4, *Technique*

Index